Corruption and Realism in Late Socialist China

Corruption and Realism in Late Socialist China

The Return of the Political Novel

Jeffrey C. Kinkley

STANFORD UNIVERSITY PRESS
STANFORD, CALIFORNIA

2007

Stanford University Press
Stanford, California

©2007 by the Board of Trustees of the
Leland Stanford Junior University
All rights reserved.

No part of this book may be reproduced or transmitted in any form or by any means, electronic or mechanical, including photocopying and recording, or in any information storage or retrieval system without the prior written permission of Stanford University Press.

Printed in the United States of America on acid-free, archival-quality paper

Library of Congress Cataloging-in-Publication Data
Kinkley, Jeffrey C.
　Corruption and realism in late socialist China : the return of the political novel / Jeffrey C. Kinkley.
　　　p. cm.
　Includes bibliographical references and index.
　ISBN-13: 978-0-8047-5485-9 (cloth : alk. paper)
　1. Chinese fiction—20th century—History and criticism.　2. Political fiction, Chinese—History and criticism.　3. Politics and literature—China.　I. Title.
PL2443.K56 2007
895.1'35209358—dc22   2006008799

Typeset at Stanford University Press in 11/13 Garamond

Dedicated to the memory of my father,
HAROLD V. KINKLEY
Honest and self-sacrificing civil servant

Acknowledgments

I have many to thank for helping me bring this book to completion. Lu Tianming, Chen Fang (who passed away in 2005), and Zhang Ping in China as well as Mo Yan, Yu Jie, and Qiu Xiaolong in America took time from their busy writing and filming careers to sit for interviews. On-site help in Beijing was arranged by Ai Qun and his staff at the Masses' Press. Valuable assistance finding written materials came from Ken Harlin, Richard Jandovitz, and others at the C. V. Starr Library of Columbia University and the Princeton Gest Library. Earlier research for *Chinese Justice, the Fiction* (Stanford University Press, 2000), to which the present book may be considered a sequel, was partially funded by the Chiang Ching-kuo Foundation for International Education Exchange.

Yet more assistance in China came from Hua Jian of Shanghai and Yu Fenggao of Hangzhou. Over the years, the Chinese Academy of Social Sciences has provided many introductions to Chinese authors and libraries. Unusual support was also rendered by the Academia Sinica of Taiwan, which hosted me for a month of research on the present project at the gracious initiative of Dr. Peng Hsiao-yen.

St. John's University provided release time for research and writing that sped the project along; further appreciation is due the University Seminars at Columbia University for their help in publication, both financial and intellectual, since the ideas in this work benefited from discussions in the University Seminar on Modern China. Understanding corruption is a tricky thing, of course; to name all the institutions in New

York City, North America, and China that have advanced my knowledge of the phenomenon is best left until later! Shawn Shieh, Helen Xiaoyan Wu, Dušan Andrs, Katherine Carlitz, William Crawford, Milena Doleželová-Velingerová, Patricia Dyson, Raoul Findeisen, Marián Gálik, Howard Goldblatt, Robert Hegel, Ken Klinker, Hans Kuehner, Charles Laughlin, Pat Laurence, Perry Link, Steve Luk, Bonnie S. McDougall, Peng Hsiao-yen, Mark Silver, James St. André, Tang Qiuyan, David Der-wei Wang, Philip Williams, Yenna Wu, Yu Haocheng, and many others meanwhile offered comments, criticisms, and the gift of collegial friendship, for which I am profoundly grateful. At the final stage, Muriel Bell and John Feneron of Stanford University Press, my copy editor Sharron Wood, and my friend and consultant Susie Corliss provided indispensable editorial advice. Not least, I am indebted to Chuchu, Emily, and Matthew Kinkley for seeing me through this project.

Jeffrey C. Kinkley
Bernardsville, NJ

Contents

1	Introduction: Corruption, Realism, and the Return of the Political Novel	1
2	The Trendsetter: Lu Tianming's *Heaven Above*	22
3	The Banned Blockbuster: Chen Fang's *Heaven's Wrath*	47
4	Climax: The Alarum and Standard-Bearer—Zhang Ping's *Choice*	78
5	Anticorruption by Indirection: Wang Yuewen's *National Portrait*	104
6	Dirt Plus Soap Equals Pay Dirt: Liu Ping's *Dossier on Smuggling*	125
7	Chinese Realism, Popular Culture, and the Critics	144
8	Conclusion: The Chinese Discourse of Corruption—and Its Limits	170
	Notes	193
	Bibliography	229
	Character List	269
	Index	275

Corruption and Realism in Late Socialist China

1

Introduction: Corruption, Realism, and the Return of the Political Novel

"Almost invariably, every book on contemporary China is about corruption."[1] A scholar writing in squeaky-clean Singapore invented that bit of hyperbole to open his review of a book printed in America. In fact, China itself, from 1995 until the inevitable clampdown in 2002, published an extraordinary number of books "exposing" its corruption. However, most of the Chinese books, or at least those trying to put all the pieces together rather than just point a finger at crime rings or flaws in the system, necessarily took the form of novels. They were a short course in corruption and its politics for the Chinese public. This book draws inspiration from the major novelist-instructors, while subjecting their observations and imaginings to critical analysis and real-world verifications. I contend that some of the novels and their mass media adaptations deserve to be examined both as social commentary and as art, or at least as popular entertainment that engages real social and moral problems. The works' historical and literary reverberations are many.

Transparency International (TI), known to be less waggish than the reviewer writing from Singapore, likewise gives China low marks in its oft-cited "Corruption Perceptions Index." In 1996, when Chinese fiction about corruption was just getting a toehold, China ranked 50th among the 54 nations TI rated (above Bangladesh, Kenya, Pakistan, and Nigeria), with 2.4 points on a scale in which 10 signifies incorruptible. China's 2004 rating was still only 3.4, up from the bottom mostly because the number of countries rated had expanded to 146. China tied with Syria and Saudi Arabia for 71st place. The United States scored 7.5, tied with Belgium and Ireland for 17th. Indonesia, original home of the provocative book reviewer, tied for 133rd, at 2.0. Singapore, in fifth place, got 9.3, which ought to dispel attributions of corruption to ethnic traits or even authoritarianism, since most Singaporeans are ethnic Chinese living under a benevolent despotism.[2]

TI's ratings are based on samplings of international businesspersons' perceptions of the illegitimate costs they incur in their global deal making. But a perception of rampant corruption in their country is just as prevalent among the Chinese at home—young and old, male and female, rich and poor, ruler and ruled, urban, rural, and migrant—and it makes them furious. More pervasive than China's discourse of reform itself, "corruption" is its evil twin. It ties into a global discussion with ancient roots both in China and abroad—one that spans the divide of oceans and continents, of capitalism and socialism. The abortive Beijing democracy movement of 1989 was partly caused by public outrage over corruption. That was before Deng Xiaoping in 1992 sped up economic reform, enabling rapid growth and what TI calls "grand," rather than simply "petty," corruption.[3] The World Bank's comprehensive "governance indicators," which compare countries according to citizen voice and legal accountability, political stability, government effectiveness, regulatory quality, rule of law, and control of corruption, revised China's position downward in all categories from 1998 to 2004, noting the sharpest decline in the nation's control of corruption and rule of law.[4]

Prosperity may have lessened the perceived damage or discomfort caused by corruption, but it probably has only heightened the impression of its ubiquity, since personal income growth has been so uneven. It is not just that China's "system" is changing in ways that many Chinese see as decay. They also feel increasingly ambivalent about what they used to see as the health of the old system. A great deal of corruption is therefore "discovered in plain sight" these days, much as "creative" CEO compensation tends to come under scrutiny in the United States for the first time during an economic downturn. Academics have described Chinese corruption as epidemic, endemic, systemic, routine, collective,[5] at a crisis level, and even as an officially tolerated form of compensation.[6] Some business sectors have been called "quasi-criminalized."[7] Informed by their own culture's age-old fears of social-moral collapse, the public is not averse to thinking of China as having entered late-stage or end-game corruption, in which behavior that used to be considered corrupt has become the new standard.[8] One implication is that the Chinese see corruption as a dynamic process, not an easily codifiable list of transgressions. Another is that they are more sensitive than ever to the concentration of political power. Outright calls for democracy are few and far between, but "excessive" power is coming to be seen as "corruption." That perception may some day threaten Communist Party rule.

"Corruption" as a General Malaise, and the Paradox of Fictionalizing It When Culture Is Considered Bankrupt, Too

The precise nature of "corruption" is a controversial question that we shall revisit in the conclusion, after viewing the full spectrum of corruption as it is popularly imagined and depicted in China's most famous recent novels with corruption themes, together with their film and television adaptations. These works tend to be thrillers, but few of the corruption cases in them were invented from whole cloth. Most of the novels are to one degree or another romans à clef. I believe that these works represent a rebirth (short-lived, perhaps) of the Chinese political novel following a hiatus after the 1989 Beijing Massacre. The novels' formal realism is debatable, but they were arguably the works of their day that "spoke truth to power." They gave the Chinese people *stories* about where their social and political problems came from, and these narratives resonated with familiar tales from Chinese history and literature. As the sanctimonious charge, these novels also made the decadent lifestyles of the rich and infamous fascinating. Corruption itself and the power struggles it causes were enshrined *as* popular culture.

We still need a working conception of corruption that will acknowledge both the concrete and the abstract, even metaphorical, manifestations of it that we find in the novels and in popular discourse generally. Lynn T. White III some years ago found "a surprising consensus on the proper definition" of corruption among Western political scientists, as *the misuse of public power for private gain*. He went on handily to demolish the utility of that formulation by contrasting Mao-era and post-Mao-era Chinese ideas of corruption in practice.[9] Still today, problems arise in distinguishing the private from the public and the less entitled "lesser public" (e.g., a firm or unit) from the "greater public" (the state or "the people as a whole").[10] And the rules keep changing. Making and keeping a profit used to be considered corrupt. Paying workers a bonus was "bribery." The very language of China's reforms can mislead. When a Chinese enterprise "goes public" (sells shares), usually it is a state firm being privatized.[11]

Despite these uncertainties, consensus that certain covert high-stakes transactions are "corrupt" is not hard to find, particularly in this age of excess. Bribery of officials, graft, fraud, and looting of the company one manages are corrupt by international standards and punished by Chinese law. Still, novelists and analysts like to examine gray areas and new kinds of malfeasance before the law catches up to them. Beyond even this, however, are much broader and yet related concepts of "corruption" (*fubai*) as a general rotting or disintegration of society, morality, and the very standards that society and morality claim to cherish. One hears of "spiritual corruption."[12] "Corruption" in practice is often a code word for any observed social injustice perceived to be caused by unjust accumulation of power, whether in the hands of an individual, individuals, or a group, not excluding the Chinese Communist Party (CCP) itself. Some scholars hypothesize a broadening of the Chinese concept of corruption since the early 1980s, in concert with an upsurge of malfeasance accompanying China's economic reforms.[13] That new forms of corruption involving vaster sums of money are now possible is indisputable, but I will argue after we examine the novels that the broadening of the idea of corruption is more a matter of linguistic usage and freedom of expression catching up with very old ideas of corruption as a general social decay. This reflects a change in values and reevaluations of recent Chinese history. Conversely, since China under Mao's socialism tended to lump corruption together with waste and mismanagement, the purview of "corruption" as a group of behaviors may have shrunk in some areas. Today, it is often the unbridled power to manage people or resources that used to be quite legitimate that is considered by many Chinese to be the root of corruption, if not its essence. The broader and the more particular meanings of "corruption" coexist in the Chinese language as they do in English, and these different fields of meaning enrich each other. Old ideas that corruption leads to regime decay and collapse (under a Mandate of Heaven theory) or to an even more cataclysmic apocalypse religiously defined[14] come quickly to mind in the Chinese case. Even the "tamer" prospect of regime change suggests something more dramatic: the final fall of communism as an international system.

Hence the larger subject of these novels is social change, negatively conceived as social-moral decay leading to citizen resistance and protest and finally to the collapse of a system and a way of life. That is what this book takes to be the Chinese discourse of corruption at its most abstract.[15] It encapsulates a general social malaise. The implications for action are paradoxical, for everyone fears regime collapse, even clings desperately to the idea of savior bureaucrats emerging to save the day—which means clinging to the status quo and all the corruption it now represents. When official Chinese propaganda denounces corrupt officials, it, too, conjures up a general miasma of economic, moral, and sexual indiscretion that bespeaks a general moral lapse (in Maoist times, it was a class or ideological lapse) and even a loss of regime legitimacy, of the Mandate to rule. In the meantime, as China moves ever closer to having a market economy, it finds itself enmeshed in other cycles besides those of the Mandate of Heaven—business cycles. This could create conditions for a "perfect storm." Corruption turns out to be, in essence, a pessimistic and teleological discourse, its own narrative of social decay and upheaval, national enfeeblement and destruction (*wangguo*), and a story of corrupt values themselves becoming the norm, all the more so because old communist ideals have come to seem hypocritical. Corruption thus conceived is itself a causal explanation for society's ills. Many a novel about corruption is an *ideological narrative* in Tzvetan Todorov's sense, in which "all actions of the characters can be presented as the products of a few very simple and very abstract rules."[16] As for Lévi-Strauss's distinction of "raw and cooked" versus "raw and rotten," demarcating the cultural sphere against the natural, metaphorical corruption as the Chinese know it applies to both.[17]

Worries about the health of Chinese society overlap and interact with a somewhat differently conceived perception of a *cultural* crisis. Culture, too, is embodied both abstractly and concretely, the latter in monuments of high culture, particularly literature. Under Mao, as under the emperors, literature had a vanguard role in popularizing correct ideology or thought (*sixiang*), formerly the Dao—the Way. Part of China's cultural crisis since the Beijing Massacre of 1989 and the freeze-frame politics that followed it is, according to high-powered social observers, that there have been few serious, no-holds-barred ideological or literary explorations of the Chinese people's fundamental concerns.

Literary critics, too, often describe Chinese literature as in crisis since the 1990s, but usually for a different, if complementary, reason: because the avant-garde creativity that won China fame in the 1980s has declined, and with it, affirmations that China is in the international cultural vanguard. Chinese culture appears now to be dominated by popular literature, the self-obsessed musings of disillusioned young people, exposés by young women trumpeting their libidinal appetites, and variously stale or trend-catching media productions—movies, television, and video and Internet games (often imported or poor examples of their type)—requiring little if any literacy.[18] Literary controversies no longer hold the public's attention. China still has famous writers, but they have lost their mystique, their romantic heroism. Many write for television. Some critics blame all this on pandering to the new market economy and the power of international capital (e.g., Hollywood) more than on the CCP and its determination to remain in power. Optimists, on the contrary, seem to think that China's new soap operas, karaoke bars, and eye-popping storefronts and advertisements are the best thing in Chinese culture since instant noodles. Celebrity critics, in Chinese as in English departments worldwide, tend in any case to celebrate that which is marginal, not what is fundamental.

Were the pundits looking without seeing? By 2000, Chinese novels about corruption were being written in the hundreds and read by the millions, including even the banned ones.[19] These works already had a generic name: "anticorruption fiction." Only the social observers and cultural critics failed to notice. Probably the critics found anticorruption novels on the whole too popular and artistically undistinguished to take seriously. I do not intend to argue that China's recent anticorruption novels are as a whole *good*, much less great. C. T. Hsia regards corrupt officials as stock characters in works that for centuries have not raised "fundamental issues about the soundness of Chinese civilization."[20] But "bad" and "popular" are not the same, and "popular in style" is not the same as best-selling. Contrary to the opinion of many Chinese intellectuals, much fiction that they deride as "popular" is not commercially successful,[21] whereas the relatively "high" novels of Wang Anyi and even the experimentalist Mo Yan sell well, as did works by Charles Dickens, Victor Hugo, and Eileen Chang in different times and places. Social commentators may have disdained the novels as "freedom of expression lite" under the impression that their "measured" scolding of the status quo helped polish "the government's reform credentials,"[22] but that is letting a political "best" that is unobtainable under present rules be "the enemy of the good." (Some skeptics take anticorruption novels' very existence as proof that they must not be very deep.) Even the optimists have ignored China's political novels. They prefer a Chinese "mass culture" at the cutting edge of a global, postmodern, postpolitical pop culture in which long-term and structural social concerns are simply not chic.

Now, many Chinese readers may well consider sex, religion, the pursuit of happiness, youth alienation, or, contrarily, the cluelessness of old people to be "fundamental concerns." Those looking for social comment, though, surely seek a literature about problems of livelihood, personal security, equity, and justice: about unemployment, unjust privilege, obstruction of justice, official corruption and incompetence, discrimination, inflation and deflation, environmental degradation, diminished health and welfare security, inadequate infrastructure, crime, urban crowding, occupational and consumer safety hazards, "social instability" (a euphemism for protests and mass unrest), declining civility, loss of home and other property by government fiat, and manipulation of the new stock markets, where the new middle class is already heavily exposed.[23] The Chinese also remain concerned about national security, prosperity, foreign investment, morality (however defined), and preventing a run on the banks. The overall health of the political system concerns many Chinese, too. This book does not mean to overturn the aforementioned conventions as to what is fundamental, though they are conventions. Like the Chinese, I worry about these problems in both our countries, and I am not displeased to see them treated in well-plotted page-turners that trace high-stakes social threats to political and social leaders.

China's discourse of corruption transcends simple bribery and graft cases, encompassing nearly all the aforementioned social problems, yet it has its limits. Fundamental concerns of Chinese readers that cannot be directly addressed include their desire for democracy (or at least greater consultation), political and civil rights, freedom to form groups to solve current problems inside and outside the workplace, and freedom to become well informed or sometimes just to work safely for a living wage. One may not suggest that the CCP should share power with other parties or depict constitutional change, much less describe nationally organized resistance to CCP policies. Excessive discussion of big losers in society, such as AIDS victims and drug addicts, is taboo, and so too, perhaps, is excessive focus on the sins of China's capitalists, professionals, and foreign investors, except those in collusion with corrupt cadres.[24] Little mention is made in the literature of the Beijing Massacre of 1989 or the freer social tendencies just prior to the massacre (including press freedoms evidently endorsed, at first, by Deng Xiaoping himself).[25] Fang Lizhi says a politically mandated amnesia about political protests is reinforced by rapid social and generational change in China.[26] After the transition to new leaders at the Sixteenth Party Congress in November 2002, license to write about corruption diminished. One needed permission. Just before the congress, China's General Anticorruption Bureau proudly announced that the spread of corruption in China was "effectively checked"![27] (In 2004 there was renewed government attention to, though not openness about, corruption. A citizen Internet poll still ranked corruption as "public enemy no. 1.")²⁸ Novels and television serials with corruption themes, which had appeared intermittently after 1995, arrived in force at the millennium, climaxed in a spurt of seemingly geometric growth in 2001, and suffered an abrupt falloff, though not a complete extinction, in 2002.

This book, then, a study of "anticorruption fiction" and its mass media adaptations, is an analysis of the rise and at least temporary fall of a genre that has been a Chinese way of addressing a variety of fundamental popular complaints and the protests and riots organized to express them (some 60,000 incidents annually by 2003, rising to 74,000 in 2004).²⁹ Anticorruption fiction was a place where the needs of Chinese officialdom and the general populace met. The officials thought the subject of this fiction was malfeasance by a limited number of its midlevel cadres; mass readers thought it was the entitlements and duties of all those in power, their right to hold power at all, and thus the system that had installed them. These are, respectively, the official and nonofficial discourses of corruption. "Anticorruption fiction" was from the first a "concept literature" or "problem fiction" at best, a wholly untransgressive formula fiction at worst.³⁰ The quasi-Malthusian proliferation and diminution of the works partly suggest the rise and fall of a market-driven fad, but raw political power was also at work.

I call the turn-of-the-millennium period and beyond "China under late socialism." That term is speculative and teleological, but terms like "postmassacre" or "postdemocracy movement" look backward, not to the inevitable coming of something new, and I am not inclined to follow current fashion in cultural studies and affirm that Chinese culture, or even its economy, was or is "postsocialist." (That term, as translated into Chinese, can mean either "postsocialist" or "late socialist.")³¹ In 2001, when the number of anticorruption novels was at its peak, state-owned enterprises (SOEs) were still "the nucleus of China's industrial and financial system," "accounting for more than one-half of industrial employment, two-thirds of industrial assets, almost one-half of industrial output, and more than two-thirds of all liabilities held by Chinese industry."³² The decentralizing thrust of reform has actually increased the resources owned by SOEs.³³ Millions of people have in recent years been laid off or retired from SOEs, their sole source of a pension. Retirees and the unemployed are much in evidence in China's anticorruption novels.³⁴ This is not to speak of the farmers and ex-farmers, variously underemployed, migrant, or working in effectively privatized township and village enterprises (TVEs)—originally capitalized by local governments—for local Communist Party bosses who now double as enterprise owners.

State and party employees in organs rather than enterprises are yet another part of socialism's unreformed payroll. According to an official Chinese source, in 2003 1 in 30 Chinese was a "civil servant," compared to "Indonesia, 1:98; Japan, 1:150; France, 1:164, or the U.S., 1:187."[35] The Chinese financial system that worries economists throughout the world is still, for want of a better word, "socialist," though not firmly under central or local control: it follows political dictates rather than market rationales. Moreover, even large-scale private enterprises, if only because they provide local employment and perks to local officials, can count on local courts and police to do their bidding in case of disputes with workers, foreign partners, or even domestic suppliers and buyers. Private money and official power remain enmeshed in complicated ways.[36] Ordinary Chinese blame both the state *and* the market, but few would follow China's New Left in thinking of the state as "neoliberal," though certain foreign and domestic players in the market may fit the label.[37]

The late 1990s and the beginning of the twenty-first century were, however, good times for China as a whole, with the private sector being China's hope. China's economic growth was nearly unequalled internationally. A newly rich middle class was developing. Observers would soon call China manufacturer to the world. The international opprobrium of the 1989 massacre had faded, and so had domestic and foreign fears that China might turn back the clock on its market reforms. China entered the World Trade Organization at the end of 2001, and Beijing was chosen to host the Olympics in 2008. But there were still all those aforementioned problems and citizen protests, as well as worries about fundamental changes in morality, family stability, and human relations, not to mention ideology, which led to contradictory yearnings for both change and social stability. And a broader question haunted Chinese citizens even as, or especially as, they contemplated the boom times. Was it all real? The seemingly contradictory coexistence of rapid economic development and stagnation or worse in social equity and reform led some to ask the same question that many Japanese were asking of their society, for different reasons: Are we a "normal" country? Are *we* for real? The question partly reflected doubts, ever more repressed in the official press, about China's "normality" in the era of Mao Zedong and the possible continuing legacy from those years.[38]

As leadership shifted to Hu Jintao in 2003, still within the political party of Mao Zedong, doubts intensified about the very reality of China's economic development. Was it just a bubble? Was it sustainable in China's overburdened environment? Were the products of China's economy themselves real or counterfeit? Was China's economic miracle, in other words, sustainable? There was also a crisis in high culture. China's culture did not match the nation's newfound power, prosperity, and international prestige, much less its past glory. Which spectacle represented China's future: Shanghai, the once and future "pearl of the Orient" with its grand opera house, or the knockoff boomtown of Shenzhen, dependent on Hong Kong and the outside world and yet fenced off from them and protected from having to obey their commercial and intellectual property laws? Foreign media and observers have largely accepted the Chinese state's narrative of future change coming from the cutting-edge cities of Shanghai, Beijing, and Shenzhen, and yet there is always room for a minority view—encouraged by China's anticorruption novels—that an upheaval might come from those parts of the country that change has left behind.[39]

Realism and Its Limitations

In addition to corruption, realism is the other major theoretical concern of this book, and it is another concept so moot that I shall hold off addressing its finer points until the penultimate chapter, when we have acquired a feel for the novels. The term "realism," as Western critics have used it, is so diffuse, encompassing now the very subjectivity that realism was originally framed against, that René Wellek writes of it as a "period concept" in French literary history, though he also defines realism as "the objective representation of contemporary historical reality."[40] (Another critic specifies that it lasted from 1848 to 1871, followed by naturalism, from 1871 to 1890.)[41] Wellek proceeds to classify the part of the "eternal realism" tradition that followed the French period (acknowledging that Auerbach's masterwork *Mimesis* begins with the ancient Greeks) into individual national traditions of realism. I think we can speak of a national Chinese tradition of realism, and now of a post-Mao mainstream realist tradition, so long as we recognize that it still competes with a related but different official dogma and practice of realism that is less critical and closer to Maoist realism. When major Chinese writers speak sympathetically of realism today, they mean the "nonofficial" critical mainstream. In chapter 7 I shall propose an inductive characterization of it according to the traits that make it admired by partisans of realism, rather than a tight definition, for the concept must fit many diverse works. When speaking of realism as an international tendency, I endorse George J. Becker's eclectic view of realism as an umbrella term for works associated with realist movement(s) variously by their (1) subject matter (unprettified, or worse); (2) techniques (slice of life, lack of a judgmental authorial voice, use of dialogue as spoken in life, and so forth); and (3) philosophy (that is, philosophies).[42] Henri Lefebvre's emphasis on themes of failure and defeat in nineteenth-century European literature suggests to me another broad marker, which like the others is potentially sufficient but not necessary: (4) mood (pessimism).[43] This book does not pursue the idea of a "real" realism; I take no stand on the ultimate nature of "reality" or the best way of conveying it. Such concerns do not necessarily inflame the authors featured in this book, either. They go for the story, the dirt, and, to their credit, the "real story" behind the unseemly appearances.

Chinese critics trace their own national tradition of literary realism not to the European and American movements, but to their own May Fourth and increasingly to their late Qing masterworks from the first half of the twentieth century. Critics today even speak of a "classic tradition" of modern Chinese realism. This implies an improbable linguistic, technical, and ideological continuity since May Fourth (and even late Qing) realism, down through the dubious socialist realism of the Mao period that followed it, and including now post-Mao realism, which is itself a very diverse practice of orthodox and relatively dissident modes of realistic writing. I find that in principle, however, even orthodox Chinese critics now expect Chinese realism to hit hard against the establishment, in the manner of not just the icon Lu Xun, but also the great contemporary realist Liu Binyan, who is still officially considered dissident. This book argues that the well-developed Chinese conceit of literary realism, shaped now by decades of socialism—not only influenced by socialist-era literary techniques, but also dependent on and symbiotic with socialism's deficit of truth telling—can be viewed as a force of its own, a force that has inspired literary achievements. It overlaps, but is not coterminous with, Western realism; it need not be seen as a divergent or defective offspring of the latter. For now, let us simply note that Chinese realists of the twentieth century, despite their ideological differences, have generally believed that literature must (1) "tell the truth" in the face of a bureaucracy not so disposed; (2) directly address and even be instructive about major and preferably problematic social trends, rather than use experimental techniques to convey subjective inner states or apolitical family psychodramas; (3) speak for the downtrodden; and (4) be accessible to a mass readership, not just an intellectual elite.

The outpouring of novels about corruption at the turn of the twenty-first century was, or perhaps under better circumstances could have been, a major "realistic fiction." Most Chinese critics favorably disposed to the novels saw them as a branch, or even the main branch, of Chinese realism of recent years.[44] Others would no doubt think this formulation an excessive compliment to the popular and sometimes racy works. To most observers, though, what stands out about anticorruption novels, if not their realism in any strict doctrinal sense, is their instructive observation of China's rapid transition from a centrally planned economy and severe, locked-down Maoist society to a "Wild East" market economy, underregulated and yet still subject to unstoppable bureaucratic whims.[45] This body of fiction does not simply describe what some see as a happy ending in a prosperous, postmodern urban society, though such a society has been described by other kinds of authors "realistically"—that is, using realistic technique (works by He Dun and Qiu Huadong are often cited).[46] The fervor with which most novels with corruption themes portray what officials call a "transitional" society (though this society is not even debating a change of political system) suggests to some the inutility and even immorality of continued CCP rule. Alternatives to sudden regime change include abolishing the CCP committees that control from within government ministries, courts, schools, and factories, a proposal of Zhao Ziyang when he headed the CCP in 1987–89, but this kind of "peaceful evolution" has been off the table for fifteen years. On one level, one sees the rapid integration of China into a postmodern world. On another, one feels the old us versus them paranoia of an internally weakening CCP organization originally steeled by civil war and global Cold War. Some critics read anticorruption novels in the manner of their forebears, who considered late Qing novels about corruption to be "novels to warn the world [of an impending catastrophe]." Critics have invoked that very phrase from a century ago. Anticorruption novels are often criticized for their all-seeing, ever-moral, incorruptible official heroes, but the villains are naturally more interesting, and they point upward, toward heroic problems of "system."

My personal slant does not favor the all-out market liberalization and privatization so often promoted by America's international institutions just now; the current CCP leadership may have more faith in markets than I. China has demonstrated that capitalism can be compatible with communist bureaucratic rule. My bias is liberal, pro-democratic, and in favor of a new global civil society. To the novelists, the current position of the CCP as a privileged, self-perpetuating, legally protected, and self-supervising elite still controlling the state, with socially egregious techniques in proportion to the very decline of its old bases of power, suggests evils that can be named without help from our neo-liberal world:

specters such as tyranny, social irresponsibility, and "feudalism." It is not simply a case of the people versus the state. Many fighters against corruption and unaccountable leadership want a stronger Chinese state that will take more responsibility for citizen welfare. It is more a case of "the people" vs. "the system"—the real system, since "the government," in CCP propaganda, is often a euphemism for the government-within-the-government, namely, the CCP. The party is now unsure enough about its legitimacy that it sometimes refers to itself in print as "the ruling party," as if there were an opposition. When it denounces the corrupt, it tends to identify them by their government position, not their rank in the party hierarchy.[47] Anticorruption novels often employ a bureaucratic euphemism for the CCP, or perhaps an immanent principle behind the godhead (the CCP) itself: "the Organization" (*zuzhi*).

"Realism"—not pornography, youth counterculturalism, or artistic experimentalism—remains the literary practice that most offends China's authoritarian regime. Realism can enlarge artists' palettes when its advocacies appear new, as they did during the May Fourth movement and the early post-Mao days, yet the commitment to "realism," I will argue in the chapters that follow, can also be charged with some of the limitations of China's anticorruption fiction. The several aspects of this can appear singly or in combination. (1) Since its European genesis, realism has in various hands eschewed certain viewpoints (subjective ones), techniques (experimental ones), and high literary languages (viewed as affectations). Realism is in principle a doctrine of self-discipline, and hence of self-limitation, as exemplified in the Jamesian unities. (2) China's own "classic" tradition of twentieth-century realism tends in practice to limit realistic themes even further, since it dramatizes conflict in terms of social clashes, often for instructive purposes. So far it has tended to pull the "realistic novel" toward melodrama. (3) In contemporary China, realistic novels invite censorship.[48] (4) Single-mindedly opposing bureaucratism imposes a focus of its own—concentration on the bureaucracy—and this, too, can be limiting. (5) The straitjacket on the imagination can be even more pronounced when literature is a substitute for journalism. The temptation for creative authors to try to do the work of journalism is great, since the news is more heavily censored than fiction, and Chinese realism privileges truth telling above all. (6) A limitation placed on realism is that Chinese fiction now has to serve market expectations, as so many critics have pointed out. Realistic "exposure," whether didactic or simply to parade the lifestyles of the rich and infamous to serve reader curiosity, caters to this.

Each of these limitations will be discussed in the ensuing chapters, in relation to one or more major novels of 1995–2002. The sequence of the next five chapters will reflect not the chronological order of the genesis of these limitations, which is hard to fix, but rather the chronology of the publication of the novels. Earlier works influenced later ones, and one can also observe a pattern, a rise and fall of the Chinese anticorruption novel as such. Let us finish with a brief historical overview of the genre before turning to the works.

The Rise of Anticorruption Fiction

The late 1990s were propitious for literature about uncomfortable social change and also corruption. Novels about unemployment, obstacles to industrial reform, and other problems of the factory shop floor and urban life appeared in mid-decade, leading to a flurry of critics' comments in 1997–98 about a rebirth of Chinese realism, or, as some put it, a "new realism."[49] One critic spoke hopefully of a rebirth "of the spirit of Chinese literature of the late seventies," before literature allegedly became divorced from reality, evidently due to the much-trumpeted Chinese avant-garde.[50] Another critic's 2001 retrospective found realism to be the literary mainstream of the late 1990s, with anticorruption novels and novels about officialdom at the head of the list.[51] Still others noted the rise of "economic novels."[52] One scholar called attention to "bankruptcy novels" of the 1930s, leaving the connection to present fiction unstated.[53] The new realism was surely buttressed by the fact that very long novels were now a mass consumer trend.[54] One Chinese critic links the upsurge of novels about officialdom in the later 1990s to a larger literary "turn from lyricism to narrative."[55] Another speaks of "an unconscious effort to return to tradition."[56]

International anxiety and pessimism about the end of a Christian millennium had little to do with the rise of anticorruption fiction. Internationally, China had gone from a reputation as a regional pariah in 1989 to one as a regional stabilizer, particularly after China easily rode out the 1997–98 economic crisis that beset other parts of East and Southeast Asia. Corruption, crony capitalism, and nontransparent financial institutions took much of the blame for the debacles of 1997–98, and this may have influenced China's writers and intellectuals, but they had to look within to buck world euphoria about China as the exception, a 100 percent successful emerging market and manufacturer for export.

Novels about corruption could become a trend only as the atmosphere for literary production and consumption improved in the wake of Deng

Xiaoping's 1992 reinvigoration of the reforms that the 1989 Beijing Massacre had almost derailed. Academic, literary, and subliterary production prospered again, popular culture above all, and by the end of the millennium even domestic cop shows were ascendant on television. Literature about corruption needed not only freedom, but also a market that indicated that consumers wanted to read about corruption. With the regime's recommitment to economic reform came the restructuring of the old industrial base (SOEs), the dismantling of the old social welfare system, mass layoffs from SOEs, and worker unrest and protests, all major topics of anticorruption novels later in the decade. In time came official anticorruption campaigns, particularly after the death in 1997 of Deng Xiaoping, the last and highest protector of the 1949 revolution's old cadres and their wayward, self-enriching children. An official anticorruption discourse was already well established, though politically seasonal in its appearance. In the 1990s, corruption was vast enough to encompass illegal privatization of whole factories, massive land grabs for private development (with kickbacks to officials), misuse of power to authorize business ventures and gain access to capital, and covert diversions of monies to real estate speculation, the new stock markets, and foreign bank accounts.

Literature bemoaning corruption of course has ancient roots. Late Qing fiction exposing a corrupt officialdom is often cited as a particular model for current anticorruption fiction. From Mao Dun to Zhang Henshui, writers after the May Fourth movement continued exposing the corruption of their age. Soon after Mao Zedong's death, China was again treated to hard-hitting works of reportage and fiction excoriating corruption, though often still from a Marxist perspective, as by Liu Binyan.[57] These fictional and nonfiction works of the late 1970s were christened, outside China, a "new realism." But works by Liu, living in exile in America since 1988, were no longer widely available or topical in the 1990s, nor were the exposure writings of his spiritual followers who came to national attention before the 1989 Beijing Massacre.

Another precedent for anticorruption fiction in the nearer past was *guanchang xiaoshuo* (fiction about officialdom), which also traced its roots to the 1890s[58]—and beyond—and was purveyed in the early 1990s by Liu Zhenyun and others. Overlapping anticorruption fiction, these works about officialdom focused on the manners of officials as a privileged group, but were not so hard-hitting about massive corruption and fraud.[59] In film, "corruption lite" was combined with the comedic talents of director Feng Xiaogang in highly popular movies about the travails of everyday life. Perhaps partly protected by his fame, in 1992 Mo Yan wrote

Jiu guo (The republic of wine), a grotesque fantasy novel about corruption. It was initially published in Taiwan. Meanwhile, space previously devoted to reportage was taken over by a fatuous product called "enterprise literature," which lauded the achievements of entrepreneurs.[60] It was prevalent in the 1990s in *Beijing Literature*, critic Li Tuo's former bastion of avant-garde fiction. Such "literature" was one more provocation that must have led to calls for realism about factory enterprises.

Zhang Ping had been publishing novels and reportage about corruption since 1991 with the powerful backing of the Masses' Press,[61] but Lu Tianming's *Cangtian zai shang* (Heaven above; 1995) appears in retrospect to have been at the head of a more defined anticorruption fiction trend.[62] It was in 1995 that Chinese growth in real wages took a nosedive, and unemployment reached the prereform level in absolute numbers.[63] It was also in April of that year that Beijng's vice mayor Wang Baosen committed suicide, providing a spectacular first act in the corruption scandal of Chen Xitong, party boss of Beijing. All this must have spurred interest in the television series based on *Heaven Above* aired in 1996, now deemed to have been the first anticorruption TV series and one of the decade's most influential contemporary TV dramas, along with *Kewang* (Yearning).[64] Lu Tianming's novel and his teleplay embody many aspects of what was to become an anticorruption formula, though the works' creative premise of a beleaguered bureaucrat returning to an old haunt that has changed beyond recognition has precedents in Ke Yunlu's *Xin xing* (New star; 1984),[65] Jiang Zilong's late 1970s stories about Manager Qiao,[66] and even Maoist stories about cadres who go down to the grass roots and are surprised by what they find there. That Lu Tianming's early novel in a nascent genre is one of its better examples suggests the unhappy possibility that anticorruption fiction's brief history may well be mostly a story of decline and variations on a theme. In his own opinion, anticorruption fiction was and is in its infancy, leaving deeper questions untouched, as China's earliest socialist war literature does.[67] A few years were to pass before another major anticorruption TV drama followed *Heaven Above*. Zhou Meisen in 1996 published a long political novel, very much in the Lu Tianming mold, about dysfunctional municipal and SOE governance; it was made into a 1998 television series, but it was largely in retrospect that the novel and teleplay were seen as the start of Zhou's now famous interest in corruption.[68]

The June 2000 release of the film *Shengsi jueze* (Fatal decision), based on a novel by Zhang Ping, finally opened the floodgates for novels exposing corruption.[69] The notions of anticorruption fiction and fiction about officialdom, which overlapped and were sometimes interchangeable, became generic trademarks or logos matching authorial output with reader interest in government malfeasance. One could enter a bookstore in most of urban China, ask for *fanfu xiaoshuo* (anticorruption fiction), and service personnel would lead one directly to the relevant books and TV series on VCDs and DVDs, though the term had come into play only after 1995–97 or so.[70] "*Fanfu*" is a slightly acronymic formulation, not unlike "anticorr." in English, so if that phrase did not communicate one's meaning, one needed only to spell it out, as *fanfubai xiaoshuo* (anticorruption fiction), or, more formally, as *fanfubai ticai xiaoshuo* (fiction with anticorruption themes). The term *fanfu xiaoshuo* appeared in China's higher literary criticism (*pinglun*) by at least 1999. Also heard was the equally acronymic phrase *fantan xiaoshuo* (antigraft fiction, or anticorruption fiction).[71] The less abrasive term *guanchang xiaoshuo* (fiction about officialdom) is probably older.[72] Once fiction about Chinese official corruption was named in literary criticism, it had legitimacy in official as well as nonofficial discourse, like the anticorruption cause itself in life. However, "anticorruption fiction" and "fiction about officialdom" were more *tifa* (formulations, programs) than recognized genres. Nor were they officially constructed critical appellations, like *fazhi wenxue* (legal system literature), though the terms were permitted in official publications. That is also to say that the terms had some conceptual validity among critics even without a full, formal push from the officials. In the bookstores, by 2001 one could go to the fiction section and pick out an armful of books with the word "power" or "black" in the title and be sure that the works had corruption themes.

The twenty-first century saw a virtual canon of full-length anticorruption novels and a growing list of authors considered masters of the genre, among them Lu Tianming, Zhang Ping, Chen Fang, Zhou Meisen, Liu Ping, Wang Yuewen, Jin Yuanping, Zhang Chenggong, and Chen Xinhao. Yan Zhen, Li Peifu, Bi Sihai, and Zhang Hongsen also contributed major works to the canon.[73] Tian Dongzhao became noted for novels and essays about low-level officialdom, like Liu Zhenyun and Chen Yuanbin before him. Ke Yunlu also entered the fray. Regarded by the public as anticorruption heroes like Liu Binyan before them (though they took fewer risks in their writing), Zhang Ping, Lu Tianming, and Zhou Meisen were besieged with fan mail from aggrieved citizens urging them to take up their cases or expose injustice. Even Chen Fang, who remained discreetly in Japan, kept adding chapters to his banned blockbuster *Tian nu* (Heaven's wrath; 1996), until he ended up with a three-volume behemoth that, for various reasons, finally could be published openly in China in 2000. Wang Yuewen and Liu Ping went on to create serial works about official life and its corruption that were greeted as relatively literary contributions, though from the point of view of exposing corruption they were less audacious than some contemporary works.

After 2000, TV series with explicit themes of official corruption burgeoned. However, they did not yet overshadow the novels. Of the seventeen best-selling novels in the first half of 2001, six were anticorruption novels, each with sales from 300,000 to one million. Major presses would have a half-dozen or more anticorruption titles in print at a time. Whole publishers' series were devoted to novels about corruption and officialdom, with the generic terms *fanfu* or *guanchang* serving as markers for customers. About a hundred relevant titles were published in 2000–2001.[74] A magazine in 2002 selected "ten classic anticorruption novels," a canon that confirmed most of the aforementioned writers (except for Chen Fang, whose reputation remained officially dubious)[75] as masters in the field, a generic association that not all of them eschewed.[76] Mainstream periodical outlets for fiction such as *Xiaoshuo jie* (Fiction world), *Dangdai* (Contemporary), and *Zhongguo zuojia* (Chinese writers) began to serialize anticorruption novels in volume in 2001–2002. They all stopped after the summer of 2002, before the CCP congress.[77]

The Fall

Readers sensed that, with so many real cases of corruption being exposed in the press, adding inordinately to the numbers with fictitious ones was bound to cross the line at some point. An interviewer asked Zhang Ping in 2002, "Teacher Zhang, how long do you think the mania for anticorruption literature can go on?"[78] Even as it created some of the excitement of a booming literary trend such as had not been seen since the 1980s, anticorruption fiction was becoming a proverbial nail that stuck out, begging to be hammered down. I believe that the heyday of anticorruption novels with real "edge" was over by 2002, if not 2000, although (and perhaps partly because) the number of titles peaked in 2001. In the twenty-first century, the novels poignantly assailing corruption were overshadowed by fiction about officialdom. The latter overlapped anticorruption fiction but tended to be tamer, as some critics acknowledge, if only because fiction about officialdom spread good and bad so evenly among all the characters and institutions, if not Chinese "culture," that individual choice and institutional revision seemed precluded.[79]

Novels about smuggling, legitimated by official propaganda about the Yuanhua case in life, became popular in literature and the media, but they tended to deflect part of the blame onto criminals from the outside, perhaps Taiwan or Hong Kong. Smuggling is "corruption" under a broad definition of the term, but only accompanying crimes such as bribery and extortion fall under the jurisdiction of anticorruption bureaus. New anticorruption television series, often about smuggling, or simple cop stories pitting bad cops against good cops, led to some new novels,[80] but this confirmed that anticorruption's social criticism was now tame enough for prime time. New themes such as the rise of female CEOs and the recapitalization of state factories by selling stock to workers entered anticorruption novels.[81] Even so, critics have yet to announce artistic or political breakthroughs in works produced since the novels in the aforementioned anticorruption canon.

Sales of anticorruption novels began to slip by 2002,[82] even as anticorruption fiction began to be printed serially in respectable journals of mainstream serious and popular fiction. Not surprisingly, earlier anticorruption novels' commercial success (and even some degree of official, or rather superficial, social status—Zhang Ping's *Jueze* [Choice] won a Mao Dun prize after Jiang Zemin extolled the film) inspired quickly produced imitations and also "pseudo-anticorruption novels" (*jiamao fanfu xiaoshuo*), which promised corruption themes on the cover but in fact were not about corruption at all.[83] Other works were said to expose social dirt journalistically, without much commentary or authorial digestion of the material. Fiction and media productions with anticorruption and officialdom themes began to get sustained bad press in July 2002. They were reportedly the subject of a clampdown in the run-up to the Sixteenth Party Congress of the CCP—a time of anxiety which, like all preludes to big party meetings, did not brook dissent.[84] It was at this time that the General Anticorruption Bureau declared victory over the spread of corruption in China.[85] Certainly some novels must have been trashy. A secondhand report tells of plots in which a corrupt official offers up his wife and daughter to a leading cadre, lingering over the sexual and violent aspects, or a high official has relations with a female personal secretary who schemes against his wife.[86] But China has laws against pornography, which are abused as it is; the main offense of these books seems to have been lèse majesté, or indeed excessive negativism—the writing of *heimu xiaoshuo* (scandal fiction), which, like pornography itself, has not so far squeezed out "healthy" serious or popular culture in free societies. The novels analyzed in this book were read predominantly by males, for whom anticorruption fiction was the top genre in 2001–2002.[87] Given that, and the plentitude of prostitutes and mistresses in the plots, the willingness of so many authors to refrain from titillating passages is noteworthy—an indication that they thought of themselves as true realist writers.

The decline, particularly in literature, was subtle enough that in 2004 workaday criticism was still being written about anticorruption fiction, and the term was still attached to new novels that the concept seemed to fit, including those by the protected Zhang Ping, who was now a deputy director of the Chinese Writers' Association and still a favorite moneymaker for the Masses' Press. The CCP renewed its commitment to fighting corruption in 2004. Anticorruption series on television hardly suffered at first.[88] Three different TV series adapted from Zhou Meisen novels with corruption themes appeared in 2003.[89] This, however, was not proof of renewed vigor, since television is generally a medium for feel-good entertainment.[90]

Why the decline? On the one hand, say some observers, the market for anticorruption fiction appeared saturated in 2002. Just too many titles were available, and one seemed much like another. On the other hand, political control was much in evidence. Books were not usually seized off the shelves, but negative criticism grew strong in the press and at forums reported on by the press. A sign of the times was a new crop of "economic" fiction, including some about bankrupt SOEs, without themes of corruption or abuse of power.[91] One could not necessarily call them less "realistic" in tone and technique than the anticorruption standard bearers, but they did seem less audacious in their truth-telling function. In 2004, the State Administration on Radio, Film, and Television announced that television programs with crime themes would no longer be shown in prime time.[92] General propaganda about state prosecution of corruption did not diminish, but neither did it appear to be gaining in transparency or depth. Accounts of the penitence of corrupt officials blossomed in 2004–2005. Chinese critics were hard put to defend that new didactic subgenre's literariness or even its authenticity.[93]

Was it CCP discouragement or market saturation that diminished controversial fiction about official corruption? Under CCP leadership, the market and political needs do not necessarily work at cross purposes—often they support each other. In this writer's judgment, written and filmed works became formulaic and mutually indistinguishable because the genre rather quickly ran up against its limits. As the quantity of works mushroomed, the limits became all too apparent as large numbers all ran up against the same ceiling. The ceiling was much lower for television productions than for novels, so to the extent that television became the main purveyor of criticism of corruption, homogenization and dilution of content were especially pronounced. Works with themes of corruption would now be judged critically only by their ability to entertain mass audiences, and chiefly by their ability to maintain suspense.

Each of the next five chapters treats a representative and influential novel about Chinese corruption with an eye to what made the novel popular, what kinds of corruption upset the author, what the novel says about the root problems (and, less frequently, possible solutions), and some of the apparent limits on the novelist's creativity and persuasiveness. The chapters examine these problems under uniform headings. At the outset is an introduction to the selected novel's (1) *storyline*, followed by an analysis of the work's (2) *corruption cases* and of the relation between (3) *the novel and realism*. Next is a look at the novel's (4) *contributions to the discourse of corruption* and what the novel reveals about (5) *limits on and of realism*. A final section, (6) *aftermath*, discusses sequels and mass media adaptations. The last two chapters of the book revisit the general questions of realism and corruption in light of the novels and academic theory. For all the limits of and on Chinese realist novels that the first six chapters elucidate, the conclusion is inescapable that Chinese realism has much unrealized potential. In the current climate, critics may overlook that. Chinese realism may well need as a foil—as its muse—a bureaucratic government that lies. Yet, even the fall of communism may not be enough to stifle that muse, unless it brings an end also to two thousand years of centralized power, bureaucracy, and greed among the bureaucratically privileged.

2

The Trendsetter: Lu Tianming's *Heaven Above*

Cangtian zai shang (Heaven above; 1995), by Lu Tianming (b. 1943), is a full-length novel with an eclectic mix of themes and narrative devices from both high art and popular culture. When Lu wrote the novel, he was already a television scriptwriter for CCTV (China Central Television), as well as a novelist and playwright.[1] He had a teleplay version of the story in mind from the start, to help CCTV remedy its excessive reliance on historical dramas. Reaching a large audience was on his mind.[2] On the first page of *Heaven Above*, Mayor Dong, a former model laborer—and a woman—mysteriously turns up dead after involvement in a corruption scandal. If that seems to promise a mystery thriller, the next five chapters, shorter still than the one-page chapter 1 (chapter 3 is six words long), suggest an artier, minimalist work. Soon, though, the novel settles into a more conventional, realistic mode, with subplots developing for pages at a time. Yet new mysteries keep popping up until the end.

In retrospect, *Heaven Above* appears to be a trendsetter, the locus classicus of numerous formulas of China's turn-of-the-century anticorruption novel. The gold standard of anticorruption novels, Zhang Ping's *Jueze* (Choice), seems particularly indebted to Lu Tianming's contribution. But many of these emergent formulas appear, upon analysis, to have been shaped by the literary past and the current environment, including China's regime of literary control, and thus to have been formulaic even when Lu Tianming "invented" them. The author was already pushing up against the political limits of realism. Successors drawn to the same political themes were restrained by the same limits. Despite the limits, *Heaven Above*, besides being a good read for a mass audience, introduces interesting dilemmas of contemporary Chinese society, drawing on conflicts of character as in the nineteenth-century Western tradition of realism, as well as the Chinese discourse of corruption. The plot is tragic, about the fall of a good man with a fatal flaw, and therefore relatively close to the Aristotelian tragic character that Marston Anderson sees as a hallmark of realism.[3]

The Storyline

In 1990, after the puzzling and foreboding death of Mayor Dong, noted engineer Huang Jiangbei, a forty-two-year-old Qinghua graduate who also has a Beijing University master's degree in philosophy, gets an emergency summons at the Sino-American chemical factory where he works to return to his native Zhangtai and become its acting mayor. Zhangtai is a fictitious northern prefectural-level city of a few hundred thousand souls. It administers four counties in a poor mountainous area that was a CCP (Chinese Communist Party) base in the 1940s revolution, notably Linzhong county. Rather improbably, in view of its isolation and backwardness, Linzhong is home to the giant Wanfang Automotive works (a Sino-American joint enterprise) and a famous old high school with big-name faculty. The teachers have gone unpaid for months and are about to launch protests on their own behalf and on behalf of a colleague in Pear Tree Hollow. The schoolmarm there teaches children outdoors in the cold because there are no funds to repair the village school's caved-in roof. Huang Jiangbei is a Zhangtai native who has made good on the outside. Now he is back, as if to answer the question: So if you intellectuals held the reins of power, how would *you* deal with corruption and rumblings among the masses?

No sooner is Huang installed than the chief of police is also found dead, cause of death unknown. The scenes of both deaths have been tampered with and evidence has been removed, seemingly with the connivance of the police, charges crusty old Zheng Yanzhang, head of the Anticorruption Bureau (under the municipal procuratorate or state's attorney, to which investigative responsibility is assigned in corruption cases). Zheng is so distrustful of the local party apparatus and its police (and procuracy, which now fires him) that he goes on the lam, reportedly with evidence incriminating higher-ups. Acting Mayor Huang gets an early premonition that the one responsible may be his old friend and mentor Vice Governor Tian (who helped get him appointed) once he visits a mansion of Tian's and observes the expensive gifts that are virtual admission fees to his parties. Huang also learns about the vice governor's bad seeds—Tian Weiming, who runs an aircraft factory in Russia and flaunts a Russian wife, and his half brother Tian Weidong. Yet the new acting mayor's biggest challenge is to reform Wanfang Automotive, a factory complex that is several years old and has yet to produce a car. During a crucial inspection, an assembly test block develops cracks in its below-contract-standards concrete, throwing the future of the whole venture into question. Huang's old teacher, Ge Huiyuan, is the beleaguered intellectual front man who manages the Chinese side of the operation. He is tired and sick. Daily operations are actually under Wanfang's pretty and voluptuous deputy manager, a savvy, and single, thirty-year-old temptress named Tian Manfang. In the meantime, Ge's daughter, Ge Ping, has run away from home, adding yet another problem to the acting mayor's desk. But Huang sees his chief mission as getting the factory into production before the Americans lose all hope and withdraw their investment. In addition to his intelligence, stamina, proactive stance, local reputation, disdain for emoluments and perquisites, and sense of justice and duty, Huang's assets are his wife, his daughter, and the special mayoral assistant Xia Zhiyuan, an old friend, associate, and fellow classmate who plays Zhuge Liang to Huang's Liu Bei. Anticorruption chief Zheng Yanzhang is incorruptible, too, but also a loose cannon who doesn't trust Huang because he compromises with the powers that be.

The acting mayor strains to be a take-charge leader. Instead of just walking out on an expensive banquet welcoming him to backward Linzhong county, he turns the tables on his guests, using the platform to issue shocking ultimatums to Wanfang Automotive, which must manufacture a car in three months, and to county officials, who must repair the Pear Tree Hollow school in forty-eight hours and not ask for new cars or other perks until all their village schools are up to par and faculty have been paid. But the fulfillment of these demands would make the local cadres, notably Linzhong county's Magistrate Qu, lose face. Zhangtai's seasoned municipal CCP secretary Lin Chengsen, Huang's immediate superior, connives with the locals behind Huang's back to sabotage Huang's goals and his subsequent, even more desperate initiatives, such as having Wanfang autoworkers go themselves to repair the Pear Tree Hollow school. (Secretary Lin sends police to block the workers' truck rather than upset the political status quo.)

Now the Tian brothers go on the offensive. No. 1, the haughty Weiming, has a private gang that kidnaps Anticorruption Bureau chief Zheng to get his evidence, but Zheng has a stroke and goes into a coma. Weidong, No. 2, adopts a conciliatory approach. Apologizing to Huang for his brother's "indiscretions," he gives the acting mayor a gift of imported mahogany furniture. Huang learns the big family secret anyway: that Tian Weiming has "borrowed" RMB 14 million (nearly US$3,000,000 at the 1990 exchange rate) from Wanfang Automotive for his now failing aircraft factory abroad, as approved on the sly by his father the vice governor, together with Mayor Dong and the police chief. The latter two committed suicide when the anticorruption chief's investigation made headway. Oddly, Acting Mayor Huang on his own authority now makes a deal with Weidong. He will leave Weiming with Weidong under informal house arrest for a short time so that the criminal brother can repatriate some of his stolen millions in hopes of escaping execution. Weidong also wants the mayor to ask Wanfang to use brake lines made in a Linzhong county village factory (in the parlance of the time, a TVE, one of the township and village enterprises). The factory serves as Magistrate Qu's slush fund, much as Wanfang is the Tians'. Still, ready-made brake lines will get Wanfang into production as fast as possible, which is Huang's number-one goal, particularly now that a meeting of the Municipal People's Representative Congress, which has the power to elect him mayor rather than just acting mayor, has been moved up. Under pressure, and determined to make Zhangtai and Wanfang not only clean but prosperous, the acting mayor cuts his deals.

It looks as if Huang Jiangbei will get away with it. Zheng's coma was faked, with assistance from hospital workers willing to help him avoid the "heat." His evidence is not lost, and Ge Ping was not really a runaway. She had seen the embezzlers' IOUs, reported her findings, and fled to Beijing, after being raped by Tian Weiming, to help Zheng summon a Central Work Team (of the Central Disciplinary Inspection Commission and the Supreme People's Procuratorate) to investigate the looting of Wanfang. And as the work team arrives, Wanfang's first manufacture, a bus, rolls off the assembly line and heads for Pear Tree Hollow, whose school has finally been restored. The teacher and more than two dozen pupils will be driven into town for a big celebration. After this double triumph, Huang is sure to be elected full mayor. But the locally produced brake lines are substandard and fail as the bus comes down the mountain. The teacher and many children die in the accident. The people of Zhangtai still see Huang as a man who meant to help them, but he will be "suspended from duties pending investigation of his case."

Hoping to divert attention from their own malfeasance to the acting mayor's indiscretion, the treacherous Tians and Magistrate Qu scheme to expose Huang's responsibility for the bad brakes. They needn't have bothered, for he is a good man ready to face the music. The amoral Tian Weiming is taken into custody and Party Central is finding evidence that the vice governor himself "borrowed" another 1.7 million yuan from Wanfang for speculation in the Shanghai and Shenzhen stock markets. Then, in another plot twist that "adds feet to the portrait of a snake" (gilds the lily), it is revealed that it was not Huang's request to buy locally that made Wanfang's manager Ge buckle and finally use parts he knew to be inferior, but instead a subsequent telephone call from Vice Governor Tian. Zhangtai and its Wanfang plant will see a brighter day, though the Americans have already pulled out of Wanfang—the more glory, in the end, for the Chinese side, to run the facility by itself.

Corruption Cases

Heaven Above has a plot that turns on corruption cases and was seminal in inspiring subsequent anticorruption fiction, partly through the television adaptation, which at one point captured 40 percent of the viewers in its time slot and may have proved *too* popular, since it was never released for home viewing on VHS or VCD.[4] The work need not be identified primarily as a generic anticorruption novel, however, even viewed in retrospect. Lu Tianming himself might deny that it is "about corruption," at least in the narrow, legal sense. Although one reads on page one that the Zhangtai Anticorruption Bureau has found evidence of the bribery of Mayor Dong and another official, the initial hook that snags the reader is the suggestion of a murder mystery, plus the political interest of a naive Huang Jiangbei facing impossible responsibilities, including detecting the mystery regarding his predecessor. The police suspect that Dong's demise is something more insidious than suicide, particularly after the death of their chief. At the other end of the novel, too, suspenseful ambiguities of character—including how particular individuals will deal with the exposure of their wrongdoing—outweigh the tangled webs of their corruption, even as new mysteries, revelations, and disappearances of characters keep the pot boiling for the popular reader.

Still, *Heaven Above* offers a virtual catalog of corrupt practices worthy of a late Qing novel. The popular reader would surely find the work informative about both the methods and the going rates of these practices—whether the novel is trustworthy about such things or not—and Lu Tianming now stands revealed as one who takes many of his plot details from life, like Chinese realists before him. He bases his plots on research, primarily from interviewing people.[5] More than most later, generic anticorruption novels, *Heaven Above* makes a point of naming offenses and the laws they break. However, the novel is hardly a reliable guide to the law. Huang's administrative interference in Wanfang is identified as *duzhi* (dereliction of duty, malfeasance), supposedly in violation of the Law of Joint Ventures, but his legal transgression seems ambiguous, if not dubious. Manager Ge felt free to ignore Huang's written request to use the local brake lines and was going to scold his former student for urging the shortcut until the following telephone call from the vice governor. *Heaven Above* develops some rather fantastic notions about law and bureaucracy—that regulations, for instance, are legalistically applied, without regard for personal or power considerations.[6] Certainly the focus is not the law enforcement professionals and how *they* crack the case (of them, only Zheng is reliable), but the plight of Huang Jiangbei and the Tians, and how Huang discovers the true nature of the world.[7]

Simple bribery is the thread of corruption that frames the plot at the beginning and end, together with the abrupt deaths (Manager Ge becomes the third suicide at the end). Page one reveals that a bribery investigation of the municipal housing corporation's general manager has uncovered evidence that Mayor Dong took a RMB 85,000 bribe for herself (US$17,800 in 1990).[8] This is a loose end, never tied to Dong's truly suicidal mortification from having authorized the siphoning of millions from Wanfang. Like the deaths on page one, the initial bribes are something of a red herring, although they also foreshadow more socially "serious" corruption themes yet to come.

After Huang Jiangbei makes contact with Tian Weidong, men come to the acting mayor's still humble abode, remove all his furniture, throw the drawers' contents on the floor (possibly searching them as they go), and replace the furniture the same day with a full set of new Thai mahogany pieces worth HK$460,000 (US$60,000 in 1990). Huang recognizes this as an attempt to entrap him with bribery. Tian Weidong, author of the scheme, sheepishly cooks up a wild story for the angry Huang about friends who speculate in the belongings of future notables, leaving behind items of greater current worth in fair trade. But Huang, too, is a little too smart for his own good. He tells Weidong to sell the furniture and deposit the proceeds into an anonymous bank account. Though it turns out to be the Linzhong County Educational Foundation's account, evidently for use in yet another of Huang's desperate attempts to mend the county's broken schools, Weidong tells a slanted version of the episode to Huang's informant Ms. Tian Manfang in hopes of convincing her that her new idol can be bribed. Having discovered that the mayor wants to trick him into donating to charity, Weidong never makes the payout. Instead he offers the same HK$460,000, plus airplane tickets, to the disgraced mayor after the bus mishap, in case Huang might find this final bribe a tempting way to get out of town. That would, of course, be very helpful to the Tians.

Laws against bribery are simply not subtle enough to halt trade in gifts, which need not be given to the vice governor personally, but might be bestowed upon his sons and clients. In an early comic scene, when the new acting mayor innocently attends a party for the vice governor, Xia Zhiyuan has to rescue Huang by providing him with a 2,000-yuan sweater that Xia was going to give his own girlfriend, so that Huang will have a gift for Weiming's Russian wife. The acting mayor was unaware that the world even had 2,000-yuan sweaters. Another well-wisher has given the bride- and groom-to-be a prepaid honeymoon suite and a lease on a Mercedes-Benz. As Chinese urban incomes have inflated, so has the cost of doing business with officials.

The biggest and most consequential crimes are those Lu Tianming refers to as *nuoyong* (*gongkuan*), or misappropriating (public funds), sometimes loosely translated as "embezzling" or "diverting funds."[9] Notable are (1) the 14 million yuan that Tian Weiming diverted from Wanfang to his aircraft factory in Russia and other ventures; (2) the 1.7 million yuan that his father "borrowed" from Wanfang to speculate in stocks; and (3) another 0.32 million yuan the father took from the city housing bureau and the Zhaofeng Construction Corporation of the municipal police bureau, whose discovery hastened the police chief's demise. But these sums, though mind-boggling for the early 1990s, are part of a far larger pathology in the discourse of corruption: the inappropriate use of public monies by officials, who, after all, have nearly unlimited legal discretionary power under the old socialist system, particularly when they stick together and can cite precedent. Rumor has it that the Linzhong schools are run down and the faculty unpaid because RMB 200,000 in education funds were diverted ("*nuoyong*") to pay for luxury cadre housing at Wanfang Automotive. Whether that is illegal or just an abuse of power is moot, as is the local cadres paying themselves before paying the teachers or putting in orders for a third personal auto each when Wanfang finally starts rolling (so as to "buy local"). However, it is surely corrupt by 1990s standards. Wanfang needed the quality housing for its visiting American investors, but Lu Tianming never raises the fact that the far vaster amounts *stolen* from Wanfang damaged the interests of, and might even have come from the pockets of, the foreign investors.

The broader question of how public spending is to be regulated is raised by the prototypical early 1980s concern about corrupt and decadent cadres wining and dining at public expense (as at a cadre hostel sporting neon lights in backward Linzhong county) and the vice governor's possession of a mansion in the Zhangtai suburbs and another well-appointed residence in town. Again, there are reasons for this spending. The elder Tian is a former Zhangtai mayor and party secretary, now entrusted with overseeing Zhangtai affairs at the provincial level. None of the expenses is illegal unless it is judged "excessive"; it is, however, corrupt from the viewpoint of popular, though perhaps not official, discourse.

Nepotism and regional favoritism, conjoined with administrative power in *guanxiwang* (webs of guanxi: personal connections and back-scratching), is another corrupt social phenomenon several steps ahead of the law that Lu Tianming illuminates in interesting ways. The use and abuse of public assets by high cadre children, or their catapulting ahead in their careers through bribes and favors to the parents disguised as gifts to the children, was a hot topic on the Chinese grapevine already in the 1980s. *Heaven Above* depicts the formation of an interlocking political elite from province to township (*xiang*, as the subcounty level was now called; it replaced the people's communes and became the locus of TVEs). All cement, even for the international auto firm, comes from a rustic plant in Linzhong's Upper Eight-Mile Village, where the vice governor originated. A distant relative of his runs it, so the locals have a bureaucratically mandated monopoly on cement production and an exemption from testing. Construction fraud is a natural consequence. Their substandard concrete leads to the fiasco of the assembly test block that is the last straw for the Americans, who are more averse to failure than the Chinese state. The brake line factory is a gravy train for the vice governor's ally Magistrate Qu and his friends and relatives (one of whom runs the TVE). More breathtaking is Wanfang Automotive itself, located in the sticks to be near the Tian clan rather than transportation lines. An outlandish proportion of its workforce is named Tian, including the unqualified head scientist Tian Enfu, who cannot be fired even after his willful failure to test the bad concrete. Plant deputy manager Ms. Tian

Manfang, a distant relative of the current vice governor, was once his children's governess (before the vice governor–to–be and his elder son raped her). The head of the American side of the enterprise naturally wonders whether the real manager is Ge Huiyuan or Ms. Tian.

In portraying the lawlessness of the new, market-oriented generation of China's high cadres and their children, *Heaven Above* suggests an underworld in the making. Tian Weidong has a private gang of enforcers. The police chief who committed suicide created a construction company for his son to run, with connivance from the former mayor and municipal housing corporation; the son wore a police uniform to help him shake down debtors and anyone else he pleased (76). At the macro level, Lu Tianming evokes the specter of old, Kuomintang-style bureaucratic capitalism. Even before and without Soviet-style privatization of public assets, particular cadres and clans, like the Tians, can milk a state-owned enterprise (or half-state-owned joint venture) and make it serve their private interests. This raises the question, was it always thus, or was it perhaps even worse (except in the amounts of money diverted, in those more penurious times) under "pure socialism," before the market reforms? Linzhong's mountainous wilds claimed precedence in development partly because they were an old revolutionary base.

The most remarkable corruption, though Lu Tianming makes little of it, is a case of obstruction of justice. The reader learns, eighty pages into the novel, that Mayor Dong and the chief of police were not murdered, but committed suicide. Yet CCP municipal secretary Lin Chengsen presides over a municipal meeting that falsely declares the cases to be unsolved murders, after having ordered his cops to spirit away crime scene evidence indicating the contrary (notably the means of death, which a suicide could not have removed). He rationalizes that Zhangtai's citizens would be less demoralized to think that they lived in a city with a high murder rate than in one with corrupt officials, and that memorial services to raise municipal (and cadre) morale can only be held for officials who are innocent victims. All suicides in the novel are victims as well as perpetrators, but their victimhood implicates higher-ups. Secretary Lin actually tells Mayor Huang that he tampered with the evidence. This privileged knowledge makes Huang complicit in outrageous judicial corruption.

The biggest individual case of corruption is one outside the law, but within corruption's more figurative discourse—that of Huang Jiangbei's character. Though immune to the lures of money, perks, the opposite sex (Ms. Tian), and the elemental power to bully, he is corrupted by another kind of power: the power to act efficiently without being obstructed by legalities or consideration of means, even if the ends are good. In time, first his wife, then his assistant, Xia Zhiyuan, notice that Huang Jiangbei has changed. In their words, he has become wrapped up in politics and his career. That is of course too simple. Still, Huang makes a number of bad choices, and many of them are the result of his penchant for going outside the rules, variously to placate or deceive the powers that be. His unilateral schemes to rebuild the Pear Tree Hollow school are an early warning, like his fondness for ultimatums, which reveal a willingness to wheel and deal. He strikes deals with Tian Weidong himself, who astutely responds by promising to help get back the money his brother stole if the mayor will just delay getting the law involved for forty-eight hours. Huang agrees, taking it upon himself to delay prosecution.

Huang puts the bribe money from the furniture to good use instead of reporting it. However, in the eyes of his wife and trusted assistant, his will has weakened. He has even begun to smoke again. Is Huang Jiangbei's ambition a tragic personal flaw that is bound to bring him down? Or does his fall come from the "natural" contamination of bad surroundings in bad times, as the discourse of corruption might have it? Huang's mentor Ge Huiyuan thinks it was both: "Huang Jiangbei has his ugly side; he is too anxious to be an official. But you can't blame him for that. In China, if you're not an official, you can't do anything at all" (387–88). What is corrupted is not Huang Jiangbei's morality, but his judgment, the very rationality and intelligence that he, as a super-intellectual and technocrat, has always held most dear. His hubris is such that at the end he begins to keep secrets from Xia Zhiyuan. Huang thinks that *he* sees the big picture and that Xia does not. Liu Bei thinks himself a better strategist than Zhuge Liang.

Looking further into the world of *Heaven Above*, one sees that doctors insist on an up-front 5,000-yuan registration fee before even looking at a patient, however pitiful her condition. Books get published, after ghostwriting if necessary, when the author is a person of influence. Reporters are given expensive "commemorative" gifts to get them to cover the news. "Theorists" propose that guanxi are a "productive force" (40). And corruption is itself corrupted. In a bit of bureaucratic lèse majesté, county-level cadres in Linzhong receive Audis (117), which ought to be reserved for provincial-level leaders. (Huang is at the municipal, Volkswagen Santana level.) These nitty-gritty details bring us to the next subject, "realism."

The Novel and Realism

The mystery themes of "who stole it?" and "will they get away with it?" quickly supplant the red herrings and even the falsified "murder" cases at the start (foreshadowing the serious corruption themes, if *Heaven Above* is read as literature), propelling the popular reader through to the climax. Key witnesses disappear, anticorruption chief Zheng's missing evidence leads to a classic quest for an unobtainable object (like the missing books of kung fu in Chinese martial arts fiction), and new mysteries bubble up even near the end. The missing 1.7 million yuan is discovered only in the final chapters, by the all-knowing Tian Weidong, who is as surprised as anyone, since his brother did not steal it. The characters are amazingly interlaced. The protesting teachers of Linzhong county are Huang's old classmates and mayoral special assistant Xia Zhiyuan's girlfriend turns out to be a cousin, roommate, and business partner of Tian Manfang. Many plotlines are improbable. Gangs negotiate with mayors. The mayor negotiates with gangs, though his boss, the party secretary, has him under surveillance. Embezzlers write IOUs for the money they steal. And Lu Tianming trades in sentiment and melodrama. Zheng Yanzhang has a fake stroke; Huang Jiangbei's wife has a real tumor. Still, *Heaven Above* can be considered within the realist tradition.

To start with, the social background is ugly. Housing for the masses is inadequate; poverty in the villages is unspeakable. Huang's daughter is groped on a bus. Ge Ping has her purse stolen at the dirty, transient-filled bus station and runs into hobos, or juvenile dropouts (*liumang*), while hitching a ride on the rails to Beijing. They try to rape her. In the meantime, Lu Tianming reveals material tidbits of bureaucratic practice such as the officials' separately wired red "hot line" telephones for security and other important party and state business. His style is conventionally realistic, with running commentaries on the characters' thoughts and reactions to each others' speech. Slangy dialogue and interior monologues, in which characters play out in their minds conversations they might have had if only they were bolder, dominate the prose. The implied narrator is himself very folksy, philosophizing from time to time in short, witty aphorisms and occasionally aiming rhetorical questions at the reader in a personal style. The text is sparsely punctuated with psychological analysis.

Evocative of classic realism in the Western tradition is Lu Tianming's attention to character, and not just that of the tragic figure Huang Jiangbei, who develops as a man and public servant through the chastening of failure. Even the mayor's private secretary develops. After a crisis of conscience, he decides no longer to spy on his boss for the municipal CCP secretary (348). But character in *Heaven Above* develops mostly through conflict; characters tend to be paired. Huang's home-picked assistant and long-time associate Xia Zhiyuan scolds the acting mayor every time he compromises with the power structure or fails to act in a straightforward, prosecutorial mode. Xia resigns before fate gives Huang Jiangbei his comeuppance. Meanwhile, Xia's sacrifices for the public engender another subplot, and in turn lessons for him, as he is chastised by his girlfriend, who has given up on public service because of its corruption. She works for the private sector, managing Ms. Tian's restaurant. The girlfriend, in the end, learns not to be so cynical. She forgives Xia for both his reckless idealism and his later cynicism, which finally result in a happy medium. The character of Huang Jiangbei's wife is revealed not so much in relation to him as to their daughter, who suspects she is having an affair with Huang's old classmate, an editor. But Mrs. Huang was doing no such thing; she simply had the prescience to get the man to publish Huang's dated Qinghua University thesis, in case his venture into politics might fail.

More interesting are the villains. The Tian brothers engage in an evil inversion of the good cop, bad cop approach to manipulating their prey. Weiming uses gangland muscle to get his way; Weidong, representing the legitimate family interests (though by birth he is illegitimate), makes amends through soft power (an apology), then tells Ms. Tian his tale of woe. As the future vice governor's bastard son, he spent his first ten years apart from the rest of the family, and after joining the Tian household he grew to love and identify with the governess that the rest of the family also abused. Perhaps he really has secretly loved her and resented the evil of his father and elder brother, as he claims; he offers Ms. Tian plane tickets to run away with him at the end. Or is this just another ruse to keep her from testifying? He also has always looked up to "Uncle Huang" (Huang Jiangbei), the Qinghua graduate whom his father held up as a role mode. Perhaps Weidong does grow, and his offer to Huang of plane tickets at the end comes from sympathy, friendship, and a sense of how unfairly fate has treated this hero of his youth. It is the same offer he has made to Ms. Tian. However, he might have been motivated by self-interest in both cases.

Tian Manfang is in the middle. Abused by the Tians, inwardly resentful of their power, and unable to respect herself for covering up their evil at Wanfang, she informs the new mayor of the misappropriated millions and, smitten by Huang Jiangbei's masculine strength, falsely confesses to his "crime" to save him at the end, having already been rescued once from suicide. Her early weakness and ultimate strength of character are another part of Huang's education. Ms. Tian's example helps her cousin to get her priorities straight, too, so that she can reconcile with Xia Zhiyuan. Getting rich in the private sector is not the purpose of life. One must sacrifice for something higher.

Ms. Tian may be Lu Tianming's artful enigma, but Secretary Lin is unfathomable. This might be due to a failure of the author's concentration. Could anything be more deleterious to the social fabric than Lin's lies and obstruction of justice in the cases of Mayor Dong and the housing director? It is Lin, as much as the vice governor (who is never directly heard from after his infamous party), who corrupts Huang Jiangbei by asking him to temporize in the cause of fighting corruption and even to kowtow to entrenched county, indeed township, cadres below them both in the hierarchy. Lin says he only wants Huang Jiangbei to succeed and not make political mistakes that might hamper his future career. That is, he must not weaken his guanxi with entrenched power above and below. As Huang begins to sink into his morass of compromises, Secretary Lin looks as if he might be one of the bad guys, working for the Tians—a touch that adds to the suspense. But when Huang fails, it is finally clear that Lin really was in his camp after all, however bad his advice. Like Huang, his temperamental opposite, he prefers the good, but in his deeds, he is part of the problem.[10]

Having told much truth and revealed much of the dark side of China, despite obligatory optimism at the very end and the deus ex machina of Party Central coming in to save the day through a work team, oblivious to the rise and fall of mere mortals on the local scene, *Heaven Above* finally remains true to the Chinese and European discourses of realism through the indeterminacy and pessimism of its ending—even though it started as a mystery thriller. Secretary Lin, the gray eminence who will make any necessary compromise with evil until the victory of the good is absolutely certain, serves out his term until retirement. It would have been more just if fate had dealt a blow to his career, not Huang's. The actual outcome is tragic. Vice Governor Tian will be prosecuted, but the reader is not reassured that he will not get off. Although Tian Weiming, the gangster, is in the party's custody, Weidong is not. He may be free to go abroad with his riches. Tian Manfang, the reformed Tian servant, is evidently forgiven by the party and allowed to go south to make a new start in business. It is unclear whether Huang Jiangbei will return to Zhangtai as a municipal worker, an automotive works executive, or a gardener, says the text. And nothing will bring back the dead: Manager Ge, the children in the bus, and Huang's wife, who dies within a year. The tone is one of forced optimism, but the actual outcomes say something else.

And yet, though *Heaven Above* is pessimistic within the parameters of Chinese realism, if not naturalism, Lu Tianming never argues that corruption *is* reality in China. Corruption is a disease, present in all facets of society, with a strength that can bring down any idealist who has a flaw. However, China's better administrators, even when tempted and corrupted, are not necessarily irredeemable. Corruption is not identical with contemporary Chinese social practice. Some later novelists will suggest that it might be.

Contributions to the Discourse of Corruption

Heaven Above goes beyond a view of corruption as mere crime and personal failure, as China's official discourse would have it, to a vision of the matter as broader but wholly manmade problems of "system." Money corrupts, but in China, power is the root of evil.[11] To Huang Jiangbei this realization comes as an epiphany, though it may strike readers as belated and banal: "The people of Zhangtai, the cadres of Zhangtai, are all quite up to the tasks before them. The problem is with a small group of people. They abuse the power that rests in their hands, so that the major players lose heart in carrying on their business" (282). Stated thus, however—as the problem of a minority—it is the official explanation of corruption in a nutshell. Yet, moments later, Huang describes a collective culprit as a "giant web of guanxi" (*pangda de guanxiwang*). China's anti-corruption novels all agree on this point, though social scientists may differ about the inherent good or bad of guanxi as a uniquely Chinese cultural phenomenon. Theorists use the term "guanxi" in reference both (1) to the biological and other "given" ties of common origination or shared experience (such as having attended the same school or labor camp)—which can, in their "naturalness," determine the *form* of power abuse, as Lu Tianming portrays so well in Linzhong county;[12] and also (2) to utilitarian guanxi, manufactured "artificially" for the specific purpose of individual or group gain (the kind of guanxi depicted by novelist Zhang Ping), sometimes for a onetime trading of favors.[13] Neither kind of guanxi relies in principle on hierarchical power, although high position always helps; both rely on conceits of kinship, honorary kinship, camaraderie, reciprocity, and mutuality, as if all Tians were Tians, regardless of their power, and apartment-granting housing bureau chiefs were equal to orchid-giving florists or grade-conferring teachers.

The guanxi that Lu Tianming criticizes, when Secretary Lin and even the presumptuous Tian Weidong admonish the acting mayor to keep his guanxi in good repair, does not suggest egalitarianism, but is instead explicitly hierarchical. This guanxi is a relationship in which an inferior seeks an all-purpose grant of power, or protection, from a superior in clearly defined ranks for his or her own all-purpose efficacy and career promotion to higher ranks. It is also, for those above, a relationship with inferiors, of course; subordinates grant general-purpose power and efficacy upwards, since some power is retained at the local levels, by permission of the hierarchy. Thus, local leaders can insist on escorting higher leaders visiting the grass roots, preventing them from meeting the common people or visiting the schools (117–19). (The opposite principle is that of the work team, by which the upper levels investigate the grass roots without observing the niceties of local power and custom.) This guanxi is, in a word, clientelism. It works hand-in-glove with paternalism, as when Secretary Lin prevents Acting Mayor Huang from doing the right thing "for his own good," so that he will not ruin his career—indeed, his chances of garnering the power, in the end, to finally do "the right thing." At the end, Secretary Lin even tries to decide for Huang Jiangbei whether or not Huang should turn himself in (his opinion is no, and is probably truly the result of his concern for Huang's sake, not Lin's own). Fortunately for society and morals, Huang is now chastened. He makes up his own mind to do the right thing.

The novel makes no obvious call for regime change, democracy, transparency, political reform, rule by pro-reform technocrats instead of career politicians, or even heightened supervision of the hierarchy, referred to euphemistically, but also realistically in bureaucratic idiom, as "the Organization."[14] The term becomes ironic and almost subversive insofar as the hierarchy comes to look like a corrupt conspiracy against the good; the term points to the Chinese Communist Party, whose Organization Department at every level in the hierarchy is the party's metonym at that level. Lu's deployment of the term "Organization" also furthers an implicit discourse of party versus government (the CCP versus "the state"). In *Heaven Above*, unlike many other anticorruption novels, the constitutionally guaranteed "leadership" (control) of the party over the state is entirely uncensored. It is in fact laid bare, as a defining characteristic of the Chinese system.[15]

Lu Tianming never dwells on Huang Jiangbei's "partiinost" (*dangxing*, party character or party-conferred character) or puts words in his mouth praising the party, though he is a party member.[16] In the hierarchy he gets his power from his place in the state apparatus. The political goal that he begins to see as his panacea for getting things done is not just to be elected regular mayor, but to become a member of the standing committee of the CCP municipal committee. Huang constantly humors and is succored by, and yet to the bitter end is stymied by, the party, personified not by Vice Governor Tian, who is known by his government rather than his party title, but by Secretary Lin, who personifies the CCP at Huang's own level.[17] That Huang is young for a mayor and only an acting mayor softens, and perhaps acts as a cover for, an implicit critique of the supremacy of party organizational rule over the state organization. Huang's kowtowing, not just for scraps of power sufficient to get things done, but for mere collegiality, is astounding. No different than Magistrate Qu, Mayor Huang stops in the middle of meetings to take telephone calls from the party secretary. Huang's own finance head, and the magistrates who are subordinate to him, will not follow his orders without prior approval from the secretary (164–65). The party secretary instructs the mayor's personal secretary Young Gao to spy on him, and when Huang discovers this betrayal, Lin has the gall to urge the mayor not to fire Gao, since he was just following Lin's orders and it would be a shame to spoil his career (192–94). Moreover, after firing him, the mayor decides to take him back! This comes after Huang has asked Lin point-blank, but respectfully, if Huang's own prescribed role is to be the party secretary's puppet (108). Even in questions of criminal investigations and prosecutions, the system is still "the secretary decides," to quote an old slogan from the Mao era (65–66). Secretary Lin uses his power ruthlessly to persecute anticorruption head Zheng and his lieutenant.

More abstractly, Lu Tianming's major contribution to the discourse of corruption, and perhaps the biggest issue he develops in the conflicts of his plot, is the idea of a trade-off between corruption or justice on the one hand and managerial efficacy on the other. Huang Jiangbei knows he is going along with corruption, even letting his own judgment be slightly corrupted, by fostering the use of substandard parts in Wanfang automobiles and buses. But if no one gets hurt, then it is but a temporary concession to "reality," a shortcut on the road to future prosperity *and* social justice. In his portentous letter to Ge Huiyuan, Huang urges that the local brake lines be used temporarily, for the greater good of bringing Wanfang into production. This gamble is an attempt to negotiate a compromise with the laws of physics (which Huang, of all people, should understand) analogous to his many prior compromises in politics. Huang, for instance, lets the evil Tian Weiming escape prosecution *temporarily* (surely an obstruction of justice; and who gave Huang the right to negotiate deals on his own authority? it is Secretary Lin's mode of operation) for the greater good of returning operating capital to Wanfang from Russia.

The idea of social justice, and anticorruption in particular, as antithetical to economic development is not new, and has its most extreme expression in social science theories that view corruption favorably as a rational choice, as grease for the irrational, squeaky wheels of socialism. Lu Tianming does not go so far, and the logic of his plot suggests that compromises do not pay. Huang Jiangbei is undone by fate, or bad luck, perhaps, but there is also an inference that Heaven (Above) has eyes—that justice will ultimately prevail. On the other hand, Huang's rationale for his actions remains compelling. He has done Wanfang a good turn in the long run by proving that it can be productive. Trade-offs are widely believed to exist in economic development, social equity, and in justice itself, as America also acknowledges in its system of plea bargaining. By raising the issue of trade-offs, Lu Tianming leaves the significance of the corruption in his novel an open-ended question, suitable for generating further thought and debate.

Heaven Above's other contribution to China's anticorruption fiction appears to be its deployment of narrative elements evidently so useful in engaging popular outrage over corruption as to prefigure a popular (which is to say, comfortable rather than entirely original) genre or formula. Let us summarize some of the elements in the paragraphs that follow. The genre is, to begin with, "epic" or long—*Heaven Above*'s 409 pages and 276,000 characters is a short preview of future, longer works in the genre. The novel describes multiple kinds of corruption at multiple levels of the party-state hierarchy, but they are caused by a limited cast of interlocking characters. (Unlike later novels, *Heaven Above* does not indulge in descriptions of sybaritic lifestyles, which may be counted as one of its sacrifices on behalf of "seriousness.") The prose is easy to read. It is heavily reliant on directly dramatized dialogue and is presented by an omniscient but generally unself-conscious narrator who is not given to editorializing, though apt once in a while to address the reader directly, as a storyteller. The point of the novel lies in the story, not in passages of ethical or theoretical discourse. The plot is structured using crime, detection, and mystery themes and devices.[18] These well serve a novel about corruption, a form of behavior that cannot stand exposure to the light of day, and yet professional crime fighters play second fiddle to the higher ranking party or state generalist bureaucrats even in the detection of corruption—as is only realistic, for civilian bureaucrats do intervene in high-level investigations. Moral consciousness outweighs legal consciousness. The interest in crime and detection, however, requires a fast-moving plot without much time for melodramatic excess, even if the villains are truly villainous. Technically ingenious scams (bearing "information" about the new China) prevail over crimes noteworthy for their wickedness. The formula is also relatively unideological in tone, though fully in favor of the economic reform cause, however much corruption has come in its wake.

Like anticorruption novels to come, *Heaven Above* is very present-minded, and even the setting is formulaic. It is a big city with a large factory under its jurisdiction, an SOE (or, in *Heaven Above*, a half-state-owned enterprise, though the novel does almost nothing with the foreign side; the American characters are offstage and never speak). The SOE is a microcosm of urban China itself, and yet the municipal/SOE divide lends a binary aspect to the plot reflecting the "organ/enterprise" distinction in life and the era's focus on economic rather than political reform. The scenes are similarly binary, tending to take place in municipal party and government offices (often in formal meetings and face-to-face exchanges in cadres' offices) or on the factory/enterprise floor, in offices, or in dormitories. Hierarchically, interplay and crossfire occur among the provincial, municipal, and submunicipal levels (this novel has the full panoply of county government, municipal level enterprise, township and village government, and TVE). Not all novels have such a clearly implied binary distinction between the party and state hierarchies as *Heaven Above*. The deep social background is fear of "social instability." Groups of the "masses" (non-CCP commoners) discontented with the performance of the socialist sector of the system are organizing, going on strike, and demonstrating in public, embarrassing the party and state. Unchecked, "social instability" can lead to revolution and regime change, a common understanding in official and nonofficial discourse that cannot be verbalized in official discourse.

Heaven Above prefigures and in retrospect typifies the anticorruption novel with its hero, a middle-aged man who nevertheless is progressive and scientific in outlook. In the larger formula, the hero is likely a bureaucrat in a difficult, unprecedented spot (he's literally in a new location in *Heaven Above*), facing hard choices of both politics and management, the latter involving responsibility not for directly running an enterprise, but for municipal production and social welfare. If the hero is in law enforcement, he is not senior in rank but is still seasoned and rational, verging on middle age. He will be, withal, a classic, incorruptible "good official" (*qing guan*), facing off against bad people at his level in the hierarchy or higher (in this novel, Secretary Lin is something of a red herring; he is not really an enemy after all, just one who makes the hero's bureaucratic success all but impossible). Being on the defensive much of the time, the hero represents justice, not crusading reformism (Huang Jiangbei is the exception, and his take-charge attitude gets him in trouble). To sternly face bad people, the hero must be not just a *qing guan* but a judicial righter of past wrongs (a *qing tian,* or "blue sky" official, like Judge Bao); here, again, Huang Jiangbei does not entirely pass the test, and he pays the price. And the hero is a technocrat, hence a man of science and good sense (he is always male). His entire career history is presented in a thumbnail sketch (here as an out-and-out résumé, which constitutes this novel's one-page chapter 4). He is practiced at commanding subordinates, and he prevails by penetrating bureaucratic human relationships, not by law work or pondering minor clues. But he still has much to learn, and the novel follows his learning process, as a sort of bildungsroman for a middle-aged man (newly arrived upon the bureaucratic stage, but no longer green in the game of life). His charisma and attractiveness to females derives from his intelligence and position in the hierarchy rather than animal magnetism or visionary plans. The novel's perspective is the hero's bird's-eye view of what is below him in the hierarchy, though much of the corruption that he must uncover, flying blind and using his own detection, is above him. Corruption as such is hierarchical, with local and municipal corruption supported by a protector one bureaucratic level above the hero in a realm whose business is not shared with him.

The Chinese discourse of corruption has always centered on the misbehavior of males in power; women are chiefly means by which males are corrupted, or at least tempted. Tian Manfang, assistant manager at Wanfang, is Acting Mayor Huang's temptress. As important as whether she is good or bad is whether she stands with Huang or with the Tian brothers. The weak link in other bureaucratic heroes' armor may be their wife, or even their maid. In realms of power, other females are likely to be mistresses. If they figure as investigative partners, they are subordinates, and perhaps romantic objects, of the "strong male" who is the hero. The genre is not feminist.

Limits of and on Realism

Why are China's popular and serious novels about corruption, in principle noteworthy for their political edge, so formulaic? We are only partway through the list of generic characteristics. Let us now begin to distinguish among formulaic elements that are politically mandatory, customary, or simply discretionary.

The first mandate from China's system of political control is so obvious that one might overlook it: fiction with corruption themes must be "anticorruption fiction," not fiction about corruption. One can show how corruption is accomplished only if this is overshadowed by a demonstration of how it is necessarily conquered in the end. Compliance with the censors is thus a matter of both the proportion of positive and negative subject matter and the final outcome in the plot. Even the relatively realistically indeterminate ending of *Heaven Above* has its tacked-on optimism: the former acting mayor still has the affection of his people, whatever turn his career may take after the party has determined how to deal with him. Moreover, if any plot with corruption necessarily has anticorruption, then the characters necessarily divide into bad and good—as Lu Tianming once astutely observed at a forum.[19]

A "good official," not mass action, is responsible for the anticorruption campaign. The "social instability" implied by mass action would reduce public confidence in party leadership and make it seem not in the lead, but in the rear guard. The intervention of Party Central at the end is a deus ex machina badly compromising the plot's realism, yet it provides reassurance and maximizes face for the party, and thus seems an obligatory part of the formula. The official discourse of corruption indeed exalts obedience, not just of the masses but of the middle-level cadres who are caught up in anticorruption in the novels as in anticorruption campaigns in life. *Heaven Above* tends to break the mold through its implicit criticism of obedience, along with party rule—of always having to check with the party before acting.[20] The supposed collectivism of such consultation is revealed to be a cover for absolutely hierarchical, top-down decision making. This is surely nonofficial discourse.

The good officials of the party and state naturally eschew luxury (corruption), and they work so hard that they have no time for family and skimp on sleep (Huang falls over from hypoglycemia after skipping too many meals). This is an old cliché from Chinese police procedurals, and it fits the old socialist discourse of serving the people. The cadres listen to the grievances of the people; this is the only place for social protest.

The defining limit of realism in anticorruption fiction, never explicitly stated but known to all authors, is the restriction on how high up the corruption can go. One powerful corrupt official may be at the provincial level, to provide protection for and even mastermind the corrupt elements at the municipal level (at which level at least some elements must be uncorrupted), but the highest position a fictitious corrupt official may hold is that of *vice* governor (e.g., Vice Governor Tian) or *deputy* provincial party secretary (e.g., Yan Zhen in *Choice*). A corrupt governor or provincial CCP first secretary is not permissible.[21] It is at that level and above that prosecution of corruption in life would be under the CCP Central Disciplinary Inspection Commission, not just one of its local branches. If one were to tread on its turf in literature, the central commission might even intervene as a censor, as it has done in regard to at least one film (see chapter 4). But anticorruption authors know where the limits are before they write.

In reaction to this restriction on expression comes a mandate that the authors impose on themselves: it is their *duty* to push the limits (become "groundbreaking heroes," in the parlance of the 1980s, when authors regularly competed to break taboos), and the ultimate expression of this is to depict corruption as high as they can get away with, even into the core party leadership, whenever that may be permitted. In the current situation, depicting corrupt provincial officials, to the extent one can get away with it, is therefore de rigueur—a formula necessity, not just for the readers, but for the author to maintain respect among his peers. This "requirement" is thus yet another limit on (and of) realism. And so, when *Heaven Above* and its television adaptation are now assessed by China's community of critics, they are remembered as the novel and teleplay that first depicted corruption at the provincial level. Even the author is content to so remember that as his creations' role in literary history. When *Heaven Above* first appeared, particularly on television, the invocation of a corrupt vice governor caused the production to take some flak.[22] However, in the teleplay's favor was the fact that its only partly named vice governor, who is never directly depicted or allowed to speak in the novel, likewise never appears on the television screen.[23] His reputation itself conveys his charismatic power. In subsequent novels and productions, Lu Tianming was able to nudge the level upward to deputy CCP provincial secretary, but no higher.

Another apparent consequence of writing in an atmosphere of censorship is that depicting corruption as a web, with protection from the top—or, better, directed from the top, as part of a hierarchical conspiracy, not just a guanxi-driven lateral conspiracy—is not just an emblem of freedom of literary expression. In the Chinese environment it is an obligation, and thus another formulaic limit on authorial freedom. And another factor drives some authors, notably Lu Tianming, to write about decision makers at the top of society: the Chinese discourse of realism, which requires attention to the "big trends" of the era. In the 1990s, Lu felt himself swimming against the tide of "pure literature." Elite critics felt that literature had to be about "individual life," whereas official critics thought literature had to be about the big trends as the party mandated them: the "main melody."[24]

Nearly all corruption in Chinese fiction is official; it is seldom initiated by the private sector (Liu Ping's *Dossier on Smuggling* is an exception). Does this reflect an unspoken ban on showing corruption in the private sector, whose market logic is the hallmark and ideological bulwark of the CCP regime in post-Mao times? Is it intended as a reflection of reality? Is it a reflection of the authors' felt obligation to excoriate official power, so long as official rather than private sector power remains hegemonic? Might it even reflect the solipsism of officials, who do not yet consider the domestic private sector powerful enough to have an active role in corruption? Or does it reflect the age-old Chinese discourse of corruption, which sees evil spreading from the top of society? One cannot say without extensive probing of the thinking of the authors. In anticorruption fiction, as opposed to crime fiction, "the butler" (or the governess, or the entrepreneur—here, Ms. Tian) is never found to have "done it." The focus on the top CCP leadership, instead of on capital and international capital, opens up a gap between anticorruption novelists and China's elite critics. But it is with the CCP, its officials, and their official discourse that the anticorruption novelists find themselves locked in an oppositional embrace—which fits the Chinese discourse of realism, as a force countering the lies of officials.

The figure of a (single) "good official," a "blue sky" official, may be as much a customary, historical, literary (and subliterary) formula as a mandated one. The tacked-on happy ending is not peculiar to Chinese communist fiction, either. In *Heaven Above* and most other novels about corruption, the social classes are still conceived in old Maoist categories, including the poor and the lower-middle peasants (38). Opening in a crisis atmosphere is also a stock-in-trade for popular mystery fiction. There is a sense that the "new man" who comes on the scene, or comes back to confront new problems in an old haunt made strange, is the last chance for a solution. Counterpoint between the hero and his master strategist is familiar from stories of Chinese history and *The Romance of the Three Kingdoms*, as well as Jiang Zilong's post-Mao classic "Qiao changzhang shangren ji" (Factory Manager Qiao takes his post). Investigative heroes have tics and mannerisms straight out of detective and cop formulas (long known to China's crime authors of the 1980s—and 1930s), such as lighting cigarettes and flicking lighters (50). There are even "good cops" who defy the organization to protect their own, such as Old Zheng in *Heaven Above*.

Of the discretionary formulaic elements, one of the most "unrealistic" (though it recurs in *Choice* and Liu Ping's *Dossier on Smuggling*) is the specter of major corruption actually being attacked, through investigation, by a secret counterconspiracy aiming to thwart the corrupt conspiracy within the party. But this, too, has roots in post-Mao crime fiction and, beyond that, Cultural Revolution fiction. More consonant with popular views of corruption on the Chinese grapevine is the vision of moral decline in younger generations, the problem of out-of-control high cadres' children.

It is formulaic for China's 1990s anticorruption fiction (as in fiction of officialdom) to provide full descriptions of political mannerisms, bureaucratic consciousness (e.g., constant brooding about one's chance for promotion), and matters of seniority, obedience, propriety, and jurisdiction. *Heaven Above* mentions Party School (24), which later authors would use as a convenient way of absenting major characters from the plot for a time. And Lu Tianming uses the technique, reflective of bureaucratic consciousness, of indicating rank not just through bureaucratic appellations, but by the type of car in which officials are driven. The provincial leaders have Audis; the mayor, a Santana (and later, evidently, an Audi; 218). Ms. Tian has her own Mazda, and the enigmatic, low-profile Tian Weidong, a compact Ford Tempo. Lu Tianming was hardly the first Chinese author to give his characters suggestive names in a Dickensian manner (the omnipresent Secretary Lin Chengsen is "Grove Becoming a Forest"), but he may have started a trend within the genre he helped found.

Perhaps the most interesting discretionary formula-element-in-the-making, considering that China is officially atheist, is Lu Tianming's patently nonofficial touch of appealing to a higher authority than the Organization itself. The book title and old Manager Ge, en route to suicide, evoke a sense of "Heaven above" that sees everything and will be the final judge. Even God (*Shangdi*, 367, 378) is mentioned. In the nervous days before the teleplay actually made it to the TV screen, censors did ask if it was appropriate for a drama set in socialist China to speak of Heaven, particularly in its title.[25] Apologists for the novel argued that "Heaven" and "God" referred to the all-seeing justice of the Communist Party!

Aftermath

Heaven Above quickly made it to television and was a hit, after overcoming objections during production that it constituted a wide-ranging attack on the party and socialist culture second only to the 1980s series *He shang* (Deathsong of the river) or was a reprise of the 1989 democracy movement's critique of society.[26] Lu Tianming vowed never to write another anticorruption work; the political risks and encumbrances were just too great. But in 2000, when the climate was improving, a film director presented Lu with some materials about a real-life case that lured him into writing the teleplay and novel *Da xue wu hen* (The blizzard leaves no trace).[27] The television series, a whodunit that actually does have a murder in it, won popular and critical acclaim by featuring ordinary contemporary urban people (notably a cop and his family) at a time when Lu's television network was still churning out historical dramas. The high cadre finally unmasked as the murderer in the novel and teleplay is psychologically complex and aberrant.[28] Despite formulaic elements such as an SOE sold for a song, protesting workers, and a slothful judicial apparatus, *The Blizzard Leaves No Trace* is more a whodunit solved by a lowly cop (though he is also a technocrat who has his own secret laboratory) than a deep or even focused probing of corruption. It also devotes much time to a love story complication involving the cop and a young reporter whom he fears is socially too far above him. The murderer, a vice mayor, carried out the deed to cover up his involvement in a stock fraud, but he committed both offenses in a fit of absence of mind. Society is troubled, but it is not as "sick" as the murderer.

Lu Tianming's new 2002 work, *Shengwei shuji* (Provincial secretary), seemed by its title to promise another advance in the portrayal of corruption at ever-higher levels. The TV drama was touted as the first to concentrate on provincial governors (three of them: past, present, and expectant). True to formula, a giant, floundering SOE figures in the plot, though it must compete with international firms after China's entry into the World Trade Organization. Lu Tianming went straight to the teleplay and composed the novel of the same name afterwards, although the book version came before the public first.[29] Viewers and readers anxious for breakthroughs in anticorruption themes may have felt suckered. The full secretaries are all good guys. Corruption still reaches no higher than a deputy provincial secretary. Lu Tianming had actually wanted to boost the "realism" of anticorruption writing to the top provincial leadership level, but he admitted to a reporter that "high official organs" warned him not to.[30] In the end, critics judged the TV series inferior to Lu's two previous TV productions. Filler about daily life and director-invented romances went overboard, weakening the main political themes.[31] In interviews, Lu now sounded defensive about having made a narrative in which corruption was a subordinate theme. He insisted his newest production was not just about corruption, which in principle sounded wise and also "realistic"; but he had, after all, made it clear in his defense of *Heaven Above* and *The Blizzard Leaves No Trace* that he was proud of their special "realism" in the contemporary, socialist sense: they told the truth in an environment averse to truth telling, and they also told people things they wanted to hear.[32]

3

The Banned Blockbuster: Chen Fang's *Heaven's Wrath*

The following is fact, not fiction. Wang Baosen, the executive vice mayor of Beijing, was found dead on a lonely wooded hillside in a Communist Party resort outside the city on April 5, 1995.[1] China's grapevine was soon abuzz with rumors that he had shot himself to avoid prosecution for embezzling funds amounting to US$37 million.[2] The scandal was said to implicate his superior, Chen Xitong. Chen was the boss of Beijing, being secretary of its municipal CCP committee. He was also a member of the twenty-person Politburo of the CCP Central Committee and a thorn in the side of the "Shanghai Gang" in power, led by Jiang Zemin (CCP general secretary since 1989, and destined to become undisputed paramount leader when Deng Xiaoping died in 1997). Having urged the hard line that led to the June 4, 1989, Beijing Massacre while he was the city's mayor (1983–92), Chen had aspired to Jiang's leadership position himself.[3] His reward instead was promotion to be Beijing's party head, "chief of the capital," but his power and his role in the massacre had also earned him enemies on his home turf. He still denied Jiang's full authority over him in deed and even in word.[4]

Chen Xitong was forced to take bureaucratic responsibility for the malfeasance of Wang Baosen, who had been his senior vice mayor and finance wizard, by apologizing and resigning from all his administrative posts twenty-two days after Wang's suicide. Once out of power, Chen was headed for increasingly rigorous forms of detention. In September

1997, he ended up in Qincheng Prison, which already held his younger son, the alleged playboy Chen Xiaotong,[5] and not a few characters Chen Xitong himself had locked away before and after the 1989 massacre. The father was not tried until July 1998, and even then the trial took place in secret.

Because of the news blackout, which exists to this day,[6] ordinary Chinese got their "facts" about the case by word of mouth and from Chen Fang's scandalous roman à clef "exposing" the corruption of the father, the son, and the unholy "Beijing Gang," *Tian nu* (Heaven's wrath). More news seeped in from the Hong Kong press. Domestically produced books that were unauthorized and of dubious origins sprang up like mushrooms after a rain, purporting to continue or supplement Chen Fang's work of presumed coded "faction."[7] Chen Xitong appeared briefly on television in 1998 when his sixteen-year sentence was announced. The list of his crimes left observers wondering why he was *really* being jailed.[8]

Heaven's Wrath came out in January 1997 and was banned three months later, in part for allegedly "leaking secrets."[9] Those who had printed and distributed the book were detained in May, but the author was not. Chen Fang (1945–2005), previously known as a journalist and magazine editor, must have had protection.[10] He had friends on the Central Committee, he said, who leaked information to him that kept his fictional exposés "about one year ahead of the news."[11] Jiang Zemin must have been happy to see his rival Chen Xitong defamed, but he could not have been happy to see the whole communist system denigrated. The book was in a gray area, having at first been published openly. The party originally dealt with it by advisories to editors telling them not to print any commentary on *Heaven's Wrath*.[12] The ban then caused sales to skyrocket to five million copies in pirated editions, claimed Chen Fang.[13] A blockbuster at home and an anticorruption icon abroad (it was translated into Japanese and Korean), *Heaven's Wrath* became a genuine *succès de scandale*.

Heaven's Wrath does not actually violate the taboo (described in chapter 2) on writing about a corrupt *provincial*-level CCP first secretary or governor, for the top villains of *Heaven's Wrath* are Jiao Pengyuan, a charismatic leader who heads the *municipal* CCP committee of an anonymous northern city, and his reckless son, hotelier Jiao Dongfang ("Orient Jiao"), who, with his band of thugs, has his hand in many illegal activities. They survive the municipality's vice mayor, whose shocking apparent suicide initiates a scandal in their city. But the city of Beijing is equal to a province in the administrative hierarchy, so if the novel's municipality is the capital, as all readers knew it to be, then the said taboo (and many more) were broken in spirit.[14]

Devoid of *Heaven Above*'s artistic pretensions, *Heaven's Wrath* is a page-turner, pure and simple. Chen Fang's vocabulary is simpler than Lu Tianming's, and his plot moves faster. On page two, the novel's hero, named Chen, holds a gun to his head, as if to commit suicide, although in fact, he is only testing bullet trajectories. Much later, the deceased vice mayor's son challenges a rival to a game of Russian roulette in yet another scenario made for filming (the rival says the challenger is imitating *The Deer Hunter*). The content is so relentlessly unflattering about the Chinese political system that it might fit the deplored category of "scandal fiction" in the eyes of official critics,[15] yet the prose is far too plain and direct to be called sensational in style. Chen Fang has no time for purple prose, melodramatic tear-jerking scenes, exploitative descriptions, or indeed cogent motivations of relations between high cadres and their cocky children. What makes the novel compelling to this reader is that every page either moves the plot forward or is crammed with commentary on corruption: details on how the thefts and scams are going down and characters' commentary on corruption and its meaning abound. As well, there are the dividends of the work being a roman à clef. Lu Tianming's *Heaven Above* was China's first contemporary anticorruption novel; *Heaven's Wrath* was the first self-conscious anticorruption novel.

The "exposure" of malfeasance and high living takes place within the frame of a conventional murder mystery, complete with chases, counterattacks, and fresh new murders, all hard-boiled mystery conventions familiar to Chinese readers. In the end everything—even a case cold after the passage of several years—is explained during an investigation by a fairly low-level "cop" (Chen Hu, or "Tiger" Chen, who is in the Anticorruption Bureau of the municipal procuratorate, but as such is a uniformed officer following clues like any police detective). All of this has a large dose of unreality; a low-level investigator cracks multiple cases seemingly on his own initiative, murders come thick and heavy, underworld gangs provide "protective custody" for turncoats, and it is discovered that the vice mayor's death is the result of "Orient" Jiao cornering him and forcing him to choose between suicide or being shot. In this roman à clef, that plotline is tantamount to accusing Chen Xiaotong of having caused the demise of Wang Baosen. No such theory has surfaced elsewhere, even in China's unofficial information network.[16]

However, despite these implausible formula plot twists and Chen's simple, "popular" style—with clipped sentences, street jingles (*shunkou-*

liu), and anecdotes—*Heaven's Wrath* has some claims to "realism" in the contemporary Chinese sense that we shall more fully and generally define in chapter 7. Chen Fang considered his novel "realistic," while of course denying that it is "documentary," as some have called it.[17] (Those who like labels might prefer fictionalized "unauthorized history," or *waishi*.) His work is known not for racy gangster language, but for bureaucratic dialogue in an idiom for which only an insider has a feel. Chen tells "truths" directly opposed to the "lies" of official discourse, not simply for the sake of scandal, but to make telling points about corruption as a social system. Even as a roman à clef, the novel does not just provide keys to implied roles in corruption played by identifiable people in life; it also enables an interface with knowledge available in the world press that was too dangerous for Chen to fictionalize. Key culprits in life were intelligence operatives. That tacit premise puts Chen's story in a new light, furthering his vision of official corruption not just as economic crime, but also as political subversion of the state. Skullduggery by out-of-control intelligence operatives in the capital of the Chinese communist empire evokes the same specter as that of the emperor's guard in the Roman Empire—praetorianism, or unsupervised power by forces with no more claim to legitimacy than their delegated geographical closeness to the center of command.

Chen Fang's page-turner favors action and dialogue; his prose is just a step away from a screenplay. And yet, a few choice pages of dialogue develop a theoretical discourse on corruption. This potted theorizing is a curious and yet relatively learned exposition that has put social science rationalizations of corruption in front of millions of popular and "serious" readers. These pages were excised from the edition of the novel that was finally distributed openly in China after 2000, though the latter edition is triple the length of the original, banned work. The original novel is also enriched by allusions to, indeed lists of, great Chinese corruption cases, ancient and contemporary, as comparative background. These lists were excised from the officially approved edition, too.[18] The revisions necessary for publication invite analysis, but the special "limit of realism" governing *Heaven's Wrath* may be Chen Fang's very passion for asking fiction to do the job of China's throttled journalism. That carries its own burden.[19]

The Storyline

Below, fictional names are followed by their presumed counterparts in life, after an "approximately equals" ($\cong$) sign, though "more or less suggestive of" would be more accurate. The major places of action are "H city" (≅ Wuxi) in "S province" (≅ Jiangsu) and the unnamed metropolis (≅ Beijing) controlled by Secretary Jiao and his cohorts. For convenience, I refer to that metropolis below as "N city," for "northern." The time is 1995.[20]

Secretary Jiao Pengyuan (≅ Chen Xitong) leads N city through the all-powerful standing committee of its municipal CCP committee. Mayor Lin Xianhan (≅ Li Qiyan), titularly his no. 2, is so ineffectual that Mayoral Assistant Qian Zhong (≅ Huang Jicheng?),[21] the no. 3, virtually takes his place. No. 4 was the executive vice mayor and finance chief, He Qizhang (≅ Wang Baosen). He has just committed suicide, like his counterpart in life (He Qizhang on May 4, or "1995.5.4"; Wang Baosen on April 5, or "1995.4.5"). The one deputy municipal secretary with spine, Fang Hao, may have no specific counterpart in life. In charge of political-legal work and concurrently secretary of the municipal Disciplinary Inspection Commission, this "good secretary" will be able to make the necessary investigations go forward—once he returns from Party School.

For now, the CCP municipal committee is content to declare He Qizhang a suicide and sweep it under the rug. However, Chen Hu, "Tiger" Chen, a lowly division chief (*chuzhang*), is more aggressive than his superior, the politically cautious Anticorruption Bureau head Zhou (who is more like *Heaven Above*'s Secretary Lin than Old Zheng, his titular counterpart in that novel). Luckily, Zhou later exchanges places with the good secretary, Fang, and goes off to Party School. Meanwhile, Tiger Chen and Ms. Tao Suling of the municipal party Disciplinary Inspection Commission go out to the lonely mountain (≅ Huairou county) where Vice Mayor He met his end. They find a second bullet casing. Chen is sure the vice mayor was murdered, especially after the brakes on his own Jeep Cherokee fail as he comes down the mountain. Ms. Tao, his partner and budding love interest, dies in the accident, becoming, if Chen's theory is correct, the second murder victim. From now on, Tiger Chen is out for revenge as well as justice.

So is the vice mayor's surviving son, He Kedai (who has no newsworthy counterpart in life). He is an out-of-control high cadre son ("princeling") with mafioso characteristics like Secretary Jiao's son Orient, Kedai's former friend but now rival (for the love of the corrupt municipal police chief's corrupted daughter, for one thing). He Kedai has lost influence since the disgrace of his father, but he still has a gang of goons. Like Chen Hu, he has concluded that his father was murdered, and by the Jiao organization. Indeed, when He Kedai almost perishes in an accident at a riding club, Kedai considers it an attempted murder by Orient himself. Meanwhile, police from S province (≅ Jiangsu), in the faraway south, mysteriously slip into N city and spirit away municipal official Li Haoyi (≅ Li Min)[22] after a sting. The N city fathers thuggishly contemplate kidnapping someone from S province in return as a hostage.

In a scene made for the movies, Chen Hu, lowly public official and son of a rickshaw puller, crashes a fancy dress ball held at Orient Jiao's base of operations, the Dipingxian, or Horizon Hotel (≅ New Century Hotel), which is half of a double-needle hotel structure joined by a skywalk with the Dongjiao, or Eastern Suburbs Hotel (≅ Xiyuan or Western Realms Hotel) in the eastern suburbs (≅ western suburbs). When Orient calls the gate-crasher "China's Holmes," it is a snide reference to his low social origins. But the Tiger meets and dances with a mystery woman of the glitterati, Qiu Siyu, and observes robber barons such as Hong Kong/Singapore magnate Wang Yaozu (≅ Li Ka-shing, one of the world's richest men and a known real estate partner with Chen Xitong even before Li made international headlines with his designs on a McDonald's property in the middle of Beijing, a subplot in the novel related below). Another celebrity present is Steel King Sun Qi (≅ Zhou Beifang, manager of Capital Steel's Hong Kong branch and assistant manager of the main Beijing complex headed by his father, Zhou Guanwu, crony of Deng Xiaoping).[23] In a side room at the ball, Orient Jiao negotiates a bribe that the Hong Kong magnate will pay to Orient's Swiss bank account, fills the reader in on various parties' corrupt ventures, and gives the Steel King and Jiao Pengyuan's personal secretary, Shen Shi (≅ Chen Jian?),[24] payouts for their previous investments or services as middlemen.

As the plot thickens by means of multiple cutaways, separate investigations by He Kedai and Tiger Chen converge and they become mutually wary allies. Kedai confronts the arrogant Orient Jiao after kidnapping a stablewoman at the scene of his accident and then one of Orient's bodyguards, a woman, who confirms that Orient meant to murder him. He Kedai hires a private detective to put Orient's rackets under surveillance (a useful novelist's device for imparting information about the Jiao scion's schemes and underworld connections, including a Hong Kong drug lord, Uncle He). Kedai conducts a memorial service for his father to see who turns up, then turns over the fruits of his sleuthing, plus a list of his father's associates, to the indefatigable Chen. "The Organization" (Chen Fang deploys the term even more ironically than Lu Tianming)[25] pulls Chen off the case because he is too successful. (And why should the procuracy be investigating murders, which is public security's job? Yet

Chen Hu, though unafraid of authority, does not bend rules like Lu Tianming's investigative hero, Acting Mayor Huang.) Luckily, Fang Hao returns to N city, providing Chen some moral and political (more than legal) direction and cover. Chen's new assistant, replacing Ms. Tao, is Ms. Jiao Xiaoyu. True to the Chinese formula, she is the Tiger's equal, more like *Heaven Above*'s Xia Zhiyuan than a mere Dr. Watson. Somehow it never dawns on Tiger Chen that she might be one of *the* Jiaos, indeed the kingpin's niece! Her charms gradually break down his reserve and he falls for her, until he learns who she is and indignantly terminates their budding romance. In fact, she is fully ready to prosecute her uncle and cousin, whom she distrusts.

Down south, Li Haoyi and his H city connection, Feng Aiju ($\cong$ Deng Bin), crack under interrogation; Chen Hu gets to go interview them. Feng is just a middle-aged female cadre, a former worker guilty of "illegal amassment of capital" (she ran a Ponzi scheme, really) with investments from greedy cadres like those in N city. Her main qualification was the good sense to be generous with bribes and interest payments—as Deng Bin was in life.[26] Li Haoyi invested RMB 100 million with Feng and lost it when the pyramid collapsed as S province heat came down on Feng. This explains why the deceased vice mayor's replacement as finance chief, Ma Zhongliang ($\cong$ Li Weihuai?), is being set up by the N city fathers as the scapegoat, unless he can return the missing 100 million. But what makes the N city municipal committee dissolve from within is the unauthorized travel to Hong Kong (which is a "crime" only in a party dictatorship) by Hao Xiangshou ($\cong$ Gao Qiming), deputy director of the Municipal Committee Office. And Hao has in fact, as his colleagues fear, fled the country to escape possible prosecution. A former Jiao mistress sets him up in Hong Kong with Uncle He, who, with Orient's connivance, strips Hao of his ill-gotten gains and sells him off to become a captive peon in Latin America. In the meantime, an informer exposes the dissolute behavior of the Steel King abroad, financed by his theft of public assets.

The last quarter of the 492-page, 380,000-character novel portrays the fall of the Jiao gang from a classic cop's perspective rather than a legal point of view. Investigators bring in a suspect, he cracks and reveals what he knows, and others are then run in, on up the line, uncovering more corruption and the story of the vice mayor's final hours. Demoralized, Secretary Jiao's personal secretary Shen Shi goes whoring, which allows the procuracy to bring him in as well. Learning that Li Haoyi has given him up, Shen gives up Steel King Sun Qi, Ma Zhongliang, and Orient Jiao. The younger Jiao knows his father signed off on the misuse of the missing RMB 100 million lost in the Ponzi scheme. Orient is willing and able to cover the loss from his own fortune to save his father (who is his protector), but Orient is unable to fool the investigators with his reimbursement, once Ma blabs about Secretary Jiao's role in the diversion of money. Jiao the elder had asked He Qizhang to be the fall guy (the Jiaos would make him mayor one day), and the vice mayor had agreed, but he retained Secretary Jiao's written authorization for the diversion as insurance. Jiao's son lured He Qizhang to the mountainside that fateful day to force him to turn over the authorization. When blackmail proved of no avail, a warning shot by Orient's henchman convinced the vice mayor he was cornered; he committed suicide to avoid being murdered.

Jiao Xiaoyu cleverly tracks down the cabbie who drove the vice mayor to the resort where he died, and from that discovers He Qizhang's secret mistress (Cui Yan), who kept Secretary Jiao's authorization for He. Hao Xiangshou repents and smuggles out of Latin America a letter of confession and accusation. Billionaire Wang Yaozu offers up evidence when allowed to testify secretly at home. Chen Hu tracks the murder of his former partner Ms. Tao and its cover-up back to Orient Jiao, while also figuring out an old, unsolved mystery called, in Chinese police bureaucratese (probably because a group to solve the crime was formed on November 2 in the relevant year), the "11.2 case." In the end, this rickshaw puller's son finally traps Orient and arrests him after an armed standoff. Secretary Jiao resigns. Heaven is wrathful, for it thunders without rain. In a scene recalling the ending of Lu Xun's story "Yao" (Medicine), Chen Hu asks for rain, which would be of use. It begins to fall, haltingly. Will there be a happy outcome in the end? Observes Ms. Jiao, "The longer pent up, the more will fall."

Corruption Cases

True to the tradition of China's novels about corruption since the late Qing, Chen Fang seems to have put every bit of corruption he has heard about regarding Chen Xitong and his gang into *Heaven's Wrath*, plus as many murders, attempted murders, and lifestyle excesses as he could imagine. Reflecting, again, a cop's-eye view rather than a legal point of view, the novel organizes corruption around skeins of characters involved, the guanxi, creating powerful images of an interlocking directorate of powerful thieves, not images of particular legal cases. Apart from the atmosphere of payoffs and covert contacts, of foreign passports and foreign bank accounts, details about who is profiting from what are often left a mystery to the reader, as they are to the low-level investigators. Repeated cutaways to simultaneous plots (in both senses of the word) reinforce the impression. The real estate development schemes that in life reportedly made Chen Xitong rich are not the focus of the novel, except for the Wucai Plaza affair, and its telling is sketchy.

The Wucai Plaza (≅ Oriental Plaza) Affair

Land development rights in the N city center (≅ Wangfujing) already leased to a foreign fast-food firm (≅ McDonald's) have been unilaterally abrogated and given to Wang Yaozu because he offered a new cash infusion to the city and bribes for individuals who cleared the way for the deal. In life, this breach of contract was notorious, for McDonald's had built its flagship Beijing restaurant there, the largest McDonald's in the world, and tycoon Li Ka-shing was the second of the "two husbands for one bride," as officials in the novel put it. In life, it was indeed said that a bride (or bribe) price paid to the Beijing municipal committee facilitated the bigamy. But this minor subplot remains a loose end in the novel. The fast-food firm has begun litigation (295–99), embarrassing N city, but neither the mayor nor Qian Zhong, who in the novel approves the new project, has been cashiered. Shopping malls were new and filled the public's imagination in the 1990s.[27] This particular scandal is launched early in the novel, providing an early warning that the work is not wholly fictitious. It is at the fancy dress ball that Wang Yaozu negotiates the bribe, with Orient Jiao, not his famous father. In life, the plaza, whose size and height ignored multiple planning regulations, was reevaluated, downsized, divided into eight separate city blocks, and finally completed in 2000. McDonald's relocated.

The Steel King's Embezzlement

Sun Qi (≅ Zhou Beifang) intends to buy steel mills in France with public money from the state steel mills he manages, laundering the funds through Japan with help from Orient's Japanese partners in his joint-venture Horizon Hotel. Yet this Chinese investment in factories abroad is openly trumpeted in the Chinese media as a triumph of the reform era. Sun keeps his SOEs' money in a private account abroad, and this, too, says the novel, is standard Chinese practice, to evade foreign taxation of public assets (410). Sun, however, draws on the money for personal use. As the N city committee comes under attack, Sun is accused by an anonymous informer at a Sino-French casino of embezzling from the overseas funds, and Secretary Jiao calls the Steel King home. He disappears with the money. In the novel, Sun becomes a U.S. citizen under a new name and joins an "investment club," really a secret society of wealthy and sinister Chinese-Americans (including lawyers—the sole mention of that profession in the book; 415–18). In the end, Interpol finds and arrests Sun Qi, though he goes free in the novel's 2000 revision. The Sun Qi subplot is not only perfunctory and quite unlike life (Zhou Beifang was arrested before Wang Baosen's suicide, in February 1995), but the fate of the money is also another loose end (which, perforce, may be realistic). Sun Qi also appears in other schemes. As princeling, he furthers the idea of a Beijing jet set that is its own interlocking directorate. Zhou did reportedly sink state assets into the Hong Kong stock market, with help from Li Ka-shing. The novel omits a link between Zhou Beifang and the Beijing municipal committee actually reported in the press: Zhou was charged with bribing Li Min ("Li Haoyi") and Chen Jian ("Shen Shi") to get his family out of China, and Zhou Beifang's fall was a domino in the fall of Chen Xitong.

The Pyramid Scheme and the "Missing 100 Million"

N city makes a killing by putting 20 million yuan into a phony H city ($\cong$ Wuxi) investment fund under Feng Aiju ($\cong$ Deng Bin). A subsequent, larger investment is not so lucky. It turns into "the case of the missing 100 million yuan," a crime that in life was posthumously pinned on Wang Baosen.[28] In the novel, Li Haoyi ($\cong$ Li Min) brokered the original N city "investment," which came in two separate RMB 10 million contributions. The first was from off-budget N city municipal monies. Vice Mayor He Qizhang approved the "loan" of these idle funds, and Finance Bureau chief Ma Zhongliang ($\cong$ Li Weihuai?) delivered them. Steel King Sun Qi provided the second 10 million yuan, via Hao Xiangshou ($\cong$ Gao Qiming). The investors illegally diverted (*nuoyong*) money from their units, though they paid it all back with interest. Exorbitantly high off-the-books interest—35 percent in two months—was the come-on for N city investors. That included 10 percent for the public (though probably really to a slush fund or "little treasury" outside the budget, according to allegations in life) and returns in the hundreds of thousands for the personal accounts of the four contributing officials, plus considerations for Secretary Jiao's present secretary Shen Shi and Orient Jiao. Li Haoyi took 1.5 million yuan from the two deals, investing them with He Qizhang's girlfriend, Qiu Siyu (193–99). The reader learns that He Kedai, too, had business dealings with Ms. Feng (200). Like father, like son.

The fund itself was phony because it was a pyramid or Ponzi scheme.

In life, fresh contributions from new investors, often officials in charge of smaller enterprises and government units in surrounding provinces, many of whom were willing to misappropriate funds from their units and earn interest rates higher than regulations allowed in order to make killer profits or crawl out of their own financial holes, supplied the capital needed to pay outrageously high dividends to prior investors—or at least the big investors from Beijing—in the nick of time. When capital ran out, prior to Deng's arrest, small investors were left holding the bag. However, the novel does not go deeply into what inspired such a hopeless scheme. How and why did it begin in H city, and what is the special link between N city and H city, whose leaders in the novel are at loggerheads? Why did rich cadres seek out a nondescript middle-aged former worker to invest their money, and what made her think she could keep the scam going forever? Did she have protection at the highest levels? Then again, we know now that postcommunist investors are often duped by such schemes, as they were also in Albania, Rumania, and Kazakhstan.[29]

These mysteries only deepen in the end, when even N city gets burned. Feng Aiju uses the windfall profits on the RMB 20 million to lure the N city fathers (Jiao Pengyuan, He Qizhang, and Ma Zhongliang) into making the much larger investment (of RMB 100 million) from off-budget municipal monies (originally allocated to build a ring road, in the revised version of the novel).[30] Feng hopes to pay it all back, with interest—it is only a two-month loan, like Deng Bin's loans in life—but the cops in S province confiscate her assets first. Whether Secretary Jiao, the boss, could have protected He Qizhang if he had become the scapegoat as he promised is dubious; anyway, the Jiaos do not feel they could take any risks. And with that, they hasten their own fall by resorting to threats and violence.

Though the 100 million yuan that N city lost is no small change, Wang Baosen in life is alleged to have spirited RMB 200 million from the Beijing treasury out of China to (then British) Hong Kong.[31] Figures in *Heaven's Wrath* allow a calculation that Sun Qi (in fiction) embezzled not just a hundred million yuan, but a hundred million U.S. dollars, which appears to be the biggest single embezzlement in the 1995 novel.[32] In his 2000 revision and enlargement, Chen Fang, echoing a number that has surfaced abroad,[33] has Secretary Jiao (now in prison) estimate that he and his vice mayor misappropriated, say, RMB 20 billion all told (793), six times the capital "illegally amassed" in the Wuxi pyramid.

Other Graft Cases

Other graft cases in *Heaven's Wrath* are not so closely related to the vice mayor's death or the surviving Jiaos. The old "11.2 case" began with an illegal transfer of foreign currency from the nation's reserves that He Qizhang enabled back when he was municipal Finance Bureau head (like Wang Baosen, in life), the job later taken by Ma Zhongliang. Bribes went to those who expedited the transfer (6–7, 239); Tiger Chen, the original investigator, was bureaucratically prevented from tracing the last missing RMB 2.5 million in bribe money, which he discovered was spirited out to Hong Kong to a man named He, perhaps "Uncle He." Although the illegal transfers ran to US$60 million, the reader is again bound to wonder why Chen Fang would invent this distracting subplot unless it exposes more details about real-life scandals of the Chen/Wang administration.

In another case uncovered by He Kedai's private eye and the son of an ex-con arrested by the Tiger, Orient Jiao borrows from his father, and then appropriates, gifts donated to N city at state ceremonies. He uses them to bribe other corruptible people and thus extend his own circle of evil (360). Most gifts were presented by foreign dignitaries, so the case might cause China to lose face in the international community (391). The crime is simple theft and the text does not waste time describing the state treasures, so this subplot simply adds plot interest while stoking reader outrage.[34] There is a whole array of digressive cases that broadens Chen Fang's portrait of malfeasance: police corruption (taking money from a third party variously to pressure suspects or let them off easy—by the police chief's daughter, no less, a "red princess") and other simple but massive alleged misuses of public funds, such as an "excessive" addition to Secretary Jiao's mansion achieved by He Qizhang's financial sleight of hand (43–44), the diversion of apartments meant for intellectuals to the use of high cadres (68), and so forth. The 2000 revision adds subplots about a crooked rural cadre and deliberately substandard construction on a ring road (*Dushi weiqing*, 216–17). Misdeeds by the vice mayor for himself and his clients that have a basis in journalistic accounts include long-term simultaneous rentals of rooms in several hotels and giveaways of apartments in dacha districts to favorite mistresses (267). In the meantime, the science of bribery has advanced. Subofficials arrange for the Li Ka-shing figure to play golf with Secretary Peng and lose. The billionaire's lost wagers are yet another payoff.

Corrupt Lifestyles

In life, Chen Xitong was convicted in 1998 of *tanwu* (graft, embezzlement) and dereliction of duty, but the former charge was trivial for one who traveled in his circles: that he received and did not report twenty-two gifts worth a total of RMB 555,000 (eight gold and silver items, six watches, four pens, three cameras, and one camcorder), plus RMB 50,000 in cash. He was also convicted of inciting Wang Baosen to misuse RMB 35,210,000 in municipal funds to build two villas for both of them, plus RMB 2,525,000 for associated expenses, including food and drink for the men's dissolute activities there.[35] Similar accusations, and the charge that Chen Xitong was *fuhua duoluo* (morally degenerate), were voiced in an August 29, 1997, decision by the Central Disciplinary Inspection Commission.[36]

Like Lu Tianming in *Heaven Above*, Chen Fang follows the Chinese discourse of corruption upward from concrete embezzlements and bullying to a more abstract vision of the corruption of character. This is where the official and the novelist's discourses of corruption intersect, though the real convergence is in the *signs* of the corruption of character—lifestyles. The concrete offense common to *Heaven's Wrath* and the state's case against Chen Xitong is the misuse of public funds to build villas. That is where the municipal bosses and their friends met their mistresses, enabling lifestyle "crimes" of gluttony, sexual license, and having more fun than any public servant ought to. Chen Fang would surely have agreed with the party's conclusion that Jiao Pengyuan/Chen Xitong is "morally degenerate," but the author seems to differ from the official discourse about the significance of the party boss's moral lapse. In both traditional and current official discourse, depravity is evil in itself. In Chen Fang's world, depravity is a sign of something that is to him more disturbing: unchecked power. Evil in Chen Fang's world spreads through the abuse of power, not by simple contagion.

Corruption means that sons and daughters will be worse than their parents. This seems implicit in official as well as traditional discourse, but in the novel corruption signifies decay of the revolution and of its power, which is inherited without conscious delegation by cadre offspring. In *Heaven's Wrath* the princelings are far worse than the parents, and even Jiao Pengyuan himself, though the latter is the linchpin protecting all the other evildoers.[37] Corruption thus weakens the bad as well as the good. Only the young (including the vice mayor's son) are so bored as to indulge in decadent pursuits like horseback competitions in "aristocratic"

British riding habits and target practice with the latest firearms. It is they who find Napoleon XO not good enough to drink (75).

Chen Fang depicts Orient Jiao making his usual entrance at his Horizon Hotel in a fleet of three black Mercedes-Benz 560s: "The hotel entrance guard hurried over to open the door of the first, and out stepped two strapping young men 1.8 meters tall, wearing black overcoats, white scarves of real silk, and dark sunglasses like General MacArthur's. The one in front held a walkie-talkie, the one in back a cell phone.[38] They protect the boss" (19). The boss is thirty-something, clad in a white windbreaker, red scarf, and crystal-rimmed shaded glasses.[39] In the third car are two tall and beautiful young women. The one with a briefcase, in a red jacket with sunglasses and free-flowing hair, is Shali [Shelley?], top secretary to the boss. The one in a black Italian leather jacket and miniskirt, big-breasted and with a masculine hairstyle, is Zhu Ni, Orient's ever-present no. 1, a martial arts expert. (She is the one kidnapped and turned by He Kedai.) The file of five travels in the same formation on foot, with the males walking point. After riding in a high-speed private elevator to the boss's penthouse office, the men stay outside, barring entrance to hotel guests and staff, while the women escort the boss to his office, which is "like a presidential suite." Bodyguard Zhu Ni stays on the lower floor, while Shali accompanies the chief up another floor via an interior staircase. The boss sits in his executive chair, "a Japanese import that cost him 200,000, about the price of a Volkswagen Santana" (20).

The vision is one of inherited class privilege transformed into criminal, underworld privilege. The princelings consort with and behave like gangsters. Orient Jiao's moral inferiority to his father is dramatized when Jiao Pengyuan is shocked to hear of his son's more outré schemes, though often the two men act hand-in-glove, the son providing plausible deniability. The father *should* be shocked. Orient Jiao, in his special hotel rooms outfitted by the Japanese with cameras, has videotaped diverse officials with their mistresses for blackmail purposes, including the vice mayor. Orient has taped his own father fornicating with a current mistress, the famous news reporter Song Huihui.[40] He uses the tape to shame her into committing suicide. The suicide deeply wounds Jiao Pengyuan, and he is ignorant of the tape. Jiao Dongfang is a criminal, a pervert, a deceiver, and unfilial to boot. He is his father's ruination. The end is surely near when a Chinese son videotapes his father's adultery.

Secretary Jiao is immoral enough; besides his wife and Song Huihui, who also services the vice mayor—and Orient—he has a "senior mistress," former municipal cadre Ge Mengmeng ($\cong$ He Ping), whom the elder Jiao and He Qizhang packed off to Hong Kong years ago to be an entrepreneur and open up secret bank accounts for them. He Qizhang is just as bad. Besides sharing a mistress with his boss (as Chen Xitong and Wang Baosen did in life, claim some Hong Kong sources), he had Ge Mengmeng find him a Hong Kong starlet (actually a call girl, Qiu Siyu) to play with, whom he set up as a hotelier. Then there is his latest and least known mistress, Cui Yan, the high-class model to whom he entrusts the disputed document that gets him killed.

Orient Jiao's virtual murder of the vice mayor (forcing a person to commit suicide is a traditional offense, but it is not a crime in the modern Chinese code), his subsequent murders and attempted murders to cover his tracks after he hires an ex-con to cut the brake lines on Tiger Chen's Jeep Cherokee, and his other violent crimes appear to be strictly fictitious,[41] products of the novelist's fertile imagination. They confirm the moral decay of the younger generation but are too extreme to fit the mold of "realism." However, as components of a separate, formulaic world, they may be discounted by the reader for what they are: motivators of the plot, not of the already manifest corruption in the "real world."

The Novel and Realism

Heaven's Wrath frames its story within a shopworn crime formula filled out by a love story on the side (that of Tiger and Jiao Xiaoyu). The plot is replete with devious murders (such as by giving cyanide-laced toothpaste to a jailed suspect before he can talk),[42] detectives, chases, and even a private eye, all segueing neatly into police procedural entrapments and confessions at the end. Few highly educated readers would think *Heaven's Wrath* "realistic," but it is a coded novel about reality in a way most other anticorruption novels are not—though many if not most of the other novels are likewise inspired by actual cases. Intellectuals read *Heaven's Wrath* for "information," like everyone else.[43] In its truth-telling function, the novel meets some of the expectations of "realism" in the restrictive world of socialist propaganda; it encodes not just alleged crimes but also deep-structure truths that may not be directly spoken. Moreover, *Heaven's Wrath* lacks many of the formulas of its particular anticorruption genre. Chen Fang may have been right when he distinguished himself from Lu Tianming and Zhang Ping as "not mainstream" (*fei zhuliu*), presumably because of his novel's frankness about official malfeasance, its lack of a savior leader, and the fact that not all the bad guys get punished.⁴⁴ The crimes and corruption cases are solved by uniformed professional detectives (however unrealistic their independence—a problem remedied in the 2000 revision), not by party secretaries or mayors, or by Party Central coming in as a deus ex machina at the end. Unlike the bad guys, the good guys are such low-level bureaucrats that they lack both bureaucratic charisma and newsworthy counterparts in life. By most accounts, in the high-level cases in life corresponding to those of the novel, high-level party and law enforcement professionals led the investigations.⁴⁵ All the characters in the novel, both the good and the bad, are flat, and not necessarily true to life. Chen Xiaotong, the son of the party secretary, is usually described as introverted in life, unlike his image in the novel.

When a revision of the novel was printed in Hong Kong in 1998, laudatory prefaces duly praised *Heaven's Wrath* as realistic. Its portraits, even of the princelings, fit many readers' jaded preconceptions of the social "reality" in China's ruling circles. Chen Fang is as conscientious as Lu Tianming in differentiating which make of foreign auto is driven by which level of official, and he instructs the reader that China computerized its fingerprint files in 1993 (363) and so forth. Chen Fang had met Chen Xitong in person.⁴⁶

Law enforcement professionals would surely fault Chen Fang for his grasp of police procedure and the law, not to mention his many fabricated "facts." Tiger Chen contemplates bullet trajectories in what he thinks must have been the murder of the vice mayor and yet he never considers powder burns. The author's forte is a good eye and ear for official culture, including its language (its euphemisms), protocol, and interpersonal dynamics in meetings. The predominant role of the party and, within the party, the party secretary in command, is never covered up. Indeed, Chen Hu reports to Fang Hao, the party superior in charge of "important cases," before he reports to his titular boss, Zhou Senlin (243). Lesser bureaucrats fear that it may be too presumptuous of them to voice their opinions. They speak when asked to speak or else humbly ask for permission to speak, and when they are done, they announce that they are done speaking. The terror of a female coroner as she addresses a gathering of party elders is apparent in the brevity of her report. It consists of three sentences and "My presentation is over" (17), as if she were a child addressing a teacher. When criticism becomes intense in a session of the standing committee of the municipal committee, the boss goes to the toilet to enforce a time-out. "After Secretary Jiao got up to go to the restroom, the meeting in effect went into recess. Some smoked, some got up

to exercise, some conversed, but only about trifles unrelated to the meeting. For small klatches of two or three to continue discussing business at such a time was very unwise, since to clam up during the meeting and go off half-cocked afterwards was often seen as behavior that contravened the Organization—the greatest taboo in official life" (336).

Sometimes the effect is comic. When the boss goes to the restroom, you must wait a few minutes before going yourself, lest you be suspected of conspiring. You must not go when your boss does, lest you harm his dignity. And in going to the toilet, as in speaking at a meeting, there is a hierarchy—those with power go first. The timid mayor confirms this; he urinates third, after the secretary and Qian Zhong, who is titularly the mayor's assistant.

Chen Fang also skewers the press, which the party bosses manhandle. Song Huihui is literally in bed with power. However, she discovers and voices the principle of *televideor ergo sum* (I am seen on television, therefore I am). She will have no more to fear from Secretary Jiao when he disappears from the screen. Conversely, being televised with a leader is a way for a Hong Kong investor to raise the price of his stock.

In principle if not in every detail, the novel's cop's-eye view of how the bad guys were run in and informed on each other has a certain structural verisimilitude to life. The arrest of Feng Aiju ($\cong$ Deng Bin, executed November 29, 1995)[47] leads the investigators to Li Haoyi ($\cong$ Li Min), who leads them to Shen Shi ($\cong$ Chen Jian?), who helps them close in on Jiao Dongfang ($\cong$ Chen Xiaotong), which causes Jiao Pengyuan ($\cong$ Chen Xitong) to offer his resignation. Zhou Beifang ("Sun Qi") is the main figure left out of this loop. In life, he was arrested between Li Min and Shen Shi, before the vice mayor's death.[48] It did take time before the party accepted the boss's resignation, and he was under house arrest and in other forms of limbo for a time before being arrested. No decision about whether Chen Xitong would be tried had been made in 1996, the year Chen Fang submitted *Heaven's Wrath* to the publisher. Chen Xitong was not even removed from the Politburo and Central Committee until September of that year.

Chen Fang altered at least one detail in his 2000 revision that amounted to the "correction" of a factual error. In the revision, Li Haoyi is a former personal secretary of Mayor Lin Xianhan ($\cong$ Li Qiyan), not the party boss. That was true of Li Min in life. Chen Fang's information when he wrote the original version of his novel must have had its limits. Asked how he could have known that the living counterpart of his Hao Xiangshou character ended up in Latin America, Chen Fang admitted that it was a lucky guess, arrived at through a process of elimination.[49]

Contributions to the Discourse of Corruption

In depicting corruption spreading through mutually reinforcing webs of guanxi, the exchange of power for money, and the deterioration of morality across time epitomized by officials' "bad seeds," *Heaven's Wrath* is true to the discourse of corruption as formularized in *Heaven Above* and in tracts, novels, and histories from China's ancient culture. A traditional formula notable in Chen Fang's novel is personal secretaries (all male) of the municipal CCP secretary running his rackets by delegation while trying to manipulate the boss and run separate schemes of their own, like the subofficials (*li*) in official histories and gazetteers. In *Heaven Above*, Huang Jiangbei's personal secretary simply spies on him for the party boss. In *Heaven's Wrath,* Li Haoyi (≅ Li Min), Hao Xiangshou (≅ Gao Qiming, in life Li Qiyan's secretary, as noted above),[50] and Shen Shi (≅ Chen Jian?), three successive past and present personal secretaries of Secretary Jiao, are major scammers operating with unsupervised delegated power. They are a mutual support group, if not a conspiracy of their own,[51] discussing what kinds of business the boss "doesn't want to know about."

Chen Fang goes much further in showing corruption to be a matter of system, not just persons—corruption *of* the party, or even the party *as* corruption, not just corruption *in* the party. He lets us overhear characters discuss two successfully prosecuted corruption cases in which 70 percent and 100 percent of the cadres at a given level, respectively, were found guilty (335). Chen Fang does not say that party rule as a system is inevitably corrupt, however. His more theoretical contributions to the discourse of corruption lie in ironic set pieces of political discourse *defending* corruption and the author's own argument that the root of corruption in China is still power and special privilege, not money.[52] The set pieces argue five common excuses for corruption. They are devil's advocate arguments, voiced mostly by villains, so at first blush they are *fanmian ziliao*, "negative examples" or intellectual straw men invoked simply to be refuted. Considered in the abstract, however, these potted theories are thought-provoking rationalizations. The defenses of corruption may be designated as follows, in social science parlance: (1) norms have changed ("everybody does it"); (2) corruption is a traditional moral economy; (3) economically, corruption is a rational choice; (4) anticorruption is just an excuse for personal and political attacks; and (5) anticorruption is a disguised attack on the post-Mao economic reforms. Perhaps it is in the argumentative excerpts below that one can in fact make a case for

Heaven's Wrath as a work of realism, in both the literary and colloquial (wise to the "real world") senses of the term.

Norms Have Changed

He Qizhang's chauffeur, who lives in a better apartment than Tiger Chen, asserts that everyone is on the take these days. Only suckers and prigs refuse to adapt (136–37). Though he disagrees, Chen at another time makes a similar observation: that corruption has entered a new stage, when some corrupt acts no longer need be done in private. An example is officials who abuse their power over housing (a power of socialist command, not money power over property). Jiao Xiaoyu marvels that unjust assignment of housing by an official power play has led to the murder of an official. Chen Hu reproves her:

> Well, well, so the woman with a full stomach can't understand a starving man. Using one's authority to siphon off too many or too good apartments, or furnish them better than regulations allow, is a kind of corruption that's almost gone out into the open. Show me a unit that's not caught up in it! Some leaders get dibs on apartments for their grandchildren before their children have married. Meanwhile you see ordinary common people living four generations to an apartment all the time. (148–49)

Corruption Is a Traditional Moral Economy

Guanxi signifies perfectly ethical exchange to some, ethical because it embodies the principle of reciprocity. But reciprocity is "form"; does the content of what is exchanged matter? He Kedai is incensed that so few people whom his father helped by providing stolen money, jobs, houses, and help with their own heists acknowledge the debt by attending his memorial service. (Naturally, they fear incrimination by association.) The debt is the greater because the vice mayor broke the law for them (232). Such a rationalization is doubly dubious when articulated by He Kedai, but the ethical nature of guanxi in all its relativity is a strongly held belief of many. Moreover, Kedai says, buying off antagonists instead of trying to eliminate them is the enlightened method of Song Jiang, hero of *Water Margin* (62, 193). It is why he prevailed against all odds. "Giving" is a good impulse.

Corruption Is a Rational Choice

The Western social science idea that graft and bribes convey price information and facilitate lateral economic exchanges that central planning stifles had appeared in Chinese intellectual journals by 1993.[53] Says *Heaven's Wrath*,

> Whatever exists is rational and necessary, and that goes for corruption, too. The current system is too rigid. If you go through proper channels and use proper procedure, a bureaucratic approval will take you three months at best. Often it will delay you a year or two. But fierce market competition won't allow an enterprise to wait patiently. The market conditions for success will pass you by while you wait. To gain a time advantage, you have to spend money to buy off some government officials, with a few hundred thousand or a few million if that's what it takes, because in having the approvals in advance, the time you save is money. You can get rich if you can act when the prices and opportunities are right. A few millions in bribe money is just an investment. . . . In these circumstances, bribe money is no longer money, it's a lubricant to grease the jammed mechanisms of government; if you don't oil them, the gears won't turn. . . . Until the bureaucrat-driven system is reformed, corruption cannot be eradicated, because entrepreneurs cannot wait for a stultified apparatus to run smoothly to do their business. The market waits for no one. . . . So corruption has a dual nature. It damages the social structure while stabilizing the social structure, all the time promoting the positive outcome of prosperity. (248–49)

Thus does the manager of a computer company defend the vice mayor, who got things cracking in N city. The businessman does not, of course, reckon with the corrosive long-term impact on public trust. Chen Hu uses social science to question social science: "This [defense of corruption by the corrupted] is not so strange. They're the ones who benefit from it. You won't hear this viewpoint from those who are hurt by it" (248).

Anticorruption Is Just a Power Struggle

As the law closes in on Secretary Jiao's diverse clients, he complains of persecution by people allegedly struggling for his power. Chen Fang would have disagreed with that analysis, but many observers believe that in life Chen Xitong was felled by a double standard because he was simply too powerful. The delay in his trial, its secrecy, and the odd assortment of stated charges suggest that his fate was politically determined, regardless of his misdeeds.

Hao Xiangshou is a corrupt official about to flee to Hong Kong, but the reader is free to separate the messenger from his compelling message quoted below. Hao's soliloquy reinforces, in Hao's own words, a point made by Leslie Holmes, that communist anticorruption campaigns are intended to discipline and reassure midlevel cadres, except that Hao stands this on its head and sees it from the corrupt cadre's point of view. To him, corruption is the sop—the cement—that the Communist Party must use to retain the loyalty of its underpaid midlevel cadres. They in turn keep the top leaders in power and prevent them from becoming wholly reliant on the entrepreneurs, as in capitalist countries. Hao's speech below also explains the thunderbolt depicted on the novel's front cover, a trope also referred to in the book's closing paragraphs.

> Right now there's a lot of anticorruption thunder and the raindrops are big. But it never rains forever. When these gusts of wind are over, even if the thunder is loud, the raindrops will get smaller. Another gust, and even the thunder will be over. Anticorruption can never be carried out thoroughly because this so-called corruption is not just the doing of one or two people. The historical conditions are just not the same as when Liu Qingshan and Zhang Zishan went down in the Three and Five Antis campaigns. In the present era of reform and opening up, would they dare get rid of us and let the capitalist class take the reins? Not a chance. Another thing, there's no way they can go full throttle with anticorruption for an extended period. Whom does this regime rely on to prop it up if not the broad middle ranks of its cadres? If they don't get a little something from it, will they still give their all? Only if they can work the system to their own advantage will they be intent on preserving it. You could say that corruption increases the stability of the regime. Can our public servants see themselves next to those in Hong Kong? Taiwan? Developed countries? Their salaries are dozens, hundreds of times ours! Not only that, if you continue anticorruption for a long time, you'll expose a lot of unpleasant things about the party. Expose too many, and the masses will lose their faith in our party, and who wants to bear the historical responsibility for that? But you can't do away with anticorruption, either. Not only would the masses not allow it, the country would collapse as the corruption increased, so not to prosecute anticorruption would lead to the end of the nation. We're between a rock and a hard place. We have to fight it a while, then let up on it a while, to protect both the party and the nation. We just want to survive and develop in the cracks between the wavering policies. (282–83)

Remembering the CCP prosecution of corruption in the 1950s, Hao sees little difference between graft and mindless waste of public assets by officials authorized to do almost anything under socialism. Compared to Mao Zedong's colossal diversion of resources to build useless air raid shelters[54] and the wasted investment in the Baoshan steel complex because no one checked the suitability of the site, N city graft is a small loss. Focus on cadre lifestyles, too, is just a political diversion. Anyone can play that game. "Successive struggles had given Orient Jiao some experience: when an opponent can't be toppled on political or economic grounds, his lifestyle problems can be very valuable" (400).

Anticorruption Is an Attack on Reform

The claim that anticorruption efforts constitute an attack on reform is a common defense heard from the corrupt, even on the socialist left. But in *Heaven's Wrath*, not just Hao Xiangshou but also the super-capitalist Wang Yaozu (≅ Li Ka-shing) fears to rock the boat. The novel takes place just three years after Deng Xiaoping's 1992 Southern Expedition returned the nation to a reform course. Jiao Xiaoyu chides Wang: surely foreign businessmen do not seek to pay bribes on top of their investments (463)? But Wang does not require freedom from "squeeze," only stability, which is the party's goal. He only fears there may be no limit to what he has to pay (466).

Chen Fang's Counterpoint: Power Is a Subversive Force

Chen Fang argues that the basis of corruption lies in power, not money. Contrary to one of his character's rationalizations above, Chen is on record as saying that "Chinese corruption is not a money problem. Raise [an official's] salary ten times and it couldn't prevent corruption, because in his eyes, the country's money is his money. He thinks it belongs to him, so he doesn't feel like a criminal."[55] *Heaven's Wrath* also points out that leaders, even the spoiled "red princess" daughter of the police chief, can use sirens to go through red lights. The book's 2000 revision clarifies the point. Power, muses Secretary Jiao to his jailer in the days after his fall from power, belongs to officials and cannot be purchased, even by the richest tycoons. They can only purchase particular policies, such as the privilege of going through a red light on a particular occasion when accompanied by an official. Thus does Jiao Pengyuan correct the theory of "rent-seeking through authority" (*quanli xunzu*), "a new concept that some theorists have translated from Western political science." He adds, ironically, that "party documents have not yet formally translated this term, and the authority to translate it does not rest in my hands" (1010–11).[56]

Chen Fang's point is that power by itself corrupts. In an interview, he faulted Chen Xitong's development plans in Wangfujing not for breaking a contract with McDonald's, but for Chen's failure to consult Party Central beforehand—lèse majesté. Press reports suggest that Chen Fang may have been right, both in this instance and in the implication that Chen Xitong's major "crime" was being too powerful.[57] At the top—or in the capital—power can subvert the state itself. That is one of the lessons of the H city (≅ Wuxi) pyramid scandal, but the details in the novel have to be supplemented with information from life.

In life, Deng Bin's base of operations in Wuxi, which after January

1993 was named the Xinxing Shiye Zong Gongsi (Xinxing industries), was one of three interlocking companies. The others were Zhongxing Industries in Shenzhen, where Deng Bin got her start in 1988, and Xinglong Industries of Beijing, the parent of both the Shenzhen and Wuxi companies. Wuxi profits went to Shenzhen and to Beijing, not only to Xinglong Industries but also to the finance bureau of the Beijing municipal government. As in the novel, Deng and others distributed generous bribes all around in the Wuxi, Shenzhen, and Beijing vicinities. Companies and government units in the Wuxi environs were ultimately victims of pyramid schemes, but they were also perpetrators, originally getting absurdly high dividends on questionable investments.[58] As the corruption progressed, the party bosses not just of Beijing, but also of Shenzhen (Li Hao) and Wuxi (Liu Jimin) were in on the scheme, and so were many of their subordinates in local party and government offices, including the police-procuracy-courts apparatus of Wuxi. As the Hong Kong journalists put it, there was not just a corrupt "independent kingdom" up north under Chen Xitong, but "three kingdoms," all getting rich in defiance of party discipline and the law.[59]

It turns out that Deng Bin and her superiors were agents of China's most feared State Security apparatus. Xinglong Industries and its Shenzhen and Wuxi subsidiaries were owned and directly managed by State Security in Beijing—though by the Beijing bureau, not the central ministry.[60] Li Min ("Li Haoyi"), chairman of the board of Beijing's Xinglong Company (and former personal secretary to the mayor of Beijing), was deputy head of the Beijing State Security Bureau, which wanted money to invest in projects overseas.[61] Li Ming, the Beijing company's general manager and another State Security cadre, was arrested before his boss Li Min and mysteriously died in custody.[62] Until the end, Deng Bin, with the privileges of being in national security work, the backing of covertly empowered agents in the capital, *and* the buffer of all those bribes to local authorities, felt she could keep building her house of cards forever.

The arrests in the Beijing State Security Bureau may have also threatened Zhu Lin, wife of Li Peng (premier, 1988–98; no. 2 man in the CCP until November 2002), and thus the premier himself. Hong Kong journalists speculated that the execution of agent Deng Bin was to keep her from telling secrets about Zhu Lin. The premier's wife had allegedly been involved in intelligence matters in her job under the State Council Office for Special Economic Zones, the head of which, He Chunlin, was Deng Bin's fellow Wuxi townsman and a protector of her crooked schemes in Shenzhen.[63]

Chen Fang did not dare mention State Security in the original *Heaven's Wrath* or in his 2000 revision, nor did media inside China.[64] But news from Hong Kong informs the Chinese grapevine, Chen Fang, and perhaps some Chinese readers. (The Hong Kong magazine *Qian shao* reported on the case as early as May 1995.)[65] That the bad guys in the novel have all kinds of surveillance equipment (Tiger Chen does not) becomes perhaps a bit more plausible. Of course, showing *good-guy* police and procurators being heavily invested in surveillance and eavesdropping is taboo in openly published Chinese crime fiction, and Chen Fang has not transgressed that boundary. One has to wonder why Chen Fang did not enliven his plot by turning Jiao Xiaoyu into a mole spying on her Uncle Pengyuan for the procuracy. Perhaps that would have crossed the line.

The upshot is that (1) N city, being Beijing, has Party Central operating on *its* playing field; (2) the villains are bound to have covert connections throughout China and overseas, including the "white" (*bai dao*) intelligence operatives and "black" underground criminal operatives that fascinate Chinese anticorruption novelists; and (3) the corrupt N city conspiracy may be read as a representation of a Beijing Gang, including not just Chen Xitong, but also Li Peng and even relatives of Deng Xiaoping, in rivalry with Jiang Zemin.[66] This is a scenario for praetorianism. At least one Hong Kong journalist accused Chen Xitong of having his own private police force (not in the State Security system) and carrying out surveillance over certain central government leaders as if they were his charge.[67]

Chen Fang may have chosen the numbers-laden and relatively undramatic pyramid scheme for the main plot because he thought it conveyed an implicit warning about corruption's power to subvert the state itself. Too, in the novel, as in life, H city/Wuxi is a major "point of entry" (*tupokou*) for prosecuting N city/Beijing corruption. The 100 million yuan was not the largest sum misspent in life, but perhaps Chen Fang's knowledge of other cases was limited. He added other cases to his 2000 revision and enlargement. In any event, those who hated and those who excused Chen Xitong would probably agree that the party brought him down primarily because he was so powerful. Absolute power in the hands of one man is not a crime, but in Chen Fang's vision (which was not the same as the party's, which in practice objects only to absolute power that it has not authorized), excesses of power are a "legal corruption" of the political system.

Limits of and on Realism

A roman à clef in principle imposes the sternest dictates of realism on the author—an adherence to researched facts second only to that in non-fiction. In a nation where journalism is so throttled by CCP control that the author's mission may be to write fiction in lieu of journalism, the burden is great indeed. Chen Fang assumed that burden, up to a point; perhaps it is the reason why he did not wrap up all his corruption case subplots in a neat solution at the end and was content simply to see the whole N city gang run in, one after another, as if from guilt by association. One interviewer has tried to impose the burden of journalism on Lu Tianming as well, by chiding him for writing novels based partly on true cases while lacking the "courage" to take it to the next step and expose "everything."[68] The interviewer may have had the reportage of Liu Binyan and his colleagues in mind.

The mandate not to make things up evidently has been an outsized burden on all Chinese realism. Many of the works appear lacking in imagination because they "stick to the facts." The paradox is that *Heaven's Wrath*, besides apparently being founded on rumor as well as fact, includes violent and incredible subplots that no informed reader would take seriously as "faction." Perhaps that was Chen Fang's strategy. The clearly fictitious crimes in his novel might have been his prepared defense against accusations of having committed character assassinations, even though he communicated a different message to informed readers—and entertained the gullible, too. If this was his strategy, it did not work. The novel was banned. Limits on expression are also clear in the aftermath, when he rewrote *Heaven's Wrath* to make it suitable for open publication. He made the villainous Orient Jiao himself a more likeable character. Chen Fang may have felt hemmed in by his mission to get his journalistic facts straight. Leaked accounts of Chen Xiaotong had by now indicated that he was hardly as aggressive as Jiao Dongfang in the novel. Of course there may have been other reasons for changing such basic aspects of the novel besides politics and journalistic accuracy. Chen Fang, in his revision, worked to satisfy the censors, the market, and even the critics. The final result is not pretty.

Aftermath

Chen Xitong was finally expelled from the party on August 29, 1997.[69] In 1998, Chen Fang once more hoped to publish his novel openly, in an expanded and revised June edition from a publisher in Qinghai. Still he could not. Reportedly the State Press and Publications Administration issued a comprehensive prepublication ban on May 1, 1998.[70] Under the title *Tian nu ren yuan* (Heaven's wrath and humankind's resentment), the book instead appeared in an August 1988 Hong Kong edition of 883 pages in two volumes, double the length of the original novel. A third printing came in September. The cover bore the subtitle "Jiang Zemin vs. Chen Xitong." This was promotional, for the enlarged book is no more about Jiang Zemin, and even less focused on Chen Xitong, than the original, though Jiang had commented positively on *Heaven's Wrath* to a *U.S. News and World Report* editor.[71] The book had done Jiang no harm as he purged his Beijing Gang rivals and strove for a reputation as a foe of high-level corruption. Maybe that is why pirated editions of the original *Heaven's Wrath* still circulated throughout China unchecked.

In May 2000, just as Jiang Zemin was revving up another anticorruption campaign, soon to be fortified by the movie *Fatal Decision* (see chapter 4), Chen Fang's magnum opus finally saw print in China. Now it was triple the original length (1,432 pages and 1.18 million characters, in three volumes), with a new title, *Dushi weiqing* (Municipal crisis), loosely translated into English on the cover as "Fighting for Power in the Metropolis."[72] Chen Fang said 100,000 copies were printed. A thirty-five-part television series was in the can even in 1999, but it has never been cleared for broadcast.[73]

Unfortunately, *Municipal Crisis* is not a victory for anticorruption fiction, but just another emblem of its decline.[74] Fans of *Heaven's Wrath* (including me) might have hoped to find in the new pages a sequel written in the same crisp style with no "fat," either continuing the saga of Secretary Jiao and his son until their secret trials, or further exposing the corruption of the Beijing Gang. Instead, Chen Fang inflated his original narrative by 50 percent without adding many new mysteries or details about major corruption (this revised "*Heaven's Wrath* half" of *Municipal Crisis* ends on page 762, in the middle of volume two). Chen's additions include a girlfriend for Orient and other human interest subplots.[75] Then follows nearly seven hundred new pages of soap opera about the conflicts, partnering, and sacrifices of Chen Fang's small-fry investigators and other characters without newsworthy counterparts in life, interspersed with fantastic stories of Hao Xiangshou (whose place in the Jiao network has been upgraded to "brains of the operation") being kidnapped by Chinese mafia back to Southeast Asia and escaping during a Cambodian civil war,[76] Ge Mengmeng's being tracked down by Scotland Yard in the Caribbean, and so forth.

Municipal Crisis is no longer an anticorruption novel in the frame of a mystery thriller, but rather a suspenseful melodrama lurching unexpectedly in the last volume into *fante* ("antispy," counterespionage) formula territory, as Chen Hu and Jiao Xiaoyu come into conflict with a vice minister, Ji Tao (≅ Li Jizhou, onetime vice minister of public security); his secret daughter Wu Aikun; and an archvillain so evil that he/it could be a godfather, a conspiracy ("a party within the party"), or an abstract aura of evil: "Wang Zhong Wang" (King of kings). (It is in fact a gang connected to Li Jizhou, Chen Fang said to me in interview.)[77] Much of the rest of the plot relates a quest for He Qizhang's "book of secrets" that will explain everything. The unifying interest is no longer the Jiaos (they are locked up in volume three, and still there is nothing about their trials), but Tiger Chen and Jiao Xiaoyu. Tiger proposes marriage, but Xiaoyu turns him down. Things are up in the air at the end—leaving room for two more volumes, Chen Fang admitted.[78] Murder is attempted on Tiger and Jiao Xiaoyu. And she, having come to feel guilty for prosecuting her uncle, is entrapped in corruption of her own.

As a novel, *Municipal Crisis* suffers from elephantiasis. Even as a comment on corruption, the book falls prey to kitchen sinkism. Counterfeit bills from abroad (North Korea?), crooked construction on a ring road, triads, smuggling of cars and heroin in and antiques out, people smuggling in Yunnan protected by cops on the take—Chen Fang's gossip dragnet now seems to cover all of China. The invocation of Li Jizhou and his smuggling shifts the arena far afield to Hong Kong (car smuggling) and particularly Xiamen and the giant Yuanhua scandal (covered in Liu Ping's roman à clef; see chapter 6), with no trace of a Chen Xitong connection; it is the investigators, Tiger and Xiaoyu, who provide the plot continuity.[79] Thus it is in his "sequel" that Chen Fang's self-imposed mandate to bare everything and write a roman à clef—fiction in lieu of journalism—limited him, not in quantity but quality, as a novelist and also as a coherent social commentator.

New Cases

Chen Fang's revision does contain big new cases, three of which (detailed below) have echoes in news sources, plus a one-line comment that Secretary Jiao once let his son, his secretary Shen Shi, and the Steel King invest public monies in real estate (967). The 20 billion yuan that Jiao estimates he and He Qizhang diverted (in the novel) had to go somewhere. But there is no follow-up on any of the cases. That could be because, paradoxically, Chen Fang was reluctant to invent more than he already had.

(1) Vice director of the N city Municipal People's Congress, Tian Xing

(≅ Tie Ying), has diverted RMB 80 million from her U.S. joint-venture air conditioner factory, bought substandard parts from a Chinese-American who bribed her, and looted the company for herself and a friend who procured male prostitutes for her. This leads to collective worker protests, a touch possibly inspired by the novel *Choice* (see chapter 4), complete with a "good official" (Fang Hao) to forestall riots. The complex trail of clues and incidents leading to "Elder Sister Tian's" exposure is more interesting than the corruption itself. The only connection to Jiao Pengyuan is that she gave him a watch as a bribe. In life, Tie Ying was a friend and ally of Chen Xitong. He was formally convicted of receiving watches; that is about all we can confirm. In life, she was sentenced to one year less than Chen.[80]

(2) Jiao Pengyuan and He Qizhang have diverted municipal monies, laundered them through a nonexistent company registered in the British West Indies, and used them to buy a publicly listed shell company in Hong Kong, the Zijin Company. In life, Chen Xitong, Wang Baosen, and Li Weihuai did ignore 1992 Finance Ministry regulations against local governments investing in Hong Kong stocks; they spent 200 million yuan from the municipal treasury to take control of a publicly listed Hong Kong company, the Xianggang Maofangqiang Youxian Gongsi (Hong Kong Woolen Mills Company, Ltd.), which they renamed the Beijing Fazhan (Xianggang) Youxian Gongsi (Beijing Development Company, Ltd.) and listed on the Hong Kong stock exchange, with Gao Qiming and others as trustees. They made a killing on the IPO. The controlling interest in the company was a nonexistent company in Tortola, British West Indies.[81] But *Municipal Crisis* does not develop the case, which it reveals through the involvement of Ge Mengmeng (≅ He Ping), or follow up on its claim that she prepared false export contracts and tax reports, cheating the Chinese government out of US$1.26 billion (1070).

(3) The military-owned Great Wall Company purports to import sensitive U.S. telecommunications equipment to modernize the army according to the "6036 Project." The goods come through a shell company, since by U.S. law and Sino-U.S. international agreement China must not import this technology for military use (1172). This is not the crime, because the novel's viewpoint is that "to screw foreigners is patriotic," to use Geremie Barmé's words.[82] The crime here is *not* deceiving the United States, and instead using army protection to smuggle in mere consumer goods. Uncle He and the King of Kings are at the bottom of it. An abortive raid on the army trucks, followed by an anticlimactic solving of the case anyway, brings Chen Fang's trilogy to its end.[83] The one link to real life that I can verify is the past existence of a Great Wall Company owned by the military.

The complicated centrifugal subplots hardly allow Chen Fang to develop his theme that power trumps money, though vignettes of military and judiciary corruption, and the alliance of cops with domestic and foreign mafias, do suggest subversion of the state. Zhou Senlin observes that procurators are destined to go bad, since by prosecuting corruption they make enemies, not friends. Without guanxi they cannot get promoted, so they go on the take. *Municipal Crisis* also criticizes institutions of "legalized corruption." Cadres in for-profit companies owned by government organs can escape the restrictions on their income, perquisites, and behavior that they must observe in parallel jobs within the government organ itself. In the novel, such companies provide slush funds out of which organs that live spartanly on the official books can arrange parties and banquets for themselves. Jiao Xiaoyu's downfall is that she has a sinecure in such a company, while also serving Vice Minister Ji Tao as his personal secretary. Moreover, the organ gets to keep 30 percent of the fines and confiscated property it acquires, as much a recipe for corruption as U.S. police departments getting to keep automobiles they seize in drug busts (according to a past law). In this case, the fines go into the private company (1174, 1213).

Methods of Self-censorship

Not all of Chen Fang's padding in the new version of the novel is there simply to tell everything he has heard. Sadly, a comparative reading of the two versions looks like a lesson in self-censorship, through five devices.

(1) *Dilution of Negativity by Padding.* Although some content is simply taboo, Chinese editors' "proportionality discourse" of censorship now allows authors to write of "nearly any" adverse social phenomena, as long as they do not do it "excessively."[84] Instead of deleting negative things, one may *add* so much innocuous new material that the negative things look small in proportion. I believe that Chen Fang adapted his work to this logic.

(2) *Amelioration of Tone and Narrative Direction.* Besides the diversion of the plot from corruption cases to conspiracies and in the end to an almost mystical miasma of evil,[85] the revised plot makes He Kedai more likeable[86] and finds chivalrous and filial aspects even in Orient Jiao's character.[87] Orient in this version does not videotape his father in bed. Jiao Pengyuan for his part seems more in-the-know, able to pose a stronger united front with his son. He Qizhang, too, is "improved." A scene about his sexual sadism is left to the imagination in *Municipal Crisis* (101–2).

(3) *Elevation and Sinicization.* When an action-dominated thriller's liter-

ary status is upgraded to "a novel in China's great realist tradition," this can provide protection not unlike the "redeeming social interest" that in American jurisprudence can save an erotic novel from being judged pornographic. Chen Fang felt defensive about the "low" style of *Heaven's Wrath*. He now freely admits to having tried to remedy it.[88] Most of his new material develops not cases but character, even if the revealing episodes turn out to be sentimental love spats. Interior monologues, psychological explanations, narrator's philosophizing, and romantic ups and downs between Tiger Chen and Jiao Xiaoyu in the second half are elevation *and* padding. There is even some irony.[89]

Taking a cue from Ming-Qing chapter-driven novels, Chen Fang reconstituted his chapters and scenes so that they end in suspense. Hence chapter endings in *Municipal Crisis* often occur in the middle of what were the old chapters. The *Heaven's Wrath* half of the enlarged novel ends in the middle of the new chapter 30. Chen Fang has also given his chapters titles for the first time, in parallel couplets. The new episodic structure and Chen Fang's plan for sequels have accelerated the centrifugal tendencies of his terribly complicated plot. But now the novel can be defended as a more authentic contribution to *Chinese* literature.

(4) *Appeals to Authority.* *Municipal Crisis* describes Jiang Zemin's devotion to anticorruption and cites his directives (14, 1282). Moreover, the plot is systematically modified to show higher authority, often Party Central itself, *authorizing* investigations, as well as the kidnapping of Li Haoyi by police from S province (45–46). Chen Hu is accompanied in his sleuthing by representatives from the Supreme People's Procuratorate and the party's Central Disciplinary Inspection Commission. Whole scenes are interpolated into the text to dramatize party and investigative group meetings that vote to give the investigators authority to pursue a line of inquiry. This may indeed add to the novel's bureaucratic realism.[90] However, Secretary Jiao's demise seems inevitable, not a matter of suspense.

(5) *Excisions.* This is only a last resort. Most corruption cases and villains from *Heaven's Wrath* have not been cut from Chen Fang's rewrite. He evidently, however, had to or felt he had to delete the information on China's computerization of fingerprints,[91] his references to other corruption cases,[92] and most of the devil's advocate speeches rationalizing corruption cited in a previous section of this chapter. Because these were set pieces, they were vulnerable on artistic grounds, but Chen Fang's work has never been an "art novel." Some readers may prefer the new version of his novel. However, it is in this aftermath that one sees Chen Fang at last accommodating overtly to limits on realism in contemporary China.

Conceptualizing the Chen Xitong case is like the six blind men describing an elephant. The government's published case was just about watches, mansions, and dalliances, a pot Chen Fang kept boiling in his elephantine revision with new material about Tie Ying's watch and a peek into one of Chen Xitong's secret mansions[93]—though now Chen Fang, the author, was just catching up with the news. Foreign businessmen know the Chen Xitong who, with his vice mayor, skimmed millions from real estate development. But to many Beijing leaders, Chen was the one who gave them luxury housing at fire-sale prices.[94] One can also draw inferences about how the party saw Chen from new national 1997 regulations against abuse by cadres' secretaries, new October 1995 Beijing municipal regulations against cadres reserving hotel suites for themselves using public funds, and so forth.[95] Then there are the millions that Chen and his vice mayor skimmed and invested in Hong Kong through their shell companies. These sides of the ex-mayor enter Chen Fang's work only in brief subplots, though he does weave an interesting picture of the power elite as an interlocking directorate. As for the pyramid scheme that is the centerpiece of *Heaven's Wrath*, Chen Xitong was not convicted for it and may have had only a secondary role—unless one draws lessons from the secret agent angle in the manner of the Hong Kong journalists. They were most sensitive to Chen Xitong's amassing of power to the detriment of Jiang Zemin. However, the gathering of power without central authorization is a crime in itself in the world of communist politics, perhaps the most important reason for the prosecution. *Heaven's Wrath*, with its focus on power, helps one understand that facet of lèse majesté. But in his revision, Chen Fang, still intent on writing à clef, makes corruption look more like a progressive dinner party, with any number of diners joining in. If the cases do not add up to a coherent whole in life, they still must do so in a good novel, even a realistic novel. Chen's elevations in style were not enough to create a good novel, much less a realistic novel. With all its love interests and psychobabble, the new version must surely strike many readers as just another potboiler.

4

Climax: The Alarum and Standard-Bearer—Zhang Ping's *Choice*

Shanxi writer Zhang Ping (b. 1954) did not contribute to China's first or second waves of anticorruption writing, in the late 1970s and late 1980s, but he published his first anticorruption book in 1991, several years before the term existed and when China was still in the grips of its postmassacre political repression.[1] Entitled *Fa han Fenxi* (The law rocks Fenxi [county]), the narrative is about rural corruption in Zhang's native province. He followed up with a companion novel, *Tian wang* (Heaven's web, 1993), then turned out a book-length nonfiction exposé of society's mistreatment of orphans.[2] Zhang Ping even in fiction bases his plots on materials acquired through on-site interviews of people who know "local conditions."[3] He has paid a heavy price for this; 241 Shanxi cadres who thought the Fenxi epics might be referring to them launched political complaints and then a collective libel suit against Zhang and his publisher, the Qunzhong or Masses' Press (an arm of the Ministry of Public Security that publishes crime fiction to make money, as well as classified police manuals). The author prevailed, but only after two years of harassment.[4] He became an idol of justice seekers and the recipient of a great quantity of fan mail. The Masses' Press stood by Zhang Ping and he stood by the press, continuing to give them manuscripts for initial publication in their popular crime and police magazine, *Zhuomuniao* (Woodpecker), even after he became famous in 2000. His masterwork is *Jueze* (Choice, 1997), a long novel (536 pages and 439,000 characters) whose setting and characters are well within Lu Tianming's formula and not so reflective as the Fenxi novels of an actual place. *Choice*'s plot unfolds in a large northern city (not named, but seemingly a place like Taiyuan, Baoding, or Shijiazhuang) with a giant failing state-owned enterprise (SOE) and a web of corruption protected at the top by a deputy CCP provincial secretary. The hero is a mayor who owes that party boss his job, so the mayor's final test is to stand up to him—and also turn on some in his own family. The heroic mayor is Li Gaocheng, who is now a household name in China. Like Lu Tianming's hero, Acting Mayor Huang Jiangbei, Mayor Li conducts investigations into municipal corruption just like a detective in a mystery. Li is also the target of threats and violence, for *Choice* is a blend of serious social novel and popular melodrama.

Anticorruption novels were not yet a trend when *Choice* first hit the stands. The 1996 *Heaven Above* television drama had no major follow-up.[5] *Heaven's Wrath* had appeared only a couple of months before *Woodpecker* put out the initial, serial printing of *Choice*.[6] Many would-be anticorruption novelists probably pulled in their horns precisely because of Zhang Ping's well-known travails in court.[7] *Choice*, too, caused Zhang Ping to encounter difficulties from bureaucrats who thought they recognized themselves among the novel's villains.[8] *Choice* had a third printing that ran to twenty thousand copies—good for a serious novel, but hardly best-selling. A television series based quite faithfully on the novel, also called *Choice*, appeared in 1998.

It was a blockbuster summer 2000 movie adaptation of *Choice* that made Zhang and his novel famous: *Shengsi jueze* (Fatal decision). High government officials had recently been charged with corruption, and news was seeping out that a prosecution of a massive corruption ring in Fujian, later called the Yuanhua case (the subject of a 2001 novel analyzed in chapter 6), was in the works. Jiang Zemin commanded China's leaders to attend a screening of *Fatal Decision* in August at their annual retreat in Beidaihe. An August 18 CCP directive enjoined the party at all levels to work on the entire membership to go see the film.[9] As the success of *Heaven's Wrath* indicates, being banned is better promotion for political art than official kudos, but *Fatal Decision* was good entertainment. It became one of the most influential and widely viewed films ever made in China, outgrossing all movies previously screened in the country with the exception of *Titanic*.[10] That may exaggerate its popularity, since many tickets were sold in blocks to government organs. Still, 25 million people viewed it in theaters, and it was extensively pirated for home viewing.[11]

This was "mass culture" politically correct enough to be released, politically brave enough to please critics, and slick enough for the market, too.

Getting the movie made was difficult, as the "aftermath" section of this chapter indicates. Zhang Ping declined to write the screenplay, yet he and his original novel benefited as much from the movie as those who actually made it. *Choice* the novel won one of the five quintennial Mao Dun awards in 2000, and *Heaven's Web* came one vote short of winning its author an unprecedented double award at the same session.[12] Zhang Ping was also elected a vice chairman of the Chinese Writers' Association in December 2001.[13] Two months after Jiang Zemin's praise of the movie, the novel's total print run was 200,000, eventually headed for 300,000, not including pirated editions and books of no relation that tricked buyers into thinking they were.[14] Although it would be years before another movie like *Fatal Decision* was made, its success and official approval gave the green light to a storm of subsequent anticorruption novels and TV dramas by diverse authors. *Choice*, the novel, became in retrospect the literary standard-bearer for a multimedia genre that was already blossoming in 2000.

The novel's original and retrospective praise were not undeserved, although politics surely explains why this middlebrow novel, which is already close to a screenplay,[15] won a Mao Dun prize next to works by Wang Anyi and Alai (though there have been worse choices in the history of the competition).[16] *Choice* is a fast-paced, unpretentious page-turner like Chen Fang's *Heaven's Wrath*. The characters, particularly the villains, are flat, and the style is easy to read. The novel lacks Lu Tianming's slang and even much differentiation between the speech of one character and another,[17] though the modulations of bureaucratic parlance are just right. Still, *Choice* is a few steps up the ladder of novelistic social prestige from *Heaven's Wrath* in style and content; Zhang Ping has written a suspenseful novel without murders, cops, gangsters, or guns. Just as morality trumps legality on a scale of literary "seriousness," so do great civilian administrators trump petty lawyers, cops, prosecutors, and even judges in Chinese media.[18] The manifestations of corruption in *Choice* are multifarious and multivariate, true to the genre and to Chinese exposé novels since the late Qing, but the deceptions are schematically political and economic, and they cohere; there are no big loose ends, as in *Heaven's Wrath*. *Choice*, with its sociological focus, provides a synoptic view of Chinese urban and factory society, indeed of social classes—the "big picture" that Chinese readers associate with the grand tradition of Chinese realism.

Critics from across the ideological spectrum hailed Zhang Ping as "the resuscitator of realism" and *Choice* as "directly facing reality," even "'a mirror held up to Chinese society,' as the experts all agree."[19] Critic Ni Zhen and others likewise praised the "realism" of the film version.[20] *Choice* deals not just with corruption, but also with one of the great economic problems of its time: the closing of obsolete rust-belt factories and the needs of those left behind. Behind all the corruption in *Choice* lies the specter of massive, corrupt privatization of public assets, as in Russia under its postsocialist reforms. This in turn evokes thoughts of the turmoil and political collapse of the old Soviet system, even if in Russia it preceded the privatization and gangsterization of the economy.

Choice openly broaches the issue of regime change. Jiang Zemin and his colleagues took note of that in the film version. It is a feel-good melodrama in which good conquers evil and all problems come from bad intentions, not bad policies,[21] but Jiang saw the film as an alarum about how the party might lose power if its current ills were not rectified. Clearly he viewed Zhang Ping's attitude as friendly, not antagonistic. The novel's own argument is couched in fairly orthodox ideological and melodramatic moral terms, indeed in the traditional garb of the Mandate of Heaven theory. The significance of such a theme will vary according to the reader's outlook on the present regime. This chapter will argue that *Choice*'s staying power, and its weakness as literature, are largely due to the limits of China's own brand of "classic" realism, which by its nature slides into melodrama. The novel and film solidified the Lu Tianming formula, while making it more dramatic. At the same time the productions made it clear that anticorruption authors who truly wanted to be original would have to find a completely different path.

The Storyline

As a young man Li Gaocheng (b. 1943) worked his way up as a factory technician, shop steward, and deputy manager in Chinese textile factories, finally to lead (as its CCP secretary)[22] the Zhongyang Textile Group, a complex of twenty thousand workers plus dependents and retired ex-workers. All are housed a few miles outside, and under the municipal jurisdiction of, a northern Chinese city of three million. In 1983, when tensions with the United States led to restrictions on China's textile exports, Li saved Zhongyang by continuing production full tilt. He gambled, correctly, that exports would some day resume and that he could sell off the accumulated inventory. Li Gaocheng was promoted up out of the factory to become vice mayor of the municipality in 1986. The successors he put in place at Zhongyang were reformers in their forties: factory manager Guo Zhongyao, CCP secretary Chen Yongming, and assistant managers Wu Mingde and Feng Minjie. Enterprise reform has now put the factory manager in command over the party secretary, as in life. The reversal leading to the current relationship occurred during Li's tenure—though in higher governance, a state organ's administrative head is still the no. 2, the party head the no. 1. The name "Zhongyang" is close enough to the Chinese word for "central," as in "Party Central," that its fate carries broad symbolic overtones, suggests Helen Xiaoyan Wu.[23] Li Gaocheng is a technocrat in the mold of his fellow mayor Huang Jiangbei in *Heaven Above*.

After 1986, coincident with the crisis of giant state-owned enterprises nationwide, Zhongyang Textiles, founded in the late Qing, declined and went deeply into debt, despite its lucrative new subsidiary ventures in transportation (Tegaote, or "Special Express"), entertainment (Green Apple), and manufacturing (Changlong Apparel and Textiles). It also went into real estate speculation, which brought enormous losses. Production ceased in 1995. Massive unperforming state loans have kept the firm afloat up to the novel's present time, 1996. The workers and retirees on Zhongyang's payroll have been unpaid for more than a year. Their factory housing is a giant slum, with electricity and water cut off due to the Zhongyang management's nonpayment of bills.

At the start of the novel, Li Gaocheng, fifty-four (fifty in the movie) and now mayor, is suddenly called back to pacify the plant when its workers assemble to march on the provincial offices (Mayor Li's municipality is concurrently a provincial capital) to protest their current managers' alleged corruption. Li goes out to listen and stop the "riot" before it can spread. Gradually he learns, to his horror, that the entire leadership team (*lingdao banzi*) he put in place at the factory has gone bad during the decade (six years, in the film version) since they succeeded him. It is a corrupt and oppressive "gang of four," to use a phrase not in the novel or film, though the potential allusion is obvious enough. There is talk of bankruptcy for Zhongyang in the name of economic restructuring and renewal, but this might cover up how much money has been looted from the enterprise by the subsidiaries and various other schemes. Mayor Li puts together his information from worker and cadre reports, documentary evidence, and finally incognito first-hand sleuthing. When he goes in person to Changlong Apparel, a piece of the old Zhongyang that has been privatized, thugs in charge of its security beat him up for intruding, not knowing he is the mayor.

The mayor lands in the hospital, even more the hero; the workers try to offer solace, but only the greedy cadres can gain admission to his room, to hover and offer insincere well wishes as in a modern-day *Volpone*. As Mayor Li struggles to expose and countermand all the corruption, he discovers that his own investigative work team has effected a cover-up, in the name of protecting him, and that his wife, who is district assistant procurator heading the Anticorruption Bureau under the municipal procuratorate of all things, plus her nephew and even the Lis' housekeeper, all feed from the Zhongyang trough. Not only that, Li's mentor Yan Zhen, deputy secretary in the provincial CCP committee and a man of no little charisma, is the evil's upstairs protector. Yan Zhen then throws down the gauntlet by stopping Li's investigations of Green Apple, Tegaote, and the Zhongyang home plant, but the so far enigmatic CCP municipal secretary Yang Cheng, who is younger and newer on the scene, emerges as a good guy. He spirits Mayor Li into a useful seclusion. The mayor and the party secretary become allies. Even in Li's absence, a still uncorrupted vice mayor, Guo Tao, parries Yan Zhen's ploy to put Zhongyang into bankruptcy, yet Yan has convinced nearly everyone that the mayor is on *his* team.[24]

Li Gaocheng thus comes to see himself as ultimately responsible for the corruption. He learns that (1) Yan Zhen promoted him up and out of Zhongyang to begin with just so Yan could more easily skim money from the enterprise through his four proxies; (2) law enforcement presumes *Li*—the mayor, after all—to be the covert protector of all municipal vice (including prostitution) that enriches Zhongyang subsidiaries; and that (3) his wife, Wu Aizhen, has taken a briefcase full of money (a RMB 300,000 "bonus" from Tegaote) that, according to a doctored tape supplied by the bad cadres, the mayor himself solicited. But Li Gaocheng makes the right choice, siding with the party and the people, not the cajoling and blackmailing forces arrayed against him. He has enough faith in providence (or, in the official discourse, enough wisdom to trust the party) to turn the briefcase over to Party Secretary Yang Cheng.

Now the Communist Party must choose. On instructions from Party Central in Beijing, Provincial CCP Secretary Wan Yongnian and Governor Wei Zhenliang descend from on high, and police detain all bosses while searching their houses (Li's included). In a surprise night meeting, the municipal leaders, with Wan and Wei in command, vote to reaffirm Mayor Li. Yet in Zhang Ping's plot, the masses must also be satisfied. Elder Sister Xia, beloved governess of Li's children back when he ran Zhongyang but now old and sick with cancer, threatens to jump off a Zhongyang building if the mayor is not acquitted. Over loudspeakers and TV hookups before massed workers, Provincial Secretary Wan is forced publicly to exonerate Li, and the mass assemblage hears for itself a second, undoctored tape, which Li's wife made "for insurance." The mayor is now vindicated from above and below. Although he evidently will not go to jail, his next post is unclear in the novel's epilogue. Zhongyang will be reopened as a joint venture.

Corruption Cases

Li Gaocheng first learns most of the nitty-gritty about scams going on at the dying Zhongyang plant long after the fact and secondhand, from reports delivered to him in person by angry workers and former plant cadres. The crooks' excuses for their odd ways of doing business, also formally stated to the mayor, are as plausible as the workers' accusations, and seemingly more modern and sophisticated. This leaves both the reader and Li Gaocheng in suspense for some time as to which side has the better grasp of reality. Li must investigate. When the facts finally become clear, one discovers, among other things, a great gap between old-style corruption and the wholesale robbery of the new era.

Penny-wise old ex-cadres, experts, and workers whose notions of corruption were formed in the Mao years open up with accusations of Zhongyang cadre corruption appropriate to an earlier era and its smaller economic stakes. An old Red Army veteran charges that the cadres abuse their official positions to eat, drink, and go abroad at public expense (27–28). The cadres say they visited cotton-growing Niger and Nigeria to find joint partners for Zhongyang and were near to closing a deal. Zhang Ping "adds feet to the snake"; excessive travel abroad, even to the less comfortable regions of Africa, is an interesting dilemma of old-fashioned socialist corruption, but that is not really the issue in this case, because Zhongyang's cadres simply lied. They spent little, if any, time in Africa. They took their families to Moscow, Paris, London, New York, and Chicago to go shopping.

Two other operational scams seem more contemporary, being indebted to the new township and village enterprises (TVEs) and market distribution of raw materials. Loaned a hundred million yuan to retool in 1992, Zhongyang sold its obsolete machines to a TVE specializing in textile manufacturing equipment. The TVE slapped a new coat of paint and new labels on the rejects, then sold them back unrepaired to Zhongyang at a profit, with big payoffs for the Zhongyang cadres (39). This is really an old-fashioned exchange of considerations between units, which could and did happen under 1950s socialism.

The cadres are also accused of having purposely bought inferior cotton at inflated prices (37). Presumably they profited from it through kickbacks from the suppliers or by overreporting the real cost and pocketing the remainder.[25] But their explanation is credible. Hundreds of millions in debt and behind in its payroll obligations, Zhongyang needed bank loans to buy raw materials, yet the loans were too little and too late. Under the newly marketized allocation of raw materials, cotton prices had soared as Zhongyang waited until late in the season, when supplies had mostly run out. After an exhaustive search, the Zhongyang leaders turned up an obscure source. It gypped them on quality, they say, and in this new, freewheeling, underregulated commodity system, how could old socialists defend themselves against such wile? They had to overpay (67–70), and also to throw in some kickbacks (premiums, or bribes?). So who was at fault? Was it the new market mechanisms that work against out-of-season buyers, or the socialist banks, who failed Zhongyang out of old-fashioned socialist ineptitude and sloth? Or was it malice aforethought by the bankers? ("If this company belonged to them, would they have acted this way?"; 70). In reality, it turns out, the bankers are co-conspirators; the cadres were taking side profits from the deal.

Like the other anticorruption novelists, Zhang Ping is also interested in new forms of bribery, and the amounts. For the birthday of a leading cadre's child, circa 1996, the going gift rate is RMB 3,000–5,000. And Mayor Li's wife, Wu Aizhen, in addition to amassing millions of yuan for their retirement and accepting giant gifts from Zhongyang, including college tuition for their daughter, has squirreled away tens of thousands of yuan in gift certificates that can go toward luxury goods, including gold jewelry. Neither giver nor seller need fear exposure; the certificates can be made out from one unit to another with no individuals named (424–25). The words for the certificates, *piaozheng* and *gouwuquan*, were not in the dictionary twenty years ago, but as a way of keeping up guanxi between organs and enterprises, these are technically just another socialist exchange between units, and cashless at that. They are nothing compared to the legal corruption of openly budgeting gifts and banquets as modern "entertainment expenses." Zhongyang spent over four million yuan on entertainment in 1995, the year it closed down (37), while its "subsidiaries" spent ten million a year, almost enough to meet the payroll for the twenty thousand laid-off workers. Yet modern business requires expense accounts for frequent business trips by dozens of specialized purchasing and marketing agents (75).

The old-timers are disturbed not just by the cadres' crimes, but also by the corruption of their whole *zuofeng*, or "work style." Expectations on both sides reflect the unprecedented pace of change in morals and culture since the days of Maoist self-sacrifice. The Zhongyang leaders' overuse of security guards, top-heavy management (one-fifth of the workforce is cadres, which a Zhongyang leader calls "universal" within China's "planned economy"; 72), and authoritarianism (what used to be called "commandism") are indicative of the change in relations between leaders and masses. But the accusers are also annoyed by cadre lifestyle offenses. Excessive consumption is a crime in itself, according to the old ways, and then there is all the sex. A charge against Zhongyang's top villain, Manager Guo Zhongyao, is that he is divorced (15). He is later found with a very young "girlfriend" in his heavily guarded private mansion (448). Feng Minjie, an assistant manager, was once jailed for visiting prostitutes on a business trip. Zhongyang never punished him and even paid his bail and 20,000 yuan fine. The sex trade hardly existed in 1980. Ironically, it is the bad cadre Yan Zhen who tells Mayor Li that television is a waste of time and a sign of decadence (*duoluo*). Not so ironically, Li Gaocheng goes to see his old mentor and catches him enrapt in a "rather vulgar TV drama from Hong Kong or Taiwan" (147).

The time lag becomes clear in a flashback to the nationwide demonstrations for democracy and against inflation and corruption in the spring of 1989. This episode of the novel means to tar the 1989 movement by association with the disorders of the Cultural Revolution. Students assume that Li Gaocheng, then head of Zhongyang, must be corrupt. Loyal workers protect their leader from the mindless accusations. Li never practiced *guandao* (official profiteering through the two-tier price system), showed favoritism to a single worker, passed out a single bolt of cloth or ration ticket, or misappropriated a single bar of steel or bag of cement. He hadn't employed a single relative. He didn't even take for himself one of the big new apartments attached to the factory (234–35). The charges are baseless in the story, but above all they seem trivial in view of present modes of malfeasance. *Real* corruption has moved on to involve bigger game.

The *big* thefts are so "modern" that they exist mainly on paper, and they are so vast that they can only be conceived in numbers. In the novel's present, Zhongyang is RMB 600 million in debt (in the film it only owes 230 million, and has laid off only three-fifths of its workforce). It is "too big to fail." But the capstone is that the four factory leaders now plan to declare bankruptcy—that is, pull off a no-fault closure of the giant enterprise that will allow them to escape all responsibility for the social tragedy as well as their crimes, with golden parachutes to boot. In the film version, they plan to sell the firm at a fire-sale price to a Wenzhou capitalist (accompanied by his secretarial "honey"). The irony, of course, is that the Chinese state was sanctioning just such restructurings at the turn of the century as a way of retiring its obligations to failing and inefficient enterprises. The problem is that the state is restructuring its enterprises without first strengthening its banks and legal system.

Parts of Zhongyang's assets and physical plant, or, alternatively, the annual state loans paid to keep it afloat (to be precise, at least RMB 22 million of the 1994 state loan of RMB 80 million to Zhongyang), are regularly poured into subsidiaries instead of kept to pay the plant's original workers. These subsidiaries are already privatized, in that the Zhongyang cadre children or other relatives who control them can use the assets to go into whatever business they want and keep all the profits. Other high cadres and bankers get salaries for sitting on their boards of directors. But in name the subsidiaries still belong to Zhongyang, so they can keep on claiming portions of Zhongyang's annual public dole. This of course requires the connivance of bankers. This is another question of socialist corruption, since bad loans are frequent in life, due to political pressure to keep SOEs solvent and thus prevent mass unemployment. But again, Zhang Ping adds feet to the snake. The bankers in the novel keep the state subsidies flowing to Zhongyang because its leaders bribe them. Since the bankers have been corrupted by illegal money, it is not clear to readers whether socialist power alone—namely, a directive from higher party bosses to keep the giant factory complex in operation no matter what—would be enough to corrupt their judgment and cause them to keep throwing great sums of public money down a rat hole.

The RMB 22 million in 1994 was put into New Tide Company, Ltd., which invested in hotels, restaurants, shops, and even coal mines spread over two dozen cities (39, 103). The subsidiaries bear a symbolic burden as indicators of the corruption of a whole city and an entire society. China's new economy needs transportation, but the profitable Tegaote provides limousine service to Beijing, presumably for the well-heeled. (It gets millions in annual state subsidies, though it makes a RMB 10 million annual profit, which it keeps.) Changlong Apparel and Textiles is simply a privatized (except insofar as it may still get state subsidies) shop from the old Zhongyang, with its original machines. Now it turns a profit in Zhongyang's core industry, which Zhongyang can no longer do. Changlong is now a dirty, noisy, and understaffed sweat shop that exploits workers who were not let go. It also employs retirees (like Elder Sister Xia) who are desperate enough to take its lower wages of RMB 5–6 for a ten-hour day (293–300, 441). Epitomizing moral decline in Mayor Li's city is the Green Apple Entertainment City, a bordello pure and simple, like Zhongyang's bars, massage parlors, saunas, and dance halls. Unbeknownst to the mayor, who visits Green Apple in all innocence to sleuth incognito but fits the role of sybaritic businessman so poorly that he cuts a comic figure, Li's wife has helped install his own country bumpkin nephew (in the film, her brother) as the manager. The illegal enterprise is free from interference from the cops because it claims, and everybody naturally assumes, that it is under the protection of Mayor Li. Even the prostitutes, some of whom are laid-off workers from Zhongyang, know enough to invoke Li Gaocheng's name. Only the mayor is not in on the racket. He is moreover shocked—shocked!—to learn the price of a bottle of cognac in such an establishment.

Not all the money went into the subsidiaries, which do at least turn a profit and offer employment, though not the social welfare benefits that SOEs provide. Also, the subsidiaries' profitability might after all rely on their official perks. The state, while doling out money to Zhongyang with one hand, takes back millions of yuan annually in taxes, including special levies for new municipal offices and such (83–84). Much of Zhongyang's missing money went into real estate speculation and was lost. The cadre thieves might even have intended to pay it all back if they could have, like the N city cadres of *Heaven's Wrath*, before the pyramid scheme collapsed. Much of the rest of the money was lost forever into cadre bank accounts overseas: RMB 170 million, including 60 million in cash (533). This proves the need for rule of law, though the panacea of anticorruption novels is simply more morality.[26]

As in other anticorruption novels, corruption in *Choice*'s world has reached the point where morals in general have declined. The only way to be sure that a bottle of wine is not fake is to choose a vintage from before 1980, after which adulteration and misrepresentation became widespread (159). So many palms have to be greased now to get things done that small amounts are no longer even considered bribery, more like "squeeze" in the old society. Factory debts needn't really be paid back; they're just a debt from one part of the state to another, say some (79). Is there any morality left? This vision of universal corruption is conservative, but not entirely consonant with official discourse. The latter holds that corruption is perpetrated by a very small minority.

The Novel and Realism

Particularly in its first 236, scene-setting pages, before action-driven chapters take over, *Choice* is in many ways a model of realism of China's own "classic" type, a realism shaped by decades of socialism. The work is a heavily researched social novel, or "problem novel," as the author likes to call it, instead of an anticorruption novel.²⁷ Zhang Ping as a rule bases his fiction on fragments of real events. He "goes down to experience life" to get his material, as have generations of socialist novelists before him. In this case, he interviewed managers and workers in a couple of dozen factories around Beijing, Taiyuan, Baoding, and other northern cities (though it was originally for another project). Workers eagerly sought out Zhang Ping when they heard of his arrival, and he kept his interviewing of them secret from the managers; the chapters of *Choice* bearing worker testimony recapitulate Zhang's experiences at the factories.²⁸ The historical context is also specified. Li Gaocheng's résumé, with his entire work history, job assignments entered year by year, begins chapter 2. New characters who enter the plot as late as page 434 are still introduced with their entire official résumés (a trait also of China's Ming-Qing novels). Li's personal history is preceded, in the opening chapter, with a complete enterprise history of the Zhongyang Group and its predecessors, year by year, in parallel with the big political events of Maoist and post-Mao history. The account keeps running tabs on the expansion of Zhongyang's payroll through the years and its mergers. Zhang Ping neglects only to detail its product lines. The novel and the TV series, but not the film, specify the factory's losses and cumulative debts in millions of yuan, and the numbers add up, for those who want to do the math.²⁹ The statistics may be fictional, inflated, representative, or an average of figures from Zhang Ping's many interviews, but it seems unlikely that they came out of thin air. The narrative is also given to listing things, and so are the characters. When Mayor Li issues directives, when the workers voice accusations and demands, and when the leading cadres justify themselves, they number their points, one, two, three. The mayor responds to the workers' opening presentations with a four-point pledge (44–46). The narrative effect is one of seeming objectivity and documentary authenticity. Since the contents of the lists are social and political, one feels at times that one is reading a policy position paper.

Yet this first half of the novel is very much a "mystery" segment, despite its sociological interest. The plot is constructed dialectically. Protesting workers in chapter 4 present their thesis of factory corruption in a private meeting with the mayor, delivering a virtual legal brief of accusations. Li ponders them until a long, sociologically well-informed antithesis appears in chapters 8 and 9, when the cadres defend themselves. At home, Li's wife chimes in with skepticism about the corruption. Could the workers have misunderstood the complex economics? Could some of them be troublemakers? Thesis and antithesis continue to alternate. The workers get two more chapters (10 and 11) to refute the cadres and petition Mayor Li. He calls the cadres on the carpet again, and so on, leading to an intermezzo of party meetings before the personal sleuthing and cadre counterattacks begin. The dialectic is therefore not just one of us versus them, but also one of two different ideas of why Zhongyang and its ilk are failing in the new era of export-led market economies. The workers' side charges corruption, but the charges require more evidence and may depend on definitions of "excess"; the leaders tell a good story about textile factories failing everywhere. Economic change has made dinosaurs like Zhongyang unviable. They, the cadres, with their old, socialist ways, are perhaps a little too backward to meet the demands of the new times.

The us versus them aspect of the conflict evokes notions of class conflict, familiar in China's old socialist realism and in modern realism from all eras and nations.[30] The factory leaders have an aggressive force of security guards and travel within the factory compound protected by bodyguards (an aspect of reality erased in the film). The "workers' side" contains representative figures from all stages of life and with experience of all stages of the Chinese revolution (but not from both genders). In fact, the "workers' side" is really a united front containing retired cadres, engineers, and Red Army veterans. It was socially astute of Zhang Ping to write about the travails of the pension-deprived retirees. Even old cadres, once retired in these dire circumstances, may be counted as having reentered the proletariat. The class dimensions of the conflict are in later chapters undone not so much by the union of people from different social backgrounds as by their ultimate definition as a *moral* united front, of upholders of good, old-fashioned morality against new forms of evil wiliness.

As a realistic novel, *Choice* represents downtrodden social types seldom seen any more in China's youth-dominated literature, portraying not just incipient class conflict but also mass unrest. The film adaptation is politically faithful enough to the novel to keep the opening "riot" scene, but the protestors on screen are much younger than the rather mature lot that have been laid off in the novel. However, the specter of out-of-control young people is a fear typical of the middle-aged—and the CCP.

Like Chen Fang, Zhang Ping depicts municipal and party meetings with an authentic feel, including the many injunctions for cadres to maintain a "sense of organization and sense of discipline" (*zuzhixing jilüxing*; 20). The culture of secrecy in party and official business is so undisguised that the good mayor Li himself is angry to learn that a petition the workers have given him is just a photocopy. He is not the only one in the loop. "Even accusations (*gaozhuang*) seem to have been modernized" (108), he says, exasperated. The supremacy of party offices over state offices at their level is also undisguised.[31] This comes straight from the party secretary, and sounds like a criticism of the system of party rule:

> Everyone says that under the current system, there's an inherent contradiction between a provincial governor and the provincial [party] secretary, a mayor and the municipal secretary, a county head and the county secretary, and a township head and the township secretary. Generally speaking, party and government organs seldom fail to come into conflict. . . . For instance, when a mayor wants to take hold of the economy and enterprise management, the crucial need is for people talented enough to lead enterprises who understand economics, can be a manager, and have a sense of the market. But the power to decide how to put these talents into play is not in the mayor's hands, but in the [municipal] party secretary's. (124–25)

Zhang Ping's plot may be formulaic in the end, but he dispenses with some formulaic touches from China's classic vernacular novels found even in *Heaven Above* and *Heaven's Wrath*, such as the good guy having a partner, sidekick, and adviser (though Yang Cheng ultimately fills this role in Zhang Ping's novel). *Choice* is intellectually independent enough to introduce, as devil's advocate, the idea that China since the revolution has elevated workers into an "aristocracy" at the expense of the peasants (241). The novel, unlike the film, does not show Li Gaocheng restored to his office at the end, so the conclusion is not entirely rosy.[32] It is the deus ex machina of Provincial Secretary Wang and Governor Wei descending from on high that finally puts the corrupt Zhongyang cadres away. But the Communist Party is, after all, a hierarchy, so this, too, is realistic. As the next section indicates, *Choice* is not equivocal about how little faith in the party and its future the party members themselves retain.

Contributions to the Discourse of Corruption

Choice lets both its positive and negative characters ponder the possibility of regime change, if only through the hoary Mandate of Heaven theory, which posits that all regimes are predestined to decline and be replaced. Zhang Ping, who depicts unauthorized worker protest gatherings at the novel's start and as a kind of reprise at the end (as the workers gather to behold Elder Sister Xia threaten suicide, a scene cut from the film version), is hardly second to Chen Fang in suggesting the magnitude of corruption in present times. His tongue loosened by liquor, Yang

Cheng confides to the mayor, "Sometimes I become more and more frightened when I think about it. What exactly can leaders like us rely on to hold up our realm (*jiangshan*, literally, "rivers and mountains," expressing the idea of China as turf)? What, in the end? For instance, if five cadres out of a hundred have a problem [of corruption], what do we do? What if it's ten? Or twenty or thirty? Can we hold up under that?" (163). Provincial CCP Secretary Wan Yongnian (who in the film is played by an actor who resembles Jiang Zemin) himself proclaims that "sooner or later, any political party or government" that fails to act against massive corruption will be "extinguished," along with its "social system" (489). Official discourse upholds the Mandate of Heaven theory as applied to regimes of the past and allows the possibility of corruption under communism, but only by a small minority insufficient to bring the larger theory into play again. *Choice*'s discourse goes well beyond those bounds. To cite another trope from the novel, Zhongyang is afflicted with a pervasive corruption like a body with "late-stage cancer. Leave it alone, and the patient will live on a few years; cure it, and the patient will expire on the spot" (93). The epilogue provides yet another warning, through the visit of a former bureaucrat from a fallen East European communist regime. *Choice* makes a point of how little China now resembles a country run for the benefit of the working class. However, Mayor Li makes no calls for heightened rule of law, and he considers democracy as simply an extremist proposal that hotheads will inevitably raise if the party does not act more responsibly. Raising China's official salaries, which are low compared to those of entrepreneurs at comparable levels, so that bribes are unnecessary is another proposal, and it is often advocated by social scientists in life, but in *Choice* the idea is voiced only by hypocrites.

In its conservatism, the novel almost comically reduces the Mandate of Heaven to a moral question. The good mayor Li is stunned—stunned!—to think that loyal communist workers would protest just because their living standards are plummeting and they have no hope of future employment: "Never could he have imagined there would be so many of them [protesting]. What really was the problem? Was it only just (*jinjin*) because they hadn't been given any wages, had no money to spend?" (14). Surely they would riot only if they were impoverished *and* thought that this was because they were being robbed! Li's absurd viewpoint might be read as a comment on his naivete and isolation from grassroots problems, but the point is repeated, without irony, by Li (24) and by the novel's highest leader, Provincial Secretary Wan, who saves the day. The implication is that the Mandate of Heaven in its full moral force must be in operation. The end is near; the masses have lost confidence.

Tradition holds that corruption, like morality, spreads from the top down, from the example set by the monarch. This would be true also of petty crime (33), which has come to afflict the Zhongyang city within a city. Crime is a symptom of coming social collapse. Model workers have fallen on hard times and technical graduates are reduced to selling eggs by the public toilets (211–13, 257). Commemorative picture books honor model workers, but the honorees cannot afford the books (262–63). Truly, society is rotting. The egg peddler could have at least repaired bicycles, but he couldn't afford the bribe to get a license (277). The local school is on its last legs, too. Its administrators left when they ceased to be paid (281). Mayor Li takes it for granted that commoners revolt because they are forced into it by the rulers, as in the classic novel *Water Margin*: "The masses must not be pressed into a 'Mt. Liang' state of rebellion, in which they figure that, having already rioted, they might as well go all the way and make it count" (6–7). And Li, in his individual but patriarchal concern for all his municipal wards, is the very image of a monarch in his realm. As under so many monarchs of Chinese history, society has come to a boil because he simply didn't know that things had grown so bad after his departure from the grass roots (33–34, 46, 59, 230, 462). Hence the necessity of his descent, in the middle part of the novel, into the bowels of the rusted-out factory and the homes of its slum dwellers, to see what their life is really like (52, 54, 248–94). The image of the factory community as an urban slum directly evokes the image of physical corruption (33). His descent into the deception of his family evokes a similar image. The morality of his own family, educated by official corruption, is at stake. The mayor is alienated from family during much of the denouement (cut from the film), for his wife leaves and the children go with her. He is, after all, accused of having taken a bribe. The plot of *Choice* devolves into a power struggle between two factions, good and bad, but that, too, fits the traditional discourse that transcends the foreign, "bright future" discourse of communism.

The crooked cadres themselves anticipate the end of Chinese communism. Thus does Zhang Ping solve the mystery of why communist officials take the risk of stealing enormous sums of cash when they already enjoy so many free perks completely within the law. "If none of these other explanations could account for their present behavior, then only one explanation was left as their motive in siphoning off so much money: they were planning an escape route. What kind of escape route? Only one came to mind: if one day there came a great change, one like that which befell the former Soviet Union and Eastern Europe, the power, position, reputation, and status of all leading cadres in authority would vanish in an instant! It would be as if they'd never existed!" (196; also 225–26). The cadres are stealing liquid assets to prepare a "base for their survival overseas" (501), leading to the overseas capital flight of RMB 170 million.

Another of *Choice*'s contributions, at least to popular discourse, is the idea of "collective corruption," of a whole leadership team going rotten. Zhang Ping knew he could not get away with portraying collective corruption at higher than an enterprise level, or surely he would have. The novel is strong in portraying the social consequences of such corruption, in the form of unemployment, poverty, and social unrest, as well as in the betrayal of development and reform (as Lu Tianming does in *Heaven Above*). And *Choice* dissects the ways in which a Confucian culture of loyalty to family and to one's mentors weakens the impulse to fight corruption. Yan Zhen effectively plays on his long-time protégé Li Gaocheng's feelings of guilt. A party member looks out for the interests of old cadres above and proves his worth as a leader by defending his subordinates, even when they have made a "mistake," like the Zhongyang cadres. Zhang Ping discourses at length on the sorry fact of how cadres in a meeting play follow the leader (151). He also criticizes a culture of dependency within Chinese political relations, epitomized by the Zhongyang cadres' acronym of *deng kao yao* ("wait, depend, ask"; 53, 64): wait for finances, appropriations, and investments; depend on the leaders, the state, and the government [for direction and aid]; and ask for whatever is still needed. This gives collective corruption vertical protection, and it is killing China.

Zhang Ping's solution to collective corruption and passing the buck is for leaders to take individual responsibility for their actions, but there is a paradox in Mayor Li's (and evidently Zhang Ping's) interpretation of this mandate. Li Gaocheng reproves the bad cadres by example because he takes comprehensive, paternalistic responsibility for everything that goes on in his municipality. He becomes the very image of a minimonarch in his realm, and thus a symbol of the Communist Party's benevolent despotism. This surely did not escape Jiang Zemin when he saw the movie version, and that may be why he liked it. Mayor Li is a *qing guan* (enlightened and just official), the kind of figure that more progressive writers (like Chen Fang) love to hate.[33] We know that Li is a *qing guan* because the narrator of *Choice* calls him that (8).

Zhang Ping voices an institutional remedy for SOE corruption, *zheng qi fenkai* (separation of government and enterprises). This is part of China's reforms, and yet in practice Li comes to regret factory autonomy and decentralization of decision making (478–79). The independence of the factory from his mayoral supervision is what allowed it to become corrupt. It also fosters unemployment. "How many years now have we hollered, 'Separation of government and enterprise, Separation of government and enterprise'? Isn't the separation of government and enterprise expressly to give enterprises and workers more autonomy? And isn't that to say, more assumption of risk?" (375). Mayor Li is still calling for total assumption of responsibility up at the top. The novel indeed is rather negative in portraying private enterprises, since they are not socially responsible. They evade taxes, ignore labor laws, and do not provide social welfare benefits (which is quite true of many of them in life), and thus offer unfair competition for SOEs (83, 494). Changlong Apparel is the exemplar of private enterprise in *Choice*.

Choice, with its focus on collective corruption and its vertical protection reaching up into the provincial party structure, is pervaded by images of corruption as a web of guanxi, as critics have noted.[34] It is chiefly the film that actually speaks of corruption as a web, indeed a "spider web." The novel writes mostly of "corruption circles." In both novel and movie, Mayor Li is entrapped by his superiors, his subordinates, and his family.

Finally, any reader of *Choice* will surely find a suggestion—a fear, really—that end-game, collective corruption, with its entertainment expenses and lucrative limousine and entertainment services, may after all be more modern, efficient, even "progressive" than old socialist SOEs. Might the new morality itself be more modern and "progressive"? Mayor Li cannot bear to see the nation's wealth sucked up by consumer pleasures, "as by a whale" (171), but his is a lonely socialist voice. That the new morality might have its own rationale is not the novel's viewpoint, but it is to Zhang Ping's credit that this viewpoint emerges in any case. Another alternative that appears between the lines is that Zhongyang is *both* corrupt *and* ripe for closure due to economic structural reasons. History does move on. Whether capitalist or socialist, growth requires "creative destruction," but *Choice* never directly considers this alternative.

Limits of and on Realism

For all the corruption it displays, *Choice*'s emphasis is on combating it, and the highest perpetrator is Yan Zhen, at the vice provincial level. Zhang Ping had to accept the standard political limits on the Chinese anticorruption novel, and he also chose to accept the anticorruption author's "sacred mission" of going to the limit; hence the job of culprit at the vice provincial level does not go vacant. *Choice* fits the formula established by *Heaven Above* in many particulars.

But *Choice* goes on for the first two hundred pages as a social novel, highly attentive to social classes, the types of people who make them up, how they live, how their welfare and morale are declining, and the financial state of their institutions, all within a detailed historical background. In these pages *Choice* may be called a thesis novel, or rather a novel with a well-argued thesis *and* antithesis: there is much testimony that Zhongyang is being looted, and also that its leadership and its product lines simply cannot keep up with the demands of a new economy. All this is in keeping with classic nineteenth-century realism. But then the novel turns into a melodrama. The "problem" is no longer corruption or simple industrial decline as a social formation, but rather the fate of Li Gaocheng, who is fighting for his political life. The transition from realism need not startle us, for by one definition, melodrama pits "personal desire and dreams [here, Li Gaocheng's idealism] against the restrictions of social realism."[35] What is lost is not plot interest or suspense, but the book's "realism"—its ability to enlighten the reader about society and also, Chinese critics agree, its believability. Also lost is Zhang Ping's deeper questioning of the system, and even his probing of whether or not Mayor Li is in some sense guilty of unintentional blindness to the realities all around him.[36]

Still, the plot's mystery dynamics take not just a melodramatic but also an unexpected "Chinese" turn, as Mayor Li goes sleuthing incognito, just like old Judge Bao in ancient stories and plays, and indeed contemporary dramatic television series about great emperors.[37] Li visits the workers in their homes and scouts for the whereabouts of promising young workers he had his eye on in earlier years. Now they are all down on their luck. He crashes the scene at the Green Apple brothel and Changlong, where he is beat up and thrown before feasting cadres, one of whom happens to be his wife, a secret trustee of the Tegaote subsidiary. There the injured Li Gaochang flies into a rage and smashes the dishes before falling unconscious. (It is a dramatic climax in the film; Li's wife is not among the diners in that version, but the mayor overturns the cadres' table like Jesus among the moneychangers. Moreover, while suffering trials and tribulations, he rests upon a bridge with arms outstretched, like Christ on the cross.)

The last third of the plot becomes a simple story of one political faction against another. The good guys are Mayor Li, joined now by Yang Cheng, who provides hidden links to higher leadership. Guo Tao, the vice mayor who is *not* on the take, and, near the end, a formulaic iron lady prosecutor, Bai Weihua (literally, "Protect China"), are also on the side of good.[38] The bad guys are the four Zhongyang leading cadres, Provincial Deputy Secretary Yan Zhen, and Wu Aizhen, Mayor Li's wife. The two-line struggle begins with a scene seemingly straight out of *Heaven Above*: a telephone call from Yan Zhen to Li Gaocheng that Li must accept during a crucial meeting. The call is both reassuring and vaguely threatening, representing Yan's two-faced position as one willing to protect Mayor Li against all threats to his position (as Yan protects all corruption in the city), if only Li will play ball and perpetrate a cover-up. That is Li's duty to his mentor above and to the factory managers that Li cultivated below, as patriarch and patron, in an old Confucian chain. Not only is Yan's protection seemingly benign, it is also inevitable; it is not so easy for Li to escape, for what investigative underling would be so foolish as to obey Li's orders to follow responsibility for corruption wherever it may lead, including to Li himself, where it does seem to reside? He is truly caught in a web.

By now, the novel has become a battle of good against bad in which one must wait for justice finally to prevail. (In John Cawelti's words, melodrama unfolds in "a world that is purportedly full of violence and tragedy we associate with the 'real world' but that in this case seems to be governed by some benevolent moral principle.")[39] The battle escalates from phone calls and reassurances to threats and blackmail, as *Choice*, like *Heaven's Wrath*, veers into more hard-boiled, counterspy territory. The mayor's enemies almost succeed in turning the investigation into an inquiry into Li Gaocheng's alleged venality. The most maudlin moment comes when Elder Sister Xia pleads for Li's innocence while threatening to commit suicide in front of TV cameras and reporters. The filmmakers may have cut this subplot from the movie because it suggests independent collective action by workers, but it is after all a rather incredible episode.

The turn away from character development and social survey toward a clash of good and evil conspiracies is the fate of realism in much fiction, even thesis stories and novels, since Mao Zedong's era and indeed since the entry of progressive themes into May Fourth fiction thirty years before the political revolution. The point of *Choice* is political reality, not character; characters do not develop. Mayor Li does not develop, though the story is refracted through his outlook; he simply descends into a maelstrom and then a nightmare. He is "steeled," as in so many socialist realist novels, and he was steely to begin with. Comparatively speaking, it is in the movie that characters turn from bad to good, including the mayor's wife and the Zhongyang cadre Feng Minjie. In China's earlier leftist novels, characters stood for political classes, or feudal and progressive ideologies. In *Choice* they simply stand for good or bad, despite a subversive implication that the bad are "up to date" and the good are "old-fashioned," as readers so often feel about corrupt cadres above them in life. If the realistic novel, to capture the spirit of the times, must become a political novel, and if in turn politics is inevitably a question of moral stance, for or against "the people" (in the official discourse, "the party and the people"), then all realistic novels must dissolve into simplistic and feel-good political-moral melodramas. This is a main outcome of China's mainstream twentieth-century "progressive" style of realism (whose defining characteristics will be postulated in Chapter 7). Not surprisingly, May Fourth, Maoist, and "realistic" post-Mao stories and novels have been adapted into melodramatic movies that develop and dramatically accentuate their bipolar political and moral tensions, without greatly changing the plotline. *Choice* was made into a Peking opera, which likewise appears to have elaborated on the melodramatic potential of the plot. The opera version gives Li Gaocheng a mother. They sing a duet.

The social problems Zhang Ping addresses remain serious, but the very meaning of "collective corruption" shifts within the novel from a criticism of the system to a criticism of a faction of political individuals. Li Gaocheng becomes an apotheosis of the good official and a symbol of benevolent monarchy within his realm. Loyalty, too, inheres in individuals in this age, since loyalty to an ideology still seems too dangerous and extremist. And yet, this was not good enough for the filmmakers, for although Li Gaocheng is a Communist Party member, he is not the chief representative of party power at his level. That honor goes to Yang Cheng.

Aftermath

In 1999, Zhang Ping followed up *Choice* with another well-reviewed, heavily researched novel with hard-hitting themes of corruption in the penal and judicial systems—all wrapped up in a detective thriller, *Shimian maifu* (Ambushed from all sides).[40] Critics have suggested that Zhang Ping's novels about corruption have tended ever more toward pessimism.[41] He has continued writing about corruption, but reviews of his 2004 novel, *Guojia ganbu* (State cadres), were not so favorable.[42]

Fatal Decision, the movie based on *Choice*, was, however, favorably reviewed—some critics preferred it to the novel[43]—even though in retrospect it is often called a "main melody" film, belonging to a vague category of works with patriotic themes approved by the party or that have at some stage been subsidized by party propaganda or cultural departments.[44] *Fatal Decision* qualified on both grounds in the end, but its seal of approval was hard won at every stage. The Beijing Film Studio began the project but failed to win clearance for its scripts.[45] The Shanghai Film Studio picked up the project, with support from the Shanghai CCP municipal committee, on Jiang Zemin's native turf. One inside source indicates that *Fatal Decision*, unlike most main melody films, was supported at the highest level not by the CCP Central Propaganda Department, but by the Central Disciplinary Inspection Commission, the party's highest organ for conducting anticorruption investigations and campaigns.[46]

Zhang Ping wanted no part of an adaptation he knew would alter his original vision. Yu Benzheng, the final director, had to be pressured to take on so political a film. The actor he cast as Li Gaocheng was fairly well known, but the others were less so. Yu claimed he cast relative unknowns to avoid the umbra of star personas. It was also difficult to find a city and factory willing to serve as backdrop. Finally Dalian accepted. Following the Beijing Film Studio's failed second draft screenplay, the script went through seven more drafts under Yu at the Shanghai Film Studio. After filming, the work underwent further revisions to suit central judicial and disciplinary inspection officials in Beijing. Even then, theaters sought local party instructions before running it.[47]

Fatal Decision is reasonably faithful to the novel, considering the latter's length. Yu Benzheng heightened the drama through what he calls "montage"[48] (frequent cutaways). He maintains suspense about Mayor Li's political fate to the end, just as in the novel. The film has fairly good acting and production values, and it has punchier dialogue than the novel, so it is fast-paced and exciting—less verbose than other officially approved films,[49] not to speak of popular TV serials with contemporary and historical themes, including the 1998 TV drama based on *Choice* that preceded the movie.[50] Surely these merits helped the film win Jiang Zemin's approval. The film also paints a warmer portrait of the Li family, though Wu Aizhen remains flawed. She gently misleads her husband as they speak in dark rooms that frame classically "noir" scenes. In the novel, she is more of a cadre than a wife; Li and Wu sleep in separate bedrooms to accommodate their different work schedules.

Because film is under tighter control than fiction, Chinese critics were not surprised to find *Fatal Decision* politically more conservative than *Choice*.[51] It was director Yu Benzheng's mission to introduce corruption gradually, avoiding previous scripts' vision of China's having gone to hell in a handbasket.[52] Elsewhere I have examined in detail, with help from the structuralist methodology of Brian McFarlane, the plot and theme transferences and alterations in the adaptation, as well as the film's unique means of enunciating them.[53] *Fatal Decision*'s departures from the novel exceed the needs of adaptation, condensation, popularization, and satisfying the censors, but this need not be taken as criticism, for the film is a work of popular political art on its own. It does, with respect to faithfulness to the original, hijack the first section of the novel by converting Zhang Ping's original dialectic of workers' and cadres' conflicting claims about the realities of Zhongyang into a simple power struggle between the mayor and Yang Cheng, who in the film is just the deputy CCP secretary. Which man will be promoted to full municipal party secretary, Li or Yang? This conflict is a red herring; Yang Cheng turns out to be as fully on the side of the angels as he is in the novel. He is not out to "get" Li. The tensions between the two leaders are only the result of a misunderstanding, based largely on Li's ignorance of the Zhongyang realities, and his ignorance has an explanation: he has just been away for a year at the Central Party School (an invention of the filmmakers).[54] Still, the dramatic result of the conflict is that the entire work is melodramatic, not just the last two-thirds, as in the novel.

The film changes some characters' functions. Mayor Li's wife, Wu Aizhen, though corrupted enough to have accepted gifts through the years from the Zhongyang leaders, does not feel that she deserves the RMB 300,000 bonus as she does in the novel, but instead is appropriately horrified when she gets a proverbial suitcase full of money. She feels guilt, creates no further trouble for Li Gaocheng, and ultimately turns herself in.[55] Their daughter Meimei is retarded in the film, "realistically" played by a young girl who is retarded in life. (Some critics found the bathos in this over the top, and thus "unrealistic.")[56] Feng Minjie transforms from villain to helper. Afflicted with liver cancer, he develops a conscience and turns state's evidence. And Yan Zhen's relative and direct contact with Zhongyang, Chao Wanshan, is a major character, renamed in the film Cao Wanshan to eliminate the Dickensian double entendre in his name ("Chao" is a homonym of a word meaning "to make money illicitly"). He takes Feng Minjie's place among the four bad cadres when Feng goes into decline. Cao plots with a doctor to have Feng murdered during an upcoming operation, but not in time to keep him from spilling the beans. Showing once again that the movie has more character development than the novel, Cao, for all his cunning, displays filial piety in the end. In the movie, he is upgraded to be Yan Zhen's foster son, whom Yan raised to fulfill a debt of gratitude to a fallen war buddy. When the jig is up, Wanshan stays in China to comfort his foster father rather than escape abroad like his siblings. He commits suicide, presumably so as not to have to testify against his father. This humanizes Yan Zhen himself. The film's triumph, most critics agree, is its realization of the Zhongyang gang of four as ordinary, down-home people simply used to their high incomes and unafraid to rationalize the means by which they extract them. Yan Zhen, who shifts into classical Chinese when lecturing his former protégé Li Gaocheng about the duties of mentorship, sounds almost like a wise and kindly grandfather. Yu Benzheng's reauthoring of the plot toys with the ages of all the characters, making the corrupt men older (more prone to decadence and more distant from the new call of reform) and Li Gaocheng younger. While Yan Zhen in the film is Li's gray-haired senior, exuding grandfatherly charisma as might be expected, Li Gaocheng is actually a year older than Yan Zhen in the novel; Yan is a figure to be feared in the novel because he is a "rocket cadre" on a fast trajectory for promotion. The age politics evident in the relative youth of the "rioting" workers in the film, though it taps a social fear, may work in the opposite direction from the adding of years to the corrupt cadres. Rioting young people plant a suspicion that seeds of corruption and self-destruction are inherent in reform itself.

The film not unexpectedly downgrades the degree of corruption and the scope of the social crisis. The number of millions of yuan owed, workers laid off, and even workers employed at the start are all decreased. The film makes the party seem to have been more alert to corruption in the earlier years of Zhongyang's decline. It portrays enticing images of the city as a dynamo by the sea, mild enough in climate for fashionable exterior dress, and already highly modernized, whether such a representation was for patriotic reasons or done to provide eye candy to film viewers (bicycles, street vendors, and smoking never appear on camera; this took some fancy editing). Perhaps the filmmakers intended to refer to Shanghai, as another tribute to Jiang Zemin and the film's patrons.[57] Apart from the "riot" at the outset, the film downplays images of independent collective action by the workers. (In the novel, the workers present the mayor with a hundred-page report on their investigations into Zhongyang. In the film, it appears in a close-up as a petition of a few pages, mostly of worker signatures.) The film deletes ironic references to the importance of "stability" voiced by the corrupt Yan Zhen.[58] Contrary even to the official discourse, corruption spreads not from the top but up from below, for it is the Zhongyang gang of four who conceive the plan of delicately bribing Yan and making him their patron, not Yan himself. And the film, unlike the novel, ends with a list of sentences for all the villains, reassuring the viewer that the bad guys will be punished. Li Gaocheng is "reelected" mayor by the Municipal People's Congress, and Yang Cheng gets the promotion to full party secretary. The novel does not relate the legal outcomes, which preserves a modicum of realism, particularly regarding Li Gaocheng. He has, however one views it, made serious political mistakes. Fortunately he awoke to them.

It is startling that the actor playing Yang Cheng is so much more handsome and decisive than Mayor Li, in an open, straightforward way, and is given so much more attention than in the novel that he almost upstages the mayor as the true savior *qing guan* (model good official) of the story.[59] Meanwhile, the film has erased any indication that Mayor Li is a technocrat. Some film posters with head shots of the two heroes made Yang's visage almost as large as Li's, with Yang looking at one confidently in the eye and Li looking askance with a worried expression. Far from erasing the party's supremacy in leading China, *Fatal Decision* takes pains to show the party organization in charge of the state and due the major credit.[60] From the film's point of view, Yang Cheng is infallible. He didn't even *have* to make a "choice."

Even if the novel had prefigured the film in shedding the early thesis chapters for more chapters about factional conflict (the theses are shoved aside in the novel for a conflict between good and bad soon enough as it is), melodrama is an arena where fiction is hard put to compete with stage and screen. Film can concentrate and concretize character types in flesh-and-blood actors, illustrate their confrontations with body language as well as speech, and keep multiple subplots moving rapidly through cutaways, at which Yu Benzheng is skilled. Mayor Li's indecisive interior monologues and self-posed rhetorical questions are gone, even at the point where he makes his "choice," for the film has few voice-overs. The viewer is, however, treated to an impassioned dramatization of the mayor's accusatory and self-accusatory speech at the end. Indeed, the fight between good and evil as dramatized is better at evoking Marston Anderson's idea of catharsis—in this case, that which comes from seeing justice finally done, after all the trials and tribulations—than the would-be realistic novel. *Fatal Decision* is not as deep or politically provocative, but it is tighter, more dramatic, withal more entertaining than *Choice*.

The film, as a "moving" document in words *and* images, is not only more memorable than the middlebrow novel. Some critics also evaluate it more highly as art.

This dilemma is common to China's mass fiction; if one wants to simplify, concentrate, dramatize, and teach while focusing on moral duty, and if one wants to deliver the lesson with a degree of suspense besides, the melodramatic potential of a visual medium such as film or television is unequaled. Much fiction today is written with dramatic adaptations in mind from the first. The success of *Fatal Decision*, commercially and even critically, suggests that if the party wanted to, by using higher budgets and better writers, it could produce slick, feel-good, patriotic movies that could compete with Hollywood for Chinese viewers.[61] Hollywood knows that audiences will pay to see patriotic films, and it also knows that sometimes nothing promotes political apathy like a feel-good film that damns the system. Meanwhile, it remains clear that fiction, because of China's censorship priorities, retains an advantage in the communication of social realism and criticism.

5

Anticorruption by Indirection: Wang Yuewen's *National Portrait*

Wang Yuewen (b. 1962) made a sensational entrance onto the Chinese literary scene in 1999 with his novel *Guo hua* (National portrait).¹ It was somewhat ahead of what would soon be a tidal wave of novels about corrupt officials, although anticorruption fiction was by now a known quantity. *Fatal Decision* was still being made, but Zhang Ping's and Zhou Meisen's novels with corruption themes were already known and being called "main melody" works, usually as a compliment to them.² "Fiction about officialdom," a category that fits *National Portrait* better, also had clear precedents in works by authors such as Liu Zhenyun, and particularly in the long novels in archaic vernacular language written at the end of the Qing by Li Boyuan and Wu Woyao. But as the anticorruption phenomenon burgeoned in fiction, many came to consider Wang Yuewen's novels about officialdom to belong to the new anticorruption genre; Wang helped blur the distinction.³ As in the Lu Tianming formula, the problem in *National Portrait* is municipal-level governance in a large city. Corruption is multifarious and pervasive, bureaucratic titles and job relationships are finely drawn, and all the action is reflected through the consciousness of a troubled municipal employee, not a mayor in this case, but a male similarly taking his identity from the state, not the CCP, apparatus. The reader's anxiety is aroused chiefly by the familiar question of whether he will prevail or go under in the world of Chinese politics.

There the similarity with contemporary formulas ends. Far from providing a big-picture synoptic account of society, *National Portrait* is a worm's-eye view of municipal corruption, of power exchanges that have become routine if not quotidian, and not just because its hero, Zhu Huaijing, begins the novel as a mere vice division chief (*fu chuzhang*). The novel observes little more than what Zhu observes, in a style that at times mimics stream-of-consciousness writing. By its themes and structural cement—the novel relies on neat segues rather than a clear plot skeleton—*National Portrait* resembles a late Qing novel of officialdom more than any other work described in this book. Wang Yuewen's masterpiece is often called a modern *Guanchang xianxing ji* (Exposure of officialdom, a novel by Li Boyuan).[4] *National Portrait*, however, is not chapter-driven. Though quite as epic as a late Qing or late socialist novel (at 690 pages, or 503,000 characters), it has no chapters, and practically no internal divisions at all.[5] This accentuates the impression of official life as an unending stream of small events.

The novel's run-on nature gives it something of an arty flavor, though it is not avant-garde, since the prose is as plain and readable as that of any novel discussed in this book. Even so, *National Portrait* was published amid critical silence.[6] This must have been due to instructions from above; some months later the legal publisher was forced to stop reprinting the book. It was, in effect, banned.[7] Ten pirated editions took up the slack, ultimately putting two million volumes into circulation, it is said.[8] Criticisms of negativity about China and its cadres in *National Portrait* and Wang's other fiction about officialdom necessarily followed.[9] Critics not toeing the party line spoke out for the novel on the Internet, praising its "realism," "critical realism," and "authenticity."[10] *National Portrait* seemed a cut above the middlebrow, crowd-pleasing melodrama and detection themes of Zhang Ping and Lu Tianming, and still Wang's novel was a great commercial success—which conservatives took as evidence that it pandered to mass taste.[11] Some critics saw it as just popular fiction (a misreading, I believe) because of its subject matter, as well as its plainness of style and seemingly documentary nature.[12] Most took it to be serious literature—again, due to its subject matter. *National Portrait* well represents the status of anticorruption fiction and, beyond that, Chinese realistic fiction as existing between serious "art" and popular "mass culture." The title, *National Portrait*, suggests that the book is a portrait of the Chinese people. Moreover, the usual meaning of *guo hua* is the national style of painting, or, as it is seen today, the *traditional* style of painting. However, I shall argue that despite its echoes of the late Qing,

Wang Yuewen's style is relatively Western, and very much like one style of Western realism. The limits of Wang Yuewen's novel, besides the usual ones imposed by the system of political control of literature, seem to come from Wang's adherence to a Jamesian discipline of realism rather than the "classic," "Chinese" kind of realism deployed by Zhang Ping.

The novel's authenticity was no doubt heightened by the fact that before devoting himself to writing Wang Yuewen had served in government. Since 1984 he had served in county and municipal offices in West Hunan and finally in Changsha, at the provincial level.[13] His apostasy no doubt stung CCP loyalists. Wang's hero, Zhu Huaijing, is corrupted by his life work, and yet he, too, manages at times to rise above it. The book has not been adapted for screen or television. If officials had allowed it, entrepreneurs would surely have leapt at the opportunity to dramatize the novel. Directors would have seen the work as one they could rewrite and make their own.

The Storyline

The plot and storyline, like the lives of the characters, are not so dramatically episodic as desultory. Nor are the villains and heroes, if one can distinguish them, charismatic. Zhu Huaijing is a bored and frustrated bureaucrat in the municipal administration of Jingdu, a large, fictitious city.[14] He has one goal: to be promoted to full division head. To that end, he gets his eccentric (and later clinically paranoid) artist friend Li Mingxi to paint a picture as a gift for his boss. As luck and considerations of face would have it, (Deputy) Head (personal) Secretary Liu Zifeng up the line decides he wants one, too, as Zhu has exaggerated the artist's fame and the monetary value of his work. But this turns out well, for Liu serves Vice Mayor Pi Deqiu, the main mover and shaker in the city, who will soon emerge as Zhu's prime new target of ingratiation (guanxi formation).

Zhu Huaijing is not just a bureaucrat, but also a family man. He helps his wife's country bumpkin nephew Si Mao (a nickname; Zhu learns his real name only halfway into the novel) when the latter is scammed by con artists, who invite poor Si Mao to a fancy meal in the Longxing Hotel to celebrate their "job offer" to him, then flee, leaving him to pay the bill. Hotel security guards then take it out of Si Mao's hide. Zhu turns even this misfortune to a profitable end. Not only the hotel manager Lei, "horrified" to have given offense, but also the chief of the local police station (*paichusuozhang*) Song, a cop on the make with underworld connections, fall over themselves to ingratiate themselves with "Big Official Zhu," the only bureaucrat they know. Zhu Huaijing has thus added to his guanxi circle a fixer on the police force, a location where he can entertain other guanxi objects gratis (because the manager of the publicly owned hotel wants the same guanxi), and a mistress, the lovely assistant hotel manager, Yu Meiqin. Indeed, Zhu acts quickly to fete Vice Mayor Pi there, together with the cop and *his* proffered connection, Magician Yuan, a modern-day fortune-teller and "miracle worker" who is a darling of the press. The vice mayor is superstitious, providing an opening for those who want to be in his good graces.

Zhu is honorary head of yet another guanxi web involving the past and current officials of Wu county, where Zhu Huaijing worked his way up to magistrate before being promoted to the Jingdu municipality. He also networks with Ruoyou prefecture, at the level of administration between the municipality and the county. The current Wu county CCP secretary, Zhang Tianqi, has ingenious ways of encouraging the bigwigs in Jingdu—and Beijing—to fund his county's pet hydroelectric project. With Zhu's help, he provides comely Wu county girls to Vice Mayor Pi and his (deputy) head secretary Liu (whose wife is an invalid) free, as "maids." In addition to servicing the municipal and Beijing leaders, the maids are to provide intelligence to the Wu county cadres. It is in Zhu Huaijing's own interest to raise his home locality's profile and simultaneously increase his influence back home. Local cadres have their own sources of income. Wu county is famous for its aphrodisiacs, which make good gifts for superiors. (Later in this often comic novel, Zhu organizes his rural relatives to grow "organic" rice for no other purpose than for gift giving.) A Wu county gofer gives Zhu his first cell phone, so he can keep in touch with the locals—and with the hope that Zhu will speak well of the gofer to his boss. This gift makes Zhu's stock rise faster at work than the Audi that Vice Mayor Pi's entrepreneurial son Pi Jie lends him for personal use, since Zhu realizes it is wise to learn to drive it himself (his lover Yuqin gives him lessons) and park it out of sight of the municipal offices lest he be suspected of graft.

The previously off-camera Jingdu mayor and eleven others perish in a plane crash, so Zhu gets his promotion, to chief of the Finance and Trade Division (*caimaochu*). His new boss, however, is a personal secretary to Vice Mayor Pi's rival for power, Vice Mayor Sima.

Zhu Huaijing has always been a fixer. He met his apolitically idealistic painter friend Li Mingxi by saving him from the local police when Li came to Wu county years ago to paint nudes, and he saved his politically idealistic former schoolmate, outspoken newsman Zeng Li, by using bureaucratic pull to call the police off him, too. Now Zhu calls in the latter favor at the request of the Wu county cadres. They insist that Zeng Li kill an exposé of Wu county corruption he wrote for the *China Legal System Daily*. (Years ago, the cadres had suckered Wu county farmers into paying for bogus peach seeds.) Zhu and Zeng comply. On another front, Zhu sends a 20,000-yuan gift to the Pi household (it goes to the wife, to avoid embarrassment), since the vice mayor's second son is about to go abroad. Zhu is upset when later there is a more open collection that makes him contribute another 5,000 yuan. He also wants to help his mistress's Longxing Hotel expand into an adjacent lot so it can keep up with the competition and build a modern entertainment complex. He hopes for help from Pi, whom the Municipal People's Congress has now elected mayor (offending Vice Mayor Sima's faction), but Pi Jie has already put in a bid for the land, to build a pleasure palace for *his* hotel. Fat chance for Longxing. Pi Jie invites Zhu, the Longxing folks—everybody—to a banquet to allay any hard feelings.

Zhu is now drawn into the circles of local entrepreneurs through his work as finance and trade chief taxing them, and through his increasing closeness to Mayor Pi and his head personal secretary, Fang Mingyuan. Pi's mah-jongg partner and chief benefactor (and Fang's, too) is Manager Pei of the Flying Man Clothes factory. His mansion makes the mayor envious, but Pei is socially insecure. Zhu gets the rich man to help sponsor his friend Li Mingxi's one-man art exhibition. Another big task with which Zhu is now entrusted is helping Fang arrange Vice Mayor Pi's secret trips to a Buddhist temple. The trips are for his old mother, but they also feed the mayor's superstition. The monks are oily bureaucrats of their realm, hankering for municipal contributions. The head monk has a salaried post in the municipal administration and wants a promotion to the vice departmental level. Zhu then accompanies higher officials in a visit to areas devastated by flood, where the officials carry on with their wining and dining. Zhu must try to kill yet another article by his friend Zeng Li to help Zhang Tianqi, now promoted to vice prefect, out of a scrape, and then help Zhang yet again when one of the old county officials, from whom he used to procure money necessary to bribe Beijing officials, gets caught up in a scandal. On a slightly sour note, that official is executed.

Many of Zhu's friends have been promoted now, and Zhu learns that he will be promoted again to the vice departmental (*fu ting*) level. He goes out with his soul mates—mistress Mei Yuqin, painter Li Mingxi, and fearless reporter Zeng Li—on an idyllic Daoist sort of picnic at an abandoned and haunted ruin, the Qie Zuo Ting (Bide-a-Wee Pavilion). Fortune turns against Zhu and his friends. Li Mingxi, confined in a mental hospital, flees and disappears. Zeng Li feels he must resign after being transferred to advertising (providing a lucrative opportunity to solicit bribes, but that is not his style) after publishing another exposé in the liberal *Southern Evening News* (whose counterpart in life would be the *Southern Weekend*). Zhu Huaijing loses face when he fails to get the promotion rumors had indicated he was up for. The other division heads, jealous of his closeness to Mayor Pi, did not ratify the promotion.

But it is Zhu Huaijing who then discovers the mayor slumped over his desk and rescues him during a heart attack. Pi's poor health is kept a secret, leading to rumors that he has been arrested until his underlings air a TV documentary praising the mayor's reform of local enterprises to show the public that Pi is still in favor. Evidently as his reward, Zhu is finally promoted to vice chief of the Finance Department (at the *ting* level), a position that has just been made vacant by anticorruption prosecutions. Zhu faces another round of congratulatory dinners from people he doesn't even know but who seek his favor, much as in Wu Jingzi's eighteenth-century novel *The Scholars*.

Zhu Huaijing is now Mayor Pi's confidant, just like a son to him, but Zhu's hopes are pinned on the wrong man. Pi Jie flees abroad after looting RMB 40 million from his enterprises. Zhu's lover Mei Yuqin, now manager of the Longxing Hotel, had felt trapped into buying the younger Pi's hotel at an inflated price of RMB 28 million, so now she stands accused of having lost the state 10 million yuan in return for a bribe. At the mayor's urging, Zhu had encouraged the sale, unaware of the terms. Heat comes down on Zhu from the Disciplinary Inspection Commission to implicate the mayor in the corrupt transaction. Zhu remains loyal, but Sima replaces Pi as mayor. Pi is kicked upstairs to chair the Municipal Political Consultative Conference. It was Pi's own secretary, Fang, allied with Sima, who betrayed Pi.

With the fall of the mayor, Zhu Huaijng has lost his niche in the political ecosystem. His extramarital affair with Yuqin is also bruited about. Zhu goes to Party School for half a year of study. But Heaven never closes off all the exits. The indomitable Zhang Tianqi, now CCP secretary of the Jingnan municipal committee, can be blackmailed by Zhu, so Zhang finds him a job at the vice prefectural level as a rural CCP deputy secretary of Meici prefecture. Local government is not so prestigious, yet its opportunities for building a power base offer potential for future promotion. Zhu Huaijing's fair-weather friends flock back, though his wife wants a divorce and his true friends are all gone, either mad, missing, or in prison. At least the shady cop Song is willing to remember a friend. He lends Zhu a car to go see his lover Yuqin in prison, where she dreams of the Bide-a-Wee Pavilion. Zhu's new subordinates come to pay respects, and he quickly learns their names to impress them.

Corruption Cases

High-profile economic crimes are not the point of *National Portrait*. It does not dramatize criminal prosecutions or have a single corruption-fighting hero. That, indeed, became a major matter of dissatisfaction among conservative critics. Good and evil are hardly part of the novel's world. Most cadre behavior is described uniformly, dispassionately, and without moral comment, as if it were all routine. The one big "case" is that of the princeling Pi Jie, who expanded his hotel into a pleasure house and brothel for cadres and their rich friends, then sold it at an inflated price with help from his father and some bribes, to Commerce Department chief Lei (for RMB 1,000,000) and Mei Yuqin, who succeeded Lei as head of the Longxing Hotel when Lei was promoted up out of it (Mei got RMB 200,000). Then Pi Jie absconded abroad with RMB 40 million. It is an abrupt ending within the relatively seamless plot, but not really shocking, nor much more than a digression setting up the fall of Mayor Pi and thus of Zhu Huaijing and his circle.

Most corruption is of the "old-fashioned" kind and appears largely in the details. In this regard *National Portrait* is formulaic. The municipal cadres live high off the hog at public expense, drinking premium *Jiu gui* ("Old Tippler," a nationally famous West Hunanese distilled liquor) as they survey flood devastation; an aide discreetly pours it into cheap-label wine bottles. But the leaders hardly outdo the Wu county crowd. When they come to Jingdu, banqueting and trawling for favors, they bring a whole retinue of wannabe apprentices and associates who aspire to power. As in *Heaven's Wrath*, the city leaders take bribes disguised as winnings from wagers on games. Zhu Huaijing himself takes a kickback from Manager Pei after helping him get his company recognized as one of the area's Ten Major Private Firms, eligible for tax breaks and government investment (549), though he turns down an outright bribe for arranging a TV spot for him (362). Zhu's long and fruitful relationship with the Longxing Hotel crowd has origins in his extortion of 85,000 yuan plus 15,000 yuan in inflated hospital fees for their maltreatment of

Si Mao. (The managers were honored to be extorted by an official.) Comic scenes have Zhu rushing his nephew to the hospital in time to substantiate his injuries and repeated visits to persuade him to feign illness as long as possible. This all seems so commonplace in the social context, though, that critics still argue whether Zhu is a "corrupt official."

As Zhu Huaijing rises in bureaucratic rank, he gets Si Mao a lucrative job heading the municipal construction brigade. Si Mao is unprepared for it, but it yields kickbacks and contracts, for restoring the Buddhist temple, building tennis courts for retired cadres, and so forth. Meanwhile, Wu county cadres stuff the brigade with patronage jobs for Wu county people. As most anticorruption novels stress, the problem of nepotism and interlocking directorates is not simply unjust enrichment of the few and the incompetent, but the building of an iron circle of power to which outsiders have no access. As a peasant, Si Mao was subject to impromptu beatings by hotel security guards. Once in the circle of power, he is beyond the law.

Corruption in the sense of decline and decay thus takes form as a betrayal of the public trust and the public servant's very profession. Serving the people is the last thing on the cadres' minds. They are intent on having a good time, getting promotions so they can enjoy themselves still more, and sponsoring banquets to celebrate each others' promotions and pave the way for the next ones. Human relations have no sincerity. Mayor Pi likes golf, so Zhu Huaijing takes it up to be near him. Pi has a weakness for sycophancy, as seen in a late Qing-style episode: going down to the flooded areas to show his benevolence, the mayor gloms on to an old lady furiously at work, who says, "The people's government is good and all the leaders are good!" (429). She is the village lunatic.

Human talent is wasted, public funds are misused, hypocrisy reigns supreme, solipsism has reached the point that officials cannot see through articles that satirize them, and the cynical and utilitarian "art of guanxi" (*guanxixue*) entails gift giving, spying, and the misuse of public facilities such as hotels. When Mayor Pi has his heart attack, responsible officials establish a "small group of curing experts," subordinate to a "*leading small group for the cure*"; Zhu himself is amused, though he is out of the loop, since mayoral health information is dispensed only on a need-to-know basis. As in the old novels, bureaucrats put on airs before commoners and form factions to struggle for power, little knowing that their personal secretaries are manipulating them and running rackets of their own on the side. The cadres are backbiting, jealous, and vengeful. Their "politics" is wholly wrapped up in personal and personnel issues without broader policy ramifications. Particularly shocking to many readers of *National Portrait* is the atmosphere of officialdom. The bureaucrats are quite comfortable in their skins, entirely blasé in their public-be-damned attitudes. Because they live as a social stratum apart from others, deceptions like putting fine liquor in cheap-looking bottles are rarely needed. Much of their activity exists in a gray area. Zhu Huaijing's big innovation on the job is to earn money for his unit by printing a book of cadre phone numbers and (ghost-written) articles "by the leaders"; this will make the book obligatory for purchase, though not, of course, reading. Zhu's most important decision is deciding annual New Year's bonuses. The leaders get RMB 5,000, at a time when Zhu as division head gets less than RMB 1,000 a month (271, 462).

In *National Portrait*, as in late Qing fiction, all professions are corrupt and hypocritical. Characters relate short anecdotes about corruption and other social oddities, sometimes for their sheer curiosity value (168–69, 271), and sometimes as a parabolic way of referring to the dangers of corruption without naming names (204, 646–47). In an apparent quotation from Wu Woyao, Zhu Huaijing reads, in the *Reference News for Cadres*, a strange and vaguely premonitory story about a couple that exude radiation and electric current. Visiting the malls, they shorted out electrical appliances (185).

The media are in the officials' pockets, having been paid off. They follow Boss Pi around in order to manufacture news for him. Manager Pei's reward for his largesse is a television spot congratulating him for rehiring laid-off state workers, filmed while Pi visits his factory (with free suits for the news staff). Reporters who tell the truth, like Zeng Li, incur a steady stream of threats, bribes, and backdoor deals intended to get their articles killed even after they have been accepted. The police, meanwhile, with their monopoly of force and underworld connections, drive around in cars better than those of midlevel municipal cadres (30). "Monkey Song," Zhu's cop "friend," stage-manages the theft of Yuqin's purse and then its return, to put Zhu in his debt and also acquire photos of Zhu with Yuqin suitable for blackmail. In a short life story worthy of a late Qing novel, a Wu county cop, in trouble from gambling, takes some girls down to Shenzhen and pimps for them. He ends up as Magician Yuan's head of security. A mere restaurant proprietor puts on airs, bragging that he served Mayor Pi. The falsehood is exposed by the braggart's inept insistence that the mayor paid his own bill! As well, *all* domestic brand-name liquor is counterfeit. Funeral home directors rip off the bereaved, until they are blackmailed by threats of being exposed as hiring undocumented workers.

The novel's representative writer, named Lu like the literary icon Lu Xun, writes fake documentary books about Magician Yuan's miracles. The monks are corrupt, and so, of course, are the miracle workers, who in life at the time were much ballyhooed in the Chinese press. The chicanery of Magician Yuan, who works voodoo on anyone who displeases him (a pregnant symbol for all those in power), occasions another exposé, because his philanthropy is self-interested. Yuan convenes a meeting to solicit opinions on how best to give away his money, but his goal is maximum media exposure, or, more precisely, to be photographed with the mayor. An indoor tennis court at a rest home for retired cadres is the solution. The mayor is sure to be there at the groundbreaking. Even in the art world, Li Mingxi's idealism is an exception. The profession is given to chicanery, puffery, and factionalism. Li is committed to the psych ward by a jealous artist heading the academy where he resides. The rival wants Li's rooms and his paintings. In academe, Zhang Tianqi uses his staff to write his master's thesis. Family and morality in the 1990s also take a shellacking. The narrative point of view of *National Portrait* is so close to Zhu Huaijing's that the reader sees every woman he would like to proposition through Zhu's lascivious eyes, including not just his wife and mistress, with both of whom he carries on passionate relations, but also the TV star Chen Yan, who is later revealed to be Mayor Pi's mistress. All hotels, not just the notorious one run by Pi Jie, offer guests the services of sauna, massage, and sex. Zhu avoids them, fearing entrapment. Ironically, his family and Liu's are chosen—by their fawning subordinates—as "model couples." Zhu and Liu have been discreet.

What brings down Pi is a silly rivalry between the Municipal People's Congress (Ren Da) and the Municipal Political Consultative Conference (Zheng Xie), which readers know to be only rubber-stamp assemblies for the municipal CCP committee anyway. Envious of the Ren Da's slightly superior food and delegate gifts when it sits, the Zheng Xie, self-righteous about the political correctness of its lesser luxury, one-ups its rival by asking for its food to be downgraded and declaring war on corruption, beginning with Pi Jie's brothel. Ironically, when Pi the elder loses his mayoralty, he is named the new chair of the Zheng Xie, evidently to save the leadership some face. It is equivalent to retirement, he confides to Zhu Huaijing. But is it really the bad guys who got their comeuppance? Or is it a kind of tragedy and not just a farce? This leads to questions of character.

The Novel and Realism

The plotting of *National Portrait* more closely fits historical and international notions of realism than modern China's "classic" realism. The novel has no great themes, no great moral hero, no grand sociological formations, and hardly any moral comment. To belittlers who prefer lessons, it is an antididactic novel. Everyone is a bit corrupt, but few characters are outstanding even in that. The narrative intelligence observes and sees through all human behavior and offers explanations for it. *National Portrait* can thus be called a comic novel. It serves up a parade of unenlightened behavior, some of it ridiculous. The novel is discursive, anecdotal, and relatively unformulaic, without crime fighting, suspense, melodrama, or indeed much drama at all. Some readers would probably consider it "plotless." Wang Yuewen's relentless attention to seemingly inconsequential detail, and his (that is, Zhu Huaijing's) compulsion to explain every conversation and gesture they encounter creates an air of authenticity, of the reader being taken into the bureaucrat's confidence, however tedious that may be. In fact, the novel might have benefited from some editorial tightening. It suffers from repetition[15] and a few too many erotic descriptions of lovemaking (of Zhu with his mistress *and* his wife). There are puzzles, rebuses, and jokes, suggesting that Wang Yuewen may have been aiming at a modern *Hong lou meng* (Dream of the red chamber), with Zhu beholding the innocence of his ruined soul mates like Jia Baoyu musing over the fates of the Twelve Beauties. That might explain surprising and lengthy digressions about the mysterious Bide-a-Wee Pavilion, a kind of Da Guan Yuan (Grand view garden) haven of peace that, local superstition maintains, holds the key to the future of all who pass through it. The overtones of a ghost story are out of character with the rest of the plot.

There is, certainly, overlap with the mainstream modern Chinese realistic novel. The prose is as plain and undecorated as any discussed in this book, merely punctuated by jingles, sayings, and anecdotes. This helped the novel acquire a mass readership, the goal of all Chinese realist authors. By dissecting official manners in detail and with seemingly no holds barred, *National Portrait* "tells the truth" in a way that official propaganda does not. The foibles of officialdom are a "dark side" of society. The reflective reader can derive from it lessons as Chinese readers always have from more didactic and event-driven fiction.

National Portrait's main claim to being a realistic novel is its attention to the development of character, particularly that of Zhu Huaijing. This is so despite the fact that the work eschews deep-structure probing of his thoughts, always preferring to relate his actions and his surface rationalizations for them, and despite the cardboard character of most other characters. Pi Deqiu becomes a little more human when he begins to confide in Zhu after his fall from power. Si Mao goes from yokel to bureaucrat and then to uppity ingrate when he finally loses his job, still without a touch of class or bureaucratic finesse, but we know this primarily from listening to Zhu Huaijing's lecturing of him. Zhu Huaijing in the end becomes a changed and sympathetic protagonist. Because Wang Yuewen lets Zhu's better nature emerge, China's conservative critics who accuse novelists of making corrupt and philandering officials into positive characters may have had Wang Yuewen in mind. The moral exemplar Zeng Li, for instance, does not approve of Zhu Huaijing's profession or his behavior, but he refuses to condemn the bureaucrats (257). He sticks up for his friend Huaijing as better than "the others" (460).

One is naturally inclined to identify with Zhu Huaijing, for one quite literally sees the world and all its characters as he does. But he quickly reveals himself capable of discreditable behavior. Having used the beating of Si Mao to rip off the Longxing Hotel for inflated damages while putting on airs as a great official, Zhu then does the unthinkable, with his wife's connivance: he lies to Si Mao, claiming that he was hard put to win him a settlement of RMB 5,000. The married couple keep the extra RMB 80,000 for themselves because they need the cash. No one is the wiser. The reader also observes Zhu Huaijing lusting after the TV reporter Chen Yan from page four, and before a hundred pages pass, he has a mistress, Mei Yuqin, with whom he spends most of his weeknights. Otherwise, Zhu's every waking thought is about his next promotion. He sinks so low as to copy the idea of a bureaucrat who devised a computer program for creating and maintaining guanxi. Guanxi target personalities are ranked, A1, A2, A3, B1, B2, etc., in order of importance to the person doing the ranking. A calendar program provides reminders of when it is time (or just a waste of time) to reinforce existing guanxi through follow-up lunches and new favors, with the frequency determined by the target's rank. When one is promoted, relations whose cultivation are no longer useful are dropped and they disappear from the calendar. Mayor Pi is an A1 for Zhu Huaijing. Zhu's new boss after he is promoted to division chief, Tan Yuan, is not the number two among municipal head personal secretaries, but he serves Vice Mayor Sima, to whom Zhu reports, so he is a B2 to Zhu. One need not go through ranks to confer favors, though, so the mayor's favored secretary, Liu, is a

Bi (264–65). Zhu Huaijing tells white lies and perpetrates small deceptions almost to the end of the novel.

But this is only one side of Zhu Huaijing. It quickly becomes apparent that he really loves Mei Yuqin *and* retains some feelings for his wife. He keeps getting his idealistic friends out of scrapes, out of sheer loyalty. Even when he persuades Zeng Li to suppress his articles exposing corruption, he does it sincerely, for Zeng's own good and the good of Wu county, including Zhu's friends there. In time, Zhu Huaijing comes to embrace two contradictory ideas of friendship. Utilitarian friends are cultivated as guanxi for the favors they can provide, which Zhu describes to Si Mao in his lectures late in the narrative (482–84). This idea culminates in Zhu's construction of an ideal guanxi web that he calls the Eight Immortals, ascending from the cop, Song, the charlatan Yuan and his bodyguard, up to the affable and generous but dangerous princeling Pi Jie, Mayor Pi's personal secretaries, and Meiqin (574–78). Zhu is more than just a fixer; he is an impresario of guanxi building (much of his time is spent planning banquets and getting the right people to attend), working for the mutual benefit of all parties. And yet Zhu becomes increasingly conscious that Mei, Li, and Zeng are his only true friends (164, 452–60, 604–6). He "wastes" time communing with and consoling Mei Yuqin, goes searching for the missing artist Li with the aim of restoring his place in the academy, and admires the dissenting Zeng Li (Zhu had once aspired to be a novelist himself). They are the ones he takes to the Bide-a-Wee Pavilion. They, and senior figures such as an artist who mounts paintings and Zhu's old professor in college, are foils to Zhu Huaijing's dark side. The professor is an ultimate truth-teller who cuts through all evasions with his reproofs, another late Qing novelistic personality. These characters see the good in Zhu. He is a fixer, not a flatterer, and he never hurts anyone out of malice. He is capable of lying and deception, but the reader also knows, from access to Zhu's every thought, how often he resists still more temptations every day.[16]

In corrupt times, this stands out as superior ethics. Wang Yuewen's readers, conscious of their times as an era dedicated to money making, may be impressed by Zhu Huaijing's relative lack of interest in piling up a fortune, though his bank account does climb into the hundreds of thousands of yuan by the end. He is a trustworthy steward of Li Mingxi's paintings insofar as Li will allow it. He is more interested in doing favors and acquiring power than wealth (that is his use for paintings; he gives them away, however precious). Even his strategic gifts and favors are increasingly rationalized as serving a higher purpose. The trickster Yuan, for instance, having become a wealthy philanthropist with bodyguards, branch companies, and a seat on the Zheng Xie, decides to stiff the writer Lu Fu on the fee promised him for a hagiographic biography of Yuan, just because Yuan can get away with it. Lu Fu threatens to write an exposé of him as a fake magician and hypocritical benefactor. Zhu Huaijing goes to great pains to get Yuan to relent, for the sole reason that any bad press for Yuan would be bad for Yuan's contact, Mayor Pi (563–68). Zhu would be responsible for any harm done to Pi, since he introduced Yuan to him, so Zhu is also self-interested, but once again he preserves a lie for "the common good." Guanxi building itself thus runs a gamut, from the relatively selfish to the relatively idealistic. In the end, Zhu is willing to give up his political ambitions and follow the fallen Pi Deqiu as personal secretary in Pi's meaningless retirement as head of the Zheng Xie, but Pi, advising him as a father, tells Zhu not to give up, to aim higher (667). As for Yuan, Zhu has for some time sensed that he has fallen into his trap; he regrets having let himself be used by Yuan to extend his guanxi for nefarious purposes (396). Zhu Huaijing in effect reflects on the evils of power. His flawed character is developing. When his friends are destroyed, Zhu Huaijing sincerely mourns.

Zhu Huaijing's belief is that everybody should help each other. His desire is to be liked. This is also his weakness. He adapts to the status quo; he cannot change it.[17] And his plan is flawed, even within the official status quo. The outcome proves that loyalty to one man and protection by way of the strongest of guanxi circles can be undone by factionalism and the corruption of others.

The novel's detail about bureaucratic manners, their rationale, and what goes on behind the scenes is another imprimatur of realism. The right haircut for a bureaucrat, the code words for naming amounts of money when discussing a deal, forms of address and flattery, bureaucratic boilerplate language, and drinking etiquette are all on display, though given the novel's slow pace, one who reads for information must sift through much narrative ore to get to the social metal.[18] Usually the manners are described as they are seen by Zhu Huaijing, who ought to know them already and not therefore consider them worth noting. He seems, thus, to be instructing the reader about bureaucracy, unless he is writing a diary or keeping himself alert. Much of the protocol preserves the hierarchy of rank. How does one approach a leader's car to enter it? Always from behind. One does not speak to leaders in the hall or beyond the door outside their home, and one always pretends to have visited them in their home before. One waits until the leader speaks before speaking and proffers a hand to shake only after the leader has extended his. (Zhu Huaijing gives the lower-ranking but potentially useful cop, Song, a warm smile but only a flaccid handshake, to keep him guessing; 166–67). At conferences, the leaders speak first, of course, but one tries to speak next, to "stake out an attitude" (*biao ge tai*) but not a position. One does not want to appear as an activist. One saves the best performance for the last day, when the TV cameras will be rolling. When giving a painting as a gift, size matters; it must match the donee's rank. The novel is full of information about the protocol of arranging banquets, including whom to ask, whom not to ask, and whom to get to do the asking. Other data are simply information for the curious. Only cadres at the departmental (*ting*) level and above are issued cell phones, and only they get twenty-four-hour heat in their homes; other cadres have it from 6 to 10 PM only. The novel provides particularly interesting vignettes of candidates putting aside their dignity to trawl for votes in Ren Da elections (e.g., for mayor). Delegates promise their votes to opposing sides. The voters will decide as the "Organization" tells them to, anyway. The book jacket states that Wang Yuewen served in the government before becoming an author; the reader naturally assumes that he is revealing what he knows.

Contributions to the Discourse of Corruption

National Portrait's relative lack of criminal cases may be taken, in its very silence, as a critique of corruption by indirection: corruption is pervasive abuse of power rather than something as codifiable as a crime. The novel's discourse is not the official one, of a few terribly bad apples spoiling the barrel. Everyone is corrupt, though few are so fully corrupt as to make it easy to assign guilt. Zeng Li thinks of the bureaucracy in terms of us versus them, or commoner versus official. This is not profound, but it may suggest that officials are a privileged social class, as under the old monarchy. One of Zeng's articles speaks on behalf of a "people-centered" (*minbenwei*) policy, which evokes the times' criticism of "official-centered" (*guanbenwei*) culture (601). Zeng also floats the idea of literati (*wenren*) as idealistic counterweights to officials, but this is unconvincing, since the two groups have been interrelated throughout history (544). Zhu Huaijing was born a peasant, and leaders today aspire for their children to become rich entrepreneurs or go abroad, transcending the bureaucratic class. Wang Yuewen points out that official salaries are too low, driving them to figure out ways to supplement their income (296). However, the professor partly refutes this by pointing out how many services officials get free. He estimates that provincial and municipal officials get the equivalent of a million yuan a year, and county heads at least one or two hundred thousand (320).

The novel is surely a sourcebook for the art of guanxi. A popular joke in China was that Wang's novel was required reading for all would-be bureaucrats; those who did not wish him well charged that he taught officials how to break the law.[19] But critique of the overuse and perniciousness of guanxi in the building of an iron circle of power is hardly original in anticorruption fiction, as the previous chapters make clear. Wang Yuewen, however, depicts an alternative to the web of guanxi: true, disinterested friendship. This may be why some critics see in the novel echoes of the chivalry better known in China's martial arts novels. Friendship, though one of the orthodox "five relationships" (the lowest-ranked of the five), like the orthodox value of chivalry (*yi* or righteousness) in the martial arts novels, becomes unorthodox and countercultural when it takes precedence over more structured and hierarchical social obligations. In *National Portrait*, Zhu's true friendships are moreover draped in enigmas of Daoism and mysticism. However, if friendship is the true remedy for the falsity and instability of factionalized bureaucracy (and society, of which bureaucracy is a microcosm), then one cannot fail to note that in *National Portrait*, the cadre Zhu is still the main mover, trying to build friendships *from the top*. Perhaps the flaw in that strategy is one of the lessons he learns.

Another, less sentimental foil to bureaucratic ambition is the figure of Deng Caigang, Zhu's vice chief, when Zhu is promoted to full chief of the Finance and Trade Department. Deng is a model public servant and the ghostwriter of an unusually perspicacious contribution "by Mayor Pi" for the cadres' vanity book. The trouble is that his eyes are not on the prize—his next promotion. Not only does Deng hold the rank at which Zhu was previously stuck, his attitude, Zhu reflects, is the same as his used to be before he saw what the bureaucratic life was all about. (In this reflection lies the seed of Zhu's future character development. Aware that he has changed, he can choose to change back.) Deng has been passed over for promotion for being frank; asked for suggestions, he pointed out that the leaders did little work and he offered serious ideas for combating corruption. Passed over again, Deng retires from government service to become a lawyer in the more open society down south (614–17). Zhu characteristically warns him against hasty decisions. He is looking out for Deng, though only within the limited confines of his social vision. As in more heavily theorized studies of systemic corruption, one can deduce that in an atmosphere of universal "collective" corruption, every individual must become corrupt or be forced out by the system. Deng, for his part, hates the system, yet like most people who know Zhu, he thinks Zhu is a cut above his colleagues.

Disinterested friendship may be considered idealistic in a time of social ambition, but in a time of rapid social change it is also an emblem of that rare and sought-after quality, *constancy*. The desire for something to rely on in personal and institutionalized relations is at the bottom of the discourse of corruption, I would argue, but it is not the same as the cynical state discourse of "social stability," the modernized version of the ancient state admonition for citizens to be *anfen leye* (content with their lot and happy at their stations). When Zhu, in one of his weaker moments, urges Zeng Li to consider the negative "social effect" of telling the truth about victimized peasants, because it might harm "social stability" (he says that spilling the beans would not remedy the problem or the system, but would only create instability that would hurt everyone), it is clearly ironic. Zeng Li holds the moral upper hand as the man of true conscience, whereas the argument about "social effect" is a tired old state discourse used to discipline and silence the people, including China's writers. The implication is that only the leaders can solve problems. The real problem, Zeng notes, is that the leaders fear the masses (260–61). Zhu himself, through his friendships, seeks a higher kind of constancy and emotional stability.

National Portrait ultimately may be taken as a tableau of corruption in the most abstract and pervasive sense: the corruption of morality and culture itself. In a startling metaphor, Mei Yuqin applies the idea of rot to romantic love: "This word love has been used a million times, a trillion times, until it's gone rotten (*fa sou le*). Now it has a putrid (*suan fu*) taste" (126). And yet Wang Yuewen also complicates, and even partly neutralizes, the discourse of corruption by diverting it into the colloquial discourse of "realism," or being "realistic" (439). Zhu Huaijing tells Zeng Li that his stubborn determination to tell the truth at any cost is divorced from "reality" (254). He compares Zeng to Lu Xun, and this is not a compliment from his viewpoint (and perhaps Wang Yuewen's), considering Lu Xun's excessive canonization (205–6). Zhu likewise tries to convince Li Mingxi to compromise with "reality" just enough to seek an exhibition, so that his painting can be sold (100–103). "Reality" and "realism" compromise not just idealism, but also the law in a discussion in which Zhu tries to cure Zeng of his ridiculous impression that some newspaper might print his photos of a social protest, since there is no law against printing them (157).

One of the reasons for compromising with reality, Zhu says, is that society is gradually getting better (254). This displays an optimism contrary to the discourse of corruption. To speak of corruption, then, is to point to behavior that is worse than simple moral compromise. Fin-de-siècle decadence is to be found everywere, even outside officialdom, as in the village where parents are happy that Head Secretary Liu will adopt their daughter, his maid, as *his* daughter—and sexpot (367–69)—shades, again, of the late Qing. Says one municipal citizen, "We ordinary folk have more faith in our country than you leaders" (372). But this "ordinary person" (meaning nonofficial) is none other than Pi Jie.

Limits of and on Realism

The style of *National Portrait* is quite uniform, showing great discipline on the author's part. Everything is related in present time without flashbacks. The tale is in principle told by the third-person omniscient narrator favored by Chinese novelists, but the narrator's omniscience is limited to his ability to penetrate the thought of Zhu Huaijing and to overhear the conversations he does. The latter are often presented in paraphrase, again as if filtered through Zhu's consciousness, sometimes in a run-on, seemingly impatient mood. Nearly all the psychology and motivation of the other characters is known through exterior signs as noted by the meticulous Zhu, or as he interprets them through his own highly informed understanding. Hardly any trivial action goes unexplained.

> Xiangmei [Zhu's wife] was still up, watching TV by herself. Evidencing no particular warmth upon his return, she just looked up at the wall clock. Zhu Huaijing understood that she was angry at him for coming home late, so he nonchalantly brought up the tragedy of Mayor Xiang and his colleagues, as an intimation that he had been busy with these matters. Xiangmei then asked him if he'd eaten. He said going so late without eating, he'd been famished for some time. At this, Xiangmei got up and poured him some water to wash his face and feet. (212–13)

This is Wang Yuewen's style in a nutshell. The conscientious documentation of small details slows down the plot and creates a sense of boredom (perhaps deliberately, reflecting Zhu's own mood), until in the end the hero changes and becomes more passionate and sympathetic. Wang's prose is far sparer and less decorated than that of Henry James, but he has, in his narrative, accepted the dicta of Jamesian realism as celebrated in the criticism of his follower Percy Lubbock[20] and gone the American critics one better, since Wang does not delve into the depths of Zhu Huaijing's consciousness. This imposes strict limits on what may be written. The run-on nature of Wang Yuewen's prose makes the narrow point of view all the more evident. It is a minimalist realism, given the further restrictions of short and simple sentences, but hardly any surface indication of motivation is too trivial to escape Zhu's notice or his habit of social comment. When politeness goes overboard into flattery, the narrative tells us so. Still, Zhu's interests have a focus. He examines his colleagues' words and gestures for their implications regarding, and possible effect on, power relations. This keeps the narrative interesting for the reader hoping for a political novel.

> Just as [Zhu] hung up, [his boss] Liu Zhongxia came in. He asked, nonchalantly, "What did Mayor Pi want to talk to you about?"
> Zhu Huaijing had to be guarded: "It was about a personal matter of his."
> Liu Zhongxia could not very well inquire further. He voiced a couple of "uh-huhs." He looked at his watch. It was about time, so he went out the door with Zhu Huaijing. They went down the stairs to eat together. It occurred to Zhu Huaijing that he had unconsciously put Liu off, perfunctorily, but that this was a good thing after all. By saying that it was a private matter of Mayor Pi's, he had both avoided hemming and hawing in embarrassment, and also demonstrated that he was quite close to Mayor Pi. (139)

> "Uh . . . approved." Mayor Pi nodded, so that everyone would know that he was in favor of Zhu Huaijing's report, and also that he had moved on to another topic. When two short words from a leader were so pregnant with meaning, small wonder that when a report came down, it was like water cascading from commanding heights, penetrating into the deepest recesses. Zhu Huaijing had worked at leaders' sides for a long time and his forte was reading the leaders' intentions. Hearing Mayor Pi say, "Uh . . . approved," he stood up without another word, respectfully and cautiously, to listen for instructions. (614)

The limitations of Jamesian realism do not allow the synoptic view or the unlimited omniscient social commentary of more formulaic anticorruption fiction (and classic Chinese realism). Zhu Huaijing and even the words of Zeng Li as heard by Zhu—indeed, large portions of articles by Zeng Li that Zhu reads into the text—are not up to such a synoptic task. A structural explanation of corruption is not the assignment that Wang Yuewen has chosen. Those who read realistic novels for "higher understanding" are bound to be frustrated. Politics itself is denatured in the portrait. *National Portrait* is all about politics with a small *p*: the nonideological jockeying for petty power advantages of people in their everyday lives. Part of the shock value of Wang Yuewen's portrait of the bureaucrats results from the fact that they are so selfish and solipsistic, seemingly unconcerned about matters of state or even local policy, the stuff of Politics with a capital *P*. But surely, one reasons, "the system" is the result not just of quotidian actions and "habitus," but also policy, even if it all comes down from the top. Moreover, if one wants to accumulate power for its own sake, this takes precedence over the motive of accumulating power to bully others. How realistic is that?

Jamesian and minimalist limitations on presenting a view of "reality" are not the only forces at work, for they are combined with political limitations. The most startlingly "unrealistic" aspect of *National Portrait* is its virtual erasure of the presence, not to mention the bureaucratic oversight, of the Chinese Communist Party. We know that the party makes all the real decisions because the other anticorruption novels are so frank about that. The party even seems to want its hegemonic role represented (and celebrated), so as to reap the glory of its *anti*corruption triumphs. Presumably the municipal party offices are in a different building in a city as large as the one in *National Portrait* (unnecessary proximity of party and state offices is now, as ever, a security risk, though they may be across the street from each other, or perhaps within the same walled compound). We do not know even that in *National Portrait*. One hardly sees a party document cross a bureaucrat's desk, one hears nothing of party instructions, and the party's role in bureaucratic promotion is almost entirely erased, except for a half-dozen perfunctory references to its Organization Department. On a few, though pivotal, occasions, the party is evidently referred to by the euphemism "the Organization." At the big Ren Da meeting, it is the Organization that decides who will be elected mayor (308–9). This is one of those aspects of circumspection to which Wang Yuewen may have alerted the reader early on, in his observation that *guo hua* (meaning here the national tradition of painting) "is very particular about the spaces left blank" (16). As every Chinese reader knows, the white spaces do not represent a vacuum. They are places unpainted, to be filled in by the observer's imagination. Wang Yuewen ultimately apologizes to the reader for his own evasions through his characters. As Zhang Tianqi explains the travails of dealing with corrupt bureaucrats in the nation's capital, he comes to a sudden halt. "Zhu Huaijing waited for Zhang Tianqi to continue. But he did not. He only sighed that it was time to change the subject, shaking his head all the while. Zhu Huaijing knew that to pursue the question might cross the line (*fan ji*, violate a taboo). He had better not inquire more deeply" (491).

Ironically, for all his caution, Wang Yuewen may have broken one of the same taboos as Chen Fang did when he set the scene for the novel's action. Jingdu governs not just its own urban districts and several counties, but also some prefectures. One might therefore conclude that Jingdu is a city under the direct control of the central government (not under the control of a province)—in other words, that Jingdu's municipal administration is equivalent to a provincial administration. This may seem a trivial point, but other anticorruption authors have observed the taboo against depicting pervasive corruption as high as the provincial level. One of Wang Yuewen's critics savaged him precisely for having depicted corruption in a centrally controlled municipality.[21] Wang had brought corruption too close to the center of power in Beijing.

Aftermath

Wang Yuewen has more or less willingly given up his bureaucratic career in order to write full time. The banning of *National Portrait* did not ruin him, though his works about officials have not been made into television dramas, and censorship of his fiction is still a problem (so is pirating that takes off where banning of open publication begins).[22] His solution in 2004 was to write a novel about officialdom and commerce "a hundred years ago."[23] Wang does continue to write critically of contemporary society in essays. In 2001, at the crest of the anticorruption wave, he published a sequel to *National Portrait* called *Meici gushi* (Stories from Meici), named after the fictitious prefecture where Zhu Huaijing resumes his bureaucratic career at a lower level. However, this novel has not won the critical acclaim of *National Portrait*. At least one commentator, novelist You Fengwei, has attributed Wang's diminished later achievement to his having become more cautious after the first novel was banned.[24]

6

Dirt Plus Soap Equals Pay Dirt: Liu Ping's *Dossier on Smuggling*

In Beijing on April 20, 1999, the CCP Central Disciplinary Inspection Commission organized a task force to investigate reports of smuggling in Xiamen (Amoy), Fujian. The first investigative team made little headway in the port city. Corruption was so pervasive that the local police tapped the investigators' phones and tipped off the suspects. The second time, in August, hundreds of Beijing personnel flooded into Fujian. They concluded that over US$6 billion in refined petroleum, vegetable oil, automobiles, cigarettes, rubber, telecommunications equipment, textiles, and other commodities had been smuggled in since 1994. Some observers calculated that a sixth of all the petroleum on the Chinese market had been coming in through the ring (the Chinese navy sometimes provided escorts). The price of oil dropped enough to shut down the Daqing oilfield.[1] This was smuggling of macroeconomic proportions—in one city!

Secret trials of the accused began on September 13, 2000. Fourteen death sentences (three with a two-year reprieve) and seventy prison terms, twelve of them for life, were announced on November 8.[2] That was just the first batch of trials. By July 2001, more than six hundred were tried, the majority of them officials.[3] The final list of those convicted included the vice provincial public security chief, Zhuang Rushun; the head of Xiamen customs, Yang Qianxian (customs is under central control, and supposedly immune to lateral corrupt influences from local government); the Xiamen chief of police; secretaries of the Fujian and Xiamen CCP committees; Xiamen vice mayors; and the heads of the major Xiamen banks (that is, the Xiamen branches of central banks). In Beijing, former vice minister of public security, Li Jizhou, who had been vice head of the National Antismuggling Leading Group under the State Council, was sentenced to death with a reprieve in October 2001. Chen Fang had already put a caricature of him into *Municipal Crisis* in 2000. General Ji Shengde, former head of military intelligence in the PLA's General Staff Department, was sentenced to fifteen years in 2000; it was rumored that some of his problems had to do with Yuanhua. Most seriously for Jiang Zemin, Jia Qinglin, a protégé whom Jiang had brought up from Fujian in 1995 to be party boss of Beijing, and particularly his wife Lin Youfang, former head of the largest state-owned import-export firm in Xiamen, were caught up in the scandal. Jiang saved Jia's reputation and his own only by ordering that investigations stop at the vice ministerial level.[4]

Allegedly at the center of all this evil was Fujian native Lai Changxing. He had moved to Hong Kong in 1991, incorporated the Yuanhua ("Fairwell") Group there as a holding company for real estate and trading, then returned to Fujian in the guise of a foreign investor. The Chinese government did not charge Yuanhua with bringing goods across the border. State-owned trading and commodities firms handled that. Yuanhua was the overlord, fixing things with customs, the police, and other investigators so that the smugglers could mislabel their goods or fraudulently declare them as tax-free items intended for re-export. Yuanhua then took its cut and arranged for domestic distribution of the underpriced goods. Many of Lai Changxing's relatives were employed by Yuanhua and later caught, but Zhuang Rushen tipped off Lai himself. He and his wife fled to Canada in August 1999, where they were detained but applied for asylum, making front-page news across the globe. They were turned down but remain in Canada, appealing the decision.

Xiamen, once as remarkably prosperous as Cali and Medellín, went into a recession after its smuggling empire was closed down. Yuanhua had built or was building many of the town's landmarks, including the notorious and exclusive Red Mansion, a pleasure hotel with secret entrances where favored cadres feasted and fornicated with call girls free of charge and allegedly were secretly videotaped for blackmail purposes.[5] The company owned a movie studio outside Xiamen with sets that duplicated the Forbidden City in Beijing and brought to town a Guangdong soccer outfit that Lai renamed the Xiamen Yuanhua Soccer Team. The team appeared headed for the big time. As if to confirm this book's view that news of corruption can itself be a form of popular culture, travel agencies organized "anticorruption tours" to Xiamen in the summer of 2001, after the Chinese government opened up the Red Mansion as a museum of the evils of corruption.[6]

Zousi dang'an (Dossier on smuggling) by Liu Ping (b. 1954) acquired a buzz as a roman à clef about the Yuanhua case much as *Heaven's Wrath* was about the Chen Xitong case. Liu Ping was head of customs in Huzhou, Zhejiang, so he was presumed to have access to privileged information. He bore the designation "anticorruption writer" proudly.[7] However, the book appeared in April 2001, after many of the trials were over, so Liu was not so clearly one year ahead of the news, as Chen Fang had been. To be sure, official media left much about Yuanhua unexplained. A promotional review of Liu Ping's novel frankly stated that it was based on what Liu had heard, his knowledge of how the business worked on both sides of the law, and what more he could imagine. It also indicated that Liu had written the book in haste. Small wonder, for he had to keep ahead of official disclosures. When a new batch of trials was announced in July 2001, the book profited, going into its fourth printing.[8] The Yuanhua scandal also inspired sensational and supposedly nonfiction tales of personalities involved in the case. These accounts appeared on the Internet and on bookstands; some of their materials came from official sources.[9] Meanwhile, Chinese Canadian reporter Sheng Xue interviewed Lai Changxing abroad. Her questions were tough and her account is neutral, but she gets Lai's side of the story on the record. He claims he was a patriot and secret agent for the Chinese government, scapegoated by a pervasively corrupt system rent with power struggles.[10]

By 2001 bookstores and kiosks were flooded with anticorruption novels, and the public wondered if some of the books about smuggling by other authors besides Liu Ping were about Yuanhua, too.[11] *Dossier on Smuggling* attracted little or no serious criticism, but then neither did most of its competition. Promotional book reviews and notices wrote of *Dossier on Smuggling*'s "realism," but it is a popular novel with as much soap opera content about the romances of both the criminals and the investigators as information about smuggling and corruption. It is all wrapped up in racy detective themes and plots, complete with a murder,[12] though that is saved for the end. *Dossier on Smuggling* represents the trend toward popularization and commercialization in the later stages of the anticorruption novel. The last 300 of its 528 pages (327,000 characters) might be compared to the old "Mandarin Duck and Butterfly" fiction. Still, the novel is a page-turner, its interest heightened by the thrill of thinking one is learning secrets about the Yuanhua scandal. The limitations of this work come less from the constraints of realism than from the evolution of Chinese anticorruption fiction into a form of ordinary Chinese popular novel. Plots with cops and robbers and smuggling in works with anticorruption themes became common at the start of the twenty-first century, in both fiction and works for television. Although the corruption in the novel's fictitious city of Haimen is as vast as Xiamen's was in life, the formulaic nature of the plot and crimes takes the edge off the social criticism.

The Storyline

Locally born Ding Wufa[13] [≅Lai Changxing] comes to Haimen city [≅Xiamen] so that his Hong Kong–based Wanli Group [≅Yuanhua] can offer the port city some "foreign investment." Haimen officials fete Ding in anticipation of his cash inflow and the day when customs will expedite imports so that Haimen can prosper. He forges friendships with Haimen's soon-to-be mayor, Chen Jiayang, and soon-to-be head of customs, Yan Hongxing.[14] Ding makes heavy investments in storage facilities, and in time bribes nearly everyone of any stature in customs and local government with money and call girls, all so that other companies—well-connected national and local state-owned firms—can smuggle goods into Ding's warehouses at will. The women come from his Wanli Club [≅Red Mansion]. Ding Wufa supplies Yan Hongxing with intelligence so that Yan can wipe out Ding's competition and meanwhile become an antismuggling hero. In a few years, Ding has monopoly power over local smuggling. He and Haimen are rich beyond their dreams. He has even given the locals a movie studio and soccer team. In Ding Wufa, the tradition of charismatic corrupt leaders in Chinese fiction reaches its pinnacle.

Those who hunt Ding, partly in search of revenge for his having bested them in a prior Hong Kong case (the subject of a prequel novel to *Dossier on Smuggling*),[15] are Yuan Ke, head of the provincial Anticorruption Bureau in the provincial capital [≅Fuzhou], and his former subordinate Hu Xinhong, now a rich and famous lawyer in the same city, heading a giant law firm of her own. Yuan helped the young woman get her start in the private sector. Presently Jin Jing, a hostess at the Wanli Club down in Haimen, comes up to the provincial capital to hire Lawyer Hu to get justice for the former head of the Haimen customs investigation division Chu Feng, who was unjustly discharged. Chu was Jin's childhood sweetheart.

Meanwhile, Ding Wufa decides he needs an heir. After getting a woman pregnant with a son (to be born and raised in the United States),[16] he stages himself an extravagant wedding with thousands of guests at the Wanli Club, with local hotels handling the overflow. The object is to entertain local, provincial, and Beijing officials. Ex-dancer Yu Shanshan, Ding's prior mistress and head of his movie studio, finds among her professional contacts gorgeous women willing to keep the rich and powerful cadres company at every table. For the most important guests, the wedding favors include cash gifts of US$5,000.

Anticorruption chief Yuan Ke and his wife Xiao Yilei are increasingly estranged. She remained in the Haimen area to nurture her own rising career as a Youth League and then CCP cadre all the years he was up in the provincial capital [≅ Fuzhou]. Now she has accepted the Haimen consensus that Ding Wufa is a great and generous visionary. Ding sets Yu Shanshan onto Xiao to befriend and spy on her, while fanning Xiao's jealousy of Yuan's closeness to the dazzling lawyer, Ms. Hu. Mayor Chen cooperates by making Xiao Yilei his head personal secretary.[17] Ding Wufa buys the company owned by Xiao's brother, saving him from possible bankruptcy. In truth, Lawyer Hu has long felt a secret attraction to Yuan, who is a strong, take-charge cadre. Their mutual friend at the pub where they often meet, who is herself having an affair, sees Hu and Yuan as a perfect match and works to raise the temperature in their relationship.

Reporting to Yuan Ke, Hu Xinhong goes to Haimen "on vacation," but really on a secret mission to get the goods on Haimen smuggling and the Wanli Group. Her discretion, fame, and worrying closeness to Yuan upset the wily Ding Wufa, but Mayor Chen asks her to join the cash-flush Haimen administration as celebrity legal adviser, so Ding hires her, too. They wonder if she can be turned. For cover, Ms. Hu pretends to be vacationing with a rich Taiwanese playboy who pursues her despite her repeated snubs. She contacts Chu Feng on the sly and finds that he truly is one of the few (ex-)customs officers not on Ding's payroll. He slipped and knowingly let through some smuggled polyester fibers to benefit a failing plant that had laid off Jin Jing's parents. He took no bribes and was simply trying to promote "social order" by benefiting the plant, so he got off with an administrative punishment. Chu Feng was puzzled by customs head Yan Hongxing's insouciant attitude toward the vast amounts of merchandise that was unaccounted for flowing out of Haimen. It could not all have been produced locally.

The second half of the novel is taken up by subplots full of romance and danger. On behalf of Lawyer Hu and Yuan Ke, Chu Feng and Jin Jing work schemes to turn around a smuggler, Ding Wufa's old friend

Cai Youqiang, who has been caught by Haimen customs often enough to sense that he is Ding Wufa's fall guy. The object is to get Cai to turn over a computer disk with smuggling data and names of Beijing officials on Ding's payroll. Chu Feng also mines customs' mainframe for data, using a home hookup. Interspersed with these initiatives are variously torrid, unrequited, and abortive love affairs and conquests. The lecherous Mayor Chen likes Xiao Yilei, but Ding warns him to leave her alone. Yu Shanshan sees in the Taiwanese playboy the rich man of her dreams and tries to blackmail him into marriage; besides, Lawyer Hu is always humiliating him.[18] Back in the provincial capital, Yuan Ke and Hu Xinhong finally consummate their long-suppressed love. But the happily married Chu Feng fends off Jin Jing's unrequited adoration when she offers him her body. Even the disciplined and cautious customs head, Yan Hongxing, finally finds true love with a call girl that Ding has offered him. As Ding Wufa's true friend, Yan warns him that he must accelerate his plans to become legitimate. His smuggling, which Yan intuits but does not officially acknowledge, cannot continue in the changing climate.

Chu and a rare Haimen cop not on the take kidnap an associate of Cai, the disgruntled smuggler, and learn enough about Cai's next delivery to have it seized by a few honest officials, so that Cai's faith in Ding Wufa's protection will be shaken once and for all. Ding is on to it and offers Cai RMB 10 million to cover his loss for the "mistake" when Cai's shipment is seized by insubordinate customs officials, but even so Cai hands over his incriminating disk to the good guys. Ding Wufa has Cai killed in a car accident and Ding's henchman, the Haimen police chief, arrests Chu Feng as a suspect in the murder of Cai after a standoff between good and bad Haimen cops.[19] But the incriminating computer data from both Chu and Cai has already reached the provincial capital and been forwarded to Beijing; Ding curses the ancestors of the people who invented the new technology called e-mail (491). Beijing then sends a work team, but it stays only two days. Ding's supporter, former provincial CCP deputy secretary Qin Jianzhong, conducts an investigation and it is a whitewash. He is angry at Yuan Ke for being oblivious to the needs of economic development and not taking instructions from the Organization.

All seems lost for Yuan Ke and Chu Feng after all. Men come to get them. But as Ding, Chen, and the Haimen police chief conspire to have Yuan, Chen, Hu, and Jin "disappear" the next time they go traveling, Yuan and Chu burst in on them. Beijing officials have sent a second team to achieve justice. They pick up Yuan and Chu not to arrest them but to let them in on the arrests of the bad guys. Yuan's and Hu's old boss Zheng, who has been wasting away since his utter defeat by Ding Wufa in *Dossier on Smuggling*'s prequel, expires with a smile on his face. Conversely, Xiao Yilei, finally aware of her dreadful misreading of Ding Wufa's motives, suffers an emotionally induced paralysis. Yuan Ke announces that he will care for his ailing wife, as is his duty.

Corruption Cases

The crimes in *Dossier on Smuggling* are the old-fashioned ones of smuggling, bribery, and debauchery, but human interest is what makes the novel. The work is short on details, even about the smuggling. They are presented in small rushes on a few selected pages.[20] Mostly it is Chu Feng who tosses off a few numbers: 800,000 tons of oil worth more than two billion yuan, more than three billion cigarettes (297), and two million tons of edible oils have come in illegally (338). The novel outlines the general division of labor as it was in life, with state-owned firms doing the smuggling and Wanli suborning the officials through bribes of money and women. The offending state firms are not given individual identities, even fictitious ones, though Chu Feng indicates that some have military connections (301). The firms are headed by the children of high cadres, which can provide protection from prosecution in a pinch. Taiwanese industrial magnates' imports of computer parts have also been going through Ding, whom the Taiwanese consider Xiamen's "unofficial customs head." They pay him 60 percent of the legal duties (266–67). Customs records are doctored and frequently erased from the computer.

Ding Wufa maintains liaisons with criminal gangs through his man Zhou (138), but there are no interesting details, and the novel has little to say about banking frauds, either, though Yuanhua in life had many outstanding loans from the state banks, leading to the criminal prosecution of bankers in on the conspiracy. Offshore money laundering is discussed, however, and the novel makes much of Wanli's business in real estate. Once the money is laundered, real estate can absorb the enormous repatriated sums in a legitimate business. The rest, about one-third of the smuggling money, goes into bank accounts abroad. Ding is so awash in cash that he can afford to spend some of it building low-priced or free housing for cadres and also low-cost housing for workers, constructed with no profit for Wanli. It boosts Ding's image as a philanthropist and friend of the Haimen common man, the same path trod by John Gotti, Colombian drug lords, and assorted Latin American criminals-cum-populists. The city housing is quite a boon for the city government, but then Mayor Chen is providing Wanli with the land at half price (131). Because Ding sells all his housing at a discount, a delegation of Haimen real estate heads barges into his office to complain that his unfair competition is driving them out of business. He floors them by offering then and there to buy them all out on generous terms (134–37). This makes his real estate monopoly in Haimen complete, so he expands the business to other cities—except for the provincial capital, the home of his enemies.

As in life, the ringleader Ding Wufa is a "nice guy," giving rewards to everyone and resorting to threats and force only as a last resort (187). All customs officials are welcome at the Wanli Club, and Ding has engineered some of their promotions. Chu Feng notes that an extraordinary number of them drive to work in cars. Bribes go out to local officials and all customs personnel down to departmental heads (*chuzhang*) in red envelopes at the New Year, though Ding sometimes comes right up to higher officials and offers them gifts of cash. He wines and dines them, bringing women for them along for lunch. He also transfers money to Hong Kong and overseas accounts he establishes for them, or pays for their children's education abroad, as Lai Changxing did in life. After the incriminating materials reach Beijing, he sends his banker to Beijing with US$5 million in bribes for each of the five leaders so they will squelch their investigations. He wires Mayor Chen US$300,000, adding to the US$1.2 million Chen already has abroad (443).

What about the characters? Chen Jiayang's friendship with Ding Wufa and Yan Hongxing is so close that they swear a kind of peach orchard oath of mutual loyalty as in *The Romance of the Three Kingdoms*, as Ding Wufa himself puts it (113). Do Yan and Chen then represent real people? Perhaps they are composite characters. Identifications made only on the basis of equivalent job titles do not seem quite right. The actual mayor of Xiamen was not accused in the scandals. Clues come from official sources such as CCTV and the New China News Service, which soon after the summer and autumn trials of 2001 leaked moralistic accounts of the Yuanhua case containing alleged details about the personalities and individual foibles of the accused parties,[21] giving the Yuanhua case legendary stature. Liu Ping (who published in April 2001) may have shared some views about the culprits purveyed in official media, for one sees reflections of them in his novel's caricatures of Yan and Chen. Whether the government's nonfiction accounts are true to life is naturally open to question.

In life, Yang Qianxian was promoted to head of Xiamen customs in

1995, after Lai Changxing came to town. Yang was young for the position, China's youngest head of a customs operation at the full division (*ting*) level. The fictional Yan Hongxing is likewise young for his position. In the end he takes a mistress that Ding Wufa dangles before him named Ye Bingbing, whose name may suggest Yang's mistress in life, Zhou Bing. Ding Wufa lets the lovers use his yacht as a hideaway for their trysts (in life, Lai allegedly built Yan and Zhou a mansion). But the notable characteristic of Yan Hongxing in *Dossier on Smuggling* is that he keeps a distance from and maintains an attitude of reserve before Ding Wufa, protecting his personal dignity and self-respect. Ding for his part is too smart to offer money and women directly to such a wise man.

Distance from the smuggling ringleader and resistance to bribes fits the description (on the grapevine—whose origins are official media) of Jie Peiyong, the vice chief of Xiamen customs, which is Yan Hongxing's position early in the novel, when he first strikes his deal with Ding Wufa.[22] The novel's head of customs thus appears to combine the heroic aspects of Yang Qianxian and Jie Peiyong. Or, one might say that this outlaw "Liangshan hero" (as Ding Wufa likes to think of him) is a heroic vision of Jie Peiyong that morphs into Yang Qianxian. Jie was concurrently head of the investigative bureau of Xiamen customs, which is the novel's whistle blower Chu Feng's position until he is fired, so perhaps some of Jie's alleged stoicism fed into Liu Ping's portrait of this hero, too.

Mayor Chen Jiayang is the other member of the troika. In life, several vice mayors were accused of taking bribes from Lai Changxing, most notoriously Lan Fu, who was in charge of foreign trade and security (Chen Jiayang is said to have come up through the ranks as a former policeman), and whose son Lai settled and supported in Australia (in the novel, Chen's son is in the United States). But the novel's depiction of Chen as an incurable lecher best fits the popular image promoted by the media of Vice Mayor Zhao Keming. And yet, just as the novel's image of Customs Head Yan is heavily indebted to images of a person one bureaucratic rung below, with whom Ding bonded in his early Haimen years, so the character of Chen Jiayang seems indebted to an image of Liu Feng, the deputy secretary of the Xiamen provincial CCP committee in charge of politics and law, who early on helped Lai Changxing obtain his oil storage facilities. (In the novel, Chen while still vice mayor provides Ding Wufa with his entrée to Haimen official society and acquaintance with vice customs head Yan Hongxing in particular.) Liu in the media was portrayed as greedy, lecherous, and ready to help Lai with all his projects at the drop of a hat. This fits the description of Chen Jiayang, the sworn ally of Ding Wufa who becomes, even in his own eyes, Ding's puppet. Mayor Chen thus looks like a composite of at least three convicted Xiamen vice municipal-level officials in life.

A high point of the novel is Ding Wufa's spectacular wedding, which costs him RMB 30 million, half of it distributed as "wedding favors." In life, Lai Changxing and his legal wife (and business confederate) Zeng Mingna married young in 1982, well before they moved to Hong Kong. The novel's wedding scenes thus appear to re-create not Lai's wedding, but the extravagant 1996 groundbreaking ceremonies for his eighty-eight-story skyscraper, the Yuanhua International Building (or Hotel). Lai reportedly invited two thousand guests from Beijing and Fujian and showered them each with gifts worth RMB 3,000, including 1,000 in cash.[23]

Haimen's *éminence grise* in the official power structure is Qin Jianzhong, deputy secretary of the provincial CCP committee, who lives in the provincial capital but is a Haimen native. He retains power over provincial political-legal affairs after his transfer to head the Provincial People's Political Consultative Conference at the end of the novel, and he has always furthered Haimen interests in the province, as in his promotion of the careers of Yuan Ke and Xiao Yilei. At the beginning of the novel he is also a promoter of Ding Wufa, which is an early warning about his corruptibility, although the extent to which he is fully aware of the corruption is ambiguous until the end of the novel. But Ding Wufa sends money to Secretary Qin's son in America, and for security he puts Qin's relatives on Wanli's payroll. There is a parallel in life to Qin's character, but with a twist in the job titles: Shi Zhaobin, who in March 2002 was convicted of taking bribes from the manager of the Xiamen Petroleum Company while Shi was party secretary of Xiamen, 1994–99.[24] In 1999, he went to Fuzhou and assumed the post Qin holds in the novel, deputy provincial secretary. When Shi was expelled from the party in September 2001, he was "held responsible for rampant smuggling activities in Xiamen, especially the case of Lai Changxing. . . . He also hampered judicial departments when they were investigating three smuggling cases."[25] By pointing a finger at Shi Zhaobin (so it seems) in the figure of Secretary Qin, Liu Ping's novel, first published in April 2001, may have in fact scooped the news.

The Novel and Realism

Dossier on Smuggling is full of social criticism and "exposure"; in the background are big social themes with structural implications for Chinese modernity, but the work's texture is heavy on quotidian life and hard to credit as "realistic," except in the very broad sense that its setting is contemporary society and the novel focuses on its dark side. Liu Ping has acknowledged that his novels are basically popular fiction and compared them to martial arts novels—for the seemingly authentic world they create—while also crediting himself with having written about current reality, not some made-up Chinese past.[26] The characters are stereotypes, with the partial exception of the villain Ding Wufa. The plot offers generous doses of melodrama, crime story developments, and multiple love interests among the heroes and heroines, besides the many sexual aggressions of the bad guys.[27] The characters and action differ so much from the Yuanhua scandal in life that Liu Ping's novel is only broadly a roman à clef. The ending is not only happy, with no loose ends, but contrary to life. As nearly any interested Chinese would know, Lai Changxing was not in fact captured, but fled to Canada before the law could catch up with him. In a sequel, Ding Wufa escapes. The plots of the sequels are generally remote from what we know about Lai Changxing in life. The major case involving Ding Wufa in Hong Kong described in a prequel has not the remotest parallel in life. Readers were more and more confused about what they were getting from Liu Ping as the books rolled out, and he responded somewhat defensively.[28]

In its technique, *Dossier on Smuggling* does sweat the details, thus adding a modicum of realism to, for instance, the fairly incredible scheme of Chu Feng and his fallen angel friend Jin Jing as they set up the sting of smuggler Cai. Chu Feng makes sure, before going into a nightclub, that his wallet is flush enough to pay the enormous sums required for entertainment in the 1990s. Liu Ping has set it up so that he has RMB 5,000, which he previously requisitioned for travel (346). The author knows bureaucratic language and uses it, and he takes time to instruct the reader in differences between childhood and adult ways for Jin Jing to address Chu Feng as her honorary elder brother (239). In addition to the many details from life that are evident as discussed above, there are a few deep-structure elements of authenticity even in Liu Ping's presentation of the investigation. In life, investigation began after Beijing's receipt of a seventy-four-page letter from Fuzhou with documents appended accusing Lai Changxing of operating a smuggling ring. Perhaps the shadow of that unknown whistle-blower is visible in the novel's character Chu Feng. And Beijing does send two teams in succession to Haimen, as it did to Xiamen in life.

But the investigative heroes are not the kind of Beijing officials who in life descended on Xiamen like locusts, but heroic local cadres like those in *Heaven's Wrath*, not necessarily having counterparts in life. They mostly solve the case before Party Central arrives. In *Dossier on Smuggling* the local officials' auxiliaries are a lawyer and a bar owner, both women, which is improbable except in a Western crime formula. The hero investigators seemingly act on their own, at times constituting a virtual secret counterconspiracy to fight the Haimen conspiracy. This is a formula with roots in early 1980s stories about good cadres hired before the Cultural Revolution and law enforcers joining forces to combat the Gang of Four. Beyond that, one senses the patriotic counterspy formula of Maoist times.

Ding Wufa is a likeable chap, not only generous but capable of friendship and of paying out favors and dividends without any immediate return in mind. To that extent, the character is complex and believable.[29] But the authenticity of Ding's portrayal as sophisticated can be faulted, since Lai Changxing in life was a peasant and by some accounts nearly illiterate. Many locals in Xiamen still remember him as a generous man who did not spend a lot of money on himself or put on airs. This is how he appears in the novel. However, this portrayal is partly contradicted by Lai's flashy behavior at gambling casinos during the early days of his Canadian exile. It attracted attention and led to his detention. Above Ding Wufa is Qin Jianzhong, who appears at the beginning and end as a possible enigmatic overlord of evil. And Qin's onetime protégé, Yuan Ke, is caught up in a revenge cycle. He must stop the overlord of Haimen, who destroyed the career of his boss, Zheng, and also made an attempt on Yuan Ke's life. Life is a story of retribution; "Heaven has eyes" (20). This is simply to say that *Dossier on Smuggling* is a popular novel for China's newly commercialized market. This does not preclude other limitations, which will be discussed below.

Contributions to the Discourse of Corruption

Dossier on Smuggling is a popular novel that does not offer a theoretical or even a synoptic view of smuggling, well organized as it is, apart from the guanxi web of Ding Wufa and his co-conspirators, which as we have seen is a staple of anticorruption fiction. The book does, however, try to grapple with some of the larger meanings and motivations of the vast corruption it portrays.[30]

Much of the human interest that lies at the center of the plot regards Ding Wufa's knack for "the art of guanxi." At a slow or rapid pace as his target's character and circumstances may dictate, he sets up social occasions—ranging from banquets, golfing outings conveniently outside the city,[31] and meetings on his yacht, to philanthropic ribbon cuttings—so that he can learn the tastes and weaknesses of every major cadre. He doles out money not in return for past or future considerations, but as gifts, at holidays and when the impulse strikes him (as did Lai Changxing). Perhaps Ding really does think of these offerings not as bribes but as gifts within a traditional framework of ethical exchange, as *renqing* ("human sentiments"). Ding Wufa is the officials' humble servant, learning what it takes to make them comfortable. Gathering this kind of intelligence is usually left to one's private secretary. In *National Portrait*, it is the county cadres' gofers who keep in their heads all the municipal leaders' clothes and hat sizes. Not unlike Zhu Huaijing as he matures in the course of *National Portrait*, Ding Wufa craves and to some extent embodies an idea of friendship that transcends the sum of all guanxi. Friendships made too easily are not solid, he philosophizes (95). At the end, he wants his confederates to crash and burn with him; he is willing to do the same for them, and they repay his trust, although Mayor Chen (but not Yan Hongxing) gets cold feet when murder is involved. In establishing friendship, however, as in establishing guanxi, there is an art and an order to gaining the other person's trust. Ding can earn the confidence of Yan Hongxing only by first winning the friendship of Chen Jiayang. He is the intermediary between Ding and Yan (and Ding and the local smugglers) from the start, in a carefully orchestrated plan of wearing down Yan's reserve. Yan does not want money or women, so Ding must learn to play on his very sense of distance and self-esteem and only then add material considerations (93). Yan's weakness, as it happens, is his desire for power and to be well known in Beijing. Ding can help him there. When Yan goes north, Ding's confederates in the capital are on board to wine and dine the customs chief.

What makes Ding Wufa special is the fact that he is not just another official playing the game, but a self-made man, a private entrepreneur. From a class point of view, as a nonofficial, he is a commoner. Officials regarded such men as little better than criminals early during the reforms, but *Dossier on Smuggling* not only makes such an entrepreneur its central figure, it elevates him into a major hero in its prologue, in which a hopeful and exultant Ding Wufa looks out on Haimen, the new world that is his oyster, in such a lordly fashion that he can pity the old Anticorruption Bureau chief Zheng, whom he defeated in the prequel. Ding Wufa was Zheng's friend. He had tried to help him, even promote his career, so that they could prosper and reach new heights together. What a pity that Zheng was too stubborn (Ding would not demean him by saying ungrateful) to accept his friendship. Instead, he tried to make Ding a criminal. But now look who is on top and who is demoted to oversee a procuratorial cadre training school. Objectively, Ding Wufa seems to be gloating, but emotionally he does seem to be sorry for the old friend who, from his point of view, inexplicably turned on him. This is subversive. Ding Wufa has turned the tables on the Communist Party as a class, status, and moral elite. He pities it.

Ding Wufa is not, of course, all about friendship and introducing friends to help other friends (even his handing off of his former mistress, Yu Shanshan, to the lecherous Mayor Chen is within a context of mutual benefit). He is on the wrong side of the law. But he sees himself as nurturing (*peiyang*) personalities and talents, as does the CCP, and he has a modern name for his strategy: "public relations" (128). Public relations is his key to success. His wedding, for instance, is in essence public relations. Even lawyers must win their cases through the use of public relations (306). This tears down the wall between the legitimate and the illegitimate. Guanxi, bribes, crime, philanthropy—what's the difference? Ding calls this "walking on two legs" (445)!

Ding Wufa's goal is to continue smuggling for another "three to five years" and then to go legit, earning all his future profits from real estate and other investments made with his ill-gotten capital (84–85). This comes from Ding's reading of his times, which is rationalized in theoretical and analytical terms. Marx taught that capital and capital accumulation are dirty in the early stages of capitalism, so they are bound to be also in the early stages of socialism (84, 232). In current policy jargon, too (and as all the intellectuals say), China is now in a transitional period. Rule of law and even democracy lie in China's future, but today China is a "pre-rule-of-law" society (3). The regime of officials will in time be replaced by an age of entrepreneurs (8). Yan holds it as axiomatic, as do many officials in China, that economic development must precede the establishment of rule of law (245). By Ding's calculation, the time for law has not yet arrived. The narrative repeats this view (19, 31, 306). And yet, Yan Hongxing is also correct in sensing that comprehensive flouting of the law is something whose time is past.

Dossier on Smuggling actually hints at a dark future for democracy under capitalism. Ding Wufa wants not only to become legitimate and all-powerful economically so as to protect himself from predatory competitors and officials, but ultimately so that he can become the kingmaker and control *everything*. Political dominion is his ultimate goal (3). He exercises power now by manipulating many an official transfer in the bureaucracy—as a favor, of course, and because he likes to nurture "talent." His love of monopoly power is already evident in his control of smuggling. No one can smuggle without Wanli's permission. The disgruntled smuggler Cai Youqiang, who persuaded Ding Wufa to move up to Haimen from Hong Kong in the first place, is of course right that Ding is using him. Tipping off Yan Hongxing to one of Cai's false cargoes helps Ding gain the (then) customs vice head's confidence early on. Ding's initial corruption of Yan was persuading him to let Cai go, so that Yan could catch him again and win still more anticorruption laurels. The deal was that Ding would pretend to remain Cai's friend, even reimburse him for some of his seized shipments for old times' sake, while keeping Yan informed of his movements. They would seize every second or third shipment of Cai's, but not so many as to put him out of business or prove to him that he was being set up (145). Yan Hongxing is now twice corrupted, for he is in effect working to protect Ding's smuggling monopoly.

The novel implicitly criticizes an institutional incentive to corruption mentioned also in *Municipal Crisis*. Local governments get to keep a portion of locally seized contraband. In *Dossier on Smuggling*, Mayor Chen turns all this booty back over to customs, and also makes annual appropriations from the municipal budget to support the customs office (207). Not only that, soon after his promotion to mayor, Chen offers money to the customs system to double the officers' salaries. Ding Wufa then volunteers to supply those funds. It is against regulations for government salaries to be subsidized by private interests, so Ding simply puts the money into a foundation (127).

The major procorruption discourse in the novel is familiar from *Heaven Above*: economic development must precede the establishment of law, which only slows down growth (31, 123). Liu Ping suggests that local officials, with their narrow bureaucratic vision and habits, are prone to overlook corruption when it seems to speed local growth. They are unconcerned with monetary losses to the state, not to mention the more abstract costs of subverting the rules of open economic conduct. This is Xiao Yilei's weakness. Ding Wufa recognizes her immediately as a "local protectionist" (305). The economic interests of the locality, narrowly conceived, may very well be opposed to state taxation if the state does not invest wisely in the locality. Xiao's position symbolizes not just a central fear of localism, but fear of private enterprise, too, which likewise sees itself as progrowth and having interests opposed to state taxation. The Wanli Group and its allies have so corrupted the local party and state that they almost represent the capture of the state by a private interest. As the social theorists of corruption point out, in such an environment it is difficult to remain uncorrupted if one wants to stay employed.

Limits of and on Realism

However far it might be from a respectable "realistic" novel, *Dossier on Smuggling* is well within the anticorruption genre or formula. As such, it is bounded by a broad range of the limits of realism that have affected the other novels. To begin with there is the obligatory overlord and protector of corruption at the vice provincial level, Secretary Qin Jianzhong, whose on-screen time is short but who appears in the plot both at the very beginning and the very end. He is not the highest culprit, but the novel is completely unforthcoming about what kind of officials might be backing Ding Wufa in Beijing; Liu Ping does not even vaguely indicate their place in the bureaucracy. Chen Fang had already dropped hints about Li Jizhou and the PLA in *Municipal Crisis*, his openly published version of *Heaven's Wrath*. Liu Ping, who was under bureaucratic and party discipline as he wrote, may have felt more bounded by limits on freedom of expression. Wang Yuewen wrote as a bureaucrat, too, and without all the evident insinuations about people in life, but his *National Portrait* was banned.

Is *Dossier on Smuggling* limited by a pretense, then, of using fiction as a substitute for journalism, or at least a desire to "instruct" the public about basic "facts"? The analytical difficulty in making such a judgment is the same as with *Heaven's Wrath*. Although many of *Dossier on Smuggling*'s details have Lai Changxing dead to rights, down to the playmate club, movie studio, and soccer team, other basic facts are altered, including even the hero's marital status. If *Dossier on Smuggling* really makes a contribution to knowledge, it surely must be in its depiction of how the real Lai Changxing went about constructing his web of guanxi or quasi-friendships. Because much of this content adheres so closely to material later disclosed in government sources, the reader may be delighted to see that he or she has after all "learned" something real—and indeed, also wonder why Liu Ping did not let his imagination wander a little further and more creatively in delineating motivations for his protagonist. Liu did, after all, change Ding/Lai from a peasant to a rather suave operator. Why did he not go further? Was it to maintain "authenticity"?[32]

China's critics would no doubt fault Liu Ping for making a popular novel out of a serious subject. Commercial it clearly is, with romantic and detective themes and a setup at the end for a sequel, plus an almost bafflingly elaborate telling in the beginning of a prequel yet to be written. But *Dossier on Smuggling* is also a good read. Its popularity must surely be partly due to its faithfulness to traditional themes loved by Chinese readers.[33] A desire for justice is not the only sentiment motivating the good guys. Yuan Ke and Hu Xinhong are modern professionals, but they are also seeking revenge—revenge for their mentor—which indicates how loyal they are. The bad guys, too—Ding, Yan, and Chen—are like sworn brothers in the classic vernacular novels. When the going gets tough at the end, the stronger characters, Ding Wufa and Yan Hongxing, dramatically renew their vows, swearing mutual fealty (495). And they *are* faithful to the end, like good Chinese outlaws. As one reviewer has already noted, *Dossier on Smuggling* has some of the character of a chivalric novel.[34] There is a rough equivalence of the officials' sentiments and chivalry with that of the book's outlaws, as there is in *Water Margin*. Ding Wufa is a kind of heroic figure, a man of epic and decisive deeds who does not show his power until he absolutely must. He sees himself not as evil but as adapting to the opportunities in the current Chinese environment and even to his vision of China's future. He is a man of great ambitions. Mayor Chen, his "puppet," is to that extent his foil. In China's new era, might it not be appropriate that audacious entrepreneurs take the place of sniveling and sybaritic bureaucrats like those who have always populated China's official class? Ding Wufa is at least due the respect of a Cao Cao. His goal, after all, is to found a dynasty. It is almost a pity that he is not legitimate.

Yan Hongxing's character is the most surprising of all. He is practically a tragic hero, incorruptible by money or sex until he meets Ye Bingbing near the end, but that is true love, the great love of a hero. He *is* a legitimate hero, being an official, and he knows enough to keep a distance between himself and Ding Wufa, the narrative keeps telling us. He is not a mere entrepreneur, and it is natural to think of him as nobler than Ding Wufa. Down deep, he even has a "correct" view of history. He realizes that China ultimately must reform to keep on growing (404). Now, however, is not the time. China is still in the stage of primitive, dirty capital accumulation. Most important, Yan Hongxing is a man of loyalty. He is loyal to his friend Ding Wufa, willing in the end decisively to cross over into illegality with him, just as in a previous test of his character, he stood by his mentor, the previous head of Haiman customs, when he was unpopular—unpopular largely because he would not expedite Haimen customs inspections and open up the floodgates to smugglers. Yan Hongxing emerges, paradoxically, as a man of principle. Through most of the novel, one can follow the narrative logic and see him as overly ambitious, another Cao Cao struggling for a more old-fashioned, bureaucratic throne than the one Ding seeks, but plausibly innocent of the smuggling his friend does. It is a paradox. Yan is not a cynical bureaucrat who does not want to know about infractions of the law. Ding Wufa never lets Yan have direct knowledge of his smuggling, and it is simply beneath a stalwart (*hao han*) like Yan to disbelieve his friend. In the end, one is sad to see a man of Yan's old-fashioned official character go along with Ding's murder plot and therefore meet his necessary end.

Aftermath

Liu Ping wrote two sequels and a prequel about Ding Wufa's exploits.[35] The components of Liu's "dossier series" are, in order: *The Dossier from the [Hong Kong] Independent Commission against Corruption, Dossier on Smuggling, Internal Dossier,* and *Overseas Dossier.* The more recent books appear to be close to complete fiction. Ding Wufa escapes to Latin America rather than Canada and he even makes trips back to China. Liu Ping is a prolific author. He has written several other books, including one about the drug trade that is to be the first in a new series.[36] In 2002 he codirected a fictional multipart television suspense drama about smuggling cases.[37]

A major obstacle to final clearance of a television series inspired by Liu's prequel, *The Dossier from the Independent Commission against Corruption* (which after shooting was called *Zhiming youxi,* or *Deadly Game*), was that the original plot was *too* fictitious; Hong Kong had never had such a case. Anyway, the teleplay's softening of the novel's original edge greatly disappointed Liu Ping. The director and original screenplay were up to his standards, but political scruples killed the first screenplay the very day that filming was to start. The director saved the project by making further drastic changes. Reading between the lines of Liu Ping's account, one can deduce that the problems with his original conception were its negativism about China, the imperfections of its law enforcement hero Zheng, and worries that the plot might hurt the feelings of the Hong Kong people.[38] The book was published only after the initial teleproduction fiasco, in a revised version (and only in a revised version, so far as I know),[39] so the book may have run into political problems, too.

Noted TV drama director Zhao Baogang bought the television rights to *Dossier on Smuggling* and started on the teleplay in July 2001, but in the fall announced that he was postponing the project to work on another TV drama about Yuanhua, *Yuanhua daan* (The great Yuanhua case). Reportedly the teleplay for the latter was already in the hands of the censors at the end of 2001. However, neither production, nor a Tianjin film version of the latter, has reached the public as of this writing.[40] In the meantime, Liu Ping's superiors in the customs bureaucracy are displeased at his preoccupation with his second career as a writer.[41]

Still, the original *Dossier on Smuggling*, by playing with the national mythology of the Yuanhua scandal, has made its own contribution to the national mythology of corruption. The Yuanhua case in all its representations, from the sublime to the ridiculous, has ratified the status of corruption itself as a spectator sport, a branch of contemporary Chinese pop culture.

7

Chinese Realism, Popular Culture, and the Critics

Chinese anticorruption fiction at the millennium hardly figured in China's high-level literary and cultural debates. Despite the desire of some to collapse binary oppositions, nearly all critics in fact drew hard and fast lines between serious elite culture (by which they usually meant avant-garde culture) and popular "mass" culture. At the time, realism's position was downshifting from the serious realm; often it was simply ignored. This suggests to me a ternary opposition: among the serious, the popular, and the realistic.[1] To elite intellectuals, who tended to be unsympathetic to it, realism was an orthodox mainstream mode not just outside serious and mass culture, but left behind by both of them. That surprising view was predicated on a reversal of mass culture's traditionally low valuation. China's mass culture was now, according to some critics, cutting-edge—a second Chinese avant-garde. China's internationally acclaimed films, for instance, were a national triumph of serious *and* mass culture. Conversely, anticorruption fiction and film were not valued as either serious *or* popular. Perhaps they were in fact a realist mode of expression outside the common literary and mass media trends of the times. My burden of proof is to show that the realism of China's works about corruption was a *critical* realism of some depth, not just a schlock realism that justified the critics' neglect. Hard-hitting criticism of China, however, would still offend some elite critics' budding national pride.

Anticorruption fiction and film need not be judged as monumental or innovative art, even in their best moments. They are, however, well situated to illuminate the ambivalences and paradoxes of China's cultural debates, for they can, in truth, lay claim to being popular, realistic, *and* serious—though seldom avant-garde, apart from avant-garde gestures such as the minimalist opening chapters of *Heaven Above*.[2] The elite Chinese critics of which this chapter speaks are celebrity and academic cultural critics and intellectuals who regularly publish in China's national literary journals, work at nationally prominent universities and research academies, and are in contact with China's expatriate academics overseas.[3] Realism, in theory and in practice, is still esteemed by China's readers, workaday scholars, and book reviewers. Realism also retains high regard in the party and state apparatuses and among their sympathizers. That support is part of realism's "problem," as the intellectual elite sees it. This chapter will explore realism as a coherent and valuable modern Chinese tradition, but not as a fixed or a superior one—for one focus of this book up to now has been, after all, the limits of realism in practice.

Chinese Realism in Theory and in History

Realism was the most prestigious mode of writing from the 1920s until the communist revolution in 1949 and again during the first few years after Mao's death in 1976. In name, it has been the orthodox Chinese literary mode in modern times, even since Mao's revolution. Realism underwent a sharp reversal of prestige in the 1980s, before China's mass culture did, though in the opposite direction. Elite Chinese critics at first came to see experimentalism or literary difficulty as the only true counterweight to "popular," down-market tastes they deemed unworthy and threatening to "art." That left realism as a backward, schlock means of "naive" representationalism, like the "realism" of paintings sold in American hotels as advertised on late-night television. This view of literary realism is hardly peculiar to China, but it was reinforced by the term's orthodox political past. The avant-garde was seen as the only counterweight to official discourse. Xudong Zhang feels that realism "degenerated into a label for literary convention and political orthodoxy within the state apparatus."[4]

Certainly China does have a strong official discourse of realism. According to official propaganda and education even today, realism is a unitary trend, the socially responsible and politically correct mainstream tendency passed down from Lu Xun and other leftist writers of the 1930s to the better communist writers of the 1950s (it is acknowledged to have died during the Cultural Revolution), down to today (the "New Era"), when widely published writers supposedly have regained the conscience and perspicacity of Lu Xun. But as virtually all critics and scholars, even those who champion realism, know, this idea of Chinese fiction as a unified trend is a fantasy. However, those who view realism favorably still link post-Mao realism to the May Fourth realism that followed the vernacular literary revolution after 1917. In those days, realism was a positive term among China's elite. This chapter will argue that Chinese realism, though hardly unified, is today an eclectic but discrete literary practice, drawing on precedents from all the presocialist and socialist periods.

In the West, major theoretical reassessments of realism in Chinese literature by Marston Anderson in 1990 and David Der-wei Wang in 1992 focused on the May Fourth period. Michael Duke, Perry Link, Bonnie McDougall, and Kam Louie, by contrast, addressed contemporary Chinese realism and its links to socialist literary practice.[5] Few analysts today would rule out the application of the term "realism" to earlier Chinese fiction as well, including some late Qing fiction. Wang's subsequent monographs push evidence of Chinese realism backward, from late Qing to late Ming fiction.[6] Previously Jaroslav Průšek, followed by Milena Doleželová-Velingerová and her students,[7] and also Joseph Levenson, Benjamin I. Schwartz, and their students in intellectual history, exemplified a trend that was general in Western sinology by the 1970s, of seeing Chinese modernity as beginning in the late Qing. Průšek pointed to a birth of subjectivism in the nineteenth century, by which he meant a liberating confessional and individualistic turn among Chinese writers that spurred them to write of their own personal thoughts.[8] This subjective blow at classical models, paradoxically (or perhaps not, since the Western sequence was in theory similar) set the stage for the realistic emphasis on objectivity, or at least the kind of impassive narration favored by nineteenth-century Western novelists such as Flaubert and Zola. It was in the twentieth century that Chinese writers acquired—beyond subjectivism, individualism, and doctrinal realism—the hubris, already present in some Western writers, to think that they could fully inhabit and represent the innermost thinking of *other people*. This is a major characteristic of realism, romanticism, and other modern literary trends. It is what Liu Zaifu referred to, in the 1980s, as the "subjectivity" of literary characters themselves, beyond the "subjectivity" of the writer and the reader.[9] China's May Fourth and post-Mao realistic movements were not so much reactions against romanticism as against formulaic writing or utopian "classicism."

Anderson confirms the consensus view, well documented long ago by Bonnie McDougall,[10] that the *doctrine* of realism came to China from the West and Japan, along with a flood of translated works representing everything Western literature had to offer, and that Chinese writers took up all of it with alacrity as a tool for transforming China and its literary culture.[11] This was followed, Anderson says, by Chinese writers' "gradual discovery of the true nature of realism and their eventual relinquishment of the mode."[12] Anderson argues that Western realism, by calling for authorial detachment, clashed both with Chinese authors' traditional views of creativity (he deemphasizes the authors' modern excitement about individualism and subjectivity) and their modern insistence that literary works arouse readers to undertake social transformation. Realism's preference for imitation of nature seemed insufficient to these writers. To them, the limits of realism were the limits of its power to stir readers to action and inner transformation. Anderson takes mimesis and detachment to be realism's necessary characteristics, yet he sees reader reception of Western realism as not very detached. Like catharsis in tragedy as explained by Aristotle, realism "performs a ritualistic purgation of the reader's emotion, specifically sympathetic identification with the figures portrayed (pity) and revulsion from the events represented (terror)."[13] We may add that catharsis outside of realism has also been valued by Westernized Chinese critics, such as Wang Guowei.

Certainly many Chinese writers, by fiat in the 1950s if not already from their own conscience in the 1930s, viewed mimetic literature as inadequate and limited in its social power. But did realism, or even the doctrine of realism, have a "true nature"? And is all realism simply mimetic, even in theory? Then there is the problem of catharsis. Although Aristotle's theory of catharsis pertains to drama and character flaws of the sort seldom seen in May Fourth's stereotyped heroes and villains, reader identification with characters clearly pertains to realistic fiction. It is often on those grounds that such fiction has been considered "bourgeois," and not just in China. Chinese readers are famous for identifying with characters in *The Dream of the Red Chamber*, which few (at least after the demise of Li Xifan's Cultural Revolution views) would call a mainly realistic work *or* bourgeois. Current criticism sometimes calls reader empathy with characters and immersion in the story "romantic," as when talking of viewer reception of Hollywood films. An old debate ponders whether realism operates intellectually, by distancing the reader or viewer from the text or performance (in a Brechtian way, or perhaps even by creating discomfort), or emotionally, by simulating reality and getting the audience to identify with the simulation. Most emotionally engaging visual and print narratives, except perhaps experimental ones, reward the reader with catharsis at the end, if only because when the words or images end, the viewer realizes that the narrative has not in fact occurred in "the real world."[14] Yet, a major problem of much canonical May Fourth fiction, McDougall points out, is that its elite male writers were in effect writing about their own social frustrations; to that extent, their heroes are not easy to identify with.[15]

The manipulation of particularly intense pity, terror, and other strong emotions in fiction is usually associated now with melodrama, by yet another transfer of theory from drama to fiction. Studies of melodrama in May Fourth films have paved the way for us to identify pervasive melodramatic aspects in May Fourth fiction, epitomized in its "tragic" stories of women, on which many films were based. Much May Fourth realism is a mix of devices from the Chinese traditions of realism and melodrama. Catharsis is also commonly used to explain the nonrealistic generic appeal of detective fiction (a frequent plot form in today's anticorruption fiction, as it was in late Qing fiction) as a purgation of social dread of injustice or the reader's own feelings of guilt and fear. Western critics have spun out many theories about reader identification or nonidentification with the role of murderer and relief at the general social or personal exculpation that comes with discovery of who is the guilty party. Chinese editors insist that their readers, like the readers of cowboy Westerns and melodramatic tales everywhere, love to see justice win in the end.

Perhaps the chief objection to Anderson's view of realism as detached is that a good deal of Western realistic fiction was itself written to have a transformative social impact, and major Chinese critics knew this, as Theodore Huters points out.[16] Moreover, many classics of realism, by Charlotte Brontë, Charles Dickens, and Stendhal, continuing down to Frank Norris, Upton Sinclair, and Maxim Gorky, are conventionally viewed as having themes of corruption. If realism has a "true nature," it is not necessarily one of disengagement. One can still agree with Anderson that by the 1930s many (though not all) Chinese authors, including most self-styled realists, changed their theories and styles away from classic justifications and practices of realism under the influence of a new sense of urgency about the need to transform society, and also under political pressure. Even their later works, however, can still be encompassed under the capacious *theory* of realism. And so they were in China. The theory was stretched to include "socialist realism," the envisioning of a glorious future existing in the present—a "reality" that was as often romantic as gritty.[17] Pessimistic it was not.

David Der-wei Wang has taken a more pluralistic view of realism in the May Fourth period that I find more congenial. He analyzes authors of such diverse styles as Mao Dun, Lao She, and Shen Congwen as realists. Each author wrote in varying styles that might or might not be considered predominantly realist, but Wang's approach avoids the dogmatism of seeing Chinese realism as having one true tradition, embodied in Lu Xun's works, as mainland Chinese critics used to argue.[18] However, even Wang puts Lu Xun ontologically at the center. He writes of Mao Dun, Lao She, and Shen Congwen as "dialogical voices arising within the discursive paradigm set by Lu Xun, voices that valorize Lu Xun's position by questioning and even transgressing its boundaries. . . . The limits reached by Lu Xun's realism are also the limits of realism for some subsequent writers, but are the boundaries where the realisms of Mao Dun, Lao She, and Shen Congwen begin."[19] Further, "We should ask how [Lu Xun's] discourse generated the conditions of writing and reading Chinese reality, and how subsequent writers tried to break away from his conditions."[20] Modern Chinese authors were a learned group, in dialogue with numerous foreign writers, if only through translations. One could in fact question that Lu Xun was a realist, except in philosophy and attitude, particularly given Wang's view of Lu Xun as a metafictional writer concerned more with literary codes than "the real," even composing *allegories* of the "real."

Wang also argues that "Melodrama and farce . . . should be regarded not as the opposites of an authentic realist narrative but, rather, as its ironic approximations."[21] In Auerbach's classic, if narrow, formulation, satire and comedy, like didacticism, are antithetical to realism.[22] But most of the novels in this book are melodramatic to one degree or another, and somewhat realistic, too. While denying the existence of an "authentic" realist narrative, I would agree that realism and melodrama are not entirely incompatible, though they need not be seen as proximate. Following Anderson, I even see shared ground with tragedy because all three modes can lead to catharsis. But melodrama and realism in ordinary parlance can still be differentiated, along at least two different spectrums: that of histrionic effects and that of moral clarity as opposed to moral ambiguity. Melodramatic elements in the novels analyzed above, at least, are not ironic.

In a later work, *Fin-de-siècle Splendor*, Wang analyzes, among other novels, the epics of the very late Qing commonly called *qianze xiaoshuo* (novels of exposure, or castigatory fiction). Masterworks by Li Boyuan and Wu Jianren (Woyao) are often cited as precedents for the anticorruption fiction of the 1990s, as when Wang Yuewen's *National Portrait* (1999) is called a latter-day *Guanchang xianxing ji* (Exposure of officialdom, which is the title of Li Boyuan's 1903 magnum opus). The relevant novels of both eras expose the dark side of society and social manners with a cornucopia of clever, unethical, and hypocritical schemes for getting ahead socially and economically, often portrayed with exaggeration, even burlesque. The 1990s generic concept of *guanchang xiaoshuo* (novels about officialdom) also has late Qing overtones. Novels from both ends of the twentieth century are political, topical, partial to the roman-à-clef conceit, and, in Wang's general sense, they have a fin-de-siècle character (the late Qing works come at the end of a dynasty). One cannot quite agree with the view once stated by the eminent scholar Chen Pingyuan that the late Qing was obsessed, as the current age is, with exposing corruption in officialdom almost to the exclusion of other trades. I believe that all professions were depicted as hypocritical and corrupt in the late Qing, as Lu Xun indicated. However, official corruption surely has primacy in both eras, at least in the now canonical novels.[23]

Most critics now trace the origins of both Chinese realism and urban commercial popular culture to the late Qing. The late Qing and late twentieth-century works exposing corruption shared this dual nature: serious in purpose because of their social criticism, but popular in form, often compromising with traditional forms and tastes. These novels of both the late Qing and the 1990s have been criticized as popular, commercial, and inferior as art—too close to the journalism of current events, which was the trade of some of the exposure writers of both the late Qing and the 1990s. All the works were written hurriedly, as is sometimes all too apparent. Furthermore, although the authors wrote their exposure novels in a relatively low idiom of their respective eras, they could and sometimes did write other works in a more literary register. Novels by the major authors of both eras also inspired inferior imitations from which the original models were sometimes at pains to distinguish themselves. Many of these qualities, except for the use of a low, vernacular idiom, also characterize Jia Ping'ao's 1993 novel about moral corruption in all walks of life, *Fei du* (Capital in ruins), and yet that novel is seldom grouped with the novels of the 1990s that this book is about. But then it is not usually called realistic, either. *Capital in Ruins*, with its references to the old classic *Jin ping mei* (The golden lotus; *or*, The plum in the golden vase), reminds us, as do critics from Robert E. Hegel to David Der-wei Wang, that novels with themes of corruption can be found in the late Ming, and of course earlier than that.[24]

Wang in his later work revisits the idea of farce as an "ironic approximation" of realism in the late Qing novels, which he says use farce and "grotesque exposé" to create a "grotesque realism." Clearly the exaggerations of farce can serve critical realistic ends, and they can be mixed with realistic prose. So can the grotesque (it is not always comic), which mimics realistic technique as a kind of surrealism, as critics have noted in Dickens, Carlyle, Forster—and Mo Yan.[25] Yet Wang sees Li Boyuan and Wu Jianren as lacking a contrastive sense of normalcy (whereas their model, Wu Jingzi, eighteenth-century author of *Rulin waishi,* or *The Scholars,* embraces Confucian normalcy). Instead, Wang imagines Li Boyuan and Wu Jianren as having a "phantom axiology" unique to the turn of the twentieth century, in which values once considered aberrant have become normal.[26] The Chinese discourse of corruption has anciently taken note of that predicament; it is simply the late-stage or end-game corruption mentioned in chapter 1, in which corrupt practices have become the new ethical standard. However, it is hard to be sure that any age is secure in its values in the eyes of perceptive authors. That is one of the difficulties of the utterly relative term "modernity"; in which recent century did authors see themselves as not living within modernity? One could argue that Wu as a failed examinee felt axiological confusion, too (only not due to Western influences), but if one accepts the divide between Wu and his late Qing followers as key, then our novels of the 1990s must be on the Wu Jingzi side of the line, for they still judge immoral behavior, even if it is now the norm, as immoral from the "old" socialist/Confucian viewpoint. Yet in form, mode, technique, and even content, the 1990s novels seem more akin to their late Qing counterparts. Cataloging immoral behavior is part of the spectatorial pleasure.[27] Their lack of humor (except in *National Portrait*) is the chief difference from the late Qing works. Or are laughter and condemnation two sides of the same coin, based, of necessity, on a sense of moral incongruity?

The writers of the 1990s on the one hand uphold old hierarchical socialist and quasi-Confucian morality above the raw power of money values, and yet they also uphold, for purposes of reform and national self-strengthening, the money values of a market economy. The authors write quickly and journalistically, for money, and then hasten to write a sequel. Wang makes much of such behavior on the part of his late Qing exposure authors, who in fact were journalists, often wrote quickly for money, and, unlike the authors of the 1990s (or at least the major authors discussed in this book), stand accused of letting others finish some of their works and even plagiarizing. Accommodations to the age's commercialism has had a devastating effect on the literary prestige of exposure literature in both eras, and I do not doubt that the authors of both ages felt ideological ambivalence, but I think we can also grant that writers can be hypocrites, compromisers, or at least compartmentalizers of their values, as of their careers. Authors of both eras wrote works in other genres that did not do them as proud as their epics of officialdom. Zhang Ping, the cynosure of 1990s anticorruption fiction, has written no late-Qing-style comic ghost fiction,[28] but he has written popular books about the supernatural. This does not contradict David Wang's insights into the ways that comic novels may have influenced Li Boyuan and Wu Jianren, as English comic novels influenced Dickens. Our novels of the 1990s, having come out of a different, "realistic" tradition or movement, may not be so like the late Qing novels after all. That leads back, full circle, to the question of whether "realism" is the most noteworthy thing that subsequent authors saw in the late Qing castigatory novels.

The Notion of China's "Classic Tradition of Realism" in Post-Mao Times

As it happened, Chinese theories and practices of realism were transformed and reified during the Mao decades. Mao's culture bureaucrats did not oppose the name "realism," but they rejected its pessimism and any visions of reality that contradicted the current party line, including dissident, subjective, and self-questioning accretions to realist writing during the twentieth-century age of modernism. The bureaucrats embraced realism's supposed transformative power, which by Marston Anderson's analysis most May Fourth writers felt they had already seen through.

In the post-Mao era, realism's politically critical and pessimistic edge came back with a vengeance, becoming the very hallmark of realism, as it had been in the May Fourth era. (Contributions to realism from modernism did not stage a comeback.) The transformation of Chinese realism, which was more political than technical, did not come all at once. Even before plain "realism" replaced Maoist "revolutionary realism," the latter had to overcome the orthodox formulation of "the combination of revolutionary realism and revolutionary romanticism."[29] Another reaction against Maoism among writers in the post-Mao era was a repudiation of realism. In general parlance, amid the flood of experimental, fantastic, and sensational popular works, "realist" came to refer to nearly any work that was neither avant-garde (for the eggheads) nor popular (catering to down-market tastes).

I believe that Chinese realism can still be defined as a more discrete realm that is not simply "mainstream," and certainly not just politically orthodox. The "mainstream," after all, includes relatively experimental writers such as Mo Yan and critically acclaimed writers such as Wang Anyi and Li Rui. Continuities exist in Chinese concepts of realism through the 1920s, 1950s, and 1990s. The classic Chinese realism that all those eras supposedly inherited from the May Fourth period is defined not just against romantic conceits, tyranny, and injustice, but also against modernist difficulty—which is to say that modernism was not unknown in early twentieth-century China. In fact, Chinese writers and critics realized that there was and is nothing extraordinary about the limits of realism's transformative power compared to the limits of other literary forms. The Chinese exception may have been to expect so much of literature. China's experimental writers of the 1980s, too, thought that their new discourses could transform Chinese culture in the broadest sense, much as their predecessors in the 1920s hoped for such an outcome by overthrowing classical Chinese. Disillusionment was the result in both cases.

Post-Mao realism with a critical and pessimistic edge owes no overt allegiance to state discourse or even necessarily to Lu Xun. It is intent on exposing the lies of all official propaganda, including that propaganda's would-be realist fiction. Chinese writers and critics began debating the nature of "true realism" and its need to tell the truth in the early 1980s. Scholars outside China articulated the notion that Chinese realism had been reborn in a guise more continuous with May Fourth realism than Mao's revolutionary realism. Li Yi and Bi Hua of Hong Kong called it "China's new realism" or "neo-realism," but political pressure led to a rejection of that concept and many of the works to which it pointed. Michael S. Duke spoke of a new Chinese "critical realism," adopting a term from Georg Lukács, but the overtones of this term also were too dissident for China in the early eighties.[30] Biting literary works continued to be written even so. One could call this combative and accusatory advocacy of antibureaucratic "honesty" the *fansi* discourse ("thought-provoking," after a 1979 trend in literature). Or call it the engaged, Liu Binyan discourse of realism,[31] which by the late 1990s was still nonofficial yet was mainstream (prestigious and not underground), even though innocuous realistic works still constituted the majority of Chinese fictional publications.

The thought-provoking style of realism inherits much from China's pre-Maoist tradition of realism, particularly as that has been reconceived in later years as a pre-Marxist-Leninist practice, and therefore even the biting contemporary realists think of their own practice as within a "classic tradition of realism" dating from the 1920s. In fact, contemporary realists, including anticorruption writers of the 1990s, are influenced not only by China's old vernacular and late Qing fiction, but also by populist, indeed Maoist, conceptions of realism, morality, social order, literary "mission," and literary instrumentality. Tensions abound within this realism, but the tension between subjectivity and objectivity is not necessarily the major one. One question is whether realism has to be pessimistic, as it typically was in the late Qing and the 1920s, or whether it can have a happy ending, as was the rule in Maoist times. Still today, official control of literature mandates that literature about corruption must have a happy ending if it is to be openly published, though literature about many other topics need not. The contradiction between the existence of corruption and a happy ending is universal in the novels analyzed above.

I believe that a Liu Binyan discourse of realism (in theory, though not always in practice) is now not only mainstream, but practically de rigueur in nonofficial writing circles devoted to realism, including anticorruption fiction. This realism retains characteristics or expectations from both the Mao and post-Mao periods, as outlined below, and it is itself now often conceived (or misconceived) as China's "classic tradition of realism"—its "real" tradition, with Maoist doctrine being aberrant. Ironically, China's classic realism needs a lying bureaucracy as its foil. Variant expectations of realism, rosier and more Maoist, have not died out, but the following ones, which add up to a "critical realism with Chinese characteristics," have become dominant in post-Mao realism, and above all in anticorruption novels.

(1) *Realism "tells the truth."* Further, *it "speaks truth to power."* Truth is, of course, subjective, but now the general Chinese presumption is that China remains a bureaucratic society and its officials lie. The precepts they circulate in all forms of propaganda, therefore, also lie. China's ancient and late Qing muckraking similarly countered the lies of a centrally organized society having a doctrine-fixing bureaucracy at its core. Lu Xun's canonical realism in May Fourth times countered alleged lies of Chinese society, politics, and culture. Even his generation, when central power was in decline, thought of itself as opposing the lies of a centrally coordinated nation that denied the class nature of society. Today, China has as many writers concerned with the deeper epistemological and cos-

mological questions of what is "real" as any other country (most of them have joined the avant-garde), but others want to postpone such abstract questions because they see *reality* in the first instance still boxed in by the raw power of a unitary bureaucracy. Directly confronting lies through realism is not, of course, the only way of rebuking bureaucratic authoritarianism. Allegory is another strategy. One may, for instance, depict the corruption of the present within a setting that seems to be the past. Great May Fourth writers such as Lu Xun, Shen Congwen, and Mao Dun have been read both as realists and as allegorists, as have Wu Jingzi and Cao Xueqin before them. However, such depth is seldom credited to the late Qing or late twentieth-century realists, and humor is seldom seen in the late twentieth-century works. They are accusatory.

(2) Bureaucracies tend to paint a rosy picture of the society of which they are stewards. Therefore, by way of telling the "truth," *realism exposes the dark side of society*, the bad things about it. It has the unprettified subject matter and pessimistic attitude characteristic of Western realism. Wellek notes that nineteenth-century realism often implied "rejection and revulsion against society."[32] Social criticism of society's dark side (Maoist society officially almost denied that there was a dark side) has for decades been codified in official Chinese criticism as the realistic literary mission of the great cultural icon Lu Xun and his followers, appropriate to *their* dark times. Realism is still a literature meant to transform society. The pessimism of this realism, to be sure, clashes with the optimism necessary to effect transformations, as well as the dictates of socialist realism. It also clashes with epiphanies about the speed and dynamism of postmodernity, including literature that conveys, often proudly, and perhaps nationalistically, real facets of China's bright and shiny postmodern culture using realistic techniques.

(3) *Realism depicts major social trends* of modern, contemporary society. Great social forces are not a mere backdrop for individual life stories and romances; individuals live amid and within the social movements of their time, though their lives need not be wholly determined by them, as they would be in naturalism. This tendency toward articulating social trends in the Chinese novel can be traced back to the Qing.[33] The charge so often leveled against Taiwan literature by mainland critics in the 1980s was that its canvas was narrow; it described quotidian domestic dramas instead of the big picture and major historical themes. When mainland literature was enriched with more works about lifestyles and concerns of personal happiness in the 1990s, these works, too, were criticized as trivial (*xiao qi*) fiction and excluded from the great national tradition of realism,

which is *da qi* (grand).³⁴ As Perry Link has noted, this fits an ancient Chinese classification of fiction as "*xiaoshuo*, or writing about 'small' affairs, which traditionally meant stories about love, family life, and the passions and problems in ordinary people's lives, which stood in implicit contrast to *dashu*, or the 'great' stories about emperors, ministers, generals, and the other events that were worthy of historical records."³⁵ Cognitive dissonance originally arose because *xiaoshuo* became the term for modern-style, including Western, *fiction*, including notably the nineteenth-century novels about great social upheavals so loved by twentieth-century Chinese. But the connotations of words change. Today, *xiaoshuo* means fiction period, including the nineteenth-century kind with grand themes. By these lights, *good* fiction, or certainly realistic fiction, must be *dashu*. Avoidance of fundamental concerns of the people in fiction is considered an evasion of reality, and even of literature's mission (as conceived by the realists). China's more avant-garde fiction is pervaded with a sense of post-traumatic stress, but it does not point to history itself, and psychological trauma in principle can originate within the family or indeed the individual psyche; it need not come from war, revolution, or social conflict. China's fiction about corruption typically evokes social conflict with very high stakes. The employment and prosperity of thousands in giant factories and of hundreds of thousands or millions in cities are on the line when the power elite make off with millions of yuan or bankrupt whole industries.

A corollary is that while short fiction can be realistic, epic realistic novels best provide the broad canvas necessary to convey social trends in all their magnitude. Another frequent corollary, which is not so necessary, is that outer social structures will take precedence over inner psychological phenomena. This is of course a latent source of tension between realism and modernism, which is known for its obsession with the private self.

Yet modern literature is about individuals. Individuals embody the great social forces and the clashes among them in China's realistic novels. Since the time of Mao, the realistic novel has been popular, didactic, moral, and political (politics being conflated with morality), and thus the characters of the novel may well be heroes and villains. It does not follow, however, that a realistic writer must believe in a telos of history or a "grand narrative." Even when writing about small folk and their everyday concerns, Shen Congwen, for instance, wrote "serious" *dashu*, like the Marxists Mao Dun and Guo Moruo.

(4) *Realism speaks for the lower orders of society*, the forgotten and the

oppressed. This is a trait of Western realism. Mao reinforced it, in theory, by calling for Chinese literature to be by, of, and for workers, peasants, and soldiers. New groups of oppressed peoples are a favorite subject of post-Mao realism in principle, and yet in practice contemporary realistic novels, like May Fourth novels, still detail mostly the behavior of the oppressors. Human flaws are simply more intriguing than righteousness.

(5) The principle that *realism requires typicality*, an early opinion voiced by Engels (realism implying "the truthful reproduction of typical characters under typical circumstances"),[36] was interpreted quantitatively in the Mao era, and it has lingering effects in the theory of post-Mao realism, though less so in its practice.[37] It is no longer necessary to concentrate on the social classes and types who are most numerous in society (ideally, if society were 70 percent of peasant origin, 70 percent of a novel's characters would be of peasant origin), although Chinese realism retains the aforementioned mandate to describe great social trends and those who make them. Today an analogous discourse of proportionality can still arise unexpectedly. The dark side of society is acknowledged and no longer blamed on remnants of capitalism, but still it must not take up a "disproportionate" number of pages. This sense of proportion is subjective, and yet is still conceived mathematically. For instance, crime fiction necessarily has murders—more than in life—but the plot must not have "too many" murders. The same goes for cadre corruption cases. A former head of the Qunzhong, or Masses' Press (the publishing arm of the Ministry of Public Security), evoked a proportionality discourse in regard to its own sales of anticorruption fiction: "We hope for hot sales, but not to win an extremely large share of the market. It would not be a good thing for society if everybody took an interest in these cases."[38]

(6) *Realism uses the techniques associated with it in history, namely those of classic works of nineteenth-century Western and twentieth-century May Fourth realism.* The newer literary techniques of modernism and the avant-garde, being fantastic or "magical," are "not realistic," except in some cases when they have been rationalized as advanced techniques of getting at "reality." Hence the identification of realism with the mainstream, though the mainstream can of course evolve.

(7) *Realism eschews "difficult" and experimental narrative structures.* Realistic works have a standard directional narrative, with a beginning, middle, and end. Though nineteenth-century realism was capable of many complications and plot deviations, and even a lack of a feeling of closure at the end (Bakhtin considered the novel in principle "dialogic"), no more than the nineteenth-century classics does China's "classic" or

even dissident realism cast doubt on its own master narrative or its relatively positivist metaphysics. The realistic novel is not given to modernist-style analysis of the nature of truth itself or of history. Even the most dissident novels have strong social ideologies. That is how didacticism and, notably, the hoary conceit of corruption can be accommodated within realism. Cinema and television about real social problems cling even more obviously to clear directional narratives. They are relatively unilinear and invariably provide a strong sense of closure at the end.

(8) The turn away from modernism, experimentalism, and conceptual or existential uncertainty at both the sentence and larger structural levels (from a twentieth- or twenty-first-century perspective) leads to another premise of Chinese realism, though it has its own historical roots in China's early twentieth-century ferment: *realism is accessible, easy-to-read "mass" literature.* (A Chinese Henry James might pose a problem of classification—though James's works have been adapted for the silver screen.) This is not so strange. Speaking of Western reading material, Peter Brooks observes that "The novel in the airport newsstand will tend to be written from a repertory of narrative and descriptive tools that come from the nineteenth-century realists."[39] Mass values were supreme in Mao's era, when all literature was required to be accessible to readers without elite education. Chinese realism remains in tension with the elitism of the old classical literature (which for modern educated Chinese is harder to read than ever) and the difficult and obscure works of the new 1980s avant-garde. (Some of the 1980s avant-garde works are as vulnerable as popular works to charges of being "kitsch"—aesthetically horrible, though they "took a lot of trouble to make.")[40] If "popular" means easy-to-read, then to some extent all Chinese literature since 1949, except for the 1980s avant-garde works, are popular.[41] That includes works that imitate the rhythms of classical Chinese in a simpler vocabulary, such as the martial arts novels of Jin Yong, novels with archaic vernacular vocabulary from Ming novels that were "low" in their time, and even fiction in semiclassical language with "base" subject matter, such as Jia Ping'ao's *Capital in Ruins.* Still, different levels or registers of style exist among novels and within novels.

(9) *The best realistic literature is not only about social trends; it also has political implications.* Some writers, in their continuing hope that realistic literature will promote action, expect realistic works to focus on the main social needs and trends of the time, as society's leaders and intellectuals define them, so that the works can be harbingers of social change. The 1980s and 1990s, for instance, were a time of economic reform, so there

was a perceived need for "reform literature," particularly in the absence of unfettered journalism. To put it benignly, realism ought to be topical, or if historical, then relevant to contemporary society. And one can in fact be quite independent in proposing how reforms should be done. The political mission of realistic novels and the primacy of political corruption (rather than more figurative or moral kinds) in novels "about corruption" may explain why *The Capital in Ruins* is seldom viewed as realistic or "about corruption," despite its dwelling on fallen sexual morality, which could be taken as an exposure of moral corruption. Many Chinese critics judge the novel as diverted from its social satire by the preponderance of romantic and sexual subplots in the text. For other critics, the primacy of sexual corruption in the novel overshadows the nonsexual corruption that seems to be seen as the proper focus of both realism and exposures of corruption.

(10) *Realistic fiction is instructive.* It may even teach facts, particularly about how the world works and the nature of society, or what might be called sociology. And it may teach moral lessons; like China's great traditional fiction, it may be didactic. This contradicts Auerbach's classic vision of Western realism, but implicit or explicit lessons are frequent in canonical novels of Western realism. In China, combative realism that speaks truth to power has even been combined, convincingly to many readers, with didactic Marxism, as it was by Hu Feng and Liu Binyan.

A provocative distinction might be that fiction about *corruption* belongs to "true Chinese realism" (in the Liu Binyan spirit), whereas "fiction about officialdom," with its psychological realism, fine but innocuous portraits of social manners, and "deep" (yet, by the same token, somehow rationalizing) explanations of corruption, is not. Anticorruption fiction, as a kind of realism, must take on the bureaucracy dramatically and combatively, pointing a finger of responsibility at real policy choices made by power holders. This fiction must be critical, willing to embrace fundamental doubts about the direction in which society is heading. And since its didacticism is more social than psychological, the life blood of the plot is "information" about how society really works: how money is skimmed, how the public and the state are kept in the dark, how guanxi circles are formed, how the money is hidden or spent. The proof that this is the realism that counts—that "hurts"—is that when this kind of realism is under bureaucratic attack, as it was in July 2002, the main weapon against it is the elevation discourse. This discourse maintains that novels about society should aim higher and delve deeper into psychology, into more abstract historical, social, and cultural factors, and be more nuanced and subtle—instead of combative, accusatory, and deeply invested in nitty-gritty details about concrete injustices (which might make the public anxious to turn the situation around).[42]

The mass appeal of this finger-pointing realism is no mystery. It accommodates social conflict and drama (often melodrama), featuring struggles between good and bad. It provides the pleasures not so much of the comedy of manners as of the technothriller, both in its "information quotient" about what goes on behind the scenes and in its plot, which tends toward unmasking conspiracies (guanxi circles).[43] And although it usually has an upbeat ending, it also unlocks social anger about injustice. It is more political than nuanced. The combativeness does finally suggest a link to Lu Xun—to the myth, more than the reality, of Lu Xun as a "fighter."

The above distillation of China's putatively "classic" tradition of realism ignores numerous internal contradictions within the discourse and the tradition's own inheritance. It is in some ways a narrowed vision of realism's techniques, philosophy, and content, and thus its potential—as became apparent in 1982, when Liu Xinwu and other creditable realist novelists defended realism against the challenge of modernism; the latter had been theoretically defended in a book by Gao Xingjian.[44] The enrichment of realistic writing by modernist and, by implication, "non-Chinese" techniques was ruled out.[45] Liu Xinwu considered "critical realism" to be China's mainstream style, though the more official line took pains to argue that China's mainstream (here meaning "correct") realism was *not* critical realism. Yet, because the CCP joined in attacking modernism, realism was once more identified with party oppression, as Xudong Zhang noted above, even though Liu Binyan, Liu Xinwu, and others had transformed it.

The reading public continues to prefer popular modes of writing, realism included, that attribute blame to concrete causes in prose that goes down relatively easily. This ratifies the divorcement of "high" intellectual and critical circles from the "masses" and their taste. As interest in realistic (here meaning no-holds-barred) writing about social themes increased in the late 1980s, primarily due to a revival of investigative journalism (reportage and documentary literature), realism and modernism became increasingly viewed as polar tendencies, with realism the favorite of the masses and modernism the cause of the critics.[46] Then, realism as politically critical as Liu Binyan's became taboo for a few years after the 1989 massacre, leaving the field of mass taste exclusively to popular fiction and nonfiction (notably, lifestyle magazines and stories about famous leaders).⁴⁷ Yet realism remained a bugaboo of the increasingly isolated progressive intellectuals, as modernist creativity for a time dried up quite as fully as critical realism.

Fantasy

Much of the popular appeal of China's anticorruption fiction naturally comes not just from its "information" or even apparent realism, but its indulgence of fantasy. We have mentioned sentiment and melodrama in the novels, luxury and decadence as eye candy and a source of the readers' or viewers' feelings of superiority (particularly in film adaptations), and the catharsis of the detective story plots—the rush one gets from seeing justice winning in the end, even if that achievement probably seems unrealistic to most readers when intellectually considered. An anticorruption novel may be enjoyed as a means of vicarious public protest. As critics of the movies point out, even when a film (or novel) has a formally unhappy ending, we typically leave the theater (or armchair) on an upbeat note, if not because of the hint of possible amelioration of the situation in the future, then because we realize that what we have just seen or read is fiction and has not actually happened to us (and, if the work is historical, the events have already happened). Furthermore, our personal narrative of reading the work, and usually the narrative of the work itself, occurs within a modern conceit of moral progress.⁴⁸

One can even see the anticorruption novel as a Chinese "mafia novel," or a more topical and partly inverted variation of the martial arts or chivalric novel. (This genre is often conceived as a Chinese form of the historical novel, though surely it is a fantasy variation in which heroes fight evil.) The chief protagonists in the anticorruption novel are evil, and yet they form an honor-bound clique of co-conspirators, a guanxi circle like a brotherhood. This circle has its own code of ethics, reflecting a counterculture that is nationwide and challenges current regime ethics. When society is thoroughly corrupt, "to rebel is justified." Rebellion might be called, by postmodern critics, a form of resistance. Moreover, the conspirators have secrets and techniques, not in using weapons but in moving around money, and these techniques (bribery, privatization, embezzlement, and development projects instead of swords, arrows, darts, and fists) have their generic attractions, as "information" for the reader. The schemes function as a sort of local color, even martial arts "magic," equivalent to jumping over rooftops in a swordfight. The plot of Chen Fang's *Municipal Crisis* turns on a quest for a coded book that will solve all mysteries of payoffs and other financial interrelations, reminiscent of the quest for a secret book of martial arts techniques that motivates many a plot in the other genre.[49]

The corrupt kingpins are larger than life, and so are their appetites and skills. The eschewal of marriage and male-female relations in the chivalric novels and earlier classics such as *Romance of the Three Kingdoms* and *Water Margin* are arguably as countercultural as the promiscuity of the corrupt 1990s municipal party bosses. Martial arts novels now are repositories of neotraditionalist pride—pride that China has a great past, whatever its content. Novels about newfangled forms of corruption are repositories of pride in China's modernization. Great is the current level of development, great enough for large sums to be skimmed off without even derailing future development. In Liu Ping's *Dossier on Smuggling*, the corrupt development in Xiamen is still development, a regional economic achievement.

Critics and China's Popular or Mass Culture

The status of China's turn-of-the-century fiction about corruption was and is problematic. Its quality did not improve over the years, and its status remained ambiguous and presumptively low even as its popularity rose. Lu Tianming's pathbreaking *Heaven Above* (1995) was originally read and reviewed as serious, realistic fiction and won a literary prize.[50] Zhang Ping's *Choice* (1997) won a Mao Dun prize in 2000 after the success of its film adaptation. Certain anticorruption novels were dignified with critical prefaces lauding them as masterpieces of realism. Even so, it was clear that many novels about corruption were written in a middlebrow style and appealed to a mass audience. Public focus on the novels' "bravery" because of their subject matter (the authors risked not just official retaliation, but also lawsuits by parties who might see themselves accused in the work)[51] was a very mixed blessing. Chinese critics like to classify even mainstream literary authors by the subject matter of their works, but in China as in the West, any hint that a work is classifiable lowers its social and critical status.[52]

Workaday criticism gathered steam in the daily press and on the Internet after 2000, as the genre began to prosper without further overt political interference.[53] Commentary ran the gamut from simple book promotion to a priori wariness of the novels' negativism and alleged appeals to low-grade tastes for sex and violence, a charge that is from time to time leveled at nearly all fiction about crime, detection, and the law, and which may have had its origins in a criticism of traditional Chinese fiction made by Liang Qichao a century earlier.⁵⁴ Some positive commentary recognized anticorruption fiction as a successor to the politically engaged "literature of the wounded" and praised the new works accordingly, as "delving into life [to make a political impact]."⁵⁵ When anticorruption fiction's "exposure" of wrongdoing became suspect as the political winds changed in 2002, minor critics and ideologists got the message and heaped criticism onto the fiction's many weak links.⁵⁶ However, the reviewing of individual novels continues, and the term "anticorruption fiction" remains in play. Some bookstores still have shelves implicitly dedicated to anticorruption fiction and nonfiction.

The reaction of China's elite cultural critics and intellectuals and their expatriate colleagues is more interesting. Most of them ignored the works.⁵⁷ (A major exception was Chen Sihe of Fudan University, to whom brief positive comments on the literature were attributed on the Internet.)⁵⁸ One can imagine why the elite critics, as guardians of cultural standards, and particularly the celebrities, many of whom view themselves as cultural radicals, may have pooh-poohed novels with corruption themes as middlebrow, melodramatic, too commercially successful, and too tepid in their social criticism. Some critics might have written off such fiction simply because Zhang Ping remained loyal to the Masses' Press,⁵⁹ Lu Tianming was a China Central Television producer, and Chen Fang wrote fast and must have had protection to keep out of jail.

The paradox is that, in the late 1990s, many of China's elite wanted to stand with China's workers, pensioners, and unemployed. They also expressed a "critical affirmation of mass culture."⁶⁰ Some were mesmerized by the opulence of China's new consumerist visual culture, a topic of research in the West's cultural studies. They delighted in fiction reflecting China's new levels of consumption and dynamic lifestyles.⁶¹ There were even intimations that a new avant-garde might be stimulated by consumerism.⁶² Such critics ignored more traditional social fiction.

China's socially critical intellectuals, steeped in Western and Marxist criticism, shared many of the critical views of mass culture held by the Frankfurt School, Antonio Gramsci, American critics such as Clement Greenberg and Harold Rosenberg, and Milan Kundera, who had savaged capitalist and communist mass culture as kitsch. It was a commonplace that mass culture was a manipulative engine mass-produced *for* the masses under the false premise that it was *of* or *by* the masses, or "folk." Already in the 1980s, China's elite critics, like their May Fourth predecessors, disdained the flood of new "popular" (*tongsu*) literature in their time. In truth, not all popular literature was commercially successful, as serious writers who went slumming by writing trashy novels for cash discovered;[63] government organs published and often had to subsidize popular fiction in the 1980s, on the grounds that the "masses" needed socially harmless material to fill their leisure time.[64] "Clean" popular fiction would divert them from sex, violence, and politics. In the 1990s, private commercial interests had acquired a bigger share of the pie, and sex and violence were everywhere. The bread and circuses strategy of the party and state still put China's authorities on the side of anything that "diverted" the masses, in both senses of the term.[65] Foreign capital was not so welcome in the making of "circuses" (entertainment), though it was a key ingredient in the CCP's profitable recipe for "bread" (manufactures). And there was already an exception to the intellectuals' disdain of popular fiction: the martial arts novels of Hong Kong writer Jin Yong, whose works were appreciated by many as a unique, national *Chinese* contribution to world popular literature.

The 1989 Beijing Massacre and subsequent harassment of intellectuals, the near desertification of new cultural production, and the endangerment of the reforms themselves rendered Chinese critics powerless and irrelevant. They found themselves outflanked by critics subservient to the party and state who, co-opting the cultural elite's radical Western theories of postmodernism and postcolonialism, mixed them with a potent brew of nationalism to justify the stable postmassacre status quo, question the good sense of the "divisive" democracy advocates and their foreign supporters, and get intellectuals back behind the party and government's agenda of unfettered economic growth and political aggrandizement, conceived as "the rise of China." Legions of expatriate PRC graduate students in North America, Europe, and Australia pursued the study of Chinese corruption in social science departments abroad, joined by a few writers at home such as He Qinglian (who, just a few steps ahead of the police, exiled herself to America in June 2001) and He Zengke, but the topic got little play in *Dushu* (Reading) and major PRC journals of literary and cultural criticism, or even international forums that published China's elite intellectuals' essays in Chinese (such as *Ershiyi shiji*, or *Twenty-first Century*). In this age of resurgent Chinese nationalism, some intellectuals may disdain not only fiction with corruption themes but the very problematic of corruption.[66]

The conversion in the 1990s, in principle, of China's elite intellectuals to a positive idea of popular culture (*tongsu wenhua*, as some called it) or mass culture (*dazhong wenhua*) was ironic and surely conflicted.[67] Western cultural studies encouraged sympathy for pop culture. So did national pride in China's new international prestige and economic ascendancy. Finding the avant-garde to have collapsed and realism old-fashioned, many intellectuals espoused, *faute de mieux*, China's vigorous new pop culture. Some critics went so far as to kiss elite culture goodbye.[68] Others were attracted to the "postpolitical" and "nonlogocentric" visual aspects of culture popular in the marketplace because they thought that these developments indicated China's liberation from the tyranny of politics.[69] Critic Dai Jinhua, known for her studies of Chinese advertisements and shopping centers as well as of movies, reminds us that much of China's popular reading matter in the 1990s was actually nonfiction and political—about international affairs, leaders, entertainers, and entrepreneurs.[70]

In revolutionary China, the terms "mass literature" and "mass culture" had in fact enjoyed positive, populist connotations from the time of Yu Dafu in the 1920s through the Mao era. The return to a positive idea of mass culture, at a time when all works still had to have the blessing of the CCP Central Propaganda Department to be sold or aired in China, even if they were produced by the capitalist West, opened a door to the revival of Maoism. A minority, including Liu Kang (who called mass culture *qunzhong wenyi*), did mythologize China's new 1990s mass culture as a non-Western, collectivist culture with a folk genius rooted in Maoism.[71] Most other elite critics preferred to see China's mass culture as part of a transnational, more-modern-than-modern cultural epiphany not centered in the West but fully conversant with and transcendent of the West. And yet, Liu's position in a way supported the old-style leftists (or conservatives) who in the 1997 debates on Chinese realism bemoaned the fact that Chinese literature had lost ground in society because it was no longer "close to the masses."[72] Liu Kang explained the patriotic basis of elite opinion. At a time when China's reputation for cultural production no longer equaled its reputation in the 1980s, or its current economic prowess, China's elite critics took comfort in the international prestige of films made by Chinese directors and what seemed to them a revival of China studies abroad.[73] Also important in the 1990s was pride in pan-Chinese culture (from Greater China).

One can thus postulate why fiction with themes of official corruption was not championed even by proponents of Chinese mass culture, despite anticorruption fiction's production within China, its potentially radical (even revolutionary) nature, its China-centered focus, its concern with familiar collective categories such as state workers, cadres, and intellectuals, and its concern for China's losers in the economic transformation. (1) Fiction about corruption is political. Some critics may avoid the topic of corruption out of caution, whereas others feel antipathy toward politics because of where it has led China in the past and out of a sense of personal exclusion from political decision making. Similarly, cultural radicals in China generally are immune to calls for revolution, which to them signify China's twentieth-century past. (2) The concept of corruption implies a state of social health before the corruption took place, a premise that radical critics may be unwilling to concede. (3) Fiction about corruption offends Chinese nationalism by focusing on the dark side of China's economic miracle and by taking an implicitly pessimistic view of the future.[74] Media productions of corruption are to that extent a negative mirror image of the popular soaps about Chinese emperors of the High Qing, when Chinese power was at its height.[75] Anticorruption fiction is typically set amid the decaying, old-fashioned state-owned economy. When it is set amid vibrant commercial enterprises (created by smuggling, for instance), the novels make those activities appear phony. Anticorruption fiction is not filled with the names of the era's pop stars or consumerist fads of young people. (4) Anticorruption fiction does not fit the postmodern theory that China's mass culture is a product of the postsocialist market or of a globalizing postmodern trend linked to international cutting-edge culture and technology. Although it is commercially viable, the fiction's popularity comes from realism's old "sacred mission" of social comment and denunciation.[76] Realism, particularly realism with a clear, directional narrative that does not problematize its own conclusions, is not fashionable among critics or literary scholars in the West. Further, Chinese anticorruption fiction does not have an obvious counterpart in the West,[77] and the Chinese works are unknown in the West. Many Chinese artistic circles regard realism not just as old-fashioned, but crypto-socialist. (6) Withal, realistic and popular anticorruption fiction suggests that China is not being transformed as fast as many might hope. The fiction uses old socialist and presocialist kinds of realism to attack aspects of China that are not postsocialist, postmodern, postcolonial, or postpolitical. And the fiction's champions are mostly outside of China's cultural elite and its younger, trendsetting generations. (7) The fact that "corruption" and "anticorruption," too, remain state discourses may in time cause intellectual elites to reject even these terms, as elites already have turned away from the terms "realism" and even "intellectual."[78]

However, even though the intellectual stronghold of culture with anticorruption themes is fiction, even serious fiction, it is distributed by new media. All of the novels discussed at length in this book have been posted in their entirety on the Internet. There are websites devoted specifically to corruption, some borrowing graphic designs from the novel *Heaven's Wrath*. Corruption is a topic of conversation in Chinese chat rooms. And the Chinese people are most familiar with the narratives about corruption through television series based on the novels, though TV productions have greatly watered down the discourse, as viewers are quick to point out.[79]

One part of the postmodern ethos that fiction about corruption in the old socialist and bureaucratic sectors did not fit was the critics' ambivalent vision of the new China as consumerist. Although that concept may have come to Chinese critics from theorists such as Jean Baudrillard, Fredric Jameson, and Mike Featherstone, to stress the impact of consumerism is chiefly to emphasize how fast China has moved from an economy of scarcity to one of plentitude—for the fortunate—and how seldom materialist values (in the colloquial, non-Marxist sense) are countered by ideologies and religion, now that faith in communism is largely dead. Even more suddenly than in the "age of realism," when Europe moved from aristocratic to mercantile values, the cash nexus and property of all kinds have emerged in China as determinants of social relations.[80] State propaganda has adopted techniques of commercial advertising and uses the pursuit of consumer goods to divert citizens from the pursuit of political power outside the party. China does appear more consumerist than postsocialist.[81] But critics' denunciations of Chinese consumerism are seldom put in global comparative terms.[82] Anticorruption novels and media productions show the masses more "realistically" than do portraits of them as consumers: as producers for consumers abroad, as employees spending much of their lives in China's factories, and as prodigious savers of their scarce wages. The CCP encourages getting rich, but spending for its own sake contradicts "socialist spiritual civilization," the CCP's last pretense that it is entitled to monopoly power because of its superior morality. The party is aware that a continued high rate of citizen savings is essential for the economy, the welfare system, state investment, and the solvency of the banking system. As China's more audacious anticorruption novels remind us, even sybaritic corrupt officials save much of their pelf—in foreign bank accounts and real estate investments—in preparation for retirement and/or emigration before or after the fall of communism. Balzac and Dickens knew that pursuit of money could be an end in itself, regardless of what it could buy. International corporate logos, advertisements, and entertainment products are everywhere in broadcasting and in most of the visual fields that confront urbanized Chinese, but so are they also in Abidjan and Dhaka. A country's elite can enjoy postmodernity before its society is postindustrial.

Anticorruption novels remind readers that consumer goods and services within the vast public sector, whether obtained as perks of office or through graft—notably cars, housing, and the service personnel to operate and maintain them—are old socialist markers of status and power. The novels detail each bureaucrat's vehicular perquisites as carefully as his facial expressions and his manners. Relative financial status or consumer savvy is not the chief reason why it matters whether a cadre is driven in a Mercedes-Benz, Audi, or Volkswagen Santana: a cadre's wheels are the chief metonym of his official rank. In feel-good anticorruption movies, consumption by the bureaucrats functions as eye candy and indicates modernization—the fact that China's officials are not "backward." Conspicuous consumption by the upper classes has since ancient times been required by Chinese society, as an emblem of rank and the prestige of the imperium. Peter Brooks tells us that attention to accumulated "things" is the sine qua non of the realistic novel.[83] That characteristic of the novel, in the age of Balzac and Dickens, came before postmodern consumerism. China's anticorruption novels likewise belong to an age not yet beholden to full-throttle consumerism.

Most fiction about corruption and officialdom does not, then, fit the high theorists' idea of China as postsocialist, postpolitical, or postbureaucratic. In a nationalistic environment still relatively uneasy with markets, self-support in the arts, lowbrow taste, and consumer choice, particularly as a form of power, China's elite critics have been quick to blame the faults of Chinese culture on the market and even international capital instead of domestic policies.[84] This has led Jing Wang to raise "the state question in Chinese popular cultural studies" in reaction.[85] China's anticorruption novels clearly uphold Wang's view that political power remains as important as money power, which is itself often linked to political privilege. But beyond the "state question" lies a "party question."[86] Many anticorruption novels call for a strong state, but one that is free of the hegemony of the Communist Party. That the party's ideological authority, social control, and internal discipline have grown weak simply makes its oppression more unbearable.

In an environment that celebrates mass culture, fault could, perhaps, be found with anticorruption novels for *not* being mass culture or purely nonofficial culture (some are published by the Masses' Press). The novels might instead be categorized as failed realism or average melodrama. Each novel is a different case; its faults do not inhere in its nature as popular or mass fiction, realistic fiction, "post" or inadequately "post" this or that, or its commercial viability. Will the novels still be widely read fifty years from now? Perhaps not. The same may be true of works by Chi Li, Jia Ping'ao, Tie Ning, Shi Tiesheng, Zhang Jie, and even Wang Meng, Wang Anyi, and Gao Xingjian, not to mention Wang Shuo, Weihui, and the (once) "later-born" lifestyle authors. Will Grisham, Turow, Ludlum, Crichton, and Clancy be read fifty years from now, or Louis Auchincloss and Tom Wolfe? Perhaps as historical documents revealing popular thinking about the Cold War, civil rights struggles, and urban mores, as Ian Fleming, Harper Lee, and Gay Talese are already. If so, their Chinese counterparts can hope at least for that.

8

Conclusion: The Chinese Discourse of Corruption—and Its Limits

China's major novels with corruption themes explore diverse forms and conceptions of corruption. What does it all add up to? Hundreds of social science books and articles have already theorized about global and regional corruption as well as corruption in developing countries, the postcommunist world, and particular nations, China prominently among them. Facing the ubiquity of corruption as a subject in public discourse and criminal codes, these treatises still find it necessary to define and reconceptualize corruption before explaining how it arises and its impact. Such analyses applied to China have been variously labeled institutional, rationalist, socio-cultural, functionalist, moralist-normative, revisionist, Marxist, or Weberian, alternatively emphasizing bureaucratic, market, or extra-market factors.[1] Some approaches attribute the enormous scale of corruption to the post-Mao reforms and marketization. Others stress inherited weaknesses from the old socialist political system that imposed the reforms, which included quick privatization of large chunks of the economy.[2] Such views are not wholly in contradiction.[3] Our novelists blame both untrammeled money and unregulated power, though they prefer to detail how power commands money rather than vice versa.

Social science approaches generally detail behaviors considered corrupt, the norms (laws, rules, or simply expectations) these behaviors defy, and how and why this defiance persists. This book has instead assumed from the start that in both daily parlance and literary performance, "corruption" refers not just to particular codifiable transgressions, but also to broad, even metaphoric perceived deficiencies of character, society, and history.[4] This is so despite the novels' nineteenth-century-style "realistic," or in other instances sensationalist, attention to detailing symptoms of corruption instead of theorizing about its causes and cures. Corruption at such levels of artistic (and popular) abstraction (and vagueness) can either reinforce or create static interference with the equally abstract constructs of social theorists, moralists, and ideologists. I believe the novels analyzed confirm that corruption at the highest level is a pessimistic discourse of social and moral change that can be trained on diverse unsettling social phenomena, both "capitalist" and remnant "socialist." Because individual transgressions fit a holistic view of progressive decay and demise, the novels and public discourse generally have little time for the idea that breaking particular rules might be good in the short run or aid "system integration"[5] and renewal through the circumvention of bottlenecks in socialist production, as the computer company manager argues in *Heaven's Wrath*. Nor are the novelists or the public intrigued by the Tammany Hall preference for "honest" over "dishonest" graft—ensuring that services are fully rendered for bribes duly paid (guanxi by another name)—although, as noted in the previous chapter, when reading in a fantasy mode, aficionados may envision an idealized, collective honor among thieves.[6] Corruption is an evil in itself. Unfairness, injustice, and the slowing of economic growth may be immanent within corruption, but corruption is not to be condemned simply because of its consequences. The novelists are uniformly incensed by unjust bureaucratic power and the antisocial exercise of it. It seems quite possible that the novels represent a revolt against bureaucratic authority as such. And with it comes a *ressentiment* about the ethos of modern times.

Chinese ideas of corruption are not only abstract, but also greatly in flux. It is not just that new institutions and the deterioration of old ones give cause for mourning a previous life and its standards. The old standards, too, often appear now as having been bankrupt or immoral from the start—and, in their persistence, more corrosive than ever, because standards *have* changed. Cultural differences between China and the West may have influenced certain mismatches between legal and moral modes of identifying corruption, but it is not only China that conflates institutional corruption and personal moral corruption. I suspect that regulation and law enforcement sometimes seem incongruent, in the absence of compensating symbolic syntheses, with citizens' desires for a stable and at the same time higher, more spiritual order and peace. China is only now reengaging with the search for a "higher" peace, the one made in "Heaven" that is invoked in the book titles.

This chapter will focus on how Chinese thinking about law, privilege, property rights, and morality affects ideas of corruption. But first, let us further examine change and other inconsistencies in the Chinese discourse.

Change and Variation in the Contemporary Chinese Discourse of Corruption

Change in Chinese concepts of corruption is reflected in the language. Chinese newspapers and magazines in the 1980s often spoke of corruption with terms such as *touji daoba* (profiteering; buying low and selling high), *guandao* (official turnaround; officials acquiring goods by quota at low state prices and reselling them for a profit at market prices, thanks to the two-tier price system of the time), and *bu zheng zhi feng* (unhealthy "winds," or tendencies, usually among cadres, referring to improper lifestyles and command relations). These China-specific terms sound as modern as the Maoist movement that spawned them, and yet also archaic, now that Maoist ideology is dead. The novels seldom invoke these terms.[7] The two-price system is history, the term "winds" recalls unsuccessful Maoist campaigns to keep omni-responsible cadres in line through exhortation, and buying low and selling high is now generally deemed good, under market principles.

The old Mandarin word *tanwu* and its root in classical Chinese, *tan*, both often translated into English as "corruption," were used in the Mao era and still are today. In law cases, *tanwu* carries narrow and technical inferences of economic crime such as bribery or misappropriation of property by public servants and so is more often rendered as "graft" or "embezzlement."[8] The word now has a legalistic ring. The first criminal code of the People's Republic of China (PRC), passed in 1979 and in effect from 1980 to 1996, named *tanwu* (in the official English translation rendered "corruption") as a crime.[9] However, the code took *tanwu* to be an offense as self-evident as robbery or murder.[10] It was in the 1996 revision, which took effect in 1997, that "crimes of graft and bribery" (*tanwu huilu zui*) were more specifically defined. The person taking the bribe (but not the bribe giver) must be a government worker or a manager of public property to be charged under that law,[11] though the PRC has recognized and punished bribery by private businesspersons in mass campaigns since the 1950s. The Chinese were aware of corruption in private charitable foundations even in imperial times.[12] Even so, no laws yet existed in the 1980s against embezzlement within privately owned firms. From a socialist point of view, one private interest's cheating another is unimportant compared to a private or "lesser public" interest cheating the state—"the people." The idea of the *state*'s being guilty of cheating private economic interests is still a difficult concept, almost a contradiction in terms. Such corruption is not the concern of Chinese novels, either.

The novels analyzed in this book, all written well after the 1980s, prefer the broad term *fubai* for corruption. *Fubai* encompasses virtually every technical and figurative meaning of corruption imaginable. Some scholars postulate that narrower Mao-era terms such as bribery (*shouhui*; literally, "receiving a bribe"), graft (*tanwu*), and privileges (*tequan*) have in the course of time been supplanted by the broader concept of *fubai* because of weakening official ethics in wake of the reforms.[13] Certainly the new linguistic usage has followed a rise in living standards and changes in business ethics in the transition to a market economy, which has witnessed new forms of grand corruption in the privatization or local seizure of enterprises, resources, and real estate.

Alternatively, however, the prevalence of *fubai* and other words beginning with the classical morpheme *fu* (to decay, to rot, rotten, corrupt, evil, worthless) can be seen as the return of very old terminology that allows abstract conceptual linkages to precommunist history and morality. *Fubai* (corrupt, rotten, putrid, decayed, to decay, to decompose) is like the English "corruption" (as in translations of the biblical Hebrew and Greek) in its retention of both biological and more figurative social applications. Popular near-equivalents of *fubai* also favored by the Chinese novelists include *fuhua* (degenerate, corrupt, dissolute, depraved, to rot), *fushi* (to corrupt, corrode, wear out), *fulan* (to rot, to decay, decomposed, corrupt, spoiled [as of fish]), and *fuxiu* (to decay [as wood], decadent, putrid, worthless [as a person]). Some observers detect nuances in the degree of rottenness.[14] The second morpheme in the dominant word *fubai*, namely *bai* (to defeat or be defeated, to decline, to go down, to spoil or be spoiled, to corrupt or be corrupted), forms other words important to the novelists and social critics: *baihuai* (rotten, to corrupt, ruin), *bailuo* (to decline in wealth and/or prestige), and *bailei* (*noun*: scum, "degenerates," including corrupt officials). The metaphoric senses of these notions of corruption are inescapable. The concept, like the phenomenon it names, tends to spread.

Rapid market reform may have brought vaster and ever more apocalyptic views of the destruction of society and social values to China, but the communist past is equally subject to reevaluation. Consider the revival of the word *guan* (official). Until the late 1970s, urban and politically well-placed Chinese seldom used the term *guan* in reference to Communist Party and government power holders.[15] They were *ganbu* (cadres). The term "official" was reserved for bureaucrats under precommunist regimes. However, "official" as a word for current power holders and their practices rapidly gained currency in the early 1980s, as in the usage *guandao* and indeed *guanchang xiaoshuo* (fiction about officialdom). Today, the term *guan* is ubiquitous. Even power holders who are not employed by the state are sometimes called officials. They are viewed as part of a unitary system of power. That inference is no longer a positive one.

Chinese public discourse, including discourse about corruption, encompasses both official and nonofficial discourses, which can be mutually reinforcing or set up interference patterns in communication. Official discourse is in principle unitary. It is a "line" emanating from the Chinese Communist Party (CCP) and its Central Propaganda Department, which is still at pains to enforce a unified and internally consistent language and viewpoint regarding actual cases and theoretical concepts of corruption in the news, literature, and Internet chat rooms. The party line also tends to maintain the pretense that it has been consistent over time. Contradictory conceptions of corruption in previous eras (attributing it to class stance, for instance) are often erased.

Besides the mass media, a prime shaper of the official discourse of corruption is anticorruption campaigns. Yet, the word on the street—call it Chinese "urban legend"—maintains, as do corrupt officials in *Heaven's Wrath*, that anticorruption campaigns are not really about fighting corruption, but about settling scores with rival political factions. Often it is the corrupt who strike, preemptively, at the uncorrupted, to protect a cozy status quo.[16] This implies that China's "politics-in-command" socialist values are poisoned at the root. The negative view of clean-ups began no later than the PRC's first great anticorruption movement, the Three Antis Campaign of 1951, in which regular courts, procurators, and even Communist Party disciplinary inspection commissions gave way to special austerity inspection commissions. They found up to 40 percent of cadres guilty at some levels and in some places, since there were no nationwide standards.[17] Still today, "strike hard" campaigns mete out summary justice.[18] Moreover, attribution of sex crimes to an offender sometimes reflects the state's decision to prosecute a minor infraction in place of the "real" political offense (a political variation on, say, convicting Al Capone for tax evasion). Conversely, public figures who have enriched themselves and yet also done good things for the locals may be forgiven the sins of their corruption,[19] particularly if they are relentlessly pursued by law enforcement from outside the region. Chen Xitong and Lai Changxing, the antiheroes of anticorruption novels analyzed in chapters 3 and 6, are prime examples. After all the official exposés, after all the novels that dished "real" dirt, numerous citizens of Beijing and Xiamen still think of these men as heroes who were prosecuted because of envy. Even *Heaven's Wrath* can lend support to such sentiments, insofar as it intimates that Chen Xitong was prosecuted because he was too powerful, not because he committed crimes. Yet gathering absolute power, even if it is delegated by the party according to correct procedures, is now generally recognized as corruption. It violates the pretense of communist democracy as well as global conceptions of democracy and fairness.

Given its inherently diverse and inchoate nature and the inadequacies of public opinion polling in China, nonofficial discourse is harder to grasp, but it may be sought in the divergences between official discourse and the public discourse as represented in anticorruption novels and other modes of public discourse. The idea of nonofficial discourse need not articulate a "Western, liberal, utopian vision."[20] Nonofficial discourse may reflect ancient Chinese predilections opposing tyranny, bureaucratism, and "feudalism" that are more ancient than the discourse of citizen rights in Roman law. In recent decades there has even been a persistent Chinese regionalist refrain criticizing "North China Plain" authoritarianism. To be sure, official discourse, in the form of documents and the writings of officials, is practically the only surviving historical record. The discourse of corruption in anticorruption novels today is still profoundly indebted to the language and concepts of official discourse. But the "official" is a paradoxical concept by modern standards. The nation's most important "public" or official business is transacted in secret, away from the eyes of "the masses," who lack *zhiqingquan* (the need to know; indeed, literally, "the right to know"). The result of this secrecy, besides making bureaucratic thrillers easy to write, is that many acts by the party are subject to interpretation or misinterpretation as self-interested by the public. In the past, the covert nature of party machinations was overshadowed by its pervasive public persona as moral educator and defender against class enemies. Much of the party's official business now is developing profit-making firms, with plans as tightly held as in capitalist societies' corporate boardrooms. Meanwhile, large-scale banqueting and gift giving are done openly as never before (China's new wealth makes lavishness more feasible than ever), which seems to bespeak end-game corruption, in which the special privileges of the elite no longer need the protection of darkness.

The novels analyzed here diverge from official discourse because they are willing to imagine corruption as a problem of system, not of a few bad officials. Because the novels see bad officials as a major social force, they seldom mimic official discourse by calling these officials *fubai fenzi* (corrupt elements), as if they were a minor phenomenon. The Mandate of Heaven is therefore in play. As corruption spreads down from the top, the whole of officialdom could become corrupt if it is not already, necessitating regime change. The traditional alternative to regime change in ancient official discourse is the restoration of good political rule, as in the Tang dynasty and the Tongzhi Restoration of the Qing. Jean-Louis Rocca has argued that in life, factory worker protests are so similar to each other and likely to end in a state-negotiated solution that they may be likened to rituals that acknowledge and thus affirm the role of the state as social arbiter.[21] If that is so, China's anticorruption novels, in their depictions of urban protests as the outcome of corruption, go a step further. The novels depict the party and state's deathly fear that protest might spread uncontrollably, leading to social disorder and the fall of Chinese and in effect global communism. Whether the masses truly desire this or fear it is moot, but within the safety of fiction they can enjoy the prospect of regime change and imagine the best possible outcome.

Law, Policy, Discipline, and the Social Compact

Evidence abounds that Chinese citizens are becoming more legally conscious in courtrooms, police stations, and lawyers' offices, in the media, on the street, and even on the farm.[22] The major anticorruption novels analyzed in this book, however, are not so concerned with law and legal institutions.[23] These works are strong in *stories* that have legal implications,[24] and they unfold mostly in cities, whose bureaucratic offices, banks, and enterprises are governed by countless thought-out rules, procedures, and "discipline," not just the trust and common understanding of some private-sector business deals in China. The novels also strive to inform the reader with nitty-gritty details, but not about laws and legal procedures. Rather, typical concerns are: How do the corrupt schemes work? How do the players know whom to bribe, and the going rate? How do they make the drop? How do they get away with it? Moreover, in these novels professionals of the criminal justice system play backseat roles to heroic CCP civilian generalists. Any police or procuratorial detective who solves a crime is bound to be just a stereotype from the Sherlock Holmes or police procedural tradition. The detective's rank is low, allowing liberties within the pretense of realism; it is plausible that such a player might be a woman, for instance. Conversely, a formula detective is generally "a hero without models"[25] in life. The more convincing novels are those in which larger-than-life mayors and party secretaries direct investigations. Below I will account for this dearth of legal consciousness in envisioning corruption and even the fight against it by referring to the breadth of the corruption discourse itself, its peculiar dual nature in the Chinese case because of CCP rule, and the novels' interest in manifestations of corruption as threats to organically conceived social health.

The legalistic discourse of corruption, or that which takes corruption to be a punishable offense or behavior rather than a larger condition, syndrome, or gestalt, overlaps at least four other discourses, only one of which is really "legal." Foremost in the West and in international organizations that must use "objective" criteria is *legal discourse* proper, the discourse of law breaking. Corruption is everywhere epitomized by crimes of bribery, peculation, and disallowed perquisites,[26] though novelists and the public may also see those as symptoms of greater corruption at the macro level. Most crimes of corruption in China are economic crimes, investigated by the procuracy rather than the police. However, in China above all, corruption is also still a part of *political discourse*, even apart from the aforementioned "urban legend." Further, many actions that may be legal are still deemed corrupt, so the discourse of corruption overlaps *moral discourse*. The importance of an official's acquisition of mistresses in branding him as corrupt furthers the idea of corruption as an accumulation not just of unmatchable money but also of unstoppable power. And yet corruption, even as a group of tangible offenses, may be part of a still broader *discourse of social hygiene* about damage to an ethos or state of social-moral well-being. Generally this has to do with transgressions against social equity, propriety (manners), and decorum.[27]

If Chinese (or Americans) were thought to be headed toward universal addictions or greed (the latter is a trend alleged to be winning out in the PRC by many of its citizens), this might be conceived as corruption, though few of the perceived defects, not even selfishness, might be called "immoral" when considered as isolated acts, nor need they be illegal. General unfairness of social, economic, and judicial outcomes, when regarded as a deterioration of a past equilibrium, may be regarded as evidence of corruption. Subservience of judges to CCP mandates may one day be deemed "judicial corruption," as court unaccountability is already. The discourse of corruption at its most abstract can be an organic, quasi-biological, or teleological discourse of deformation, malady, rot, and finally death.[28] Yet there seems to be less consensus in China about what is "unhealthy" than what is immoral. The nature of the good society is not something people agree on yet. The consensus is simply that China is sick, particularly in its official realm. Globalization and legalization of Chinese norms (as under the WTO) may well shrink the purview of corruption to a sphere of specific, if numerous, outlawed acts. Lapses in lifestyle, party and bureaucratic ethos, and "socialist spiritual civilization"—selfishness and dissoluteness—may fall below the radar screen of

China's trading partners and international organizations, but not necessarily that of the Chinese themselves. To the Chinese Communist Party and state, social protest itself must appear very much like corruption, as a *contagion*.[29] But so, too, does unhealthy concentration of power appear to be a spreading disease, in both official and nonofficial discourse as we have seen it in the novels. Let us pursue the limits of these discourses further, from the legal to the hygienic.

A major pattern of interference in the Chinese discourse of law breaking is the dual structure of law. The state has laws, but party discipline (obedience to the leadership) and policies take precedence over laws.[30] In the following exchange from *Heaven's Wrath*, the words of the corrupt Jiao Pengyuan may seem legally indefensible to us, but they evidently have much persuasive power within the CCP. The exemplary official whom he reproves is another party secretary, who presumably shares Jiao's view of the proper role of the CCP and policy.

> [Fang:] "We will handle these problems according to the legal process."
> Secretary Jiao Pengyuan slammed his cup down on the table. "Comrade Fang Hao, do not forget that there is a still higher principle: I ask you, which takes precedence, the party or the law? Is the party above the law, or the law above the party? Laws are laid down by the party. The one and only fundamental principle is that the party leads all." (375–76)

Secretary Fang, the "good guy," may actually disagree, but he (and the author?) dare not refute Peng's logic. Fang can only return the conversation to the matter at hand, which is Secretary Jiao's insistence that the arrest of Jiao's private secretary, Shen Shi, be rescinded. Fang Hao treats that matter, too, as political, not legal. He will demand a collective decision from the party standing committee first. He is following party procedure, but that is different from following the law that governs all citizens.

Rule of law is nevertheless an obvious possible solution to corruption and abuse of power, and it is dimly advocated by name in these novels, as by Fang Hao in the opening sentence cited above. *Dossier on Smuggling* faces the question directly. It poses rule of law as the ultimate solution, but only to be realized a few years in the future, because it seems simply impossible to achieve now.

Reflecting the divided nature of the legal process in China so clearly visible in the novels is the fact that in most corruption investigations, the uniformed agents of the procuracy are joined by members of the civilian Central Disciplinary Inspection Commission of the CCP. Being of the party, the commission is outside and above the state, though it has local branches parallel to the state's triumvirate of police departments, procuratorates, and courts, which are themselves subordinate to the unitary leadership of the CCP committee at their level (province, city, county).[31] China also has a supervisory system in the state apparatus, under a Ministry of Supervision, that investigates economic crimes such as theft, waste, and smuggling, which are outside the more narrowly defined crimes of bribery, graft, and misappropriation, which belong to the jurisdiction of the procuracy.[32] Further confusing the public is the fact that when corrupt officials are under pressure to clean up their act, so usually are nightclubs, pornographers, and even pets, which are for the police to deal with, often without recourse to the legal system.[33] The various kinds of crackdowns are initiated by the same top civilian CCP officials in Beijing, so they come and go together in waves.[34]

At any rate, legal discourse is the professional realm of cadres and, more recently, lawyers. None of the institutions or social groups associated with the law is prestigious yet, not even socialist judges, and certainly not the police. At times, corruption can seem to be simply the display of a bad attitude. This is so even in official discourse, and particularly in a frenzied anticorruption campaign that expedites legal procedures and depicts the accused as morally degenerate (as in the case of Chen Xitong in life). To the extent that corruption or *tanwu* becomes a legal concept, it may well lose its force in a nation in which citizens often claim that they are not under the rule of law and that "real" official corruption (*fubai* or *tanwu*) is seldom prosecuted. They mean that the law itself, or the judicial system that enforces it, is corrupt—diverted from its original impartiality, so that it serves the selfish interests of the powerful.

Besides a unitary code or a common law, another presumed prerequisite of the rule of law is "thinking in cases." The idea of cases is ancient in China, and the habit of thinking in cases has long been present in medical as well as legal practice, though Chinese law has always privileged rule-based reasoning from legal codes rather than case-based reasoning from precedents, as in Anglo-Saxon law.[35] Popular, more or less nonfiction "casebooks" flourish in China today. However, they are often casebooks of crime, not law. They illustrate the ingenuity of the criminals.[36]

Yet, anticorruption fiction is a moral literature focusing on sin, with few signs of legal reasoning. *Heaven's Wrath* and its enlargement ought to be the prime example of thinking in legal cases, because it is a collection of diverse instances of malfeasance in Beijing under Chen Xitong—originally written, to be sure, without benefit of published details about the prosecution of actual crimes, and even in the revision without much guidance from the highly selective details publicly aired from Chen's secret prosecution. But the cases as presented by Chen Fang do not have clear boundaries; it was I who divided them into the discrete "Wucai Plaza Affair," "pyramid scheme," "case of the missing 100 million," and so forth. *Heaven's Wrath* is a study not of discrete violations of rules, but of the all-around malevolence of a party boss, his private secretaries, and particularly his ne'er-do-well son, including all their sexual infidelities and betrayals of friends and comrades. In its legal stance, the nonofficial corruption discourse of the novel varies little from the official discourse implicit in the offense of "moral degeneracy" for which Chen Xitong was prosecuted in life.

Morality, I have argued elsewhere, is a "higher" discourse than the discourse of law, in the West and in China.[37] It is interesting that in China's nonofficial discourse of corruption, and in official discourse, too, which often promotes "rule of law" as a utilitarian measure to promote social order and economic growth, violations of law are still often sublimated into the more "important" question of their moral impact on society.

The party is concerned with corruption as a violation of its discipline (obedience; political morality) or the "Organizational concept" (*zuzhi guannian*), as *Choice* and *National Portrait* put it, rather than as rule breaking per se. In the form of insubordination, factionalism, and ultimately rebellion, indiscipline threatens the existence of party rule. Simply doing other than what higher leadership wishes in appointing personnel, whether or not it is motivated by corruption, nepotism, or factionalism, is paradigmatic of disobedience in Chen Fang's depictions of party meetings in *Municipal Crisis*. Corruption and forms of deviance can occur amid great respect for procedure in the form of conducting the proper meetings and duly receiving directives from higher up. Ironic portraits of corrupt high officials' diligence in maintaining a facade of collective decision making to legitimate their foul deeds is a triumph of anticorruption works as realistic novels of manners. The major novels discussed in this book, consciously or unconsciously assimilating a Communist Party viewpoint, still tend to "escalate" cadres' economic crimes into matters of disobedience—how dare the lower levels of governance endanger the regime's relationship with the masses—for that is a greater offense than breaking rules as such. Thus the novels also suggest the theory of the Mandate of Heaven—another political and moral discourse, not a legal one.

As Leslie Holmes has observed of postcommunist Eastern Europe, official anticorruption discourse has dual purposes and audiences. The discourses are more moral and organizational than legal. Anticorruption is aimed at "educating" the masses (the general populace outside the Communist Party) and disciplining the party and state bureaucracy's own middle cadres. Some paradoxes flow from this. Being the sovereign's (the Communist Party Politburo Standing Committee's) instrument of disciplining its own privileged bureaucratic elite, the contemporary official discourse of (anti-)corruption is like the legal code in imperial China, whose statutes were preoccupied with crimes that could only be committed by bureaucrats. But the modern tool of prosecuting corruption is quite unlike penal law in imperial China and the modern law of the People's Republic. Such laws appeared and appear mostly aimed at regulating common imperial subjects and the masses, respectively. The examination elite and CCP members, respectively, in theory (though not always in practice) were and are a privileged class above penal punishments. CCP members tend to be judged and punished by civilian disciplinary inspection commissions, not the courts, unless their infractions are severe. When they mismanage public assets, they are brought down with anticorruption campaigns in high-profile, educative circumstances, not just by trials, which are sheltered from public scrutiny. And yet, given the inadequacy of discipline and regulation to rein in outrageous behavior in China's new market economy (e.g., the lack of sophisticated bankruptcy and foreclosure procedures to prevent the stripping of assets from dying enterprises), criminal prosecution may be the only resort left for reckoning with "the bad guys." The result is spectacular prosecutions and, reflecting them, novels full of awful "crimes"—even in the absence of much legal consciousness in either venue. Legal punishment remains, as of old, distinguished by its severity, as a tool of organizational and moral regulation of last resort.

Is corruption then not so much a generally shared *moral discourse*, as simply a political one? Political discourse changes. In Mao's day, corruption indicated problems of class stance and disobedience to political orientations that are now obsolete.[38] The idea of wrongdoing as a manifestation of class stance and wrong political choices was supposed to be replaced, under the reforms of Deng Xiaoping and Jiang Zemin, by the idea of wrongdoing as a matter of law and "socialist spiritual civilization." Political correctness is seen by China's rulers today, more than ever, as a moral choice in favor of socialist spiritual civilization.

Yet, Chinese morality today is uncodified, as much in flux as the law. It is mostly the party that sees moral significance in all its policies. For most people, extra-legal "corruption" in official discourse, even as conceived at the micro-level as individual indiscretions, need not always be as serious as political-moral offenses. That goes also for overconsumption, gambling, and sex outside of marriage. Oddly, such activities are still punishable, not under the criminal code or local laws and regulations, but at the discretion of the police and other political-legal authorities. The offender is given the administrative punishment of reeducation through labor instead of being put through the court system.

Hence the importance in nonofficial discourse of a view of corruption as something broader than immorality itself: a fundamental decay of the social compact, tending ineluctably toward the fall of the system, if not apocalypse. This is the quasi-biological, hygienic vision of corruption, still embodied in the selfish transgressions of individuals. The novels are interested in the pattern of contagion. Corruption spreads horizontally and also vertically, to younger generations. Chinese officials fear the fall of the system even more than the novelists, but they dare not point out omens of it.

The organizing concept for unhealthy lateral contagion is corrupt guanxi, a web of unhealthy human associations and actions that cannot risk exposure to the light of day. Tiger Chen of *Heaven's Wrath* puts it well even as he speaks of "cases" in N city: "This is a great spider web: old cases and new cases are all intricately linked together. At present, we have not even ripped open a corner of this great web" (124). This echoes the old Chinese detective story formulation of "cases within cases" (*an zhong an*), and it is as in the original Lu Tianming formula. In Lu's *Heaven Above*, all malfeasance, including crimes and simple mistakes of judgment in the use of public funds, originate in a great power web of Tians that originated in a mountain county whose scions came to power in the communist revolution. Likewise, corruption in *Choice* appears organized according to concepts that come from business school rather than law school: they are encompassed in a flow chart, that of the Zhongyang Group and its multifarious subsidiaries. Whosoever has taken a bribe or a job they did not deserve, including the mayor's wife and relatives, took it from Zhongyang. In *National Portrait*, influence peddling is so ingrained in bureaucratic culture that there is not even any clear narrative stance on what might be corruption, much less a breach of the law and ethics. The novel appears to be an "objective" report on business as usual. *Dossier on Smuggling*, written by a uniformed customs officer, gets anticorruption discourse back on a legal track by focusing on discrete cases rather than webs, but its real focus is social relations: cops and robbers and the love interests of both.

The vertical dimension is the spread of corruption to younger generations, the "princelings." Orient Jiao is more evil than his father, on whose power his own relies. He has the will and the means to further corrupt his own father. This, perhaps unconsciously, mimics official discourse when the latter intimates that lower-level cadres can cause corruption, or at least its ill effects, to spread upward to the originally innocent top leadership, as in the film *Fatal Decision*, whose basic-level Gang of Four initiated the corruption of deputy provincial CCP secretary Yan Zhen. The spectacle of Orient Jiao the son corrupting Jiao Pengyuan the father in *Heaven's Wrath* is an extraordinary inversion of filial piety. It also inverts the traditional Chinese discourse of immorality spreading down from the top, and the equally hierarchical Mandate of Heaven discourse itself, into a more fully biological discourse of contagion, in which corruption can spread in any direction: up, down, or laterally. In *Fatal Decision*, Yan Zhen's stepson is likewise more evil than his stepfather, plotting a murder and so forth, but in that politically vetted production, the stepson is an exemplar of filiality. He chooses not to flee prosecution so that he can comfort his guilty father.

Changing Attitudes toward Privilege, Property, and Morality

Michael Johnston and Yufan Hao have named "privilege" (*tequan*) as a major category of corruption in the prereform era of Mao Zedong.[39] Special access to goods and services under the original communist central supply system and to special shops closed to the public epitomizes privilege better than the seemingly more damaging power of cadres to make or break other people's futures at will. It seems right, therefore, that this privilege of private consumption should be considered corruption in the narrow sense of using public office for private gain. But "privilege" as corruption in Mao's era meant under-the-table *special privilege* not available to other cadres at one's rank rather than ordinary privileges of office. The privilege of shopping in separate stores stocked with foreign and other goods not available to the public at any price was like a system of sumptuary laws. Such privilege, indeed sumptuary law, was a legal aspect of traditional social orders in China as elsewhere. It is only today that all systematically privileged cadre consumption is considered corruption. This is due to a change in values.

Shuntian Yao construes privilege differently, as a major category of corruption in the current era that comes as an ordinary concomitant of power, inasmuch as officials retain the privilege of control over China's resources and capital. Before the communist revolution, this was called bureaucratic capitalism. On the basis of their economic power, Yao defines China's "privileged class" as "the leading members of the CCP central committee, the top-level government officials, the highest-ranked military officials, the heads of the provincial governments, and the heads of the major state-owned enterprises, except for a very tiny percentage."[40] Foreign reporting has exposed the heavy hand of officials even in allocating and profiting personally (or profiting on behalf of their organization) from foreign direct investment. Mary E. Gallagher postulates that the initial impact of foreign investors, who have little interest in democratizing China and can afford bribery and other inefficiencies of corruption, has been to delay China's democratization.[41] An independent business class has not developed to monitor and protest official corruption from its own viewpoint, much less compete with bureaucratic capital outright. Moreover, workplace despotism in Chinese factories, both foreign and domestically managed, bespeaks a tyranny that anticorruption novels "speaking for" China's workers (such as *Choice*) view as corruption of the social system.[42] Here, privilege is unjust power, the power to break people, not just special access to goods and services.

Monopoly control of capital and resources is a major concern in the current theorization of corruption, as by Robert Klitgaard, who finds corruption to be based on "monopoly plus discretion minus accountability."[43] This definition has proved particularly attractive to scholars of corruption in developing and postcommunist states. Cliques and "mafias" on occasion privatize or monopolize much of the economies of weak states and the government itself, to the point of "state capture."[44] The irony of looking at the not-really-postsocialist *polity* of an economically "postsocialist" China in these terms is that the state and national economy were "captured" in 1949—by the Chinese Communist Party. From this point of view, legalized corruption in the Chinese case is precisely the system described in the state constitution. The negative concept of state or economic "capture" by the party or party elite is not of course seen in anticorruption novels, which pay lip service to the party as the constitutional leader of the revolution. But the idea of state capture seems an inevitable inference in a time of changing values, even as party control—and discipline—decays. Citizens like Chen Fang disdain party leaders who go through red lights even if, and perhaps all the more because, their overall power has decayed.

The novels are as one in depicting China as ruled by an interlocking power elite. "The exchange of power for money" is a shibboleth in China's internal debates about corruption, but Chen Fang has explicitly named power as the controlling factor, and most other novelists do so implicitly by tracing all corruption to political leaders. These elites are variously identified as the Tian empire of *Heaven Above*; the municipal party and state apparatus of N city and its clients in *Heaven's Wrath*;

Zhongyang's Gang of Four and their upstairs protectors in *Choice*; the administration of Jingdu and its clients, down to the Buddhist abbots, in *National Portrait*; and the Ding Wufa (Lai Changxing) empire in Haimen (Xiamen). Liu Ping's *Dossier on Smuggling* is the sole novel to depict the money of a private citizen, Ding Wufa, rather than the power of party or government officials, as the initiator of official corruption. But without official protection, Ding's empire would fall. In the end he has to seek higher protection in the provincial capital and Beijing.

The corruption of the ruling elite spreads like a web in every novel, including *Dossier on Smuggling*, with illegitimate transfers of money and power holding the web together. It might seem that such corruption, spreading unchecked, might reach a point of universal participation, if not modest redistribution of wealth downward, when it gets to the chauffeurs, call girls, and Mayor Li Gaocheng's maid. However, the novels clearly attest that these guanxi networks, often celebrated in the theoretical literature, are not just ad hoc and organized for utility rather than social solidarity, but they are also hierarchical. They are akin to clientelism, as dramatized in the film *Fatal Decision*. Yan Zhen tries to induce Mayor Li to become not just his pupil, but also his client. He also tries to persuade him that it is Li's patriarchal duty, as a leader in his own right, to succor the men he has raised up in the bureaucracy, whether or not they have done evil. The exception that proves the rule is the princelings. They have acquired power through the fathers and will fall if the fathers fall, yet the evil spawn (by blood or adoption) of Vice Governor Tian, Yan Zhen, Pi Deqiu, and of course Jiao Pengyuan are more fearsome and have often acquired more illegitimate money and criminal gangland power than their fathers. This inversion of filial piety and seniority recapitulates the nightmarish Cultural Revolution lèse majesté of young people. It also conjures up a vision of the corrupt elite illegitimately perpetuating itself in the future.

Are corrupt officials a class, then? They are more of a ruling elite or ruling class, a group defined politically rather than economically. *Heaven's Wrath*, *National Portrait*, and *Dossier on Smuggling* delight in portraying the sybaritic lifestyles, freedoms, and legal protections shared by all the major corrupt players. They speak a common language. The conversations even of the entrepreneurs in *Dossier on Smuggling* and the hoteliers and private textile manufacturers in *National Portrait* take their cue from official business: they are all about kickbacks, contracts, permits, and go-aheads for construction and demolition, apart from incidental mentions of driving, golf, and yachting lessons. It is in fact the officially vetted *Choice* and its media adaptations that stress class divisions, through the display of official leisure and consumption and the melodrama of poor workers barely hanging on in their slums. But how is the privileged class to be defined? Lifestyles are so important in class differentiation that the elite appear now to be defined by income. Organizationally, however, the major players are officials, with a hierarchy of top leaders necessary even for the existence of rich private entrepreneurs. Party position trumps state office and enables the amassment of money and power. This occurs also in the countryside, out of sight, as *National Portrait* and *Municipal Crisis* are intent on pointing out.[45] Whether the Communist Party as such, or its top echelons, will be seen as the privileged elite that has "captured" the state and national wealth remains to be seen. For now, that view is taboo.

Property rights is another changing realm nebulous enough for corruption always to be suspected. Rights to develop parking lot space for expansion of an entertainment center go to Mayor Pi's son's hotel instead of to the hoteliers in cahoots with Zhu Huaijing, but either way, the public is deprived of its share of the profits from the state-owned land, not to speak of the nepotism and bribes involved. Under the old system of the municipal clique's "capture" of municipal property rights, the mayor was entitled to dispose of the property however he saw fit anyway. The enormous pelf brought into Haimen by Ding Wufa is entrepreneurial value added, ownership of which was always moot under socialism.

One right of property is the right to agree to a sale price. Traditionally, few exchanges of money were impersonal; they were often negotiated, and those in command of assets might feign a *noblesse oblige* attitude toward them, such as letting their servants take a portion of household expenses for themselves (Westerners called it "squeeze," a form of corruption).[46] One sees survivals of the attitude when communist managers rationalize, in a patronizing as much as a socialist spirit, that it is all right for shop clerks to pilfer a little from inventory, since they are poorly paid.[47] The property pilfered is public, but the managers still see it as belonging to themselves. They see themselves as poorly paid, too.

The big stakes, however, are the giant state-owned enterprises (SOEs) capitalized with the public's (largely the peasants') taxes, now being turned into private or partly privatized enterprises. *Choice* details how SOE assets, including entire factories, can be privatized without shutting down the whole enterprise. Much of the scam, however, involves capital allocated by state banks to the SOE. It is diverted to the new subsidiaries before it ever reaches the old SOE; if the subsidiaries are kept as publicly owned on the books, they can even apply for funds of their own, in an old-fashioned socialist kind of scam. The flashpoint is the final disposal of Zhongyang, including its unemployed workers and housing compounds. By this time Zhongyang has negative worth; the workers ask, retrospectively, where did all the factory assets and productive power go? A common solution of the late 1990s was to sell SOEs to their workers in the form of stock, which might keep them employed but would be of no comfort to the taxpayers who originally capitalized the enterprise. The common argument of the novels and mass media productions is that the workers are owed equitable portions of SOE assets because they built the SOE with their labor. Zhang Ping actually gives the taxpayer a voice, by letting Mayor Li Gaocheng wonder if the supremacy of the working class in the Maoist era wasn't overdone, due to Marxist ideology. In any case, questions of ownership, productive power, real estate, and indeed debt are clearly in transition and a source of citizen disillusionment in a time when economic development requires the shutting down of sunset industries. This leads to yet another question, which is in principle divisible from the corruption question: What minimum welfare does the Chinese state owe the worker, above all the unemployed worker, in a time of marketization? In *Choice*, even the public schools are closed, as if they, too, had been privatized. They are expected to pay for themselves, but of course they cannot. In the end, questions of property lead to political questions: to whom does *China* belong?

A final consideration, conceivably outside the corruption discourse and yet within the concerns of ethics and criminal law, is personal morality and decorum judged on their own terms, not necessarily because as bacilli of social contagion they have the power ultimately to rot away the state as an organism. Ancient and socialist Chinese morality tended to portray the corruption of personal character as of a piece, and thus to link together embezzlement, whoring, gambling, drug addiction, and just having an outrageously good time. If one is morally depraved in one sphere, one may be corrupted and prey to other vices.[48] Under Maoism, having lots of women friends, money, and unofficial power, or just having a high standard of living, was proof of corruption. Living a life of extreme luxury and sexual dissipation was evidently among the main charges that brought down Chen Xitong. Many societies besides China's are ambivalent about wealth and pleasure seeking. Moreover, whoring signifies a power over women that ramifies the anticorruption authors' outlook on corruption as something ancient and upheld as much by concentrated power as by concentrated wealth. And yet, prostitution or "sex work" suddenly became so prevalent again in late twentieth-century China that the spread of this police-protected illegal—and unhygienic—activity made it an increasingly appropriate symbol of general social decadence. The patrons are mostly officials and businessmen.[49] However, despite all the ambiguities and the fact that adultery, gambling, and many other forms of dissipation trotted out in anticorruption campaigns are technically noncriminal matters not even within court jurisdiction, any of them can get an offender sent to a reeducation camp by the police.

Indeed, not being able to "control" one's wife or girlfriend(s), particularly if one is an official, appears as a primary concern in novels such as *Heaven's Wrath* and *Dossier on Smuggling*. The women engage in crime, but the problem seems partly to be one of social decorum. Whether this is a corruption of social norms is a moot point. Old social norms, as pointed out previously in the analysis of the film *Fatal Decision*, require that officials live in a style appropriate to their rank. And now, to preserve China's face, they must live in the style of leaders of richer nations. Moreover, in quasi-Confucian style, an official must take care of his family as a model for other families.[50] Morality begins in the family and spreads from the more refined to the less refined. Chinese morality has long found expression in the giving of appropriate gifts and reciprocity toward those who act with kindness. To act morally and according to social norms, officials must observe these niceties. At some point, this behavior can be seen as bribery and influence peddling.

The Discourse of Corruption: An Evasion of Social Controversy?

This study has not taken "corruption" to be a discourse as Michel Foucault would define it: a set of limitations on expression determined by a power structure. Still, can discourses and other habits of language, even if one can break out of them, lead to forms of blindness and evasions? The discourse of corruption can be an avant-garde discourse that awakens and sensitizes societies to new ethical problems that have previously gone unnoticed or unarticulated. For instance, prison overcrowding and violence and abuses from the privatization of prisons may come into public consciousness through novelistic portraits of them as a corruption of the judicial system. Outrage at the sexual indiscretions of officials as portrayed in anticorruption novels, on the other hand, may play a rearguard role by inflaming passions that most of society considers obsolescent (except when the focus is the abuse of women). Fomentation against corruption in a Chinese society increasingly governed by market forces may even serve as a moralistic evasion of difficult political choices. Anticorruption novels might create nostalgia for anticorruption campaigns of the Maoist type.[51] A focus on corruption can thus serve as an evasion or redirection of inquiries about such fundamental issues as power sharing, the interests of dispossessed social groups, and antisocial behavior by the growing private sector. With its focus on official wrongdoing and social ethos, the corruption discourse sidesteps alternative discourses emphasizing structural economic change, marketization and globalization, reform and opening up, and beneficial or inevitable change in values and laws, to name a few. The novel *Choice* posits the theory of structural economic change as an explicit alternative to its vision of corruption, but it takes the easy path of rejecting this alternative out of hand, since its factory managers are in fact evil. *Heaven's Wrath* (the banned version) cites a wealth of alternative explanations in order to reject them, although once stated, the alternatives are on the table for consideration. In the end, one may wonder if China's anticorruption discourse does not represent something even more basic: for better or worse, a growing resistance to authority, despite concurrent fears of social anarchy.

To speak of corruption is to have in mind a previous baseline of social health under communism. But when was that? As a historical notion, corruption is inevitably complicit with officially enforced amnesia about recent Chinese history. Although fiction and reportage of the late 1970s created images of corruption during the Cultural Revolution, that viewpoint is now little seen. To argue that corruption, conceived as an abuse of power, existed in 1949 is to condemn the communist regime. It is little wonder that corruption is so facilely attributed to the new intrusion of market values. Yet, there is no modern counterpart to Mao Dun, who in the 1930s wrote of China's crooked stock exchange. Indeed, corruption as a negative discourse of change runs the risk of lagging behind necessary social change and degenerating into a general fear of change as such. However, worries about corruption do not seem to have fed the cynicism sometimes heard in China today. Corruption gets people angry.

When the discourse of corruption leads to notions of regime change under a Mandate of Heaven theory, the image of history evoked is cyclical. The psychological associations of this Chinese idea of cyclicalism may bear reinvestigation in the modern age. The West, too, has propagated cyclical visions of history. The uniqueness of Chinese versions, from a Western perspective, is their focus on decadence of the ruler instead of the common people, and on regime decay without reference to imperial expansion. Imperial oppression of minorities, of women, of country folk, and of many other social groups gets short shrift within the Chinese discourse of corruption.

Perhaps the most often criticized "failing" of China's anticorruption novels is their reliance on savior heroes. For all the similarities of China's end-of-millennium anticorruption fiction with late Qing novels about corruption, contemporary China seems not to have found its Liu E to write about terrible bureaucrats whose error lies in the misguided strength of their certitude as opposed to the weakness of their flesh or the excessive cleverness of their accounting methods.[52] The errors of the self-righteous might summon up the errors of Mao Zedong and also implicate the current leaders of the Communist Party. Not all of them are corrupt, but they rule only because they have risen to power within Mao Zedong's political party.

Yet faith in a savior at the top of the bureaucracy reflects views widely held in China today, even among protesters. They seem to think that if only rotten officials at the lower, middle, and even high levels were exposed for the leaders to see, the leaders would fire and punish them and the corruption would be eliminated.[53] At first glance, this is the view of the anticorruption novels analyzed in this book. Such views fit the official discourse. But is that view shared by the whole public, and is it really the final viewpoint of the novels? To rely on savior communists to halt corruption in a dysfunctional system now so often viewed as corrupt from its communist start is to render the corruption discourse irremediably pessimistic. In this time of religious and ethical turmoil, perhaps we should take the novels' titles and the words of the characters seriously: perhaps they are pointing up beyond the leaders, to a moral force above humankind, toward "Heaven." From this point of view, China's anticorruption fiction, a transitional literature in a transitional era, may represent a hunger for a yet unrealized spiritual transcendence beyond politics, law, and even secular ethics.[54] However, other Chinese may see faith as the ultimate evasion of reality. Faith and reality as such are primed to be debated directly in fiction and nonfiction again, but "the Organization" is not yet ready for it. Until then, the test of wills is bound to continue.

Reference Matter

Notes

Full author's names and publication information for works cited in short form may be found in the Bibliography, pages 229–67.

Chapter 1: Introduction

1. Wibowo, 762.
2. Shang Ying emphasizes that freedom from corruption does not always coincide with democracy. Oddly, the Burmese have accused China of "corrupting" Myanmar. Mark Landler, "For Many Burmese, China Is an Unwanted Ally," *New York Times*, Dec. 30, 2001. In 2003, China had the same Transparency International point rating of 3.4, tied for 66th place among 133 countries. Indonesia tied for 122nd at 1.9. The United States, at 7.5, tied for 18th place. Singapore, at 9.4, was in fifth. For links on global corruption, see http://groups.msn.com/Sequitur/corruption.msnw.
3. Jing Wang's "The State Question" emphasizes 1992 as a watershed date also in popular culture.
4. Kaufmann et al.
5. Shieh; Gong, "Dangerous Collusion"; Wedeman, "The Intensification," 895n1.
6. Fan and Grossman, "The Uses of Corruption," 8–11.
7. Ding, "The Quasi-criminalization."
8. Or, as the evil factory manager Guo Zhongyao says in the fifth draft screenplay of *Fatal Decision*: "If the majority do it, then you can't call it corruption any more." *Shengsi juezi*; Screenplay ("Fifth draft"), scene 155.
9. White, 50. Nye, 119, defines corruption as "behavior which deviates from the formal duties of a public role because of private-regarding (personal, close

family, private clique) pecuniary or status gains; or violates rules against the exercise of certain types of private-regarding influence." For a good synopsis of definitions of corruption, and a convincing argument as to why broader definitions, such as "against the public interest," are hard to apply to China, see Lü, 14–22.

10. Lü, 48.

11. Conversely, much money making that appears to be private enterprise in China may really be an entrepreneurial activity undertaken on behalf of bureaucratic or corporatist local interests. See Duckett; Wank; Walder and Oi; and Rocca, "The Rise of the Social," 13.

12. As in the title of Liu Haimei's article, "Jingshen de fubai" (Spiritual corruption).

13. Hao and Johnston, 3; Johnston and Hao, 87–88.

14. A popular novel involving corruption and envisioning nonreligious, political-environmental apocalypse is Wang Lixong, *Huang huo*, analyzed by Kinkley, "Modernity and Apocalypse"; and Barmé, 261.

15. Here "discourse" simply denotes associated words, phrases, beliefs, and explanations that a group of people considers mutually consistent and uses frequently. The elements of a discourse turn on interpretation, but I do not intend to follow Michel Foucault in implying that discourses determine "knowledge," "power," or beliefs, or that a discourse is a self-contained world. On the contrary, discourses overlap and are unstable—subject to being altered, undermined, and overturned by new information, other discourses, the revelation of inconsistencies, and ideological persuasion, for example.

16. Todorov, 42, cited in Rong Cai, 151.

17. Lévi-Strauss, 143.

18. See, for instance, Chen Xiaoming, "Xianfengpai zhi hou"; Dong Zhilin. Henry Zhao, "The River Fans Out," sees many of these trends as ephemeral, but also sees promise in new literary trends. On transformations of Chinese mass media, see Lynch.

19. Richard Levy, "Corruption in Popular Culture," is one of the few works on this subject. See also Helen Xiaoyan Wu, "Anticorruption Literature and Television Dramas." Perry Link, *The Uses of Literature*, covers corruption in 1970s and 1980s literature. Many books about pop culture (e.g., Huot) tend to stress those that are avant-garde or linked to international trends.

20. Hsia, 42.

21. Lin Jianfa.

22. This was some critics' view of Zhou Meisen and other anticorruption authors reported on in Howard W. French, "A Gadfly Criticizes China's Powerful, Within Limits," *New York Times*, May 22, 2004.

23. There have been civil protests; see Areddy and Wonacott.

24. For instance, malpractice suits against doctors are booming (though many doctors work for the state, their malpractice is not "of the state"), but it

remains to be seen if this subject will become the topic of current anticorruption fiction, as it surely would have been in late Qing novels (which satirize quack native doctors). See Leslie Chang, "In China, Courts Find New Muscle as They Take on Medical Cases," *Wall Street Journal*, Jan. 7, 2002, A1, A6. Interestingly, lawyers are not the butt of anticorruption novels, though in life judges and police often try to neutralize them. The hands-off attitude toward entrepreneurs may reflect defensiveness in the face of attacks on them by "leftists."

25. Liu Binyan, "Sellout by China's Intellectual Elite," 32.
26. Fang Lizhi.
27. Xinhua News Agency, "Fantan zongju," October 14, 2002, release.
28. In a March 2004 Internet poll, 86 percent of respondents "clicked on government corruption when asked to name 'the issue that needs to be addressed the most' by the current N[ational] P[eople's] C[ongress]." Wang Wu, "Corruption Seen as Public Enemy No. 1," *China Business Weekly* (of *China Daily*), March 16, 2004, 1. Notes Yan Sun in *Corruption and Market*, 2, "Almost every public opinion survey since the late 1980s has shown corruption to be the top concern among the general public."
29. Hutzler, citing a researcher at the CCP's "top training academy," provides the 60,000 figure, coming after 17 percent annual increases. Howard W. French, "Land of 74,000 Protests (But Little Is Ever Fixed)," *New York Times*, August 24, 2005, A4, gives the 2004 number, from China's Minister of Public Security.
30. The classic treatment of formula fiction is Cawelti.
31. In Chinese, the term *hou shehuizhuyi* usually means postsocialist, but linguistically it could be construed not just as "since the advent of socialism," but also as "late socialist." Likewise, *hou zibenzhuyi* is sometimes translated as "late capitalism."
32. McNally, 2.
33. Wenhao Cheng, 79.
34. On their plight, see Yongshun Cai; Hurst and O'Brien.
35. Chen Lumin, cited in "Getting at the Root of Corruption."
36. See Buckley.
37. See New Left thinker Wang Hui for views of the Chinese party-state as "neo-liberal."
38. Terrill cites smugness in "academic and foreign policy circles" that China surely must be a "normal country" in view of its smooth economic success. For another pessimistic view, see Feigon.
39. Johnson, 15, sees revolutionary potential in China's backward rural areas; the Chinese state is even more concerned about the backward industrial cities, home to those once called the proletariat.
40. Wellek, 240–41.
41. Stromberg, "Introduction," ix.
42. "Introduction," in Becker, ed., 3–38.

43. Lefebvre, 105.

44. As late as 2002, after the novels had taken considerable flak, Gu Fengwei and Wu Yumin referred to anticorruption fiction as a "shock wave of realism."

45. Williams and Wu, 6, usefully borrow Gregory Kazsa's concept of a "conscription society" of "administered mass organizations" to describe Mao's locked-down society. In fact, a conscription society, like the army, can provide existential comforts if the mission is clear; the loss of the Chinese "unit" as a paternalistic caregiver is another source of anomie and a feeling of social loss and corruption. See Tang and Parish.

46. See Zhang Yiwu, "Postmodernism"; Chen Xiaoming, "Wufa shenhua." This "new realism" is a different kind of realism than the mainstream Chinese realism defined in chapter 7. The focus on present realities as tokens of a bright future has ironic parallels to socialist realism.

47. I thank Helen Xiaoyan Wu for this important observation in a personal communication.

48. Perry Link's works, notably *The Uses of Literature*, offer the best expositions on CCP control of Chinese literature.

49. A digest of the debates is offered by Li Zimu. See also Chen Jiangong et al.; Sun Xianke; Tong Qingbing and Tao Dongfeng; Xiong Yuanyi; Xiong Yuanyi and Dong Jieying; and Chen Liao. Some critics saw the new realism as more sociological and less concerned with individual viewpoints than previous realism. Somewhat different is the view of Zhang Yiwu, "Postmodernism and Chinese Novels of the Nineties," 252, who focuses on realistic technique and the realism of China's postmodernity and fast economic development—not the old SOEs. Xiao Xialin, "Zhuang zai taozi li," bemoans the tendency of 1990s "new realism," possibly Zhang's kind of realism, to describe daily life without the critical edge of the old realism; Xiao also discusses anticorruption works as realistic fiction, but inadequate ones.

50. Sun Haiwen, 94, speaking particularly of Zhang Ping's *Jueze* and other economic novels.

51. He Zhenbang, "Changpian re," 15, singles out Wang Yuewen's *Guo hua* (discussed in chapter 5 of this book) and Zhang Ping's *Shimian maifu* for praise. See also Mao Keqiang.

52. Lu Kan provides a list, including Zhang Ping's *Jueze*. See also Lei Da, and Yao Huanji, rapporteur.

53. Jin Hongyu, both articles.

54. Xiao Xialin, "95 nian"; He Zhenbang, "Jiushi niandai" and "Changpian re." Even in this there is politics. In 1993, Jiang Zemin asked that novels be a priority in fiction production.

55. Yang Xia, 9.

56. Henry Zhao, "The River Fans Out," 195.

57. Liu Binyan, *People or Monsters?* See Perry Link, *The Uses of Literature*, 260–63.

58. Literary historian Chen Pingyuan, in *Ershi shiji Zhongguo*, considers "fiction about officialdom" an old late Qing category.

59. Mao Keqiang and others, however, seem to view anticorruption novels (e.g., Zhang Ping's *Jueze*) as identical with novels about officialdom.

60. Kong, 154–61.

61. Zhang Ping, *Fa han Fenxi* (1991), *Tian wang* (1993).

62. Han Kuancheng, rapporteur. Sichuan author and former official Li Taiyin's *Beihun* (1995) is tagged as an early and influential anticorruption novel now that the author has been arrested for corruption. See Zhu Zhaolong; You Di. References courtesy Helen Xiaoyan Wu.

63. Harman, 16–18.

64. Wang Fanghua. On the importance of *Kewang*, see Zha, 25–53.

65. Chen Zhiang, "*Cangtian*," 24–25, also notes this work as a major precedent, emphasizing the TV adaptation. It was broadcast in 1986. Sheldon Lu, 26. Liu Yi agrees with me that there is a link between anticorruption fiction and previous works by Jiang Zilong.

66. Jiang Zilong, both stories. Ma Yixin also notes the kinship of the social novels discussed in this book (which he calls reform novels) with the Manager Qiao stories and *Xin xing*.

67. Liu Yi.

68. Zhou Meisen's *Renjian zhengdao* (1996) came to be seen as the first of a trilogy that also included *Tianxia caifu* (1997) and *Zhongguo zhizao* (1998). See Ma Yixin. Zhou's later novels, *Zhigao liyi* and *Juedui quanli*, have clearer corruption themes. Amid the anticorruption mania, all his novels have been swept into the same bin.

69. Jiang Xiaoling. Says Wang Dehou, 67: "The first significance of *Shengsi jueze* is that [such a film] was shot, passed inspection, given affirmative criticism, and openly distributed and screened. This is a historical breakthrough." Many novels looked as if they had been written for television adaptation; Luo Gang.

70. Ai Qun, of the Masses' Press, affirms that the term, and concept, did not exist when Lu Tianming wrote *Cangtian zai shang* in 1995. Personal interview, March 15, 2002. The term was half germinated by the time a preface to Zhang Ping's *Jueze* (1997) called the novel a work that might bring *fan fubai douzheng ticai de wenxue* (literature with themes of the anticorruption struggle) to a new high point. Yan Zhaozhu, "Yi qu fan fubai." He Zhenbang's late 1997 piece "Shidai fuyu," 141, shortens the term slightly, to *fan fubai ticai wenxue* (literature with anticorruption themes). Both call these novels "literature," not just fiction.

71. Li Yunlong; *Yangcheng wanbao*.

72. In 1999 the Zhongguo dianying chubanshe of Beijing was already instituting a "Zhongguo dangdai guanchang xiaoshuo xilie" (Contemporary Chinese officialdom fiction series).

73. Li Yuntuan, "Lun xin shiqi wenxue," provides a different canon of more elite, less generic authors, including Mo Yan and Liang Xiaosheng.

74. Yu Xiaoshi, "Fanfu xiaoshuo"; Wan Lingyun, "Fanfu tushu."

75. Previously, in January 1989, a screenplay by Chen Fang won a commendation in the First Woodpecker Literary Prize competition. "Zhuomuniao wenxuejiang."

76. Chen Fang, "*Jijian yu jiandu* zazhi pingchu Zhongguo shi da jingdian fanfu xiaoshuo."

77. Even *Shouhuo* (Harvest) printed Zhou Meisen's classic, *Zhongguo zhizao* (Made in China), in its first 1999 issue. Anticorruption did not become a staple of the magazine. But *Xiaoshuo jie* began serializing Wang Yuehua's *Guo hua* (see chapter 5) in January 1999, and, in early 2002, Zhou Meisen's *Juedui quanli* (Absolute power), Jin Yuanping's *Quanli de pingtai* (Platform of power), and Lu Tianming's *Shengwei shuji* (Provincial secretary). *Dangdai* in 2001 printed novels by Yan Zhen (*Canglang zhi shui*; Deep blue breakers) and Wang Yuewen (the sequel to *Guo hua*), then in 2002, Ke Yunlu's *Long nian dang'an* (Cases of the year of the dragon). *Zhongguo zuojia* in 2000 printed Bi Sihai's noted *Caifu yu renxing* (Riches and human nature) and in 2001, Wang Yuewen's "Bian ge gushi" (Make up a story) and Liu Guoqiang's "Quanli" (Power). The capstone was the 2002 printing of a novella about officialdom (but not corruption) by Wang Yuewen, "Jieju huo kaishi" (Ending or beginning) in *Renmin wenxue* (People's literature). Periodicals sometimes printed most of a novel except for the ending, then summarized the ending.

78. Yan Yujiao, 25. Zhang Ping ducked and said it could go on as long as people hated corruption.

79. Hao Yu, "Fanfu da qushi xia de guanchang xiaoshuo," 73; Chen Xihan. Preferring literature about officialdom for its putatively greater subtlety than anticorruption fiction is Jiakechong. Zhang Zhizhong simply notes that anticorruption fiction is a subsection of fiction about officialdom. A seeming example of "literature of officialdom lite," about a bedrock Chinese culture of influence peddling spreading up from the peasants to infect officials who are their relatives, is Sun Chunping's story, originally printed in *Renmin wenxue*, December 2003.

80. See Du Ruoyan.

81. I thank Katherine Carlitz and William Crawford for advising me of some of these trends, which they noted in their research on recent anticorruption novels and television series.

82. Yu Xiaoshi, "Fanfu xiaoshuo."

83. A notable example is *Shiwei shuji* (Municipal secretary), whose title made it look like a sequel to *Shengwei shuji* by Lu Tianming. Zhang Aijing, "Maochu." Many books were also made to look as if they were by Chen Fang or Zhang Ping.

84. *Shijie ribao*. Wen Bo writes of a July 2002 Shanghai Academy of Social Sciences panel convened evidently to criticize unhealthy trends in recent anticorruption and officialdom literature; the moderator announces that the *Wen-*

huibao was getting lots of reader letters "sharply criticizing" bad anticorruption fiction. Other articles about the same or other denunciatory conferences in Shanghai are reported on by Wu Juan; Wen Bo; and Lu Mei, "Hu shang wentan." For a summary of bad press for anticorruption fiction, see "Tanguan biyou huai nüren he dakuan," from Xinhua. See also Xiang Wei.

85. Xinhua News Agency, "Fantan zongju," October 14, 2002, release.

86. Xiang Wei. When the climate for freedom of expression is bad, anticorruption fiction, like all crime fiction, is blamed for teaching crooks how to commit crime. See Wan Lingyun, "Fanfu wenxue."

87. Wan Lingyun, "Fanfu wenxue." On the predominance of male readers, see the interview with Ai Qun and others of the Qunzhong chubanshe, March 15, 2002. Colleagues opine that the television series may be more popular among females.

88. See Xiao Yang and Meng Jiangxiong; Qi Dianbin.

89. Yu Kai.

90. See Hu Zihong's devastating critical review of Zhang Ping's epic 2004 anticorruption novel, "*Guojia ganbu*." Xiang Jun seems obliquely to attack Lu Tianming's latest novel as a work of formula fiction because Lu titled it *Provincial Secretary*, and Xiang Jun notes the improbable incorruptibility of Lu's and Zhang's characters in that position. Another sign of lessening freedoms after 2003 is that the *Fanfubai daokan*, or *Anticorruption Herald*, founded in 2001, became "internal" (classified) in January 2004, as indicated in a notice in the November 2003 issue. Helen Xiaoyan Wu made me aware of this journal. An ad in the journal indicates that nearly every province has its own journal run by supervisory and disciplinary organs, often with "*dangfeng*" (the state of the CCP) in the title. I do not know whether any or all of them also became internal.

91. As Wang Zhiping, 39–40, describes Chen Qiwen's novella *Bai de yaoyan de shijian* (A time of dazzling white).

92. Xin Dingding.

93. Li Shi. A transparent attempt to repeat the success of the film *Shengsi jueze* was the release in 2005 of a film of similar name, *Shengsi jiexian* (Between life and death). It was about a real case. See Fan Hongguo. I thank Helen Wu for these references.

Chapter 2: The Trendsetter

1. Lu Tianming, born in Kunming and raised in Shanghai, in his youth was sent down to the countryside twice and only completed the first year of high school. His plays, novels, and CCTV teleplay productions date from the early 1980s. His younger sister is Lu Xinger, and his son, known for *Xun qiang* (Searching for the gun), is Lu Chuan. Hou Xiaoqiang; Miao Chun; Zhang Aijing, "*Shengwei shuji*"; Dai Xiu and Zhuang Xin.

2. Personal interview, March 15, 2002.

3. In Anderson, *The Limits of Realism*.

4. Hou Xiaoqiang. Lu Tianming wrote the teleplay; Zhou Huan directed. Chen Zhiang, "*Cangtian*."

5. Liu Yi. Lu Tianming admitted, in 2003, that the villain of his *Da xue wu hen* was based on a former Natural Resources minister, Tian Fengshan, who was accused of corruption after the TV program aired. Bu Changwei. Lu went up to Heilongjiang to interview the cadre who turned in Tian. *Caijing shibao*. When I interviewed him on March 15, 2002, Lu Tianming said the lawsuits against Zhang Ping for exposing rural corruption had caused him not to model *Cangtian zai shang* too closely after real-life cases.

6. In the novel it is explained at length that safe deposit boxes are sacrosanct under the law, to be opened only by the owner or the insurance company providing the box (316). This hardly squares with common knowledge about police powers in China. It might be deemed an authorial plea, expressing an ideal in hopes of attracting attention to it as a future goal.

7. Law enforcement professionals duly complained that Lu Tianming slighted the procuracy and showed party committees too much in command in the TV adaptation of his next novel, *Da xue wu hen*. *Fazhi pinglun*.

8. Calculated at RMB 4.78 to $1.

9. According to the "Supplementary Provisions of the Standing Committee of the National People's Congress Concerning the Punishment of the Crimes of Embezzlement and Bribery" (January 21, 1988), Art. 3, "State personnel, personnel of collective economic organizations or other personnel handling or administering public property, who, by taking advantage of their office, misappropriate public funds for their own use or for conducting illegal activities, or misappropriate a relatively large amount of public funds for conducting activities to reap profits, or misappropriate a relatively large amount of public funds and fail to return it after three months, shall be guilty of misappropriation of public funds." From http://www.chinalaw114.com/englishlaw (July 3, 2004).

10. Chen Zhiang, "*Cangtian*," 25, 26, and Yun De, 191, praise the portrait of Lin.

11. This point is general in the novels about officialdom, argues Chen Chengcai.

12. For a view of guanxi as a traditional form of recognizing "natural" or "given" relatedness, see Kipnis.

13. Mayfair Yang discusses instrumental guanxi and its extreme form, one-time-only, single-purpose guanxi. Thomas Gold et al., eds., tend toward a view of guanxi as instrumental but also enduring, the basis of a "gift economy," as Yang would have it.

14. For references to the Organization and the principle of the Organization, see 50, 51, 124, 232, 245, 291, 379, 399. Lu Tianming uses the same euphemism in interviews; see Hou Xiaoqiang.

15. See 13, 50, 291.

16. Uncharacteristically, Huang tells the wayward Ms. Tian to "Rely on the party and the people." She snorts, turns on her heel, and heads for the door (185). *Dangxing* is a concept important to Secretary Lin (33).

17. Indeed, Lin tells Huang it was Lin who recommended him to Vice Governor Tian (199).

18. Li Chun, 66.

19. Wu Juan, moderator.

20. See 28, 33, 50, 108.

21. I deduced this rule from my reading of the novels. Zhang Ping and Chen Fang confirmed it explicitly in separate interviews, March 15, 2002, as does Xiang Jun's article. When interviewed separately by Liu Yi, Lu Tianming said he went no higher than vice governor because he was afraid of lawsuits by administrators who might imagine they were the model for the character.

22. Liu Yi; Xiao Xialin, "Zhuang zai taozi li de xianshizhuyi," pt. 3. Lu said in a personal interview on March 15, 2002, that the Central Disciplinary Inspection Commission had wanted to coproduce the drama with CCTV. Lu refused, not wanting to have to answer to them, so they retaliated by demanding that the television series not be put up for a particular prize consideration.

23. Chen Zhiang, "*Cangtian*," 25. Chen compares Tian to the mastermind Jin Ba in Cao Yu's *Richu* (Sunrise).

24. Lu Tianming's last comments in Wu Juan, moderator. He has inveighed against the literature of self-absorption in many interviews; see Bu Changwei. For an explanation of "main melody," see chapter 4 in this book, note 44.

25. Liu Yi.

26. Chen Zhiang, "*Cangtian*," 26.

27. Tong Liqun. Reference courtesy Helen Xiaoyan Wu.

28. A rave review of the novel is Chen Zhiang, "*Da xue*." The TV series won the Golden Eagle award for best TV drama series in 2001. Yu Kai.

29. Kui Long.

30. Liu Yi.

31. Tao Lan; Miao Chun. Still, 250,000 copies of the novel were issued before the TV series was broadcast, including a large type edition. *Cangtian zai shang* went through at least a second printing (for a total of 40,000 copies) in 1995, and a sixth printing (130,000) in 1996. Yun De, 190. *Da xue wu hen* reportedly had been issued in 180,000 volumes by 2002. Miao Chun.

32. Hou Xiaoqiang; Lu Tianming, "Zai Zhongguo shehui biange zhong."

Chapter 3: The Banned Blockbuster

1. Cui Yuping, 48–52, suggests Wang chose the location to shame the party.

2. Beijing prosecutors floated this amount after the suicide. Tempest, "Beijing Prepares."

3. Faison.

4. Gilley, 242–43.

5. Griffin. Xiaotong was sentenced to twelve years for misappropriating (*nuoyong*) government funds of RMB 35,000,000. *Xinbao*.

6. Even the Hong Kong journalists could not penetrate the secrecy. Ji Wei's insightful book, whose English title is *The Trial of Chen Xitong*, was mostly written before the trial. This book, 97–101, and *Fazhi ribao*, "'98 shi da fazhi xinwen," do not even agree on the dates of the trial and what came from it.

7. On grapevine rumors, see Gittings. A flurry of books followed *Tian nu*, some about Chen Fang's subject matter and some not, including Chen Xiaotong's alleged memoirs and two 1998 books of reportage (not novels, even in form) by Shi Yan (pseud.; not Chen Fang), *Tian yi* (the cover says it is "a companion and sequel to *Tian nu*") and *Tian huo*. Those books' subtitles mimic *Tian nu*'s subtitle. Ling Fei in 2000 published *Tian qiu*, which has no relation to *Tian nu* or the Chen Xitong/Wang Baosen case, but is tagged on its front cover, title page, and spine as an "anticorruption novel." The same is true of Mu Yilin's *Tian pan* (Heaven judges) and Tian Tian's *Tian cheng* (Heaven punishes). Ren Yanfang's *Ren yuan* (Humankind's resentment) is reportage about a man with a grievance against Chen Xitong, the unnamed target of Chen Fang's novel (the phrase "Heaven's wrath" has origins in the classical expression "Heaven's wrath and humankind's resentment"). Zhang Ping's *Tian wang* (Heaven's net), published in 1993, preceded Chen Fang's *Tian nu*, and the phrase "*tian wang*" appears near the end of the movie *Fatal Decision*, but Chen Fang's novel is better known, and it was no doubt the inspiration for websites and website columns exposing corruption entitled *Tian nu* or "Heaven's Wrath," some of them copying or imitating the cover art of Chen Fang's novel, showing lightning bolts from heaven or fiery characters saying "heaven's wrath." Websites still existing in 2003 (many have expired) were at http://members.tripod.com/-cora_2/index/about.htm and http://members.fortunecity.com/tiannu/.

8. Chen was allowed some dignity; he appeared on TV in his own clothes, head unshaven, according to Patricia Dyson, a consultant for the American Center for International Labor Solidarity.

9. In April 1997, the CCP Central Propaganda Department, Ministry of Culture, and State Press and Publications Administration issued a joint circular banning *Tian nu*. Unattributed officials' statements claimed that the novel "leaked secrets," had the potential to damage the leaders' relationship with the masses, and hurt the leaders' morale. "China: Book Banned," on the "Hong Kong Voice of Democracy" website, August 21, 1997, at http://www.democracy.org.hk/pastweek/97_aug/ hrw970821.htm (June 7, 2001), citing a Reuters release of April 13, 1997. Reportedly, police from the Beijing municipal authority seized printing negatives of the novel from its press in suburban Beijing in April 1997, and on May 21, 1997, detained six people involved with publication. In Inner Mongolia, the press's head and its general editor lost their jobs, according to

http://www.aan.net/webzine/tiannu/tiannuo.htm (July 24, 2001) and *Mingbao*, June 16, 1996, accessed at the same time on the same site. The ban did not extend to Hong Kong. Chen Fang claimed being threatened in the years since. Weng Changshou; *Mingbao*, "Xie *Tian nu* chunu dangshiren."

10. Birth and death dates courtesy Ai Qun. For Chen Fang's biography, see Xia Congzhi. Chen Fang's father, who translated Russian and had been to the USSR, was accused of being a Russian spy, and Chen Fang was barred from university. Personal interview, March 15, 2002. Before writing his novel, Chen served as editor of *Huaren shijie* (The world of Chinese), a magazine of the Central United Front Department of the CCP. He was also deputy managing editor of *Xingguang yuekan* (Starlight monthly), a joint publication of the *Renmin ribao* and Hong Kong's *Xingdao ribao*. Both magazines that Chen edited were closed down due to excessive liberalism (Griffin). The Japanese Foreign Ministry invited Chen Fang to teach in Japan for all of 2001. Zhi Hui. Chen Fang said that after 2000 he "entered into" the work of the Central Disciplinary Inspection Commission. Weng Changshou. He struggled to recover from a stroke in 2005. McGregor.

11. Personal interview, March 15, 2002.

12. From a source in the Qunzhong chubanshe (Masses' Press), interview, March 15, 2002.

13. Long Lihua. Chen Fang felt only a tenth as many copies would have sold if the book had not been banned. Personal interview, March 15, 2002.

14. Chen Fang believed his book was banned not because it tells about real people, but because he criticizes the system—and because he dared to criticize an official at the Politburo level. Personal interview, March 15, 2002.

15. "Official critic" is a term made popular by Helmut Martin.

16. Chang Chuan, 71, mentions rumors that more than one bullet hole entered Wang Baosen.

17. Xu Jingbo, iv–v. The August 6, 1998, *Mingbao* article uses the term "documentary novel."

18. *Tian nu*'s list at 183 does not appear in *Dushi weiqing*. Reference to the Great Wall scandal of Shen Taifu (*TN* 193) goes missing in *DSWQ* (365–66). Real cases are at 183, 194, 195, 335, 450.

19. David Der-wei Wang, *The Monster That Is History*, 324n53, cites PRC scholars such as Luan Xiang who have studied the representation of contemporary events in novels during the late Ming. Largely allegorical treatments of recent history in literature are of course ancient in China.

20. There is a letter dated June 1995 at 288. See also 241, about 1993 events. The city is not far from Beidaihe (192) and northern (242).

21. Sentenced to ten years for taking bribes of RMB 220,000.

22. Sentenced to life imprisonment for taking bribes of HK$800,000. See below for his posts in life.

23. The son was sentenced to execution with a two-year stay (in effect, a

suspended death sentence) for taking bribes of RMB 9,280,000 and paying out bribes of RMB 1,200,000. *Xinbao.*

24. In life, concurrently vice director of the Municipal Committee Office. Sentenced to fifteen years for taking bribes of HK$200,000 and US$30,000. Strengthening my identification of the ineffectual Shen Shi is Chen Fang's opinion of him as someone only good at Ping-Pong. Zhang Yifan, xii.

25. Obedience to the Organization (the party hierarchy) or having "the Organizational concept" (knowing that one should let the Organization lead) is counterposed to obeying the law. See 53–54, 81, 93, 151, 174–75, 247, 250, 277, 286, 375.

26. *Dangjian wenhui*, 28–30; Jiang Xiaoqing, 16.

27. Dai Jinhua, "Behind Global Spectacle."

28. Wang Baosen was posthumously convicted of having misappropriated (*nuoyong*) RMB 100 million. *Xinbao.*

29. Jiang Xiaoqing, 12–14; Lushan, "Chen Xitong duli wangguo neikui," 32–33.

30. Thanks to his son's machinations, when Secretary Jiao approved the diversion of RMB 100 million of city funds, 50 million was in theory an unsecured loan to a friend of Orient's who wanted in on the investment, one of Feng Aiju's mysterious high official backers. In return for not providing capital up front, the other partner would let the city take some of "his" interest out of the 35 percent. But any interest to him was just a payoff, for none of the capital loaned to H city was his to begin with (424–25). The introduction of such technical and superfluous details is enough to convince the reader that the details come from life and make the reader wonder, "can you make this stuff up?" But one can, of course.

31. Jiang Xiaoqing, 13.

32. Sun Qi wires US$50 million to Orient's and Uncle He's secret accounts to pretend compliance with their demanded recompense for letting him escape China, though he keeps the greater part of the pelf for himself (*Tian nu*, 415–16). That means he must have embezzled over US$100 million, not counting the millions the novel says he had already lost in casinos. The RMB 100 million of municipal funds lost by the whole municipal committee in the main case is but a fraction of that. It is odd that the money Sun invested remains a loose end in the novel.

33. A government official reported in the *Beijing ribao* in April 1996 that RMB 18.3 billion (US$2.2 billion) was the total missing in the Chen Xitong/Wang Baosen case. Tempest, "Beijing Prepares." Also Ji Wei, 55, 60. A figure of RMB 18 billion is cited in "Shiji tanwufan," evidently after findings of the Central Disciplinary Inspection Commission about Wang Baosen.

34. The precious objects Chen Xitong was convicted of receiving at his secret trial included gifts he received in his official capacity and did not report, but this was a relatively minor charge, and the trial lay in the future when Chen Fang wrote.

35. Ji Wei, 141–42; *Xinbao*.

36. It was delivered to the Fifth Plenum of the Fourteenth Central Committee. Ji Wei, 41, 55.

37. The Chinese reader would presume Orient to be a gatekeeper for Secretary Jiao's graft, though Chen Fang's novel is vague about this, showing the princelings and kingpins operating in different circles. Foreign businessmen reported that Chen Xiaotong in life arranged audiences with his father for US$93,000 a pop. Tempest, "The Scions."

38. *Dageda*, literally "mob boss," after the kind of people who mainly used the phones in the mid-1990s.

39. Note the glasses in the picture of Chen Xiaotong on the front cover of his no doubt fake autobiography and apology (see Chen Xiaotong).

40. An internal Chinese report on Chen Xitong in 1997 found that he entertained "young female television presenters" in his mansions. Faison. Chen Xiaotong, 187, speaks of the son having relations with a TV personality named Zhu. Lushan, 68, speaks of a mistress who consorted with both Chen Xitong and Wang Baosen (Song Huihui does with Jiao Pengyuan and He Qizhang in the novel). She is not identified except as the manager of a Holiday Inn, which would seem to indicate He Ping. Ji Wei, 65, indicates that there were many rumors about Chen Xitong and his women, including one to the effect that he and his son had a mistress in common. When the Hong Kong magazine *Qian shao* named the TV personality Du Yu as a mistress, she sued and won in Hong Kong courts (Shi Yan, *Tian yi*, 524–30). A mistress of Wang Baosen named Zhao Lijiang from Haerbin reportedly went on the lam after his suicide (Xiao Li).

41. An appendix in Chen Xiaotong, 266, mentions the death of an investigator in an auto accident.

42. Maybe Chen Fang read about this in alleged plots to assassinate Patrice Lumumba. See De Witte.

43. Evidently the U.S. Embassy in Beijing felt instructed by *Tian nu* about how crooked Chinese (here, Sun Qi) learned to acquire fraudulent L-1 visas. U.S. Embassy (anonymous).

44. Personal interview, March 15, 2002.

45. Arrests of municipal cadres in 1995 in life were made by organs of Party Central, not by the local police and procuratorial characters who find all the clues in *Tian nu* (see Chang Chuan, "Beijingshi duli wangguo kaizui yuanlao rehuo," 79)—though a Chinese source credits the municipal Disciplinary Inspection Commission with putting together and heading a 117-person investigative task force in 1995, with participation by the municipal Disciplinary Inspection Commission, procuracy, police, and auditing office (Huizhou Municipal Committee Party School and Huizhou Municipal Administrative Academy, September 9, 2001, at http://www.hzdx.gov.cn/zt/jsjy2-2.htm [September 9, 2001]). Other sources speak of the Public Security Ministry's having organized a "5.11" special task force, presumably on May 11, 1995, with a detective Yang Feng-

rui, deputy head of the detective bureau, of the ministry (Ji Wei, 68). Ji Wei also speaks of a central "2.13" task force founded in Beijing on February 13, 1995 (32, 43). Top investigators included Ms. Liu Liying of the CCP Central Disciplinary Inspection Commission, Cao Keming, secretary of the Jiangsu provincial committee's Disciplinary Inspection Commission, and Luo Ji, head of the Anticorruption Bureau of the Supreme People's Procuratorate (Ji Wei, 32). When party leaders like Chen Xitong are under suspicion, the party's Political-Legal Commission usually gives approval to investigate. Later, Luo Ji was "arrested for 'collective graft taking' linked to the misappropriation of funds discovered during the Chen case." At http://www.asiaweek.com/asiaweek/98/0828/feat_6_passage.html (June 7, 2001).

46. Xu Jingbo, ix.
47. Amnesty International, 59.
48. On the arrests, see Ji Wei, 25, 31, 33, 73, 132, and Wang Gui, 53.
49. Long Lihua; personal interview, March 15, 2002. Chen Fang told me he knew Gao Qiming's wife.
50. Like Hao Xiangshou, Gao Qiming collaborated with the Beijing party boss's senior mistress He Ping ("Ge Mengmeng"), handled business for the vice mayor in Hong Kong, and absconded to Hong Kong when in the hot seat. Lushan, 55. On Chen Xitong's secretaries, see also Yi Ming.
51. Secretaries can plot conspiracies, says Chen Fang, in Zhang Yifan, 11–12. In the novel, see 49–51.
52. It is not in the novel, but Chen Fang in an interview cogently explicated three costs of corruption: it raises the cost of business, throws the legitimate economy into chaos, and diminishes the prestige of the party and government. Xu Jingbo, iii–iv.
53. As in Zheng Yefu's influential article in *Dushu*. Fan and Grossman, "Incentives and Corruption," argue the positive effects of corruption in China, citing Samuel P. Huntington as an early theorist of it.
54. Judged to be politically deficient while a student, Chen Fang was assigned to dig air raid shelters in the 1960s. Personal interview, March 15, 2002.
55. Weng Changshou.
56. Chen Fang speaks of the "renting of authority" in Xu Jingbo, iii.
57. Xu Jingbo, v; Gittings. The Oriental Plaza contract was just too large to neglect consulting the central government, particularly since it was in the capital.
58. Officially, 368 units and thirty-one individuals in seven provinces were involved. *Dangjian wenhui*, 27.
59. Lushan, "Li Peng baobi Wuxi feifa jizi anfan," 33–37.
60. Jiang Xiaoqing, 12–14; Lushan, "Li Peng baobi Wuxi feifa jizi anfan," 32–33.
61. Ji Wei, 24.
62. Jiang Xiaoqing, 21, speculates that Li Min was taken to Jiangsu (Nan-

jing) after his arrest (as is Li Haoyi in the novel) to save him from the fate of his State Security colleague Li Ming. Ji Wei, 29, says Li Ming had a terminal illness; an appendix in Chen Xiaotong, 256, says he died of cancer.

63. Jiang Xiaoqing, 14–19; Lushan, "Li Peng baobi Wuxi feifa jizi anfan," 31–32; Lushan, "Li Peng furen bei diaocha," 38–47.

64. Jiang Xiaoqing, 12–13; *Dangjian wenhui*, 26.

65. Xiao Chong, *Zhongguo fantan*, 26.

66. Lu Chen.

67. Lushan, "Chen Xitong duli wangguo neikui," 67.

68. Liu Yi. The reporter chides Lu, for instance, for setting *Shengwei shuji* in "K province." China has no province beginning with "K." Couldn't Lu have dropped a hint by using the real letter, while still leaving his readers guessing? See Qiu Xiaolong, who testifies that censors changed "Shanghai" to "H City" in a Chinese translation of his English-language mystery *Death of a Red Heroine*. (Shanghai was once called Haishang.)

69. Ji Wei, 40–41, 100.

70. Long Lihua; *Mingbao*. *Tian nu ren yuan*, 883, indicates that Chen revised the final Hong Kong version in June 1998, three months after the CCP announced that Chen Xitong would be tried. A prior draft, presumably that seeking publication in China, was completed in December 1997.

71. Xu Jingbo, vii.

72. Without having done a line-by-line reading of the Hong Kong version, as I have of *Dushi weiqing*, I would say that the latter more or less uses the Hong Kong edition as a basis and adds the third volume, except for chapter forty-six, the first chapter in volume three, which is the last chapter of the Hong Kong edition. *Dushi weiqing* lacks the front matter of the Hong Kong book.

73. Mi Jiashan was the director of this March 1999 production (from a *Dushi weiqing* publicity folder, provided me by Chen Fang, March 15, 2002). See also Voice of America.

74. However, Zhong Xinshe, xxvi–xxvii, likes at least the Hong Kong version better than the original.

75. The first half of the novel, containing the material from *Tian nu*, has a new subplot about a corrupt rural county boss, who may represent Liu Jinsheng, whom Chen Xitong made party secretary of Yanqing county over local CCP objections (Ji Wei, 80–87). Vice Mayor Li Shangmin ($\cong$ Li Runwu?—I suggest this identification because he dies on the job), originally a bit player, is elevated into a Jiao Yulu sort of hero. See Lushan, "Wang Baosen anjian manyan Xianggang," 55. But Shi Yan, *Tianyi*, 532–33, suggests that Li Runwu committed suicide because of his own misconduct. In the second half of the revision, a poor county in Northwest China has passed out RMB 960,000 in one year as gifts (1105).

76. Pressed about the incredible Cambodian episodes, Chen Fang said that these subplots are in life about someone other than Gao Qiming. He conflated the two in fiction. Personal interview, March 15, 2002.

77. Personal interview, March 15, 2002.

78. Personal interview, March 15, 2002. Meanwhile, Chen Fang wrote a novel, *Hai nu* or *The Sea's Wrath*, about corruption in Japan. Zhi Hui.

79. In November 2001 Li Jizhou, vice minister of public security, 1995–99 (assistant to the minister in 1994), was sentenced to execution with a two-year stay (in effect, a suspended death sentence; that he lived caused many to think he got off easy). He was convicted of taking more than US$600,000 in bribes from the notorious Lai Changxing. A case of cars smuggled from Hong Kong also involved bribes to Li Jizhou, so this is probably the car smuggling case in *Municipal Crisis*. Xinhua, "Smuggler Sentenced to Death."

80. Fifteen years, for taking bribes of RMB 430,000. *Xinbao*.

81. Jiang Xiaoqing, 13; Lushan, "Wang Baosen anjian manyan Xianggang," 54–55. *Dushi weiqing* follows the Hong Kong sources closely here; Ge Mengmeng (≅ He Ping), the party boss's older mistress in Hong Kong, gives up the game. In the novel, she is captured in the British West Indies—a fiction, probably, since the company was just a mailbox.

82. Barmé; this is the title of his chapter 10.

83. Ostrov, 45, notes that "starting in the 1980s, the license plates of military transports were rented out and then used for smuggling," and that by 1998 the PLA had a "smuggling empire" in Guangdong. See also Mulvenon.

84. Kinkley, *Chinese Justice*, 279, 293, 297, 300. See also Jiang Xiaoling. Lu Tianming cited a similar proportionality logic to defend his *Shengwei shuji* for not having more about corruption. His object was "comprehensively to write about high-level political persons," so it couldn't be all about anticorruption, nor could anticorruption be its main thread. Hou Xiaoqiang. Chapter 7 of this book revisits the notion of proportionality.

85. Chen Fang admits to being slightly mystical in his writing in Xu Jingbo, vii.

86. When he goes to Dongfang's hotel to settle scores, he takes pains so that innocent bystanders don't get hurt (426).

87. In the revision, Jiao Dongfang speaks good French, declares customers to be "gods," and shines the shoes of a sloppy doorman (27–28). Much of his relation with Tian Congying, a newly invented girlfriend, is also chivalrous. He marries her and makes provisions for their child to live abroad.

88. Long Lihua; personal interview, March 15, 2002.

89. Secretary Jiao convenes a "last supper" for himself, at which he announces that one of his apostles on the standing committee (Fang Hao) will betray him (612–25).

90. However, at one point in the first half of the revision, the good guys go to a secret military base to dedicate themselves—under orders from Party Central (435)!—to becoming a new, secret conspiratorial group to investigate corruption. This group opposes the new conspiratorial municipal committee investigatory group set up by Secretary Jiao to look into (really, to cover up) the real cor-

ruption scandals. The latter is headed by He Xiangshou, whose status is upgraded in the revision. The good guys' "conspiracy" may be counted as one of the revision's bows to "national forms"; Zhou Senlin, Chen Hu, and Mie Baozhu (a newly identified hero from the old 2.11 case, brought back into action in the revision and killed off, as is the private investigator, both in scenes good for cinema or television) take the equivalent of a peach blossom vow (cf. *Romance of the Three Kingdoms*), and at a Judge Bao temple (351–55).

91. *Tian nu*, 363; there is no mention in *Dushi weiqing*, 579.

92. *Tian nu*'s list at 183 does not appear in *Dushi weiqing*. The reference to the Great Wall scandal of Shen Taifu (*TN*, 193) goes missing in *DSWQ* (365–66).

93. It has giant photos of Song Huihui; this would match Chen Xitong's secret hideout in Shunyi county, not his giant retreat at Daoxianghu. See "Shiji tanwufan."

94. This enters Chen Fang's plot when He Qizhang gives away apartments (61–63, 92).

95. Zhiyue Bo, ed., 66–76; Ji Wei, 57.

Chapter 4: Climax: Alarum and Standard-Bearer

1. On the advent of anticorruption fiction, some time between 1995 and 1997 or so, see chapter 1. For Zhang's biography, see Lu Mei, "Lichang," 4; *Beijing qingnianbao*; Tang Nan; Shu Jinyu. Zhang Ping's father was a professor who as a rightist was sent to the countryside, so Zhang knew the peasant life. During the Cultural Revolution, Zhang Ping was enlisted to write propaganda plays, and in 1978 he entered Shanxi Normal College. He earned money during vacations laboring in coal mines. He graduated in 1982 and was appointed to cultural units in Shanxi. His early stories won awards; in 1985 his story about a negligent police station, "Xuehun," was his first about corruption, but he continued with more modernist pieces. (On Zhang's modernism, see *Beijing qingnianbao*; Lu Mei, "Lichang," 5. Zhang liked *The Sound and the Fury* and *One Hundred Years of Solitude*.) In the Shu Jinyu interview, Zhang Ping notes that many press interviews are fabricated from other interviews and Zhang's books' afterwords, etc. Note the similarity of Lin Hong's piece to Jiang Xiaobo's.

2. *Tian wang*'s and *Fa han Fenxi*'s print runs ultimately ran to about 200,000. Shu Jinyu; Yi Menglin. Zhang Ping's *Guer lei* is about orphans.

3. As noted in the title and content of *Beijing qingnianbao*, "Zhang Ping: Wo de xiaoshuo shi caifang chulai de."

4. Tang Nan, 7; Lin Hong, 213. Zhang Ping's retrospective is his "Yi ge xianwei shuji de zibai." Ai Qun and Wu Xiaolong's account of the suit and what led up to it won a commendation in the fourth Woodpecker Literary Prizes of 1999, in the documentary literature category.

5. Zhou Meisen's novel *Renjian zhengdao* (1996) provided the next major TV series with some corruption themes. It aired in 1998.

6. *Zhuomuniao*, nos. 2, 3, 4 (March, May, July 1997). Reportedly, the *Jiefang ribao* also printed the novel.

7. The lawsuits dissuaded Lu Tianming from writing strict romans à clef; see Liu Yi.

8. Zheng Bonong, 45; Wang Jianmin, 29.

9. Wang Jianmin et al.; "*Caifu yu renxing* tixian fantan xiaoshuo"; "Zhongyang Jiwei, Zhong Zu Bu, Zhong Xuan Bu."

10. Officially, *Shengsi jueze* grossed US$14.5 million, the record for a domestic film until 2003, when Zhang Yimou's *Yingxiong* (Hero) surpassed $25 million. *Titanic* still held the record in 2003, at $38.6. Jones; Rosen.

11. Jones; Craig S. Smith, "Piracy a Concern as the China Trade Opens Up," *New York Times*, Oct. 5, 2000.

12. Lu Mei, "Lichang," 4.

13. *Jueze* shared the October 2000 Mao Dun award, for novels published between 1995 and 1998, with three other novels. In November, the movie version won a Golden Rooster award for best feature film (shared with two other films). In the fall of 1999, the novel won first place for fiction in the fourth Woodpecker Literary Prize competition, for public security literature. In 1994, Zhang Ping's *Tian wang* won a first prize for fiction in the third Woodpecker competition; in 1999 again, Zhang Ping's *Guer lei* won a second prize for documentary literature. See "Zhuomuniao wenxuejiang."

14. An ad on the back cover of *Zhuomuniao* 106 (October 1, 2000) gives the 200,000 figure. Some sensational titles appeared under the name of "Zhang Ping"—another Zhang Ping, was the explanation. See, for instance, "Zhang Ping bei *Lü maozi* kunrao." The 300,000 figure comes from "Gei fubai haokan."

15. Wan Yongnian's long speech is even written with stage directions, including "applause" and "enthusiastic applause" (488–91).

16. Wang Zheng, 20.

17. As noted by He Zhenbang, "Shidai fuyu," 142.

18. Zhang Ping's standard defense for writing a novel with so little legal consciousness is that to portray a China ruled by law would be unrealistic, a "fantasy." Zhong Xiaoyong.

19. Zheng Bonong, 45, 47; Zhang Jiong, 7 (Zhang is an orthodox CCP critic); Yi Menglin, 6.

20. Ni Zhen, "Xianshizhuyi de beizhuang." Liu Zengrong agreed.

21. Simplistically tracing all problems to bad people was part of the film's attraction (hence it was liked by Miao Junjie, 32), but, as we shall see, the novel already has tendencies in this direction.

22. Li was concurrently factory head in charge of production. In both the novel and film, Li's old subordinates at times revert to calling him simply "Factory Head Li" (Li *changzhang*).

23. From a personal communication. One can detect Dickensian puns or suggestive hints in many names. The villain Guo Zhongyao sounds like "important offenses." Gaocheng could be "tall and accomplished," or "tall accomplishments." His greedy wife, Aizhen, sounds like "in love with treasures" (this was changed in the film version). The previous, good factory manager was Yuan Mingliang, "originally clear and bright." Wan Yongnian suggests a man for the ages, a man of a myriad, eternal years.

24. Yan Zhen makes this a point of benevolence in the film. He will protect Li from all charges.

25. Li Yanchun indicates that incidents of an exchange of old machines between factories and the purchase of cotton at inflated prices are phenomena that Zhang Ping uncovered during his research into North China factories. The novel reads as if they were; Zhang is providing "information."

26. Despite inferences to the contrary by me and other interviewers, Zhang Ping insists that his novel is not about morality, but about "the system." Personal interview, March 15, 2002.

27. Personal interview, March 15, 2002. Zhang sees "problem literature" as between "pure literature" and "popular literature."

28. Zhong Xiaoyong; Wang Jianmin, 29; Zheng Bonong, 44; Lu Mei, "Lichang," 5; Tang Nan, 7 (on secrecy). The cities are specified in "Xinwen lianjie" (News roundup), *Chengdu shangbao*, October 20, 2000[?], http://www.cdsb.com/2000/200010/20/html/006.htm (August 16, 2001).

29. Sun Zhao has counted the statistics; there are 105 "important numbers" in the plot.

30. The workers are so at odds with the factory bosses that they will not even accept relief if they know the factory bosses are distributing it (246). Mayor Li's "dangerous" alternative solution, then, is to go through the workers' and protestors' own leaders.

31. As noted by Jiang Xiaobo, 208.

32. It is rumored that in life, judicial officials in Beijing caviled over these (film) punishments, delaying the release of the picture.

33. Even before the film *Shengsi jueze* brought him fame, Zhang Ping was sensitive to charges that he had written *qingtian xiaoshuo* (fiction with uncorruptible officials). Jiang Xiaobo, 208.

34. Zheng Bonong, 43, 45; Sang Ningxia, 112–13.

35. Corrigan, 13.

36. Dongfang.

37. As noted by Hu Ke, 16.

38. Bai Weihua may be modeled on Liu Liying, deputy secretary of the Central Disciplinary Inspection Commission and daughter of the CCP elder statesman Liu Bocheng. She headed investigations of the Chen Xitong case and of a smuggling ring in Zhanjiang, then set up the 420 task force (founded April 20, 1999) that ended the miasma of malfeasance in Xiamen. Fewsmith, 224.

39. Cawelti, 44–45. See also Pickowicz; Nick Browne et al., eds.; and Dissanayake, ed.

40. He Zhenbang, "Changpian re," 15–16. He Zhiyun liked the novel's realism, as did Mao Keqiang. Its print run was 300,000; Shu Jinyu. On the research, see *Beijing qingnianbao*.

41. Zhong Xiaoyong.

42. Hu Zihong.

43. I tend to prefer the film version, and so does Zhang Tianwei. In addition to the 162-minute version of *Shengsi jueze* shown in theaters and available on VCD and DVD, there is a 93-minute abridgment on VHS that I find still more gripping, and also a "Fifth Draft Screenplay" (*wu gao*) of June 3, 1999 (when Yu Benzheng was already in charge; the film is directly descended from this script) posted on the Internet with material for a three-hour epic. Even the 93-minute version has episodes not in the novel.

44. Conceison, 191, notes that the term "main melody" (*zhuxuanlü*) appeared in drama and film publications as early as 1987. Tao Dongfeng, 116, cites promotion of the term at a March 1989 national film conference. But because the term connotes stressing the "main melody" of the CCP and socialism amid the cacophony of voices in China, it is thought of as a term primarily used during the conservative period after the June 4, 1989, massacre. In its elaboration since then, the term has been associated with films heavy in CCP propaganda, like historical epics about the Chinese revolution that convey patriotic CCP heroism. However, China's litterateurs and artists naturally resist the whole concept, thinking it a throwback to Maoism. Because Jiang Zemin embraced "main melody" works for showing mainstream positive aspects of China during its cacophonous development, some critics hold that the main melody is not so political, but simply about today's ordinary people coping with a rapidly modernizing China in an "idealistic" (upbeat) way (overcoming aggravations that China can be proud of, like cell phones). Director Feng Xiaogang thus claims his own feel-good comedic hits to be China's "real" main melody films, and ads for cassettes of his films on the Internet sometimes describe his films as "main melody." But the clincher is if a film is thought to have been initiated by a local cultural or propaganda department and state subsidized in production and/or through block ticket purchases. Corruption certainly was not a "main melody" theme in film; *Shengsi jueze* needed heavy local and central support, and perhaps the blessing of Jiang Zemin, to be made. However, Conceison notes, 202, that the theme of exposing systemic party corruption did exist in certain Shanghai spoken art dramas, in the guise of praising the CCP.

45. Also, in the plot the mayor's wife is corrupt; at the time, the wife of Beijing party boss Jia Qinglin (Chen Xitong's second successor) was suspected of corruption in the Yuanhua affair.

46. Said an officer of the Masses' Press, March 15, 2002. This contradicts

Wang Jianmin et al., 27, who say the CCP Central Propaganda Department suggested to its Shanghai branch that *Choice* be filmed.

47. See "Yingpian ge an fenxi," esp. He Zizhuang and Song Jigao, 10, and Ni Zhen, "Yu Yu Benzheng," 5. See also Lan Ying. As to the actors, Wang Qingxiang, who plays Mayor Li, had played a model official in a 1999 TV series, *Zouguo Liuyuan* (Passing by Liuyuan). After *Shengsi jueze* he was typecast in such roles. See Li Yan; Chen Bin.

48. Yu responding to web fans in Zhao Bing.

49. My favorable opinion is more or less shared by Derek Elley in *Variety*.

50. Called *Jueze*, like the novel. Yu, who began his work in October 1998 after the TV drama aired (Yu began filming in July 1999), says he viewed the TV version only after finishing the film (Zou Jianwen, 30). But there are odd similarities. Both versions invent a handicapped Li child and a Li-Yang talk at a scenic overlook. Slower in pace and very faithful to the novel (from which much dialogue is taken whole), the teleplay hardly had to invent new subplots to fill up the time, until the second half. Yet even Zhang Ping preferred the film version. See Hu Yinhong and Zhao Xiaozhen. Li Xuejian played Mayor Li on TV, and he was a movie star, having personified the model official Jiao Yulu in the movie of that name (1990). Like Wang Qingxiang, he was typecast. The novel *Jueze* was also made into a radio play by 1998; Sun Haiwen, 94.

51. Hao Jian, 12.

52. Ni Zhen, "Yu Yu Benzheng," 5; Zou Jianwen, 30. In the fifth draft screenplay, Cao Wanshan at the end jumps out of a window to his death, and the girls in the brothel wear bikinis. They are better covered up in the film as released.

53. Kinkley, "*Choice* in Film Adaptation"; McFarlane.

54. Like me, some Chinese critics found this a poor excuse. See Bai Lian.

55. For more on how the film transforms the family dynamics of Li Gaocheng, Wu Aizhen, and their children, see Kinkley, "*Choice* in Film Adaptation." Hao Jian, 13, 14, sees Wu as an "unintentional" corrupt element, even a victim. A possible political reason for ameliorating Wu Aizhen's evil might have been fear of allusions to actual CCP leaders with corrupt wives. Investigation of Beijing party boss Jia Qinglin's wife delayed the film's release in Beijing. Wang Jianmin et al., 28.

56. Zhang Tianwei.

57. The film's panoramic vista, with skyscrapers and a Ferris wheel in the distance, was filmed on Dalian's Green Mountain. See http://www.skyscraperpicture.com/dalian.htm. The film's time is moved forward to after April 1997, after Deng Xiaoping's death in February 1997, and anticorruption plaudits could go uniquely to Jiang. The "Hai[zhou]" on the film's license plates would suggest a provincial-level city like Shanghai. Ai Qun, in a personal communication, indicates that the film was partly filmed in Shanghai, but of course that was where the film studio was. The city of the novel is northern; the

action takes place before the New Year, and it is cold (as in the teleplay, shot in Baoding).

58. An irony noted by Sun Wuchen, 9.

59. Film audiences saw it as I do. At the premiere, their greatest applause was for the actor who played Yang Cheng. Hu Yinhong and Zhao Xiaozhen.

60. The general gestalt of a two-man party-state team of corruption fighters, Yang and Li, instead of individuals pitted one against another as in other anticorruption works, was pleasing to at least one "responsible comrade" of the Central Disciplinary Inspection Commission that helped the film get clearance. "Zhong Ji Wei fuze tongzhi." The CDIC intervention on this point seems confirmed by Zou Jianwen, 30.

61. I would thus refute those who think Chinese film's main problem is not quality (as shaped by lack of freedom of expression and other factors) but lack of protection from Hollywood competition—as argued by, for example, Dai Jinhua in "How about China's Hollywood."

Chapter 5: Anticorruption by Indirection

1. Previously Wang published *Guanchang chunqiu*, but its sales did not take off. Liu Liming. Biographical information on Wang Yuewen is scarce, but see Huang Bin. Wang's father was a rightist. Wang Yuewen, "Fumu"; Phoenix TV Web.

2. Li Liqun.

3. In May 2002, after *Guo hua* had been banned, Wang lent his name and two of his other novels to a ten-volume anticorruption series. See Wang Yuewen et al., *Zhongguo fanfu xiaoshuo daxi*.

4. Huang Bin.

5. There are thirty-five blank lines at points that provide minor breaks in the novel. These take the place of natural segues.

6. Liu Xuyuan.

7. The National Library in Beijing retains copies of *Guo hua*, though it does not of Chen Fang's *Tian nu* or Wang Lixiong's *Huang huo* (discussed in Kinkley, "Modernity and Apocalypse").

8. Fu Guoyong; Yu Jintao. Wang Yuewen says only 105,000 copies of the legal edition were printed.

9. Chu Tian; Li Liqun.

10. Liu Xuyuan. The term "critical realism" is used in "Nairen xunwei."

11. Li Liqun.

12. Yu Jintao reports on this kind of criticism.

13. Reportedly he gave up bureaucratic work in favor of writing in 2000. Hu Peng and Bai Junfeng. Wang served in the Xupu county government, 1984–92, then in the nearby Huaihua municipal government, before moving to Changsha around 1994. He was working for the Hunan provincial government in 1999,

when he wrote *Guo hua*. Huang Bin; Yu Jintao; Phoenix TV Web. He began writing in 1989, say his book jackets, and wrote in earnest about the bureaucratic life after 1994, says Huang. He began with short stories.

14. There are indications that the city is in the south (249), though it can snow (248), as it does sometimes in Changsha (capital of Wang's native province) and cities in neighboring Hubei (the "Jing" of Jingdu suggests Hubei).

15. For instance, the text points out at several times that Mei Yuqin, Li Mingxi, and Zeng Li are Zhu's only true friends, as in passages as close together as pp. 201 and 208.

16. The notable example is Zhu's seduction by the call girl Li Jing, to whom he is strongly attracted, in Pi Jie's pleasure city near the end of the novel.

17. That this is ultimately bad is revealed in a parable about how cop Song got to be the way he is (685).

18. Liu Liming faults the novel for being so informational, at the expense of probing of character.

19. Hu Peng and Bai Junfeng.

20. As in Lubbock's *The Craft of Fiction*.

21. Li Liqun.

22. See Peng Lun; Hu Zihong, "Daoming shenyu daoban." References courtesy Helen Xiaoyan Wu.

23. "Wang Yuewen xie xinzuo." Reference courtesy Helen Xiaoyan Wu.

24. "Changpian xiaoshuo bu fanrong?" Likewise, see Wang Xiangdong, 24, and Zhang Zhizhong.

Chapter 6: Dirt Plus Soap Equals Pay Dirt

1. Shieh; Lawrence; Fewsmith, 224–25; Mulvenon, 28–33.

2. Lawrence.

3. "She an renyuan 600 duo."

4. Fewsmith, 226; Mulvenon, 31, on Ji Shengde.

5. An official source on the Red Mansion is Han Yanrong. Various websites have pictures of the place. Sheng Xue, 260–77, questioned Lai and telephoned four ex-employees of the Red Mansion long-distance. They denied the official news accounts of illicit activities and videotaping there. However, videotapes made somewhere were allegedly used to identify Lai Changxing's cronies.

6. Rose Tang.

7. Liu Ping, "Wo xie fanfu xiaoshuo." This article has a summary of Liu's career.

8. Zhao Lanying. According to my copy of *Zousi dang'an*, the third printing took the copies issued from 18,201 to 23,300. One must wonder if Liu Ping delayed work on *Lianshu dang'an*, which is a story of events that took place before the events of *Zousi dang'an* and whose plot is partly summarized in *Zousi dang'an*, but was published after *Zousi*, to get *Zousi* out as fast as possible, before

it was overtaken by revelations about Yuanhua in the news. That *Lianshu* was released after work began on a TV adaptation of the novel might have been a marketing ploy.

9. A book-length piece of reportage on the Internet by Liu Zhiwu, who seems to have written a lot of reportage about philandering officials, is *Yang Qianxian duoluo shimo*, about the downfall of the head of Xiamen customs and his mistress. This may have been published previously in book form. Official or semiofficial sources, which I thank Shawn Shieh for bringing to my attention, are the books by Zhang Xianhua and by Hai Yun, and the VCDs called *Xiamen teda zousi an*. Much government dirt on Lai Changxing and his confederates was available to a wide public on the Internet, including in the sources cited below.

10. Sheng Xue.

11. I thank Shawn Shieh for mentioning *Hei dong*, by Zhang Chenggong (an Anhui provincial police cadre with a long record of service) and Lu Chuan (director of the movie *Xun qiang*, or *Looking for the Gun*, and son of Lu Tianming, discussed in chapter 2). Some readers thought this novel might have been inspired by the Yuanhua case, but Zhang Chenggong in an interview surprisingly revealed exactly which criminals and law enforcers from an Anhui case it was based on. See Bei Qing. *Hei dong* sold many more copies than Liu Ping's works; after the first printing in September 2001, a seventh printing in January 2002 brought the number of copies issued from 70,000 to 85,000. *Hei dong* was by then profiting from the popularity of its television version, and it was no. 2 in a series (the first being *Hei bing*, or *Black Ice*). I am not sure that the TV version did not precede the novel. *Hei dong* is by any estimate a popular novel, with noticeably less complex and ornamented prose even than *Zousi dang'an*.

12. There is also an intimation that the villain did away with two people in a previous case (6).

13. "Wufa" could be construed literally as "my law," but better yet it is homophonous with the first part of *wufa wutian*, "defiant of the laws below and Heaven above." Ding Wufa's cousin, who manages "public relations" for him, is named Ding Wutian. Together, they are *wufa wutian*.

14. When Ding initially pulls them into his guanxi web, Chen is deputy party secretary of Haimen and Yan is vice chief of customs. Haimen customs has been elevated from *chu* (division) to *ting* (department) rank.

15. Namely *Lianshu dang'an*.

16. To be safe, Ding impregnates two women. Only one can be his wife, but with his customary chivalry he sends the other mistress and son to the United States, too, where he will support them for life.

17. Guo Xiaoling, the sole female member of the Xiamen municipal CCP standing committee, was demoted for corruption, but Xiao may be a composite character. Guo's husband was a Xiamen University professor accused of economic crimes of his own.

18. To paraphrase Geremie Barmé again, the novel's viewpoint is that it is

Notes to Chapter 6

"patriotic" to "screw" Taiwanese compatriots who are too rich for their own good and want to take advantage of mainland girls' purer morality. Hu abuses her pursuer mercilessly.

19. Shawn Shieh wonders if this police chief resembles Zhuang Rushun, but I do not have sufficient details for either figure to hint at a match.

20. By a generous count, at 83–84, 128–32, 179–80, 267–68, 284, 297, 336–38, 454, 496.

21. Yu Yingrui; Zhongyang Dianshi Tai. In Sheng Xue's presentation of Lai's side of the story, 283–94, Lai argues that Yang Qianxian was a scapegoat.

22. Yu Yingrui; Zhongyang Dianshi Tai. Jie Peiyong in the end accepted precious books and antiques from Lai Changxing and so was convicted at trial. Lai honored Jie by using his calligraphy for the brand name on packs of Wanli cigarettes; this seems characteristic of the respect between Ding and Yan in the novel.

23. Xie Hong. The 3,000 yuan figure is widely cited in various newspaper accounts listed at http://www.ccadp.org/laichangxing.htm. The novel's subplot about Ding impregnating two women and sending them to the United States to have their children (which would make them U.S. citizens) may reflect Yang Qianxian's handling of the pregnancy of Zhou Bing, if we are to believe Yang's alleged confession as excerpted in Sheng Xue, 289.

24. Xiao Luntian.

25. "Former Fujian Provincial Deputy Party Secretary Expelled from CPC."

26. Liu Ping, "Qian yan," esp. at 5.

27. Interestingly, Ding Wufa is said to be, but not really depicted as, a former lecher tending toward sexual sadism who has lost interest in sex by the time of his marriage (his only interest now is acquiring an heir). Why Liu Ping chose to develop this line of characterization instead of depicting a fictionalized image of Lai's wife and alleged confederate, Zeng Mingna, is a mystery to me. Indeed, Internet gossip attributes to Lai Changxing one or more mistresses before he returned to Fujian from Hong Kong.

28. "Qian yan." The ambiguity was all the greater since Liu's audience knew the prequel from its television adaptation, which drastically departs from the novel's plot.

29. He was a big spender with a Robin Hood reputation. Beech.

30. In an interview, however, Liu uses the term "rent-seeking" and argues, as in the novel, that localities often find smuggling to be in their economic interest. Lu Xingsheng.

31. The proximity of the golf course described at page 97 suggests that its model may be the one at the Xiamen Haiceng Taiwanese Investment Zone, at a time when it was not so accessible by bridge.

32. It is interesting that Liu Ping's narrative never takes a clear stand on whether or not Chu Feng was actually set up in the case of the polyester fibers. Is this because there is some true case behind this subplot (assuming that Chu

Feng represents a real person) and Liu Ping did not want to go beyond his "knowledge"? See 239.

33. The book was not a best-seller, however. Its third printing brought the number of copies issued to 23,300. That was before the July Yuanhua trials created a demand for a fourth printing. Otherwise, *Zousi dang'an*'s market timing was not so good, for the market was saturated with anticorruption books and series in 2001.

34. Zhao Lanying.

35. They were praised in *Renmin ribao*. Yan Zhaozhu, "Fanfu changlian."

36. This is *Gudu lüren* (2004). In 2001 he said he would write novels of the merchant life and of love in a "tears" series, *Tears of Officialdom*.

37. Ge Fei and Liu Ping wrote the screenplay for the 2002 TV series, *Jisi yaoanzu* (Anti-smuggling team for serious cases). That was also the title of a 2000 book by Ge Fei, published by the Zuojia chubanshe in Beijing. I do not know which came first, the TV series or Ge Fei's book.

38. Liu Ping, "Qian yan," 1–2.

39. The front book jacket flap, but not the cover or title page, indicates that the May 2002 "first edition" is a revised edition. I have found no evidence of an earlier edition in print.

40. Yang Binbin; "Yuanhua daan jiang cheng yingshi redian."

41. Liu Ping, "Hou ji," 489–90.

Chapter 7: Chinese Realism, Popular Culture, and the Critics

1. In fact Zhang Yiwu, "Zhongguo baixing lanpishu," points out, rightly I think, that there has been further polarization of mass versus avant-garde literature. Dai Jinhua, in "Huo de zhishi," maintains the distinction between elite and mass culture. In works that mix the two, she speaks of one having compromised with the other. However, collapsing binary distinctions is otherwise fashionable; see Jing Wang's "Guest Editor's Introduction," 1–7. Another dichotomy seldom collapsed is that of modernism/postmodernism. Words beginning with "post" typically refer to concepts that are historicist and teleological; "postmodernism" is rarely argued to exist without "modernism" before it.

2. Lu Tianming, a little fed up with the greater attention paid his three anticorruption novels than his other three, nevertheless told an interviewer that the former were "closer to reality" and yet also more like mass literature (*dazhonghua*, "massified," made for the masses, and *pingminhua*, suitable for common people). Hou Xiaoqiang. He Zhiyun calls Zhang Ping's *Shimian maifu* a "massified social novel, a political novel."

3. "Modern Chinese literary practice in the 1920s, but also in later decades, is characterised by collectivity." Hockx, "Playing the Field," 76. My conception of China's elite intellectuals is indebted to Hockx and, before him, to the many writings of the late Helmut Martin.

Notes to Chapter 7

4. Xudong Zhang, *Chinese Modernism*, 112. It is unclear whether Zhang means that it was in the state apparatus that the term degenerated or that the term was a label for orthodoxy in the state apparatus.

5. Anderson, *The Limits of Realism*; David Der-wei Wang, *Fictional Realism*. Duke and Link address the post-Mao period, when realism's prestige was about to wane. McDougall and Louie also take post-Mao realism seriously, while finding in it continuities with Maoism.

6. David Der-wei Wang, *The Monster That Is History*, 209. However, at 272–73 he seems to see "a modern realist discourse" as a late Qing project and a holistic cultural one, not so pluralist. He cites Yü-sheng Lin's evocation of holistic cultural change; Lin took the New Culture Movement of the early republic as the turning point, unlike his mentor Benjamin Schwartz. At 279, Wang writes of a "phantasmagoric realism" of the late twentieth century and possibly of the end of the previous century, too.

7. Another example is Huters's research to this end, beginning with "A New Way of Writing."

8. Průšek, 1–28. Doleželová-Velingerová and her pupils, in *The Chinese Novel at the Turn of the Century*, saw modernity's arrival more in terms of literary structures than ideological ones.

9. For an excellent exposition of this aspect of Liu's thought, see Rong Cai, 38.

10. McDougall, *The Introduction of Western Literary Theories into Modern China*.

11. See Denton, 36–41.

12. Anderson, 25.

13. Ibid., 18.

14. Rosenstone, 39.

15. This is a general theme of McDougall, *Fictional Authors*, notably chapter 7.

16. Huters, "Ideologies," 154, adds that realism was appealing in China precisely because of its identification with social reform movements of nineteenth-century Europe. See Wellek, 242, on this "contradiction" in the theory of realism.

17. Unlike Anderson, 202, I believe that socialist realism at its best (though in its melodramatic, not its realistic, aspects) did inspire audience identification with heroes against the villains, and catharsis.

18. As pointed out by Xiaobing Tang, 51–52, who prefers not to emphasize Lu Xun as a realist.

19. Wang, *Fictional Realism*, 1–2.

20. Ibid., 10.

21. Ibid., 16.

22. As noted by Wellek, 234, 236. See Auerbach, e.g., 24–26.

23. Chen Pingyuan, *Ershi shiji Zhongguo*, 192–99. I believe he has revised this view in more recent writings. Lu Xun, *Zhongguo xiaoshuo shilüe*, chapter 28.

24. Hegel; David Der-wei Wang, *The Monster That Is History*, 200–223.

25. David Der-wei Wang, *Fin-de-siècle Splendor*, 183–251, takes a Bakhtinian view of a "grotesque realism" that dates back to the Renaissance and ancient times, which Wang values positively.

26. In *The Monster That Is History*, 218, Wang indicates that the late Qing writers projected a "complacency" about the moral changes and a feeling that they were "palatable."

27. As noted in regard to a late Qing Li Boyuan novel, by David Der-wei Wang in his *The Monster That Is History*, 50.

28. David Der-wei Wang, *Fin-de-siècle Splendor*, 205.

29. Duke, *Blooming and Contending*, chapter 2 (and its opening notes), provides a guide to the debates.

30. See Li Yi; Bi Hua; Duke, "Chinese Literature." Duke, *Blooming and Contending*, esp. 29–97, discusses the debates, here adopting the term "neorealism" instead of "critical realism." As Duke notes, the term "critical realist" was too hot for Chinese writers to apply to themselves. For instance, Jie Min, 55, takes the orthodox class stand that critical realism belongs to capitalist society. The combination of "new" and "realism" happens periodically in many cultures, of course, and it did so previously in China, to connote proletarian writing. See David Der-wei Wang, *The Monster That Is History*, 83.

31. Epitomized by the title essay in Liu Binyan's *People or Monsters?*

32. Wellek, 242.

33. Huters, in *Bringing Home the World*, 135, points out Wu Jingzi's dismissal of famous scholars who were not given to "serious concerns."

34. Lu Tianming calls literature about big social themes "Great China literature," which is unlike *sirenhua xiezuo*, or "self-absorbed writing." Bu Changwei. Lu Tianming and Liu Zhenyun have used the idea that "main melody" literature embodies the major trends of the times to dissociate the main melody concept from government propaganda. Instead they emphasize that the main melody amounts to a focus on major trends (as defined independently by authors).

35. Link, "Introduction to the Revised Edition," xxii.

36. Friedrich Engels, Letter to Margaret Harkness, retitled "On Socialist Realism," in Becker, ed., 484.

37. The phrase from Engels is still cited by Wang Xiangdong in regard to novels about officialdom.

38. Wu Xiaoming, quoted in Zhu Xiuliang. The same editor noted these taboos in the press's popular publications: "Don't put criminals and bloody scenes on the cover; Don't go into details of investigative procedures; Don't write anything that would encourage crime; Don't diminish readers' sense of security; Don't puff up the arrogance of criminals; Don't display the details of crime or try to shock readers." Another application of the notion of proportionality is broached in chapter 3 of this book, at note 84.

39. Brooks, 5.

Notes to Chapter 7

40. Highet, 211.

41. Kinkley, *Chinese Justice*, 267. Zhang Yiwu, in Chen Xiaoming and Zhang Yiwu, "Shichanghua," J3, 6, backs this view with his judgment that "literature of the wounded" was a branch of "mass literature." The difference arrived with the avant-garde in 1985–86, in works by Yu Hua and Ge Fei, for example.

42. See, for instance, Hao Yu, "Guanchang zuowei ren de yizhong chujing"; Li Yuntuan, "Guanchang xiaoshuo"; Wen Bo. I thank Helen Xiaoyan Wu for these references.

43. Wang Lixiong's *Huang huo*, analyzed in Kinkley, "Modernity and Apocalypse," is a popular novel about global apocalypse. It is a thriller, yet it was also written to exemplify and promote Wang's new conception of democracy, later adumbrated in his nonfiction book *Rongjie quanli*.

44. Gao Xingjian.

45. Jing Wang, *High Culture Fever*, 145–47. Bao Chang, for one, wrote an article to show that China had never had much interest in modernism; realism was modern Chinese literature's "law of development."

46. Ibid., 162–69.

47. These included books about exemplary bad political leaders such as the Gang of Four, but seldom corrupt leaders, like those featured in the nondissident book by Ling Fei, *Xia yi ge shi shui?*

48. Rosenstone, 55–56, 61–62.

49. Hamm provides superb description and analysis of the martial arts novel.

50. Second prize in the 1994–95 Shanghai municipal competition for mid-length and full-length novels. I thank Hua Jian for this information.

51. Among the major anticorruption authors, not just Zhang Ping was sued, as related in chapter 4, but also Zhou Meisen. Forty Jiangsu officials sued him for defamation in his novel *Renjian zhengdao* (1996). McGregor (date of novel amended).

52. Chi Li, called "a writer for the commoners" in a symposium pamphlet (the phrase was intended as praise), blew up over the categorization of writers by subject matter ("rural writers, city writers, military writers and even anticorruption writers") and "whether they write about the lives of commoners or of intellectuals, etc." (quoted from the rapporteur's paraphrase); see "Hot Debate in Literary Circles." See also Guoguo.

53. Positive comments are typified by the opinions of He Hong; Hu Zihong, "Fanfu xiaoshuo"; Li Yuntuan, "Lun xin shiqi wenxue." Chen Meilan's 2002 retrospective on diverse novels of the 1990s gives an important and positive role to *Cangtian zai shang* and *Jueze*. Positive retrospectives on literature of officialdom come from Shen Jiada and Zhang Zhizhong. Fang Xuesong sees a positive start followed by a decline, as I do.

54. Cited in Chen Pingyuan, "Literature High and Low," 119.

55. Zhang Lei, Han Kuancheng.

56. See Jiang Hu; Lu Mei, "Fanfu xiaoshuo"; Jian Lushi.

57. Lu Tianming was particularly stung by the refusal of critics to review his works, perhaps because of the initial positive reception of *Cangtian zai shang*. Miao Chun.

58. Chen Sihe is widely cited on the web as having made positive remarks about anticorruption fiction, as in "*Caifu yu renxing* tixian fantan xiaoshuo xin tese," and Yu Xiaoshi, "Naqi wenxue de wuqi." In print, Fu Qingxuan cites Chen Sihe as praising the TV series *Hongse kangnaixin* at a conference. In literary journals, one saw Tang Zhesheng favorably analyzing novels with corruption themes as popular fiction, and Gu Fengwei and Wu Yumin praising them as a "shock wave of literary realism." In 1999, Zhang Yiwu, in "Quanqiuhua," J3, 20, noted themes of "layoffs, corruption, transnational capital investment behavior, and inequalities of wealth" in novels that he considered optimistic because they showed new opportunities for group identity. These seem not to be the more pessimistic anticorruption works. Lu Tianming and Zhou Meisen voiced resentment at critics' refusal to take them seriously; see Yu Kai. Celebrity creative writer Mo Yan also speaks favorably of "literature about officialdom" in Wang Jun.

59. Qunzhong chubanshe also publishes Zhang Chenggong. It previously published "bad boy" Wang Shuo.

60. Dirlik and Zhang, 14. See also Fu Ping; Zhang Yiwu, "Zhongguo baixing lanpishu." China's academic critics were actually rather diverse in their opinions; see Dong Zhilin. Rong Cai, 181, offers the theory that intellectuals in the late 1990s, as opposed to the early 1990s, were resigned to the new commercialization of culture.

61. Chen Xiaoming, "Wufa shenhua"; also "Wugen de ku'nan."

62. Chen Xiaoming, "Nuoyong, fankang."

63. Lin Jianfa.

64. Jing Wang, "Guest Editor's Introduction," 8–9, also reminds us that best-sellers in China may not fit the stereotype of "popular culture," but may reflect momentary trends, distribution, and practical needs—such as the need for cadre manuals.

65. I was pleased to find the "bread and circuses" figure of speech in Kraus, 225; I used it about the same time, for Ken Klinkner's 2002 conference on China Pop.

66. The volumes edited by Gloria Davies, Chaohua Wang, and Xudong Zhang (*Whither China?*) well represent elite intellectual thought in general and their lack of engagement with the corruption discourse in particular. "Corruption" does not even appear in the indexes of these books, nor that of Liu Kang's *Globalization and Cultural Trends*. *Dushu* printed articles on corruption by Feng Xiang, Fu Ping, and Zheng Yefu, with a rebuttal by Zhang Shuguang, in 1993–2003, but I consider this treatment limited.

67. Jing Wang, "Guest Editor's Introduction," 5–6, discusses the distinction between "popular" and "mass," opting for the latter.

68. See Henry Y. H. Zhao, "Post-Isms," 36–37; Zhao convincingly argues that nationalism and a knowing "postist" "transcendence" of 1980s democratic and liberal "follies" have turned many of China's would-be radical elite intellectuals into cultural conservatives. Chen Xiaoming, in "Xianfengpai zhi hou" (1997), viewed the fall of the old avant-garde as if it were a historical necessity, but found in new young authors' self-absorbed enmeshment with China's new market-driven urban culture a new serious literature for China.

69. Zhang Yiwu, in Chen Xiaoming and Zhang Yiwu, "Shichanghua shidai," J3, 3. My view is that reticence about politics is in this case caused by CCP political control. I question the argument, which the Chinese critics attribute to influence from Derrida, that visual culture is more liberating than written culture.

70. Dai Jinhua, "Behind Global Spectacle," 164.

71. Liu Kang, "Popular Culture and the Culture of the Masses." Works by Zhang Xudong describe other viewpoints that oppose local culture to global culture.

72. Li Zimu, 54.

73. Liu Kang, "The Short-Lived Avant-Garde," 101. China and other area studies were actually under attack in the 1990s, from the left, the postmodernists, and the new globalizers.

74. On 1990s Chinese nationalism, see Dai Jinhua, "Behind Global Spectacle."

75. The TV dramas about the Kangxi, Yongzheng, and Qianlong reigns, however, depicted corrupt official behavior that could be appreciated as allegories of current times.

76. "Defended by the official criticism as the backbone of the architecture of the literature of the New Era, realism was viewed by the newly emerging subject positions as a restored and lingering bureaucratic formula of representation." Xudong Zhang, *Chinese Modernism*, 111. This well captures the "subject positions'" dismissive attitude.

77. The United States had a made-for-TV movie about the Enron scandal, but that seems to be the exception.

78. Huters, *Bringing the World Home*, 307n28.

79. Ma Yutao; Zhou Mingjie.

80. On Europe, see Brooks, 14.

81. Barmé; Jing Wang, "Culture as Leisure."

82. Chen Xiaoming, "Nuoyong, fankang."

83. Brooks, 16.

84. Hence Dai Jinhua, cited in "How about China's Hollywood," argues for protectionism to keep Hollywood blockbusters from overwhelming China's domestic film industry.

85. Jing Wang, "The State Question in Chinese Popular Culture Studies."

See also Jing Wang, "Culture as Leisure." David S. G. Goodman supports Wang, and brings the focus closer to mine, by discussing the bureaucratic cultural capitalism (if I may coin a phrase) of not just the state but the "party-state."

86. Kraus's recent book on the visual arts concurs with my emphasis on party, not state, hegemony.

Chapter 8: Conclusion

1. The studies are so classified by, e.g., Xiaobo Lü, 14–29, and Peter Nimerius, Introduction, 1–4. See also Michael Johnston, "The Search for Definitions." Notable Chinese studies of and comment on corruption are by He Qinglian, He Zengke, Lu Shi (rejoinder by Lu Zhoulai), Shen Yuanxin, Wan He, Zhang Shuguang, and Zheng Yefu. Others are appraised in Yan Sun, *Corruption and Market*, 2–3, 10. Overseas and Hong Kong studies include, besides those of Johnston, Lü, Nimerius, and Sun, works by Feng Chen, Joseph Y. S. Cheng, Chengze Simon Fan and Herschel Grossman, X. L. Ding, Hill Gates, Ting Gong, Yufan Hao, Rasma Karklins, Julia Kwong, Richard Levy, Alan P. L. Liu, T. Wing Lo, Stephen K. Ma, Melanie Manion, Connie Squires Meaney, James Mulvenon, Jean C. Oi, Elizabeth J. Perry, Jean-Louis Rocca, Hilton Root, Shawn Shieh, Andrew Wedeman, Lynn T. White, III, Helen Xiaoyan Wu, Shuntian Yao, and many others. Corruption in eighteenth-century China is analyzed by Nancy E. Park. On other Asian countries, see David C. Kang.

2. Yan Sun in *Corruption and Market* and Xiaobo Lü exemplify these two emphases.

3. Wedeman, "Great Disorder," notes that corruption has grown in scale, but so has the Chinese economy.

4. Johnston, "The Search for Definitions," 2–3, notes ancient Greek and Renaissance uses of the term "corruption" to indicate deficiencies in the political equilibrium of societies. Biological images of rot and contagion do not seem to be involved, however.

5. For a summary of such theories, see Yan Sun, *Corruption and Market*, 13–19. In the Chinese case, see Johnston, "The Political Consequences," 464.

6. George Washington Plunkitt of Tammany Hall spoke of "honest graft." Cited by Randy Cohen in "The Ethicist," *New York Times Magazine*, April 10, 2005, 24.

7. *Bu zheng zhi feng*, however, occurs in *Choice* (231). A fascinating study of language about corruption is Helen Xiaoyan Wu, "Wining and Dining."

8. Another colorful Chinese word is *lao* (to get by improper means), as in *da lao te lao* (skim big-time). The root meaning of *lao* is "to dredge up."

9. So did the "Supplementary Regulations on Suppression of Corruption and Bribery," promulgated on January 21, 1988. However, as in the case of the constitution, "corruption" is a translation of *tanwu*.

10. Ch. 3, Sec. 5, Art. 155 of the 1979 criminal code states, in the official English, that "State personnel who take advantage of their office to engage in corruption involving articles of public property are to be sentenced to not more than five years of fixed-term imprisonment or criminal detention"; under more serious circumstances, one can be sentenced up to life imprisonment and death. This makes the crime seem vague and yet also limited, since state personnel and public property must be involved. *The Criminal Law and the Criminal Procedure Law of China* (1984), 53–54 (Chinese text, 102). A separate section on bribery is Ch. 3, Sec. 8, Art. 185 (62, 108).

11. In Sec. 2, Ch. 8, "Crimes of Graft and Bribery" (Arts. 382–96), http://www.nsjc.net/1004_xingfa.htm and in Wei Luo, 197–203; 300–303. See also "Supplementary Regulations on Suppression of Corruption and Bribery" and "Zuigao Jianchayuan guanyu xinghuizui li'an biaozhun."

12. Item eight of the regulations of You Zhi's mid-nineteenth-century Infant Protection Society (trans. by Clara Yu) begins, "With time, it is expected that corruption will occur." Ebrey, 315.

13. Hao and Johnston, 3; Johnston and Hao, "China's Surge of Corruption," 87–88.

14. The word *fubai* is a noun (as in *gao fubai*, engage in corruption), adjective (corrupt), and verb (to become corrupt). In Chen Fang's *Dushi weiqing* 2:809, the concept of *fuxiu* (rotten, decaying, decadent) is referred to as a stage beyond *fubai*. Many of the nuances cited here are from the Lin Yutang dictionary.

15. When I spoke of *guan* in the PRC in 1980, as I did among Taiwanese and overseas Chinese, PRC academic friends corrected me. The term was offensive.

16. T. Wing Lo likewise regards the censure of corruption in the PRC as a political act, indeed an act of Gramscian "hegemony."

17. Lü, 55. As in the novel *Tiannu* discussed in chapter 3, a major crime was *nuoyong gongkuan*, the diversion of funds for unintended uses.

18. Tanner.

19. As argued by Rocca, "The Rise of the Social," 10. In fact, a noted anticorruption novelist whom I interviewed (not Chen Fang) thought that Chen Xitong was in effect persecuted.

20. Jing Wang, "Guest Editor's Introduction," 2, takes this opposing view.

21. Rocca, "The Rise of the Social," 17–18.

22. For dramatic recent examples, see Ian Johnson.

23. These matters are taken up more pointedly in regard to Chen Fang's *Tian nu* in Kinkley, "Jiedu yingshe xiaoshuo *Tiannu*."

24. One branch of legal theory and practice emphasizes legal storytelling instead of conventional legal reasoning. See Kinkley, *Chinese Justice*, 22, 369n3.

25. The phrase is Roger Rosenblatt's, from his television essay on the detective story on the *Lehrer News Hour*, August 23, 2004. His original meaning is

that heroic private detectives, so common in fiction, have few if any models in life. I believe the same logic applies to heroic Chinese police detectives.

26. Part of the problem with perquisites, however, is not the aspect of theft, but that the bureaucratic sense of rank may be disturbed if lower bureaucrats get more than is appropriate for their level.

27. Wedeman, 897, notes that Ting Gong, Julia Kwong, and Alan P. L. Liu tend to include any form of "improper" behavior by an official as corruption, including living lavishly, gambling, drunkenness, womanizing, and selling state secrets. Ethnically Chinese scholars appear to have a broader definition of corruption than other social scientists.

28. See Huang Ziping on "social hygiene" in modern Chinese literature. On judicial corruption, see Ting Gong, "Dependent Judiciary."

29. Rocca, "The Rise of the Social," 20.

30. Conflict between state law and party discipline and policy in earlier post-Mao fiction is a main theme of Kinkley, *Chinese Justice*, notably at 126–31.

31. Police still make the arrests, while procurators draw up the accusations, as they do as a matter of law in criminal cases generally (those that go to court). Manion, "Lessons," criticizes the overlap of disciplinary inspection and procuratorial legal activities.

32. Wedeman, "Great Disorder," 5.

33. Shanghai's nightclub scene was the subject of a big and long-term crackdown after the summer of 2000. Lily Tong, "In a Chinese City, Partyers No Longer See the Dawn," *Wall Street Journal*, August 13, 2001, A11.

34. Chen Fang, *Tian nu*, 15, has the chief of police submit his report on the investigation of He Qizhang's suicide to the municipal party committee for suggestions. The committee will decide whether to report the death as suicide or not. When it comes to a missing persons case, the municipal first secretary's personal assistant is the one who mobilizes the police hunt (51).

35. See Zeitlin et al.

36. Examples are the books edited by Bi Shengde and Yue Zhihong; Wang Lijuan and Ma Lan; and Xu Bin and Cheng Tiejun. Hong Kong compilations seemingly interested in mainland China as the home of "the strange" include the three books edited by Xiao Chong.

37. Kinkley, *Chinese Justice, the Fiction*, chapter 2.

38. See Lü, 127–30.

39. Johnston and Hao, "China's Surge," 86; Hao and Johnston, 3.

40. Shuntian Yao, 283.

41. Gallagher, 338–43. Yufan Hao, "From Rule of Man," surmises on the contrary that corruption may stimulate calls for rule of law.

42. See Ching Kwan Lee.

43. Klitgaard, 75.

44. World Bank, esp. 3. Karklins, 23.

45. See also Jean C. Oi.

46. Fairbank and Goldman, 182.

47. Mei Zhang, 77.

48. Lü, 128–29, suggests that sexual and economic misconduct are linked in the political mind due to their common presumed roots (in Mao's day) in failings from one's class standing. But this identification transcends the communist era and is not unique to China.

49. Elisabeth Rosenthal, "With Ignorance as the Fuel, AIDS Speeds across China," *New York Times*, Dec. 30, 2001, A1, A8.

50. This, too, is not peculiarly Chinese. Samuel Johnson wrote, "A man should first relieve those who are nearly connected with him, by whatever tie; and then, if he has any thing to spare, may extend his bounty to a wider circle." Boswell, *Journal of a Tour to the Hebrides*, Monday, 1st November, at http://etext.library.adelaide.edu.au/b/boswell/james/b74t/chap80.html (July 10, 2005). Reference courtesy Randy Cohen, "The Ethicist," *New York Times Magazine*, October 31, 2004.

51. Lianjiang Li sees nostalgia for the old anticorruption campaigns in rural China.

52. Mo Yan may have come the closest, with his portraits of pigheaded officials in *Tiantang suantai zhi ge*. Wang Lixiong's *Huang huo* creates visions of ideologically crazed tyrants in a science fiction realm.

53. This is a theme of Ian Johnson's remarkable book, as at 59, 221.

54. The 1999 *Dushi weiqing* publicity booklet for the never-released TV series based on Chen Fang's novel provides the English title "The Wrath of God" (after *Tian nu*).

Bibliography

The following abbreviations are used in the Bibliography:

J3: Zhongguo Renmin Daxue shubao ziliao zhongxin 中國人民大學書報資料中心 (Chinese People's University Book and Periodical Center), compiler. *Zhongguo xiandai, dangdai wenxue yanjiu* 中國現代，當代文學研究 (Research on modern and contemporary Chinese literature). Series J3. Monthly. Beijing.

J8: Zhongguo Renmin Daxue shubao ziliao zhongxin 中國人民大學書報資料中心 (Chinese People's University Book and Periodical Center), compiler. *Dianying, dianshi yishu yanjiu* 電影，電視藝術研究 (Research on film and television art). Series J8. Continued under the title *Yingshi yishu* 影視藝術 (Film and television art). Monthly. Beijing.

Ai Qun 艾群 and Wu Xiaolong 吳小龍. "Fating wai de huhuan—Lai zi *Tian wang*, *Fa han Fenxi* shesong an de baogao" 法庭外的呼喚—來自《天 網》,《法撼汾西》涉訟案的報告 (Shouts outside the courtroom—A report on the lawsuit involving *Heaven's Web* and *The Law Rocks Fenxi*). *Zhuomuniao* 啄木鳥 72 (November 22, 1995): 4–40.

Amnesty International. "China: Death Penalty Log: July to December 1995." June 5, 1996. http://library.amnesty.it/aidoc_everything.nsf/Index/ASA 170641996 (July 19, 2001).

Anderson, Marston. *The Limits of Realism: Chinese Fiction in the Revolutionary Period*. Berkeley: University of California Press, 1990.

Areddy, James T., and Peter Wonacott. "Volatile Issue: As China Rises, Sinking Stocks Spark Middle-Class Protests." *Wall Street Journal*, April 21, 2005, p. A1.

Auerbach, Erich. *Mimesis: The Representation of Reality in Western Literature*. Willard Trask, trans. New York: Doubleday Anchor, 1957 [1953].

Bai Lian 白蓮. "Wo kan yingpian *Shengsi jueze*" 我看影片《生死抉擇》 (My view of the film *Fatal Decision*). *Dianying yishu* 電影藝術 276 (January 5, 2001): 116.

Bao Chang 鮑昌. "Xianshizhuyi de kaige xingjin—Lüe lun Zhongguo xiandai wenxue de yi ge fazhan guilü" 現實主義的凱歌行進—略論中國現代文學的一個發展規律 (The forward march of realism amid songs of victory—Brief discussion of a law of development of modern Chinese literature). *Tianjin shehui kexue* 天津社會科學 3 (1982): 71–79. Reprinted in J3 13 (1982): 21–29.

Barmé, Geremie. *In the Red: On Contemporary Chinese Culture*. New York: Columbia University Press, 1999.

Becker, George J., ed. *Documents of Modern Literary Realism*. Princeton, NJ: Princeton University Press, 1963.

Beech, Hannah. "Smuggler's Blues." *Time Asia* 160.14 (October 14, 2002). http://www.time.com/time/asia/covers/1101021014/story.html (August 11, 2004).

Bei Qing 北青. "*Hei dong* muhou de hei dong" 《黑洞》幕後的黑洞 (The black hole behind *Black Hole*). *Shishi ribao* 石獅日報, January 30, 2002. Google cache of http://www.ssrb.com.cn/paper/20020130/GB/paper%5E1426%5E7%5Ea30 b0001.htm (March 26, 2004).

Beijing qingnianbao 北京青年報. "Zhang Ping: Wo de xiaoshuo shi caifang chulai de" 張平：我的小說是採訪出來的 (Zhang Ping: My novels come from interviewing). *Beijing qingnianbao*, August 23, 2000. http://www.people.com.cn/GB/channel6/32/20000824/200552.html (September 2, 2001).

Bi Hua 璧華. "Xin xieshizhuyi wenxue de yishu chengjiu" 新寫實主義文學的藝術成就 (The literary accomplishments of new realistic literature). In Li Yi 李怡 and Bi Hua, eds., *Zhongguo xin xieshizhuyi wenyi zuopin xuan xubian* 中國新寫實主義文藝作品選續編 (A selection of China's new realistic literary works, sequel), pp. 3–9. Hong Kong: Qishi niandai zazhi she, 1980.

Bi Shengde 畢勝德 and Yue Zhihong 岳智宏, eds. *Shi da tanguan xianxingji* 十大貪官現形記 (The real stories of ten major corrupt officials). Haerbin: Heilongjiang renmin chubanshe, 1998.

Bi Sihai 畢四海. *Caifu yu renxing* 財富與人性 (Riches and human nature). Nanjing: Jiangsu wenyi chubanshe, 2000.

Blecher, Marc J. "Hegemony and Workers' Politics in China." *China Quarterly* 170 (June 2002): 283–303.

Bo, Zhiyue, ed. and trans. "Selection and Appointment of Leading Cadres in Post-Deng China." *Chinese Law and Government* 32.1 (January–February 1999).

Brooks, Peter. *Realist Vision*. New Haven, CT: Yale University Press, 2005.

Browne, Nick, et al., eds. *New Chinese Cinemas*. Cambridge: Cambridge University Press, 1994.

Bu Changwei 卜昌偉. "Lu Tianming xin xiaoshuo 'yiru jiwang fanfu'" 陸天明新小說"一如既往反腐" (Lu Tianming's new novel is "as against corruption as always"). *Jinghua shibao* 京華時報, December 5, 2003. http://www.zuojia.

com.cn/epublish/gb/paper279/14/class027900002/hwz1352359.htm (July 10, 2004).

Buckley, Chris. "A Legal Battle Exposes Tangled Dealings in China." *New York Times*, January 18, 2005, p. C6.

Burns, John P., and Stanley Rosen, eds. *Policy Conflicts in Post-Mao China: A Documentary Survey with Analysis*. Armonk, NY: M. E. Sharpe, 1986.

Cai, Rong. *The Subject in Crisis in Contemporary Chinese Literature*. Honolulu: University of Hawai'i Press, 2004.

Cai, Yongshun. "The Resistance of Chinese Laid-off Workers in the Reform Period." *China Quarterly* 170 (June 2002): 327–44.

"*Caifu yu renxing* tixian fantan xiaoshuo xin tese" 《財富與人性》體現反貪小說新特色 (*Riches and Human Nature* embodies new characteristics of the antigraft novel). *Zhonghua dushubao* 中華讀書報, January 3, 2001. http://www.gmdaily.com.cn/01ds/2001-01/03/GB/2001^333^0^DS122.htm (September 12, 2003).

Caijing shibao 財經時報. "Tian Fengshan shi she Heilongjiang fubai daan" 田鳳山事涉黑龍江腐敗大案 (The Tian Fengshan affair involves a big corruption case in Heilongjiang). *Caijing shibao*, October 25, 2003. http://big5.china.com.cn/chinese/2003/Oct/429074.htm (July 10, 2004).

Cawelti, John G. *Adventure, Mystery, and Romance*. Chicago: University of Chicago Press, 1976.

Chang Chuan 常川. "Beijing si suo daxue chuxian dazibao" 北京四所大學出現大字報 (Big character posters appear at four universities in Beijing). In Xiao Chong, ed., *Zhonggong fantan*, pp. 70–75.

———. "Beijingshi duli wangguo kaizui yuanlao rehuo" 北京市獨立王國開罪元老惹禍 (The Beijing independent kingdom offends the elders, courting disaster). In Xiao Chong, ed., *Zhonggong fantan*, pp. 76–81.

Chang, Gordon C. *The Coming Collapse of China*. New York: Random House, 2001.

"Changpian xiaoshuo bu fanrong? Fanrong? Xujia de fanrong?" 長篇小說不繁榮？繁榮？虛假的繁榮？ (Is novel writing flourishing? Not flourishing? Only ostensibly flourishing?). Part 1 of 3. *Book 11 web*, December 24, 2003. http://www.185e.com/list/shopworld_detail.asp?Nclassid=441&pt=1&articleID=129950 (August 8, 2004).

Chen Bin 陳濱. "*Shengsi jueze* nan zhujiao Wang Qingxiang: Huo zai jiaose zhong" 《生死抉擇》男主角王慶祥：活在角色中 (*Fatal Decision* lead Wang Qingxiang: Living in his roles). *Beijing wanbao* 北京晚報, n.d. http://www.bookinfo.net/chinese/toshi/c.8.28.03.htm (April 14, 2001).

Chen Chengcai 陳成才. "Yi guan wei ben de guanyuan xingxiang" 以官為本的官員形象 (Images of bureaucrat-centric officials). *Guangxi Daxue xuebao (Zhexue shehuikexueban)* 廣西大學學報（哲學社會科學版）24.4 (August 2002): 69–73.

Chen Fang 陳方. "*Jijian yu jiandu* zazhi pingchu Zhongguo shi da jingdian fanfu xiaoshuo"《紀檢與監察》雜誌評出中國十大經典反腐小說 (*Discipline Inspection and Supervision* magazine picks ten great classic Chinese anticorruption novels). *Jijian yu jiandu* 紀檢與監察, October 2002. http://www/oh1000.com/art/wenxue/eye/express/200210/23070407011080.html (September 14, 2003).

Chen Fang 陳放. *Dushi weiqing* 都市危情 (Municipal crisis; cover has English title, "Fighting for Power in the Metropolis"). 3 vols. Beijing: Zhongguo dianying chubanshe, 2000.

———. *Tian nu ren yuan* 天怒人怨 (Heaven's wrath and humankind's resentment). 2 vols. Hong Kong: Taipingyang shi ji chubanshe, 1998.

——— [pseud. Fang Wen 方文]. *Tian nu: Fantanju zai xingdong* 天怒：反貪局在行動 (Heaven's wrath: The anticorruption bureau in action). Huhehaote: Yuanfang chubanshe, 1996.

Chen, Feng. "Subsistence Crises, Managerial Corruption and Labour Protests in China." *The China Journal* 44 (July 2000): 41–63.

Chen Jiangong 陳建功, He Xilai 何西來, and Qin Jin 秦晉. "'Xianshizhuyi' wenti san ren tan" "現實主義"問題三人談 (Three-way conversation on the question of "realism"). *Wenxue pinglun* 文學評論 2 (March 15, 1997): 86–93.

Chen Liao 陳遼. "Cong kaifang xianxhizhuyi dao lixing xianshizhuyi—Du '97 bufen zhongduan pian xiaoshuo" 從開放現實主義到理性現實主義—讀'97部分中短篇小說 (From liberated realism to rational realism—Reading some of the mid-length and short fiction of 1997). *Nanjing shehui kexue* 南京社會科學 2 (1998): 59–62, 73. Reprinted in J3 6 (1998): 90–94.

Chen Meilan 陳美蘭. "Zheige shidai hui xiechu shenme yang de changpian xiaoshuo" 這個時代會寫出什麼樣的長篇小說 (What kind of novels could be written in these times). *Wenyibao* 文藝報, August 25, 2001. Reprinted in J3 9 (2001): 8–9.

Chen Pingyuan 陳平原. *Ershi shiji Zhongguo xiaoshuo shi; Diyi juan, 1897–1916* 二十世紀中國小說史；第一卷, 1897–1916 (A history of Chinese fiction in the twentieth century; vol. 1, 1897–1916). Beijing: Beijing Daxue chubanshe, 1989.

———. "Literature High and Low: 'Popular Fiction' in Twentieth-Century China." Michel Hockx, trans. In Hockx, ed., *The Literary Field of Twentieth-Century China*, pp. 113–33.

Chen Xiaoming 陳曉明. "Nuoyong, fankang yu chonggou—Dangdai wenxue yu xiaofei shehui de shenmei guanlian" 挪用, 反抗與重構—當代文學與消費社會的審美關聯 (Diversion, resistance, and reconstruction: Aesthetic interrelations of contemporary literature and consumer society). *Wenyi yanjiu* 文藝研究 139 (May 21, 2002): 4–16.

———. "Wufa shenhua de ziwo yu xianshi—jinqi xiaoshuo de shenmei yishi liuxiang" 無法深化的自我與現實—近期小說的審美意識流向 (A self and a reality that cannot be made deeper—The direction of aesthetic consciousness in recent fiction). *Henan Daxue xuebao (shekeban)* 河南大學學報（社科版）3 (2002): 17–24. Reprinted in J3 11 (2002): 86–93.

―――. "Wugen de ku'nan: Chaoyue feilishihua de kunjing" 無根的苦難：超越非歷史化的困境 (The distress of the uprooted: Transcending the predicament of dehistoricization). *Wenxue pinglun* 文學評論 5 (September 15, 2001): 73–79.

―――. "Xianfengpai zhi hou: Jiushi niandai de wenxue liuxiang jiqi weiji" 先鋒派之後：九十年代的文學流向及其危機 (After the avant-garde: Literary currents of the nineties and their crisis). *Dangdai zuojia pinglun* 當代作家評論 81 (May 25, 1997): 35–53.

Chen Xiaoming and Zhang Yiwu 張頤武. "Shichanghua shidai: Wenxue de kunjing yu ke'nengxing" 市場化時代：文學的困境與可能性 (A marketized age: Literature's predicament and potential). *Dajia* 大家 3 (2002): 116–27. Reprinted in J3 7 (2002): 3–14.

Chen Xiaotong 陳小同 [sic; authorship dubious]. *Chen Xitong zhi zi Chen Xiaotong zishu* 陳希同之子陳小同自述 (The account in his own words of Chen Xiaotong, son of Chen Xitong). Hong Kong: Huanqiu shiye gongsi, 1998.

Chen Xihan 陳熙涵. "Fanfu xiaoshuo digu xianxiang burong hushi" 反腐小說低谷現象不容忽視 (The depths to which anticorruption fiction has fallen must not be ignored). *Wenhuibao* 文匯報, July 25, 2002. http://www.oh100.com/art/wenxue/eye/talk200207/2507040703402.html (December 15, 2002).

Chen Yuanbin 陳源斌, Chen Shixu 陳世旭, et al. *Guanchang baogao* 官場報告 (Reports from officialdom). Changsha: Hunan wenyi chubanshe, 1999.

Chen Zhiang 陳志昂. "*Cangtian zai shang* de zhongda yiyi" 《蒼天在上》的重大意義 (The great significance of *Heaven Above*). *Wenyi lilun yu piping* 文藝理論與批評 58 (March 1996): 24–27.

―――. "*Da xue wu hen* de 'wu ge yi' " 《大雪無痕》的"五個一" (The five "outstandings" of *The Blizzard Leaves No Trace*). *Wenyi lilun yu piping* 文藝理論與批評 88 (March 2003): 85–91.

Cheng, Joseph Y. S. "Guangdong's Challenges: Organizational Streamlining, Economic Restructuring and Anticorruption." *Pacific Affairs* 73.1 (Spring 2000): 9–35.

Cheng, Wenhao. "An Empirical Study of Corruption within China's State-owned Enterprises." *China Review* 4.2 (Fall 2004): 55–80.

China Labor Watch. "Hundreds of Chinese Factory Workers Protest Job Cuts and Corruption." Press release, December 11, 2000. http://www.chinalaborwatch.org/releases/releases.htm (August 9, 2003).

Choi, Eun Kyong, and Kate Xiao Zhou. "Entrepreneurs and Politics in the Chinese Transitional Economy: Political Connections and Rent-seeking." *The China Review* 1.1 (Fall 2001): 111–35.

Chu Tian 楚天. "Huian de guanchang wenren Wang Yuewen" 灰暗的官場文人王躍文 (The gloomy literatus of officialdom, Wang Yuewen). *Zuopin yu zhengming* 作品與爭鳴 243 (March 17, 2001): 70.

Ch'ü, T'ung-tsu [瞿同祖]. *Local Government in China under the Ch'ing*. Cambridge, MA: Harvard University Press, 1962.

Conceison, Claire A. "The Main Melody Campaign in Chinese Spoken Drama." *Asian Theatre Journal* 2.2 (Fall 1994): 190–212.

Corrigan, Timothy. *Film and Literature: An Introduction and Reader.* Upper Saddle River, NJ: Prentice-Hall, 1999.

The Criminal Law and the Criminal Procedure Law of China. Beijing: Foreign Languages Press, 1984.

Cui Yuping 崔玉平. "Wang Baosen yi si chou Zhonggong" 王寶森以死臭中共 (Wang Baosen died to defame the Communist Party). In Xiao Chong, ed., *Zhonggong fantan*, pp. 48–52.

Dai Jinhua [戴錦華]. "Behind Global Spectacle and National Image Making." *positions: east asia cultures critique* 9.1 (2001): 161–86.

———. "Huo de zhishi—Lun dazhong wenhua yanjiu" 活的知识—论大众文化研究 (Living knowledge—On the study of mass culture). April 8, 2003. http://www.culstudies.com/rendanews/displaynews.asp?id=375 (June 3, 2004).

———. "Invisible Writing: The Politics of Chinese Mass Culture in the 1990s." *Modern Chinese Literature and Culture* 11.1 (Spring 1999): 31–60.

Dai Xiu 代琇 and Zhuang Xin 庄辛. "Zuojia Lu Tianming" 作家陸天明 (The writer Lu Tianming). *Xiamen ribao* 廈門日報, September 25, 2002. http://www.people.com.cn/GB/wenyu/223/9103/9105/20020925/830885.html (December 15, 2002).

Dangjian wenhui 黨建文匯 (Collected documents on party building) editorial board. "Deng Bin feifa jizi an" 鄧斌非法集資案 (The case of Deng Bin's illegal raising of capital). *Dangjian wenhui*, November 1995. In Xiao Chong, ed., *Zhonggong fantan*, pp. 26–30.

Davies, Gloria, ed. *Voicing Concerns: Contemporary Chinese Critical Inquiry.* Lanham, MD: Rowman and Littlefield, 2001.

De Witte, Ludo. *The Assassination of Lumumba.* Ann Wright and Renée Fenby, trans. New York: Verso, 2001.

Denton, Kirk A., ed. *Modern Chinese Literary Thought: Writings on Literature, 1893–1945.* Stanford, CA: Stanford University Press, 1996.

Ding, X. L. "The Quasi-Criminalization of a Business Sector in China: Deconstructing the Construction-Sector Syndrome." *Crime, Law and Social Change* 35 (2001): 177–201.

———. "Systemic Irregularity and Spontaneous Property Transformation in the Chinese Financial System." *China Quarterly* 163 (September 2000): 655–76.

———. "Who Gets What, How? When Chinese State-Owned Enterprises Become Shareholding Companies." *Problems of Post-Communism* 46.3 (May–June 1999): 32–41.

Dirlik, Arif, and Zhang Xudong. "Introduction: Postmodernism and China." *boundary 2* 24.3: 1–18.

Dissanayake, Wimal, ed. *Melodrama and Asian Cinema.* Cambridge: Cambridge University Press, 1993.

Doleželová-Velingerová, Milena, ed. *The Chinese Novel at the Turn of the Century*. Toronto: University of Toronto Press, 1980.

Dong Zhilin 董之林. "Dangdai wenxue yu 'dazhong wenhua shichang'xueshu yantaohui ceji" 當代文學與"大眾文化市場"學術研討會側記 (Sidelights from an academic conference on contemporary literature and "the market for mass culture"). *Wenxue pinglun* 文學評論 1 (2003): 131–38.

Dongfang 東方 [pseud.]. "*Shengsi jueze* banshang jingju wutai" 《生死抉擇》搬上京劇舞臺 (*Fatal Decision* moves onto the Peking opera stage). *Jiangnan ribao* 江南日報, October 17, 2000. http://www.booktide.com/News/20001017/200010170008.html (August 1, 2004).

Du Ruoyan 杜若岩. "Fanfu xiaoshuo tuxian yuedu xin liangdian" 反腐小說凸顯閱讀新亮點 (Anticorruption fiction raises a new bright spot in reading). *Zhonghua dushubao* 中華讀書報, February 27, 2002. http://www.gmdaily.com.cn/ds/dshomepage.nsf/documentview/2002-02-27-07-65B8230B92FCB3F648256D00056A32?OpenDocument (December 19, 2002).

Duckett, Jane. *The Entrepreneurial State in China: Real Estate and Commerce Departments in Reform Era Tianjin*. London: Routledge, 1998.

Duke, Michael S. *Blooming and Contending: Chinese Literature in the Post-Mao Era*. Bloomington: University of Indiana Press, 1985.

———. "Chinese Literature in the Post-Mao Era: The Return of Critical Realism." In Duke, ed., *Contemporary Chinese Literature: An Anthology of Post-Mao Fiction and Poetry*, pp. 3–6. Armonk, NY: M. E. Sharpe, 1984.

Dushi weiqing 都市危情 (Municipal crisis). 14-page publicity booklet for a never-released 35-episode television series planned and written by Chen Fang 陳放, based on his novel of the same name. Beijing: Beijing dianying zhipianchang, March 1999.

Ebrey, Patricia Buckley, ed. *Chinese Civilization and Society: A Sourcebook*. 2nd ed. New York: Free Press, 1993 [1981].

Elley, Derek. "*Fatal Decision*" (review). *Variety*, February 26, 2001. http://www.findarticles.com/cf_dls/m1312/2_382/71558733/print.jhtml (December 19, 2003).

Fairbank, John King, and Merle Goldman. *China, a New History, Enlarged Edition*. Cambridge, MA: Harvard University Press, 1998 [1992].

Faison, Seth. "Jailing of Ex-mayor Shows a Tougher China." *New York Times*, August 1, 1998, p. A4.

Fan, Chengze Simon, and Herschel Grossman. "Incentives and Corruption in Chinese Economic Reform." *Journal of Policy Reform* 4.3 (2001): 195–206.

———. "The Uses of Corruption in China." *Taipei Times*, July 11, 2001, p. 8.

Fan fubai daokan 反腐敗導刊 (Anticorruption herald). Zhejiang Provincial Disciplinary Inspection Commission of the Chinese Communist Party 中共浙江省紀律檢查委員會 and Zhejiang Provincial Department of Supervision 浙江省監察廳, eds. Hangzhou.

Fan Hongguo 範宏國. "Dianying *Shengxi jiexian* guan hou" 電影《生死界綫》

觀後 (After viewing the film *Between Life and Death*). *Renmin ribao (Haiwaiban)* 人民日報（海外版）, September 14, 2005, p. 8.

Fang Lizhi. "The Chinese Amnesia." Perry Link, trans. *New York Review of Books* 37 (September 27, 1990).

Fang Xuesong 方雪松. "Fanfu xiaoshuo yu xiaoshuo de fanfu" 反腐小說與小說的反腐 (Anticorruption fiction and fighting the corruption of fiction). *Wenyi lilun yu piping* 文藝理論與批評 3 (May 2002): 65–69.

Fazhi jibao 法制日報 (*Legal System Daily*). "'98 shi da fazhi xinwen" '98 十大法制新聞 (Ten biggest legal system news items of 1998). Reprinted by *Zhongguo jingji shibao* 中國經濟時報 (China economic times), May 1, 1999. http://www.cet.com.cn/FALU/99010504.htm (July 24, 2001).

Fazhi pinglun 法制評論 (Legal system critique [monthly]). "Fanfu dianshiju *Da xue wu hen* ye you 'shanghen'" 反腐電視劇《大雪無痕》也有"傷痕" (The anticorruption TV series *The Blizzard Leaves No Trace* leaves its own "scars"). Summary in *Zhongguo xinwen wang* 中國新聞網, March 14, 2001. http://www.chinanews.com.cn/2001-03-14/26/78349.html (June 2, 2004).

Feigon, Lee. "A Harbinger of the Problems Confronting China's Economy and Environment: The Great Chinese Shrimp Disaster of 1993." *Journal of Contemporary China* 9 (2000): 323–32.

Feng Xiang 馮象. "Fubai huibuhui chengwei quanli?" 腐敗會不會成為權利？(Might corruption become a right?). *Dushu* 讀書 8 (August 2000): 3–9.

Fewsmith, Joseph. *China Since Tiananmen: The Politics of Transition*. Cambridge: Cambridge University Press, 2001.

"Former Fujian Provincial Deputy Party Secretary Expelled from CPC." *People's Daily*, September 27, 2001. http://english.people.com.cn/english/200109/27/eng20010927_81139.html (August 11, 2004).

Freedom House. "Freedom in the World 2002: The Democracy Gap." December 18, 2001. http://www.freedomhouse.org/research/freeworld/2002/essay 2002. pdf (December 23, 2001).

Fu Guoyong 傅國涌. "Bu yiyang de xiaoshuojia Wang Yuewen" 不一樣的小說家王躍文 (Wang Yuewen, a different kind of novelist). *Dajiyuan* 大紀元, April 14, 2004. http://www.epochtimes.com/gb/4/4/14/n509728.htm (May 22, 2004).

Fu Ping 符平. "Zoujin dazhong wenhua chang" 走進大眾文化場 (Entering the mass culture market). *Dushu* 讀書 1 (2000): 122–28.

Fu Qingxuan 傅慶萱. "'Zhuxuanlü' zuopin haokan le" "主旋律"作品好看了 ("Main melody" productions have gotten better). *Wenhuibao* 文匯報, February 27, 2001, p. 12. Reprinted in J8 2 (2001): 92.

Gallagher, Mary E. "'Reform and Openness': Why China's Economic Reforms Have Delayed Democracy." *World Politics* 54 (April 2002): 338–72.

Gao Xingjian 高行健. *Xiandai xiaoshuo jiqiao chutan* 現代小說技巧初探 (A preliminary exploration of the art of modern fiction). Guangzhou: Huacheng chubanshe, 1981.

Gates, Hill. "Eating for Revenge: Consumption and Corruption under Economic De-reform." *Dialectical Anthropology* 16.3–4 (1991): 233–49.

"Gei fubai haokan—Fanfu duwu pandian" 給腐敗好看—反腐讀物盤點 (Giving corruption a once-over—An inventory of anticorruption reading matter). *Beijing wanbao* 北京晚報, October 18, 2001. http://book.peopledaily.com.cn/gb/paper17/31/class001700006/hwz177679.htm (December 15, 2002).

"Getting at the Root of Corruption." *China Daily* (Hong Kong edition). August 6, 2003. http://www3.chinadaily.com.cn/eb/doc/2003-08/06/content_252503.htm (August 19, 2003).

Gilley, Bruce. *Tiger on the Brink: Jiang Zemin and China's New Elite*. Berkeley: University of California Press, 1998.

Gittings, John. "Beijing's Ex-mayor Faces Lurid Corruption Trial." *The Guardian*, July 17, 1998, p. 16.

Gold, Thomas, Doug Guthrie, and David Wank, eds. *Social Connections in China: Institutions, Culture, and the Changing Nature of* Guanxi. Cambridge: Cambridge University Press, 2002.

Gong, Ting. "Dangerous Collusion: Corruption as a Collective Venture in Contemporary China." *Communist and Post-Communist Studies* 35.1 (March 2002): 85–103.

———. "Dependent Judiciary and Unaccountable Judges: Judicial Corruption in Contemporary China." *China Review* 4.2 (Fall 2004): 33–54.

———. *The Politics of Corruption in Contemporary China: An Analysis of Policy Outcomes*. Westport, CT: Praeger, 1994.

Goodman, David S. G. "Contending the Popular: Party-State and Culture." *positions: east asia cultures critique* 9.1 (2001): 245–52.

Griffin, Michael. "Murder, He Wrote . . ." *Index [on Censorship] Online*. August 1997. http://www.oneworld.org/index_oc/news/china260897.html (June 7, 2001).

Gu Fengwei 顧鳳威 and Wu Yumin 巫育民. "Wenxue xianshizhuyi de chongjipo—Fanfu changlian xiaoshuo xilie yanjiu zhi yi" 文學現實主義的衝擊破—反腐倡廉小說系列研究之一 (A shock wave of literary realism—A study of series of novels countering corruption and advocating honesty). *Dangdai wentan* 當代文壇 3 (2002): 15–18.

Guoguo 蟈蟈. "Shusheng baoguo yu xiaoshuo fanfu" 書生報國與小說反腐 (Intellectuals repaying their country and anticorruption in fiction). *Nanfeng chuang* 南風窗. Sichuan zai xian 四川在綫, April 2, 2004. http://focus.scol.com.cn/mkzx/20040402/20044294552.htm (May 27, 2004).

Hai Yun 海韻. *Xiamen Yuanhua daan: Chaji Lai Changxing zousi fanzui jituan jishi* 廈門遠華大案：查緝賴昌星走私犯罪集團紀實 (The great Xiamen Yuanhua case: A record of the investigation and arrest of Lai Changxing's criminal smuggling clique). Beijing: Zhongguo haiguan chubanshe, 2001.

Hamm, John Christopher. *Paper Swordsmen: Jin Yong and the Modern Chinese Martial Arts Novel*. Honolulu: University of Hawai'i Press, 2005.

Han Kuancheng 韓寬程, rapporteur. "Ruhe tigao 'fanfu xiaoshuo' de shendu" 如何提高"反腐小說"的深度 (How to increase the depth of "anticorruption fiction"). *Xinmin wanbao* 新民晚報, October 25, 2000. http://www.xmwb.com.cn/xmwb/20001025/GB/14129^24102511.htm (December 18, 2002).

Han Yanrong 韓燕榮. "'Hong lou' jingshi lu" "紅樓"警示錄 (Account of the warning in the "Red Mansion"). *Fazhi ribao* 法制日報, August 30, 2001. http://www.ahut.edu.cn/~jiwei/w/w-hljul.htm (August 14, 2004).

Hao Jian 郝建. "Bei jieshou de shi hao de" 被接受的是好的 (It's good to be accepted). In "Yingpian ge an fenxi," pp. 11–15.

Hao Yu 郝雨. "Fanfu da qushi xia de guanchang xiaoshuo" 反腐大趨勢下的官場小說 (Fiction about officialdom amid the big anticorruption trend). *Zuopin yu zhengming* 作品與爭鳴 255 (March 17, 2002): 73–76.

———. "Guanchang zuowei ren de yizhong chujing" 官場作爲人的一種處境 (Officialdom as a human predicament). *Dangdai wenxue yanjiu ziliao yu xinxi* 當代文學研究資料與信息 5 (2002): 14–16.

Hao, Yufan. "From Rule of Man to Rule of Law: An Unintended Consequence of Corruption in China in the 1990s." *Journal of Contemporary China* 8 (1999): 405–23.

Hao, Yufan, and Michael Johnston. "Reform at the Crossroads: An Analysis of Chinese Corruption." http://people.colgate.edu/mjohnston/MJ%20papers%20o1/asiaper.pdf (September 7, 2003). Published in revised form in *Asian Perspective* 19:1 (Spring–Summer 1995), pp. 117–49.

Harman, Joshua Alexandr. "Relative Deprivation and Worker Unrest in Mainland China." Paper for the Pacific Regional Body of the Association for Asian Studies. http://mcel.pacificu.edu/aspac/papers/scholars/Harman/Harman.htm (May 22, 2004).

He Hong 何弘. "Fanfu da qushi xia de fanfu wenxue" 反腐大趨勢下的反腐文學 (Anticorruption literature amid the big anticorruption trend). Changchun xinxi gang 長春信息港, n.d. [late 2002]. http://www.changchun.jl.cn/CCCMS/Main.nsf/HTMLS/ywxts&wxpl&5&167 (December 18, 2002).

He Pin 何頻 and Gao Xin 高新. *Zhonggong "taizidang"* 中共"太子黨" (CPC princes [title page translation]). Rev. ed. 2 vols. Brampton, Ont., Canada: Mingjing chubanshe, 1996.

He Qinglian 何清漣. *Xiandaihua de xianjing—Dangdai Zhongguo de jingji shehui wenti* 現代化的陷阱—當代中國的經濟社會問題 (The pitfalls of modernization: Contemporary China's economic and social problems). Beijing: Jinri Zhongguo chubanshe, 1998.

———. *Zhongguo de xianjing* 中國的陷阱 (The pitfall for China; title page has English title, "The Primary Capital Accumulation in Contemporary China"). Carle Place, NY: Mingjing chubanshe, 1997.

He Zengke [何增科]. "Corruption and Anti-corruption in Reform China." *Communist and Post-Communist Studies* 33.2 (June 2002): 243–70.

———. "Fighting against Local Corruption through Institutional Innovations in Current China." http://www.indiana.edu/~workshop/colloquia/spring2000_colloquia.html (December 27, 2001).

———. *Zhengzhi zhi ai: Fazhan zhong guojia fuhua wenti yanjiu* 政治之癌：發展中國家腐化問題研究 (The political cancer: A study of problems of corruption in developing countries). Beijing: Zhongyang bianyi chubanshe, 1995.

He Zhenbang 何镇邦. "'Changpian re' dailai de fengshou" "長篇熱"帶來的豐收 (The bumper harvest brought about by the mania for full-length novels). *Xiaoshuo pinglun* 小説評論 2 (2001): 34–40. Reprinted in J3 5 (2001): 15–21.

———. "Jiushi niandai 'changpian re' toushi" 九十年代"长篇热"透视 (Perspective on the 1990s fad of full-length fiction). *Guangming ribao* 光明日報, February 26, 1998. Reprinted in J3 3 (1998): 60–64.

———. "Shidai fuyu de yi zhuang shensheng shiming" 時代賦予的一樁神聖使命 (A sacred mission conferred on us by the times). *Guangming ribao* 光明日報, November 25, 1997, p. 6. Reprinted in J3 12 (1997): 141–42.

He Zhiyun 何志雲. "Guanyu *Shimian maifu* de biji" 關於《十面埋伏》的筆記 (Notes on *Ambushed from All Sides*). *Gongren ribao* 工人日報, July 16, 1999. http://www.gmw.cn/01wzb/1999-07/22/GB/wzb^1664^6^WZ3-2216.htm (September 18, 2003).

He Zizhuang 賀子壯 and Song Jigao 宋繼高. "Rang guanzhong qu pingshuo" 讓觀衆去評説 (Let the audience decide). In "Yingpian ge an fenxi," pp. 10–11.

Hegel, Robert E. *The Novel in Seventeenth-Century China*. New York: Columbia University Press, 1981.

Hendrischke, Hans. "Corruption, Networks and Property Rights: The Demise of a Local Leader through Love and Greed." In Christina Neder, Heiner Roetz, and Ines-Susanne Schilling, eds., *China in seinen biographischen Dimensionen: Gedenkschrift für Helmut Martin*, pp. 517–34. Wiesbaden: Otto Harrassowitz, 2001.

Highet, Gilbert. "Kitsch." In *A Clerk of Oxenford*, pp. 210–19. New York: Oxford University Press, 1954.

Hockx, Michel. "Playing the Field: Aspects of Chinese Literary Life in the 1920s." In Hockx, ed., *The Literary Field of Twentieth-Century China*, pp. 61–78.

Hockx, Michel, ed. *The Literary Field of Twentieth-Century China*. Honolulu: University of Hawai'i Press, 1999.

Holmes, Leslie. *The End of Communist Power: Anti-Corruption Campaigns and Legitimation Crisis*. New York: Oxford University Press, 1993.

"Hot Debate in Literary Circles." Beijing: Foreign Languages Press. http://www.chineseliterature.com.cn/newsandevents/hot.htm (June 5, 2004).

Hou Xiaoqiang 侯小強. "Duihua Lu Tianming: Wo xie fanfu xiaoshuo" 對話陸天明：我寫反腐小説 (In dialogue with Lu Tianming: I write anticorruption fiction). *Beijing qingnianbao* 北京青年報, July 17, 2002. http://people.com.cn/GB/wenyu/223/9103/9105/20020925/830910.html (December 17, 2002).

"How about China's Hollywood." *Zhongguo zhoukan* 中國週刊 6 (November 11, 2002). http://edu.sina.com.cn/en/2002-11-11/7014.html (January 3, 2004).

Hsia, C. T. *C. T. Hsia on Chinese Literature*. New York: Columbia University Press, 2004.

Hu Ke 胡克. "Fan fubai ticai de dianying biaoxian fangshi" 反腐敗題材的電影表現方式 (Forms of expression in films with anticorruption themes). In "Yingpian ge an fenxi," pp. 15–19.

Hu Peng 胡鵬 and Bai Junfeng 白俊峰. "Zhuanfang Wang Yuewen: You xie ren ceng shuo wo de zuopin huiyin huidao" 專訪王躍文：有些人曾說我的作品誨淫誨盜 (Exclusive interview with Wang Yuewen: Some have said that my works stir up sex and violence). *Meiri xinbao* 每日新報, October 17, 2001. http://www.people.com.cn/GB/wenyu/66/134/20011017/583516.html (December 19, 2002).

Hu Ping. "On Corruption with 'Chinese Characteristics.'" Association for Asian Research. September 30, 2002. http://asianresearch.org/articles/939.html (August 13, 2003).

Hu Yinhong 胡殷紅 and Zhao Xiaozhen 趙曉真. "'Fubai de benzhi jiushi quanli de lanyong'—Zuojia Zhang Ping fangtan" "腐敗的本質就是權力的濫用"—作家張平訪談 ("The essence of corruption is the abuse of power"—Interview of writer Zhang Ping). *Wenyibao* 文藝報 [2000]. http://www.bookinfo.net/chinese/toshi/c.8.29.02.htm (April 2, 2001).

Hu Zihong 胡子宏. "Daoming shenyu daoban" 盜名甚於盜版 (Pirated author names outstrip pirated texts). *Renmin ribao (Haiwaiban)* 人民日報（海外版）, August 6, 2004, p. 8.

———. "Fanfu xiaoshuo de liang da 'paibie'" 反腐小說的兩大"派別" (Two major "schools" in anticorruption fiction). *Hunan ribao, San Xiang dushiban* 湖南日報，三湘都市版, October 28, 2002. http://www.hnol.net/gb/content/2002-10/28/content_1656583.htm (December 19, 2002).

———. "*Guojia ganbu* de baibi zhi zuo" 《國家幹部》的敗筆之作 (Flaws in *State Cadres*). *Xingchen zai xian* 星辰在綫, April 19, 2004. http://www.csonline.com.cn/changsha/cbpl/t20040419_162427.htm (May 21, 2004).

Huang Bin 黃斌. "Wang Yuewen yinxiang" 王躍文印象 (Impression of Wang Yuewen). *Renminwang* 人民網, October 15, 2001. http://www.people.com.cn/GB/wenyu/223/6659/6660/20011015/581848.html (December 19, 2002).

Huang, Ray. *Broadening the Horizons of Chinese History: Discourses, Syntheses, and Comparisons*. Armonk, NY: M. E. Sharpe, 1999.

Huang Ziping 黃子平. "Wenxue zhuyuan ji—Ding Ling 'Zai yiyuan zhong' ji qita" 文學住院記—丁玲"在醫院中"及其他 (Literary hospitalization: Ding Ling's "In the Hospital" and others). *Jintian* 今天 3 (1993).

Huot, Claire. *China's New Cultural Scene: A Handbook of Changes*. Durham, NC: Duke University Press, 2000.

Hurst, William, and Kevin J. O'Brien. "China's Contentious Pensioners." *China Quarterly* 170 (June 2002): 345–60.

Huters, Theodore. *Bringing the World Home: Appropriating the West in Late Qing and Early Republican China*. Honolulu: University of Hawai'i Press, 2005.

———. "Ideologies of Realism in Modern China: The Hard Imperatives of Imported Theory." In Liu Kang and Xiaobing Tang, eds., *Politics, Ideology, and Literary Discourse in Modern China: Theoretical Interventions and Cultural Critique*, pp. 147–73. Durham, NC: Duke University Press, 1993.

———. "A New Way of Writing: The Possibilities for Literature in Late Qing China, 1895–1908." *Modern China* 14.3 (July 1988): 243–76.

Hutzler, Charles. "China's Workers Vent Anger." *Wall Street Journal*, April 18, 2004, pp. A16–A17.

Ji Wei 季偉 [pseud.] (for the Zhongguo jushi fenxi zhongxin 中國局勢分析中心 [Center for the Analysis of the Chinese Situation]). *Shenpan Chen Xitong* 審判陳希同 (The trial of Chen Xitong). Brampton, Ont., Canada: Mingjing chubanshe, 1998.

Jia Ping'ao 賈平凹. *Fei du* 廢都 (The capital in ruins). Taibei: Fengyun shidai chubanshe, 1994.

Jiakechong 甲殼蟲 [pseud.]. "Manhua Zhongguo dangdai guanchang wenxue" 漫話中國當代官場文學 (Informal discussion of China's contemporary literature about officialdom). *Guangming shuping* 光明書評, April 12, 2002. http://www.gmdaily.com.cn/gmsp/gmsphomepage.nsf/documentview/2002-04-12-03-AS5C79A97932A453248256B98002E99E5?OpenDocument (September 6, 2002).

Jian Lushi 蹇廬氏. "Shi fanfu wenxue haishi fubai wenxue" 是反腐文學還是腐敗文學 (Is it anticorruption literature or corrupt literature?). *Guxiang* 故鄉, May 25, 2002. http://www.guxiang.com/wenxue/pinglun/dushu/200205/20020525 0029.htm (September 16, 2003).

Jiang Hu 江湖. "Xianshi ≠ fanfu" 現實≠反腐 (Reality does not equal anticorruption). *Wenyibao* 文藝報, March 26, 2002. Reprinted in J3 5 (2002): 92–93.

Jiang Xiaobo 蔣小波. "Guanzhu xianshi: Cong *Fa han Fenxi* dao *Shimian maifu*—Zuojia Zhang Ping fangtanlu" 關注現實：從《法撼汾西》到《十面埋伏》—作家張平訪談錄 (Paying attention to reality: From *The Law Rocks Fenxi* to *Ambushed from All Sides*—Interview with writer Zhang Ping). *Shu yu ren* 書與人 6 (1999): 33–38. Reprinted in J3 2 (2002): 205–9.

Jiang Xiaoling 姜小玲. "'Fanfu xiaoshuo' chengwei chuangzuo redian" "反腐小說" 成為創作熱點 ("Anticorruption fiction" is becoming a hot medium). *Jiefang ribao* 解放日報, August 21, 2001. http://news.fm365.com/yule/yuleh/20010821/360862.shtml (December 19, 2002).

Jiang Xiaoqing 江小青. "Wuxi jizi pian'an jingtian da neimu" 無錫集資騙案驚天大內幕 (The earthshaking inside scoop on the fraudulent Wuxi capital raising case). In Xiao Chong, ed., *Zhonggong fantan*, pp. 12–21.

Jiang Zilong 蔣子龍. "Qiao changzhang hou zhuan" 喬廠長後傳 (Follow-up to the story of Manager Qiao). *Renmin wenxue* 人民文學 2 (1980).

———. "Qiao changzhang shangren ji" 喬廠長上任記 (Manager Qiao assumes office). *Renmin wenxue* 人民文學 7 (1979).

Jie Min 潔泯. "Xiang xianshi de shendu kaijue" 向現實的深度開掘 (Digging deeply into reality). *Wenxue pinglun* 文學評論 8 (1981): 3–18. Reprinted in J3 10 (1981): 51–61.

Jin Hongyu 金宏宇. "'Jingji pochan' zuowei xushi laiyuan" "經濟破產"作為敘事來源 ("Economic bankruptcy" as a narrative source). *Zhongguo xiandai wenxue yanjiu congkan* 中國現代文學研究叢刊 2 (1998): 113–23. Reprinted in J3 10 (1988): 84–91.

———. "Wenxue de jingji guanhuai" 文學的經濟關懷 (Literature's concern for the economy). *Wuhan Daxue xuebao, zheshe ban* 武漢大學學報, 哲社版 1 (1998): 76–82. Reprinted in J3 4 (1998): 68–74.

Jin Yuanping 晉原平. *Quanli de pingtai* 權力的平臺 (Platform of power). Tianjin: Baihua wenyi chubanshe, 2002.

Jisi yaoanzu 緝私要案組 (Antismuggling team for serious cases; television series). Xu Geng 徐耿, dir. Screenplay by Ge Fei 革非 and Liu Ping 劉平. Hairun yingshi zhizuo youxian gongsi 海潤影視製作有限公司, Zhongguo haiguan chubanshe 中國海關出版社, Beijing zijincheng yingye youxian zeren gongsi 北京紫禁城影業有限責任公司, 2002. 23 VCDs.

Johnson, Ian. *Wild Grass: Three Stories of Change in Modern China.* New York: Pantheon, 2004.

Johnston, Michael. "Corruption in China: Old Ways, New Realities and a Troubled Future." http://people.colgate.edu/mjohnston/MJ%20papers%2001/currhist.pdf (August 7, 2005).

———. "The Political Consequences of Corruption: A Reassessment." *Comparative Politics* 18.4 (July 1986): 459–77.

———. "The Search for Definitions: The Vitality of Politics and the Issue of Corruption." http://people.colgate.edu/mjohnston/MJ%20papers%2001/issj2.doc (December 23, 2001).

Johnston, Michael, and Yufan Hao. "China's Surge of Corruption." *Journal of Democracy* 6.4 (1995): 80–94.

Jones, Arthur. "'Hero' Worship Lifts Pic to Top." *Variety*, January 20, 2003. http://www.findarticles.com/cf_dls/m1312/9_389/97060336/print.jhtml (December 9, 2003).

Jueze 抉擇 (Choice; television series). Chen Guoxing 陳國星 and Zhu Decheng 朱德承, dirs. Beijing Jinyingma Studio, Beijing Film Studio, Liaoning TV Station, and Tianzheng Studio of the *Chinese Procuratorial Daily*, coproducers. Guangdong: Baile, 1998. 17 VCDs.

Kang, David C. *Crony Capitalism: Corruption and Development in South Korea and the Philippines.* Cambridge: Cambridge University Press, 2002.

Karklins, Rasma. "Typology of Post-Communist Corruption." *Problems of Post-Communism* 49.4 (July–August 2002): 22–32.

Kasza, Gregory J. *The Conscription Society: Administered Mass Organizations.* New Haven, CT: Yale University Press, 1995.

Kaufmann, D., A. Kraay, and M. Mastruzzi. "Governance Matters IV: Governance

Indicators for 1996–2004." World Bank Institute, 2005. http://www.worldbank.org/wbi/governance/pubs/govmatters4.html (November 26, 2005).

Ke Yunlu 柯云路. *Long nian dang'an* 龍年檔案 (Cases of the year of the dragon). Beijing: Renmin wenxue chubanshe, 2002.

———. *Xin xing* 新星 (New star). *Dangdai* 當代 supplementary issue no. 3 (August 1984).

Kinkley, Jeffrey C. [金介甫] "Author Interviews: Qiu Xiaolong." *Mystery Scene* 72 (2001): 54–57.

———. *Chinese Justice, the Fiction: Law and Literature in Modern China*. Stanford, CA: Stanford University Press, 2000.

———. "*Choice* in Film Adaptation." In Ken Klinkner, ed., forthcoming.

———. "Jiedu yingshe xiaoshuo *Tiannu* (zhi 2): *Tiannu* zhong de zhengyi guannian" 解讀映射小說《天怒》（之二）：《天怒》中的正義觀念 (Interpreting the roman à clef *Heaven's Wrath* [Part Two]: Concepts of Justice in *Heaven's Wrath*). Tang Qiuyan 湯秋妍, trans. *Newsletter of the Institute of Chinese Literature and Philosophy, Academia Sinica* 14.4 (December 2004): 107–24.

———. "Modernity and Apocalypse in Chinese Novels from the End of the Twentieth Century." In Charles A. Laughlin, ed. *Contested Modernities in Chinese Literature,* pp. 101–20. New York: Palgrave Macmillan, 2005.

———. "A Talk with Chinese Novelist Mo Yan." *Persimmon* 1.2 (Summer 2000): 62–65.

Kipnis, Andrew B. *Producing Guanxi: Sentiment, Self, and Subculture in a North China Village*. Durham, NC: Duke University Press, 1997.

Klitgaard, Robert. *Controlling Corruption*. Berkeley: University of California Press, 1988.

Kong, Shuyu. *Consuming Literature: Best Sellers and the Commercialization of Literary Production in Contemporary China*. Stanford, CA: Stanford University Press, 2005.

Kraus, Richard Curt. *The Party and the Arty in China: The New Politics of Culture*. Lanham, MD: Rowman and Littlefield, 2004.

Kui Long 奎龍. "Lu Tianming *Shengwei shuji* dianran dianshiju yu xiaoshuo 'shuangxiangpao'" 陸天明《省委書記》點燃電視劇與小說"雙響炮" (Lu Tianming's *Provincial Secretary* ignites a double-barreled shot in television and fiction). *Chengshi wanbao* 城市晚報, March 18, 2002. http://ent.sina.com.cn/v/2002-03-18/76394.html (June 2, 2004).

Kwong, Julia. *The Political Economy of Corruption in China*. Armonk, NY: M. E. Sharpe, 1997.

Lan Ying 蘭英. "Paishe dianying *Shengsi jueze* de muhou xinwen" 拍攝電影《生死抉擇》的幕後新聞 (Behind the scenes: News on the filming of *Fatal Decision*). *Dazhong ribao* 大衆日報, n.d. [summer 2000]. http://www.bookinfo.net/chinese/toshi/c.8.28.09.htm (April 14, 2001).

Lawrence, Susan V. "A City Ruled by Crime." *Far Eastern Economic Review* 163.48 (November 30, 2000): 14–18. http://www.globalpolicy.org/nations/corrupt/governmt/0011svl.htm (August 11, 2004).

Lee, Ching Kwan. "From Organized Dependence to Disorganized Despotism: Changing Labour Regimes in Chinese Factories." *China Quarterly* 157 (March 1999): 44–71.

Lefebvre, Henri. *Critique of Everyday Life*. Vol. 1. John Moore, trans. London: Verso, 1991 [1947, 1958].

Lei Da 雷達. "Quan kao women ziji—*Chejian zhuren* zai jintian de jingshen jiazhi" 全靠我們自己—《車間主任》在今天的精神價值 (Relying entirely on ourselves—The spiritual value today of *Shopfloor Director*). *Wenxue pinglun* 文學評論 5 (September 15, 1997): 97–100.

Lévi-Strauss, Claude. *The Raw and the Cooked*. John and Doreen Weightman, trans. New York: Harper and Row, 1969 [French ed., 1964].

Levy, Richard. "Corruption, Economic Crime and Social Transformation Since the Reforms: The Debate in China." *The Australian Journal of Chinese Affairs* 33 (January 1995): 1–25.

———. "Corruption in Popular Culture." In Perry Link et al., eds., *Popular China: Unofficial Culture in a Globalizing Society*, pp. 39–56.

Li Boyuan (Li Baojia) 李伯元 （李寶嘉）. *Guanchang xianxing ji* 官場現形記 (Exposure of officialdom). Changchun: Shidai wenyi chubanshe, 2000.

Li Chun 李春. "Shilun Lu Tianming fanfu juzuo de tongsu xushi" 試論陸天明反腐劇作的通俗敍事(Preliminary discussion of popular narrative in the anticorruption dramas of Lu Tianming). *Dangdai dianying* 當代電影 112 (January 15, 2003): 65–68.

Li, Lianjiang. "Support for Anti-corruption Campaigns in Rural China." *Journal of Contemporary China* 10 (2001): 573–86.

Li Liqun 李立群. "Zhi *Guo hua* zuozhe Wang Yuewen: Fanfu wenxue haishi mohei wenxue?" 至《國畫》作者王躍文：反腐文學還是摸黑文學？ (To Wang Yuewen, author of *National Portrait*: Anticorruption literature or mudslinging literature?). *Renminwang* 人民網, October 12, 2001. http://www.people.com.cn/GB/wenyu/223/2029/5561/20011012/579602.html (October 13, 2003).

Li Shi 李石. "Tanguan chanhui lu de jiazhi pinggu" 貪官懺悔錄的價值評估 (Assessment of the value of corrupt official's accounts of their penitence). *Fanfubai daokan* 反腐敗導刊 52 (April 5, 2005): 14–15.

Li Yan 李彥. "Wang Qingxiang: Cangtian zai bang" 王慶祥：蒼天在幫 (Wang Qingxiang: Heaven is helping). *Dazhong dianying* 大衆電影 570 (December 1, 2000): 10–12.

Li Yanchun 李彥春. "Zhang Ping: Yi bi wei qiang fan fubai" 張平：以筆為槍反腐敗 (Zhang Ping: Using his pen as a spear to counter corruption). *NetEase*, August 25, 2000. http://culture.163.com/edit/000825/000825_40913.htm (September 2, 2001).

Li Yi 李怡. "Wenyi xinzuo zhong suo fanying de Zhongguo xianshi" 文藝新作中所反映的中國現實 (The Chinese reality reflected in new literary works). In Li Yi, ed., *Zhongguo xin xieshizhuyi wenyi zuopin xuan* 中國新寫實主義文藝作品選 (A selection of China's new realistic literary works), pp. 2–9. Hong Kong: Qishi niandai zazhi she, 1980.

Li Yunlong 李雲龍. "Fantan xiaoshuo huobao Zhongguo" 反貪小説火爆中國 (Antigraft fiction explodes across China). *Zhong Xin she* 中新社, December 12, 2000. http://edu.sina.com.cn/wander/2000-12-12/16966.shtml (September 12, 2003).

Li Yuntuan 李運摶. "Guanchang xiaoshuo duo mian kan" 官場小説多面看 (A many-sided look at fiction about officialdom). *Dangdai wenxue yanjiu ziliao yu xinxi* 當代文學研究資料與信息 5 (2002): 12–13.

———. "Lun xin shiqi wenxue dui quanli fubai de pipan" 論新時期文學對權力腐敗的批判 (On criticism of the corruption of power in literature of the new era). *Guangming ribao* 光明日報, April 11, 2001. http://www.booker.com.cn/big5/paper18/15/class001800001/hwz115292.htm (June 5, 2004).

Li Zimu 李子木. "Guanyu 'xianshizhuyi xiaoshuo' de taolun" 關於"現實主義小説"的討論 (On the discussion of "realistic fiction"). *Zuopin yu zhengming* 作品與爭鳴 10 (1997): 75–79. Reprinted in J3 12 (1997): 52–56.

Lin Hong 林紅. "Guanzhu xianshi, guanzhu baixing" 關注現實，關注百姓 (Pay attention to reality, pay attention to the common people). *Zhongguo wenhuabao* 中國文化報, July 29, 2000, p. 4. Reprinted in J3 9 (2000): 212–13.

Lin Jianfa 林建法. "Zhongguo you changxiaoshu ma?" 中國有暢銷書嗎？(Does China have bestsellers?). *Dangdai zuojia pinglun* 當代作家評論 91 (January 25, 1999): 124.

Lin, Yi-min, and Tian Zhu. "Ownership Restructuring in Chinese State Industry: An Analysis of Evidence on Initial Organizational Changes." *China Quarterly* 166 (June 2001): 305–41.

Lin Yutang 林語堂. *Lin Yutang's Chinese-English Dictionary of Modern Usage* 當代漢英詞典. Hong Kong: The Chinese University of Hong Kong, 1972.

Ling Fei 凌非. *Tian qiu* 天囚 (Heaven's prisoner). Changchun: Shidai wenyi chubanshe, 2000.

———. *Xia yi ge shi shui? Cong Hu Changqing, Cheng Kejie liang'an kan Zhongguo fanfu douzheng* 下一個是誰？從胡長清，成克傑兩案看中國反腐鬥爭 (Who's next? A perspective on China's anticorruption struggles, from the two cases of Hu Changqing and Cheng Kejie). Beijing: Dazhong wenyi chubanshe, 2001.

Link, Perry. "China: Wiping Out the Truth." *New York Review of Books* 52.3 (February 24, 2005): 36–39.

———. "Fiction and the Reading Public in Guangzhou and Other Chinese Cities, 1979–1980." In Jeffrey C. Kinkley, ed., *After Mao: Chinese Literature and Society, 1978–1981*, pp. 221–74. Cambridge, MA: Council on East Asian Studies, Harvard University, 1985.

———. "Introduction to the Revised Edition." In Chen Ruoxi, *The Execution of Mayor Yin and Other Stories from the Great Proletarian Cultural Revolution*, pp. xi–xxxii. Howard Goldblatt, ed. Bloomington: Indiana University Press, 2004 (1978).

———. *The Uses of Literature: Life in the Socialist Chinese Literary System*. Princeton, NJ: Princeton University Press, 2000.

Link, Perry, Richard P. Madsen, and Paul G. Pickowicz, eds. *Popular China: Unofficial Culture in a Globalizing Society*. Lanham, MD: Rowman and Littlefield, 2002.

Liu, Alan P. L. "The Politics of Corruption in the People's Republic of China." *American Political Science Review* 77.3 (September 1983): 602–23.

Liu Binyan [劉賓雁]. *People or Monsters? And Other Stories and Reportage from China after Mao*. Perry Link, ed. Bloomington: Indiana University Press, 1983.

———. "Sellout by China's Intellectual Elite." Perry Link, trans. *China Rights Forum* 2 (2004): 32–33.

Liu Guoqiang 劉國強. "Quanli" 權力 (Power). *Zhongguo zuojia* 中國作家 3 (2001): 148–67.

Liu Haimei 劉海梅. "Jingshen de fubai" 精神的腐敗 (Spiritual corruption). *Zuopin yu zhengming* 作品與爭鳴 289 (January 17, 2005): 72.

Liu Kang [劉康]. *Globalization and Cultural Trends in China*. Honolulu: University of Hawai'i Press, 2004.

———. "Popular Culture and the Culture of the Masses in Contemporary China." *boundary 2* 24.3 (1997): 99–122.

———. "The Short-Lived Avant-Garde: The Transformation of Yu Hua." *Modern Language Quarterly* 63.1 (2002): 89–117.

Liu Liming 流麗明. "Wang Yuewen de guanchang xiaoshuo" 王躍文的官場小說 (Wang Yuewen's novels of officialdom). *Renminwang* 人民網, October 15, 2001. http://www.people.com.cn/GB/wenyu/223/6659/6660/20011015/581777.html. (September 16, 2003).

Liu Ping 劉平. *Gudu lüren* 孤独旅人 (The solitary traveler). Shanghai: Dianban chubanshe 演办出版社, 2004.

———. *Haiwai dang'an* 海外檔案 (Overseas dossier). Shanghai: Shanghai wenyi chubanshe, 2004.

———. "Hou ji" 後記 (Afterword). *Neibu dang'an*, pp. 489–94.

———. *Lianshu dang'an* 廉署檔案 (The dossier from the Independent Commission against Corruption). Shanghai: Shanghai wenyi chubanshe, 2002.

———. *Neibu dang'an* 內部檔案 (Internal dossier). Shanghai: Shanghai wenyi chubanshe, 2001.

———. "Qian yan" 前言 (Preface). *Lianshu dang'an*, Preface pp. 1–5.

———. "Wo xie fanfu xiaoshuo" 我寫反腐小說 (I write anticorruption fiction). N.d., posted after 2002. http://www.booker.com.cn/big5/paper21/19/class002100007/hwz140513.htm (August 18, 2004).

———. *Zousi dang'an* 走私檔案 (Dossier on smuggling). Shanghai: Shanghai wenyi chubanshe, 2001.

Liu Xuyuan 劉緒源. "*Guo hua*" 《國畫》 (review). *Dangdai zuojia pinglun* 當代作家評論 97 (January 25, 2000): 13–14.

Liu Yi 劉易. "Lu Tianming xie fanfu bu wang 'xiaocongming'; you hen shen lingyu wei chuji" 陆天明写反腐不忘"小聪明"; 有很深领域未触及 (Lu Tianming writes about anticorruption but doesn't forget "sly tricks of the trade"; there are some deep realms left untouched). *Beijing yule xinbao* 北京娛樂信報, November 9, 2003. http://learning.sohu.com/05/61/article215366105.shtml (July 9, 2004).

Liu Zengrong 劉增榮. "*Shengsi jueze* chumu jingxin" 《生死抉擇》觸目驚心 (*Fatal Decision* startles). *Dianying yishu* 電影藝術 5 (September 5, 2000): 108.

Liu Zhiwu 劉志武. "Yang Qianxian duoluo shimo" 楊前綫墮落始末 (The whole story of Yang Qianxian's degeneration). *Meiri xinbao* 每日新報, November 28, 2001 (?). Installment 1, with 50 or more installments following irregularly. http://www.mrxcm.com.cn/search/result.asp?DOCID=87392&PUBNAME=%C3%BF%C8%D5%D0%C2%B1%A8&KEY=%C1%F5%D7%CE, (August 17, 2004).

Lo, T. Wing. *Corruption and Politics in Hong Kong and China.* Buckingham: Open University Press, 1993.

Long Lihua 龍麗華. "*Tian nu* zuozhe Chen Fang xiansheng fangtanlu" 《天怒》作者陳放先生訪談錄 (Transcript of an interview with Mr. Chen Fang, author of *Heaven's Wrath*). http://www.shulu.net/net/wz/sky.htm (August 14, 2001). Long interviewed Chen in Japan for *Tangrenbao* 唐人報 on July 18, 1998.

Lu Chen 陸沉. "Jiang Zemin yu Beijing shiwei de jiuhen xinchou" 江澤民與北京市委的舊恨新仇 (Old and new resentments between Jiang Zemin and the Beijing municipal committee). In Xiao Chong, ed., *Zhongguo fantan*, pp. 96–105.

Lu Kan 路侃. "Jiushi niandai de jingji xiaoshuo" 九十年代的經濟小說 (The economic novel of the nineties). *Guangming ribao* 光明日報, January 28, 1999, p. 6. Reprinted in J3 3 (1999): 78–79.

Lu Mei 陸梅. "Fanfu xiaoshuo chulu hezai?" 反腐小說出路何在？ (Where lies the future of anticorruption fiction?). *Wenxuebao* 文學報, August 1, 2002. Reprinted in J3 9 (2002): 6.

———. "Hu shang wentan pingshuo fanfu xiaoshuo" 滬上文壇評說反腐小說 (Criticism and discussion of anticorruption fiction in the Shanghai literary world). *Dangdai wenxue yanjiu ziliao yu xinxi* 當代文學研究資料與信息 5 (2002): 9, 16.

———. "Lichang bi huojiang geng zhongyao—Fang *Jueze* zuozhe Zhang Ping" 立場比獲獎更重要—訪《抉擇》作者張平 (The standpoint is more important than prizes: Interviewing Zhang Ping, author of *Choice*). *Wenxuebao* 文學報, October 26, 2000, p. 2. Reprinted in J3 11 (2000): 4–5.

Lu, Sheldon H. "Soap Opera in China: The Transnational Politics of Visuality, Sexuality, and Masculinity." *Cinema Journal* 40.1 (2000): 25–47.

Lu Shi 魯石. "Fubai de jingjixue fenxi: Ling yizhong guandian" 腐敗的經濟學分析：另一種觀點 (Economic analysis of corruption: Another view). *Wencui zhoukan* 文萃週刊, October 16, 2000. http://www.cc.org.cn/old/wencui/oldwencui/zhoukan/1013adac03.htm (November 14, 2005).

Lu Tianming 陸天明. *Cangtian zai shang* 蒼天在上 (Heaven above). Shanghai: Shanghai wenyi chubanshe, 1995.

———. *Da xue wu hen* 大雪無痕 (The blizzard leaves no trace). Changchun: Jilin renmin chubanshe, 2000.

———. *Shengwei shuji—K sheng jishi* 省委書記—K 省紀事 (Provincial secretary—Annals of K province). Shenyang: Chunfeng wenyi chubanshe, 2002.

———. "Zai Zhongguo shehui biange zhong 'daochang'" 在中國社會變革中"到場" ("Being present" at the transformation of Chinese society). *Wenhuibao* 文匯報, February 17, 2001, p. 9. Reprinted in J3 3 (2001): 152.

Lu Xingsheng 陸幸生. "Zhejiang Huzhou haiguan guanzhang, zuojia Liu Ping: Zousilian jiushi fubailian" 浙江湖州海關關長，作家劉平：走私鏈就是腐敗鏈 (Liu Ping, customs head at Huzhou, Zhejiang and writer: A smuggling ring is a corruption ring). *Xinmin zhoukan* 新民週刊, August 28, 2001. http://sina.com.cn/c/2001-08-28/341087.html (March 7, 2004).

Lu Xun 魯迅. "Yao" 藥 (Medicine). In Lu Xun, *Nahan* 吶喊 (Outcry). Hong Kong: Xinyi chubanshe, 1967 [1922].

———. *Zhongguo xiaoshuo shilüe* 中國小說史略 (A brief history of Chinese fiction). Beijing: Renmin wenxue chubanshe, 1973 [1923]. Trans. by Yang Hsien-yi and Gladys Yang as Lu Hsun, *A Brief History of Chinese Fiction*. Peking: Foreign Languages Press, 1964.

Lu Zhoulai 盧周來. "Guanyu fubai de jingjixue fenxi" 關於腐敗的經濟學分析 (About the economic analysis of corruption). *Sixiang geshihua* 思想格式化, May 14, 2001. http://www.028cn.com/forum/messages/412.html (August 14, 2001).

Lubbock, Percy. *The Craft of Fiction*. New York: Viking, 1957 [1921].

Luo Gang 羅崗. "Dianshi qizhe wenxue zou? Jian dui dangqian fanfubai ticai yingshi he wenxue chuangzuo de ji dian sikao" 電視騎著文學走？兼對當前反腐敗題材影視和文學創作的幾點思考 (Is television hitching a ride with literature? Some reflections on current film, television, and literary creation with anticorruption themes). *Wenhuibao* 文匯報, April 27, 2002. http://www.china.org.cn/chinese/RS/139005.htm (December 15, 2002).

Luo, Wei. *The 1997 Criminal Code of the People's Republic of China: with English Translation and Introduction*. Buffalo, NY: William S. Hein, 1998.

Lushan 盧山. "Chen Xitong duli wangguo neikui" 陳希同獨立王國內窺 (An inside peek at Chen Xitong's independent kingdom). In Xiao Chong, ed., *Zhonggong fantan*, pp. 62–69.

———. "Li Peng baobi Wuxi feifa jizi anfan" 李鵬包庇無錫非法集資案犯 (Li

Peng's protection of criminals in the Wuxi illegal capital accumulation case). In Xiao Chong, ed., *Zhonggong fantan*, pp. 31–37.

———. "Li Peng furen bei diaocha" 李鵬夫人被調查 (Mme. Li Peng investigated). In Xiao Chong, ed., *Zhonggong fantan*, pp. 38–47.

———. "Wang Baosen anjian manyan Xianggang" 王寶森案件蔓延香港 (The Wang Baosen case spreads to Hong Kong). In Xiao Chong, ed., *Zhonggong fantan*, pp. 53–57.

Lü, Xiaobo [呂曉波]. *Cadres and Corruption: The Organizational Involution of the Chinese Communist Party*. Stanford, CA: Stanford University Press, 2000.

Lynch, Daniel C. *After the Propaganda State: Media, Politics, and "Thought Work" in Reformed China*. Stanford, CA: Stanford University Press, 1999.

Ma, Stephen K. "Reform Corruption: A Discussion on China's Current Development." *Pacific Affairs* 62.1 (Spring 1989): 40–52.

Ma Yixin 馬以鑫. "Lun gaige shidai de gaige xiaoshuo" 論改革時代的改革小説 (On reform fiction in an age of reform). *Wenyi lilun yanjiu* 文藝理論研究 2 (2000): 58–63. Reprinted in J3 7 (2000): 67–72.

Ma Yutao 馬玉韜. "Dianshi vs xiaoshuo; dianshiju ba *Shengwei shuji* pai 'ruan' le" 電視vs 小説；電視劇把《省委書記》拍"軟"了 (Television vs. fiction: The teleplay *Provincial Secretary* is a weak adaptation). Renminwang 人民網, October 10, 2002. http://people.com.cn/GB/wenyu/64/130/20021010/838786.html (June 2, 2004).

Manion, Melanie. "Correction to 'Corruption by Design.'" *Journal of Law, Economics, and Organization* 14.1 (April 1998): 180–82.

———. "Corruption by Design: Bribery in Chinese Enterprise Licensing." *Journal of Law, Economics, and Organization* 12.1 (April 1996): 167–95.

———. "Lessons for Mainland China from Anti-corruption Reform in Hong Kong." *China Review* 4.2 (Fall 2004): 81–97.

McDougall, Bonnie S. *Fictional Authors, Imaginary Audiences: Modern Chinese Literature in the Twentieth Century*. Hong Kong: Chinese University Press, 2003.

———. *The Introduction of Western Literary Theories into Modern China, 1919–1925*. Tokyo: The Centre for East Asian Cultural Studies, Toyo Bunko, 1971.

McDougall, Bonnie S., and Kam Louie. *The Literature of China in the Twentieth Century*. New York: Columbia University Press, 1997.

McFarlane, Brian. *Novel to Film: An Introduction to the Theory of Adaptation*. Oxford: Clarendon, 1996.

McGregor, Richard. "Art and Graft: Chinese 'Anti-corruption Novels,' Melding Fact with Fiction about Crooked Officials, Are a Hit with Readers." *Financial Times*, April 23, 2005, "Weekend Magazine," p. 27.

McNally, Christopher A. "China's State-Owned Enterprises: Thriving or Crumbling?" Pamphlet in the series *Asia Pacific Issues, Analysis from the East-West Center* 59, March 2002.

Mao Keqiang 毛克強. "Chongzhu xianshizhuyi wenxue de linghun" 重鑄現實

主義文學的靈魂 (Resmelting the soul of realistic literature). *Xi'nan minzuxueyuan xuebao, zhesheban* 西南民族學院學報，哲社版 4 (2001): 124–28. Reprinted in J3 6 (2001): 195–99.

Meaney, Connie Squires. "Market Reform and Disintegrative Corruption in Urban China." In Richard Baum, ed., *Reform and Reaction in Post-Mao China: The Road to Tiananmen,* pp. 124–42. New York: Routledge, 1991.

Miao Chun 苗春. "Ta shi yi ge rexue de ren" 他是一個熱血的人 (He's a warm-blooded fellow). *Renmin ribao (Haiwaiban)* 人民日報（海外版）, November 28, 2002. http://www.luckup.net/n/ca23973.htm (May 25, 2004).

Miao Junjie 繆俊傑. "Zhenlong fakui de jingshi zhi zuo—Ping yingpian *Shengsi jueze*" 振聾發聵的警世之作—評影片《生死抉擇》 (An alarum that will lead the deaf to hear and the blind to see—Critique of the film *Fatal Decision*). *Wenhuibao* 文匯報, July 8, 2000, p. 12. Reprinted in J8 5 (2000): 31–32.

Mingbao 明報. "Xie *Tian nu* chunu dangshiren, Chen Fang ceng jie kongxia dianhua" 寫《天怒》觸怒當事人，陳放曾接恐嚇電話 (Having enraged concerned parties by writing *Heaven's Wrath*, Chen Fang has received threatening phone calls). *Xiao cankao* 小參考 151, August 6, 1998, item 9. http://www.bignews.org/980806.txt (December 20, 2001).

Mo Yan 莫言. *Jiu guo* 酒國 (The republic of wine). Taibei: Hongfan shudian, 1992. Trans. by Howard Goldblatt as *The Republic of Wine*. New York: Arcade, 2000.

———. *Tiantang suantai zhi ge* 天堂蒜薹之歌 (The garlic ballads). Beijing: Zuojia chubanshe, 1988. Trans. by Howard Goldblatt as *The Garlic Ballads*. New York: Penguin, 1995.

Mu Yilin 穆宜林. *Tian pan: Sangna mi an* 天判：桑拿謎案 (Heaven judges: The mysterious sauna case). Beijing: Dazhong wenyi chubanshe, 1999.

Mulvenon, James. "To Get Rich Is Unprofessional: Chinese Military Corruption in the Jiang Era." *China Leadership Monitor* 6 (Spring 2003): 21–35.

"Nairen xunwei de guanchang xiaoshuo" 耐人尋味的官場小說 (Novels of officialdom that offer food for thought). *Remin wang* 人民網, October 15, 2001. http://www.people.com.cn/BIG5/wenyu/223/6659/6660/20011015/581828.html (December 19, 2002).

Ni Zhen 倪震. "Xianshizhuyi de beizhuang—Tan yingpian *Shengsi jueze*" 現實主義的悲壯—談影片《生死抉擇》 (Realistic tragedy—On the film *Fatal Decision*). *Dianying yishu* 電影藝術 5 (September 5, 2000): 63–66.

———. "Yu Yu Benzheng tan *Shengsi jueze*" 與于本正談《生死抉擇》 (Interview of Yu Benzheng on *Fatal Decision*). In "Yingpian ge an fenxi," pp. 5–10.

Nimerius, Peter. *Daring to Fight Tigers? Anti-corruption Work in Contemporary China*. Stockholm: Department of Political Science, Stockholm University, 1997. Web-published thesis. http://home4.swipnet.se/~w-48538/tableofcontents.html (23 July 2001).

Nye, J[oseph] S. "Corruption and Political Development: A Cost-Benefit Analysis." *American Political Science Review* 61.2 (June 1967): 417–27.

Oi, Jean C. "Partial Market Reform and Corruption in Rural China." In Richard Baum, ed., *Reform and Reaction in Post-Mao China: The Road to Tiananmen,* pp. 143–61. New York: Routledge, 1991.

Ostrov, Benjamin C. "The Anti-Smuggling Investigation Bureau's War on Smuggling in China." *Police Practice and Research: An International Journal* 3.1 (March 2002): 41–54.

Park, Nancy E. "Corruption in Eighteenth-Century China." *Journal of Asian Studies* 56.4 (November 1997): 967–1005.

Peng Lun 彭倫. "Wang Yuewen wukenaihe shuo 'xinzuo'" 王躍文無可奈何說"新作" (Wang Yuewen is obliged to discuss his "new work"). *Wenhui dushu zhoubao* 文匯讀書週報, May 28, 2004, p. 2.

Perry, Elizabeth J. "Crime, Corruption, and Contention." In Merle Goldman and Roderick MacFarquhar, eds., *The Paradox of China's Post-Mao Reforms,* pp. 308–29. Cambridge, MA: Harvard University Press, 1999.

Phoenix TV Web. "Wang Yuewen yu *Guo hua*" 王躍文與《國畫》 (Wang Yuewen and *National Portrait*). *Fenghuang wang* 鳳凰網, January 19, 2003. Cached at http://www.google.com/search?q=cache:a-WLU-6RCSMJ:210.51.8.60/home/program/mrmdm/200301/21/24579.html+%E7%8E%8B%E8%B7%83%E6%96%87%EF%BC%9B%E7%A6%81&hl=en (August 7, 2004).

Pickowicz, Paul G. "Melodramatic Representation and the 'May Fourth' Tradition of Chinese Cinema." In Ellen Widmer and David Der-wei Wang, eds., *From May Fourth to June Fourth: Fiction and Film in Twentieth-Century China.* Cambridge, MA: Harvard University Press, 1993.

Potter, Pitman B. "Guanxi and the PRC Legal System: From Contradiction to Complementarity." Washington, DC: Woodrow Wilson International Center for Scholars, 2000. Archived at www.chinaonline.com/PremiumSolutions/com_guanxi_C00021599Wilson-S.asp (July 19, 2001).

Průšek, Jaroslav. *The Lyrical and the Epic: Studies of Modern Chinese Literature.* Leo Ou-fan Lee, ed. Bloomington: Indiana University Press, 1980.

Qi Dianbin 齊殿斌. "Redu shengwen: 2003 yingping fanfuju zhiji zhenshi anli" 熱度升溫：2003 熒屏反腐劇直擊真實案例 (Rising temperatures: TV anticorruption programs in 2003 directly take on true cases). January 5, 2004. http://www.people.com.cn/GB/news/9719/9720/2278627.html (June 2, 2004).

Qiu Xiaolong [求小龍]. "In Another Language of Crime and Detection." *Japan Times,* October 17, 2004. http://search.japantimes.co.jp/print/features/life2004/fl20041017x6.htm (November 2, 2005).

Ren Yanfang 任彥芳. *Ren yuan: Yi ge shouhaizhe de shouji* 人怨：一個受害者的手記 (Humankind's resentment: Notes from a victim). Beijing: Zhongguo dianying chubanshe, 1998.

Rocca, Jean-Louis. "Corruption and Its Shadow: An Anthropological View of Corruption in China." *China Quarterly* 130 (June 1992): 402–16.

———. "The Rise of the Social and the Chinese State." *China Information* 17.1 (2003): 1–27.

Root, Hilton. "Corruption in China: Has It Become Systemic?" *Asian Survey* 36.8 (August 1996): 741–57.

Rose-Ackerman, Susan. *Corruption and Government: Causes, Consequences and Reform*. Cambridge: Cambridge University Press, 1999.

Rosen, Stanley. "The Wolf at the Door: Hollywood and the Film Market in China from 2000." http://www.asianfilms.org/china/xuyan.html (December 15, 2003).

Rosenstone, Robert A. *Visions of the Past: The Challenge of Film to Our Idea of History*. Cambridge, MA: Harvard University Press, 1995.

Sang Ningxia 桑寧霞. "Wenxue zou chu gan'ga—Zhang Ping chenggong qishi lu" 文學走出尷尬—張平成功啓示錄 (Literature escapes its quandary—A record of Zhang Ping's success). *Wenyi lilun yu piping* 文藝理論與批評 3 (2000): 15–21. Reprinted in J3 7 (2000): 111–17.

"She an renyuan 600 duo; she an jin'e shubai yi—Jujiao Xiamen zousi an" 涉案人員600多；涉案金額數百億—聚焦廈門走私案 (Over 600 people and several tens of billions involved in the case—Focus on the Xiamen smuggling case). *Beijing qingnian bao* 北京青年報, July 23, 2001. http://www.ahut.edu.cn/~jiwei/w/w-xmaj.htm (August 14, 2004).

Sheel, Kamal. "Understanding 'Human Relationships' in China." In Tan Chung, ed., *Across the Himalayan Gap: An Indian Quest for Understanding China*. New Delhi: Gyan Publishing House, 1998.

Shen Jiada 沈嘉達. "Lun guanchang xiaoshuo" 論官場小說 (On fiction about officialdom). *Fangcao* 芳草 7 (2002): 73–76. Reprinted in J3 9 (2002): 7–10.

Shen Yuanxin 沈遠新. "Biange shiqi fubai chixu buzhi de chengben xiaoyi fenxi" 變革時期腐敗持續不止的成本效益分析 (Analysis of the costs and benefits of permanent corruption in time of change). *Bai nian* 百年, January 2000. http://mysixiang.myetang.com/000310/3.htm (August 14, 2001).

Sheng Xue 盛雪. *"Yuanhua an" heimu* 「遠華案」黑幕 (Unveiling the Yuan Hua case [English title on cover]). Hong Kong: Mingjing chubanshe, 2001.

Shengsi juezi 生死抉擇 ("Fatal decision" in release; lit., "Life and death decision"; film). Yu Benzheng 于本正, dir. He Zizhang 賀子壯 and Song Jigao 宋繼高, screenplay. Shanghai Film Studio, 2000.

———. 162-minute version for home viewing. Shanghai: Shanghai shengxiang chubanshe, 2000. VCD.

———. 93-minute version for home viewing. Taibei: Longteng [Long Term] guoji duo meiti youxian gongsi, for Zhongyang dianying shiye gufeng youxian gongsi, 2000. VHS.

———. Screenplay ("Fifth draft"); "*Shengsi jueze* dianying wenxue juben" 《生死抉擇》電影文學劇本 (Teleplay text, *Fatal Decision*). Signed "June 3, 1999, Wu gao" 五稿 (Fifth draft). Posted on *Xiangjian huanxi dianying wang* 相見歡喜電影網 (Mutual pleasure film web). http://g01.163.com/~hzzh/jueze/a.htm (March 23, 2001).

Shi Yan 實言 [pseud.]. *Tian huo: Jianchayuan zai xingdong* 天禍： 檢察院在行動 (Heaven's disaster: The procuracy in action). N.p.: Xinjiang Daxue chubanshe, 1998.

———. *Tian yi: Zhongjiwei zai xingdong* 天意： 中紀委在行動 (Heaven's intent: The Central Disciplinary Inspection Commission in action). N.p.: Xinjiang Daxue chubanshe, 1998.

Shieh, Shawn. "The Rise of Collective Corruption in China: The Xiamen Smuggling Case." *Journal of Contemporary China* 14 (February 2005): 67–91.

"Shiji tanwufan: Chen Xitong fanzui jishi" 世紀貪污犯: 陳希同犯罪紀實 (Graft-taker of the century: A record of Chen Xitong's crimes). http://www.acsu.buffalo.edu/~jw9/ChenXiTong and http://www.acsu.buffalo.edu/~jw9/ChenXiTong/index2.html (June 7, 2001).

Shijie ribao 世界日報. "Shijie ribao: Zhonggong fengsha guanchang xiaoshuo Shiliuda qian shou er nanjin" 世界日報: 中共封殺官場小說 十六大前收而難緊 (*World Journal*: Chinese Communists suppress fiction about officialdom; clampdown in advance of the Sixteenth Party Congress is not so easy). *Shijie ribao*, June 30, 2002. http://xinsheng.net/xs/articles/gb/2002/6/30/15731.htm (September 16, 2003).

Shu Jinyu 舒晉瑜. "Wei zuguo he renmin xiezuo—Fang zuojia Zhang Ping" 為祖國和人民寫作—訪作家張平 (Writing for the fatherland and the people—Interview of writer Zhang Ping). *Zhonghua dushubao* 中華讀書報, September 27, 2000. http://www.booktide.com/News/20000927/200009270030.html (July 31, 2004).

Smith, Craig S. "Piracy a Concern as the China Trade Opens Up." *New York Times*, October 5, 2000.

Solinger, Dorothy J. "Why We Cannot Count the 'Unemployed.'" *China Quarterly* 167 (September 2001): 671–88.

Steinfeld, Edward S. *Forging Reform in China: The Fate of State-Owned Industry*. Cambridge: Cambridge University Press, 1998.

Stromberg, Ronald N., ed. *Realism, Naturalism, and Symbolism: Modes of Thought and Expression in Europe, 1848–1914*. New York: Harper and Row, 1968.

Sun Chunping 孫春萍. "Shuo shi gao guan" 說是高官 (They say he's a high official). *Zuopin yu zhengming* 作品與爭鳴 280 (April 17, 2004): 3–11.

Sun Haiwen [孫海雯]. "'A Hard Choice'—A Novel that Reflects China's Social Reality." *Chinese Literature*, Winter 1998, pp. 91–94.

Sun Wanning. "A Chinese in the New World: Television Dramas, Global Cities, and Travels to Modernity." *Inter-Asia Cultural Studies* 2.1 (2002): 82–94.

Sun Wuchen 孫武臣. "Gongchandangren bidajuan" 共產黨人必答卷 (A book that communists must answer). In Zhang Ping, *Jueze*, first preface, 13 pp.

Sun Xianke 孫先科. "Yingxiongzhuyi zhuti yu 'xin xieshi xiaoshuo'" 英雄主義主題與"新寫實小說" (The theme of heroism and "new realistic fiction"). *Wenxue pinglun* 文學評論 4 (July 15, 1998): 54–60.

Sun, Yan [孫燕]. *Corruption and Democratic Governance: The Asian Paradox*. Occasional Paper No. 69. Washington, DC: Woodrow Wilson International Center for Scholars, 1996.

———. *Corruption and Market in Contemporary China*. Ithaca, NY: Cornell University Press, 2004.

———. "Reform, State, and Corruption: Is Corruption Less Destructive in China Than in Russia?" *Comparative Politics* 32.1 (October 1999): 1–20.

Sun Zhao 孫釗. "Hexie—duizhuang—hexie" 和諧—對撞—和諧 (Harmony—collision—harmony). *Taiyuan ribao* 太原日報, March 2001? *Renmin ribao wang*. http://www.qglt.com/wsrmlt/jbzl/2001/03/zhp/00b.html (October 13, 2003).

"Supplementary Regulations on Suppression of Corruption and Bribery." Promulgated by the National People's Congress, January 21, 1988. http://www.qis.net/chinalaw/prclaw52.htm (June 20, 2001).

Tang Nan 塘楠. "Jiedu 'fanfu zuojia' Zhang Ping" 解讀"反腐作家"張平 (Interpreting the 'anticorruption author' Zhang Ping). *Zhengfu fazhi* 政府法制 98 (November 1, 2000): 6–11.

Tang, Rose. "China Turns Corruption into Tourist Attraction." CNN, August 27, 2001. http://www.cnn.com/2001/WORLD/asiapcf/east/08/27/china.tourism/ (August 12, 2004).

Tang, Wenfang, and William L. Parish. *Chinese Urban Life under Reform: The Changing Social Contract*. Cambridge: Cambridge University Press, 2000.

Tang, Xiaobing [唐小兵]. *Chinese Modern: The Heroic and the Quotidian*. Durham, NC: Duke University Press, 2000.

Tang Zhesheng 湯哲聲. "Lun jiushi niandai Zhongguo tongsu xiaoshuo" 論九十年代中國通俗小說 (On Chinese popular fiction of the 1990s). *Wenxue pinglun* 文學評論 1 (January 15, 2002): 109–15.

"Tanguan biyou huai nüren he dakuan? Meiti renwei fanfu xiaoshuo tai digu" 貪官必有壞女人和大款？媒體認爲反腐小說太低谷 (Must corrupt officials have bad women and moneybags? The media judge anticorruption fiction to have hit new lows). *Xinhua wang* 新華網, July 30, 2002. http://news.xinhuanet.com/newscenter/2002-07/30/content_503421.htm (August 14, 2004).

Tanner, Murray Scot. "State Coercion and the Balance of Awe: The 1983–1986 'Stern Blows' Anti-Crime Campaign." *The China Journal* 44 (July 2000): 93–125.

Tao Dongfeng 陶東風. "Guanfang wenhua yu dazhong shimin wenhua de hudong—Lun 20 shiji 90 niandai Zhongguo de 'zhuxuanlü' dianying" 官方文化與大衆市民文化的互動—論20世紀90年代中國的"主旋律"電影 (Interaction between official culture and mass urbanite culture—On Chinese "main melody" films of the 1990s). *Qiusuo* 求索 127 (May 20, 2002): 116–21.

Tao Lan 陶瀾. "Lu Tianming bu jin shi 'fanfu zuojia'" 陸天明不僅是"反腐作家" (Lu Tianming is not just an "anticorruption author"). Xinhua net, October 21, 2002. http://news.xinhuanet.com/ent/2002-10/21/content_602562.htm (June 2, 2004).

Tempest, Rone. "Beijing Prepares for Corruption Trial." *Los Angeles Times*, April 4, 1996, p. 16.

———. "The Scions Still Rise in China." *Los Angeles Times*, February 13, 1996, p. 1.

Terrill, Ross. "Thought Police at Work in the New China." *International Herald Tribune*, September 30, 2003.

Tian Dongzhao 田東照. *Pao guan* 跑官 (Running for office). Beijing: Zhongguo dianying chubanshe, 2000.

Tian Tian 田天 (Tian Mingke 田明科). *Tian cheng* 天懲 (Heaven punishes). Changchun: Shidai wenyi chubanshe, 2001.

Todorov, Tzvetan. "The Two Principles of Narrative." *Diacritics* (Fall 1971): 37–44.

Tong Liqun 童莉群, excerpter for *Baokan wenzhai*. "Lu Tianming: Wo weihe zai xie 'fan fubai'" 陸天明：我爲何再寫"反腐敗" (Lu Tianming: Why I wrote about "anticorruption" again). *Wenxuebao* 文學報 1184. Reprinted in *Baokan wenzhai* 報刊文摘, December 14, 2000, p. 3.

Tong Qingbing 童慶炳 and Tao Dongfeng 陶東風. "Renwen guanhuai yu lishi lixing de queshi—'Xinxieshizhuyi xiaoshuo' zai pingjia" 人文關懷與歷史理性的缺失—"新現實主義小説"再評價 (The loss of human solicitude and historical reason—Reassessing "new realistic fiction"). *Wenxue pinglun* 文學評論 4 (July 15, 1998): 43–53.

Transparency International. "Corruption Perceptions Index 2003." http://www.transparency.org/pressreleases_archive/2003/2003.10.07.cpi.en.html (August 13, 2004).

———. "Corruption Perceptions Index 2004." http://www.transparency.org/pressreleases_archive/2004/2004.10.20.cpi.en (January 21, 2005).

U.S. Embassy (anonymous). "PRC Anti-Corruption Novel 'The Wrath of God': Insights into Official Corruption." http://www.usembassy-china.org.cn/english/sandt/wrath.htm (June 7, 2001).

Voice of America. "Heavenly Rage: Anti-corruption TV Series Produced but Not Ready for Show Yet." September 15, 1999. http://www.voa.gov/chinese/archive/worldfocus/sep1999/thur/091699heavenlyrage.htm (August 14, 2001).

Walder, Andrew G., and Jean C. Oi. "Property Rights in the Chinese Economy: Contours of the Process of Change." In Oi and Walder, eds., *Property Rights and Economic Reform in China*, pp. 1–24. Stanford, CA: Stanford University Press, 1999.

Wan He 皖河. "Fubai zhong de zhuanxing jiang chansheng shenme yang de zhidu?" 腐敗中的轉型將產生什麼樣的制度 (What kind of system will the transmutation of corruption produce?). *Dangdai Zhongguo yanjiu* 當代中國研究 70 (2000). http://160.79.248.165/luntan/fubai/wanhe.txt (August 14, 2001).

Wan Lingyun 萬凌雲. "'Fanfu tushu' you yinyou" "反腐圖書"有隱憂 (Hidden worries about "anticorruption book series"). Reprinted from *Zhongguo wenhuabao* 中國文化報, on or before July 29, 2002. http://www.gmdaily.com.

cn/gmsp'gmsphomepage_sza.nsf/documentview/2002-07-29-04-1B8B5D7736 07546648256C0100oEEB87?OpenDocument (September 6, 2003).

———. "Fanfu wenxue: Moluo de haomen?" 反腐文學：沒落的豪門？ (Anti-corruption literature: A bastion of wealth in decline?) *Zawenbao* 雜文報 12 (December 24, 2002): 2.

Wang, Chaohua [王超華], ed. *One China, Many Paths*. London: Verso Books, 2003.

Wang Chunyu 王春瑜, ed. *Zhongguo fantan shi* 中國反貪史 (A history of China's fight against corruption). 2 vols. Chengdu: Sichuan renmin chubanshe, 2000.

Wang, David Der-wei [王德威]. *Fictional Realism in Twentieth-century China: Mao Dun, Lao She, Shen Congwen*. New York: Columbia University Press, 1992.

———. *Fin-de-siècle Splendor: Repressed Modernities of late Qing Fiction, 1849–1911*. Stanford, CA: Stanford University Press, 1997.

———. *The Monster That Is History: History, Violence, and Fictional Writing in Twentieth-Century China*. Berkeley: University of California Press, 2004.

Wang Dehou 王得后. "*Shengsi jueze* de yiyi" 《生死抉擇》的意義 (The significance of *Fatal Decision*). *Dianying yishu* 電影藝術 (Film art) 5 (September 5, 2000): 67–69.

Wang Fanghua 汪方華. "Fanfu juzuo: dianshiju yishu de yi ba lijian 'tuwen'" 反腐劇作：電視劇藝術的一把利劍"圖文" (Anticorruption drama: A sharp-edged "graphic" in television art). *Renmin ribao* 人民日報, November 22, 2001. http://beijing.sohu.com/87/34/news147243487.shtml (May 24, 2004).

Wang Gui 王檜. *Toudeng yaoan* 頭等要案 (Banner cases). Beijing: Zuojia chubanshe, 1997.

Wang Hui [汪暉]. *China's New Order: Society, Politics, and Economy in Transition*. Theodore Huters, ed. Cambridge, MA: Harvard University Press, 2003.

Wang Jianmin 王建民 (interviewer). "Qian quan jiaoyi shi fubai genyuan—Zhuanfang Zhongguo dalu zuojia Zhang Ping" 錢權交易是腐敗根源：專訪中國大陸作家張平 (The exchange of money and power is the root of corruption: Interview of Chinese mainland writer Zhang Ping). *Yazhou zhoukan* 亞洲週刊, August 21–27, 2000, p. 29.

Wang Jianmin, Jiang Xun 江迅, Wang Ruizhi 王睿智, and Xiao Ersi 蕭爾斯. "Shengsi bianyuan dianying jiu dang" 生死邊緣電影救黨 (A movie to save the party at the brink of life and death). *Yazhou zhoukan* 亞洲週刊, August 21–27, 2000, pp. 26–29.

Wang Jie 王杰 and Liu Zhenhua 劉振華. *Jiaoliang: Zhongguo fantan licheng* 較量：中國反貪歷程 (Test: The course of anticorruption in China). Nanchang: Jiangxi jiaoyu chubanshe, 2002.

Wang, Jing [王瑾]. "Culture as Leisure and Culture as Capital." *positions: east asia cultures critique* 9.1 (2001): 69–104.

———. "Guest Editor's Introduction." *positions: east asia cultures critique* 9.1 (2001): 1–27.

———. *High Culture Fever: Politics, Aesthetics, and Ideology in Deng's China*. Berkeley: University of California Press, 1996.

———. "The State Question in Chinese Popular Culture Studies." *Inter-Asia Culture Studies* 2.1 (2001): 35–52.

Wang Jun 王軍. "Guanchang wenxue: Guanjian zaiyu zenyang baolu fubai" 官場文學：關鍵在於怎樣暴露腐敗 (Literature about officialdom: The key is *how* it exposes corruption). *Banyuetan* 半月談, December 2, 2003. http://www.21cbi.com/Article/200312/1724.htm (January 21, 2004).

Wang Lijuan 王麗娟 and Ma Lan 馬蘭, eds. *Shi da heidao renwu fumieji* 十大黑道人物覆滅記 (How ten major syndicate personalities met their doom). Haerbin: Heilongjiang renmin chubanshe, 1998.

Wang Lixiong 王力雄. "Bao Mi" 保密 (Keep it a secret) [pseud.]. *Huang huo* 黃禍 (Yellow peril). 3 vols. Taibei: Fengyun shidai chubanshe, 1991.

———. *Rongjie quanli—Zhu ceng di xuan zhi* 溶解權力—逐層遞選制 (Dissolving power—A successive multilevel electoral system). Brampton, Ont., Canada: Mingjing chubanshe, 1998.

Wang Shuo 王朔. *Qian wan bie ba wo dang ren* 千萬別把我當人 (Please don't call me human). Changsha: Hunan wenyi chubanshe, 1993. Trans. by Howard Goldblatt as *Please Don't Call Me Human*. New York: Hyperion East, 2000.

Wang Xiangdong 王向東. "Jinnian guanchang xiaoshuo manping" 近年官場小說漫評 (Informal criticism of recent fiction about officialdom). *Yangzhou Daxue xuebao (Renwen shehuikexueban)* 揚州大學學報（人文社會科學版）6.5 (September 2002): 21–27.

Wang Yuewen 王躍文. "Bian ge gushi" 編個故事 (Make up a story). *Zhongguo zuojia* 中國作家 3 (2001): 133–47.

———. "Fumu yu wo de xiezuo shenghuo" 父母與我的寫作生活 (My parents and my life of writing). *Beijing qingnianbao* 北京青年報, October 16, 2001. http://www.people.com.cn/GB/wenyu/66/134/20011016/582359.html (December 19, 2002).

———. *Guanchang chunqiu* 官場春秋 (The spring and autumn era of officialdom). Tianjin: Bai hua wenyi chubanshe, 1998.

———. *Guo hua* 國畫 (National portrait). Beijing: Renmin wenxue chubanshe, 1999.

———. "Jieju huo kaishi" 結局或開始 (Ending or beginning). *Renmin wenxue* 人民文學 515 (July 3, 2002): 13–43.

———. *Meici gushi* 梅次故事 (Stories from Meici). Beijing: Renmin wenxue chubanshe, 2001.

Wang Yuewen 王躍文, Qi Zhi 祁智, et al. *Zhongguo fanfu xiaoshuo daxi* 中國反腐小說大系 (Compendium of Chinese anticorruption novels). 10 vols. Hohhot: Inner Mongolia People's Press, 2002.

"Wang Yuewen xie xinzuo yu Shanghai duzhe jianmian" 王躍文攜新作與上

海讀者見面 (Wang Yuewen, new work in hand, meets Shanghai readers). *Wenhui dushu zhoubao* 文汇读书週报, June 4, 2004, p. 2.

Wang Zheng 汪政. "Kending yu yihan dou shi heli de" 肯定與遺憾都是合理的 (Both affirmation and regret are reasonable). *Zhongshan* 鍾山 2 (2001): 141–42. Reprinted in J3 4 (2001): 19–20.

Wang Zhiping 王治平. "Zhenshi shijie de jingji xianxiang" 真實世界的經濟現象 (Economic phenomena in an authentic world). *Zuopin yu zhengming* 作品與爭鳴 272 (August 17, 2003): 39–40.

Wank, David L. *Commodifying Communism: Business, Trust, and Politics in a Chinese City.* Cambridge: Cambridge University Press, 1999.

Weber, Eugen. *Apocalypses: Prophesies, Cults, and Millenial Beliefs through the Ages.* Cambridge, MA: Harvard University Press, 1999.

Wedeman, Andrew. "Great Disorder under Heaven: Endemic Corruption and Rapid Growth in Contemporary China." *China Review* 4.2 (Fall 2004): 1–31.

———. "The Intensification of Corruption in China." *China Quarterly* 180 (December 2004): 895–921.

Weijigan 危機感 [pseud.]. "Shengsi bianyuan dianying jiudang" 生死邊緣電影救黨 (On the brink between life and death, a movie saves the party). *Yazhou zhoukan* 亞洲週刊 (*Asiaweek*, Chinese edition), August 21–27, 2000, pp. 26–29.

Wellek, René. "The Concept of Realism in Literary Scholarship." In Wellek, *Concepts of Criticism*, pp. 222–55. Stephen G. Nichols Jr., ed. New Haven, CT: Yale University Press, 1969 [1963].

Wen Bo 文波. "Wentan redian liangti" 文壇熱點兩題 (Two hot topics on the literary scene). *Dangdai wenxue yanjiu ziliao yu xinxi* 當代文學研究資料與 信息 4 (2002): 8–9, 13.

Weng Changshou 翁昌壽. "*Tian nu* zuozhe shuo shu chuban hou jingchang shou kongxia" 《天怒》作者說書出版後經常受恐嚇 (Author of *Heaven's Wrath* says he has often been threatened since book's publication). *Zhonghua dushuwang* 中華讀書網, July 4, 2000. http://www.booktide.com/News/20000618/200006180032.html (September 6, 2003).

White, Lynn T., III. "Changing Concepts of Corruption in Communist China: Early 1950s vs. Early 1980s." *Issues and Studies* 24.1 (January 1988): 49–95.

Wibowo, Ignatius. Review of *Cadres and Corruption* by Xiaobo Lü. *China Quarterly* 171 (September 2002): 762–63.

Williams, Philip F., and Yenna Wu. *The Great Wall of Confinement: The Chinese Prison Camp through Contemporary Fiction and Reportage.* Berkeley: University of California Press, 2004.

World Bank. *Anticorruption in Transition: A Contribution to the Policy Debate.* Washington, DC: The World Bank, 2000.

Wu, Helen Xiaoyan [吳小燕]. "Anticorruption Literature and Television Dramas." In Jing Luo, ed., *China Today: An Encyclopedia of Life in the People's Republic*, pp. 27–31. Westport, CT: Greenwood, 2005.

———. "Wining and Dining at Public Expense in Post-Mao China from the Perspective of Sayings." *East Asia Forum* 5 (Fall 1996): 1–37.

Wu Jianren (Wu Woyao) 吳趼人 （吳沃堯）. *Ershinian mudu zhi guai xianzhuang* 二十年目睹之怪現狀 (Strange things eyewitnessed in the last twenty years). Beijing: Renmin wenxue chubanshe, 2000.

Wu Jingzi 吳敬梓. *Rulin waishi* 儒林外史 (The scholars). Fuzhou: Haixia wenyi chubanshe, 1995.

Wu Juan 吳娟, moderator, with Zhang Shengyou 張勝友, Lu Tianming 陸天明, and Zhou Zhengbao 周政保. "Yu fanfu ticai chuangzuo zhuanjia duihua: Fanfu chuangzuo ≠ zhanshi fubai" 與反腐題材創作專家對話：反腐創作≠展示腐敗 (Dialogue with specialists in creative writing with anticorruption themes: Anticorruption writing is not the same as displaying corruption). *Wenhuibao* 文匯報, July 10, 2002. http://www.people.com.cn/GB/wenyu/223/9103/9105/20020925/830842.html (December 15, 2002).

Xia Congzhi 夏從只. "Poyi Zhongguo zhengju mima" 破譯中國政局密碼 (Decoding China's political scene). *Mingbao* 明報, August 10, 1998. Reprinted in Chen Fang. *Tian nu ren yuan*, pp. xiv–xvii.

Xiamen teda zousi an 廈門特大走私案 (The great Xiamen smuggling case [documentary]). Zhongguo guoji dianshi zong gongsi 中國國際電視總公司, 2002? 2 VCDs.

Xiang Jun 湘君. "Bu hui fubai de shengwei shuji" 不會腐敗的省委書記 (Provincial party secretaries who can't be corrupted). *Huawei wang* 華徽網, February 21, 2004. http://www.hhw.com.cn/news/asp?key=36122 (May 22, 2004).

Xiang Wei 項瑋. "Jingti! Fanfu zuopin yongsuhua—Tan wentan yige bixu yinqi guanzhu de xianxiang" 警惕！反腐作品庸俗化—談文壇一個必須引起關注的現象 (Be on guard! The vulgarization of anticorruption works—On a literary phenomenon of concern). *Xinmin wanbao* 新民晚報, July 5, 2002. http://www.people.com.cn/GB/wenyu/223/9103/9105/20020925/830854.html (December 15, 2002).

Xiao Chong 曉沖, ed. *Zhonggong fantan daan zhongan* 中共反貪大案重案 (Big and important anticorruption cases in Communist China). Hong Kong: Xiafeier guoji chuban gongsi, 1998.

———. *Zhonggong guanchang daan* 中共官場大案 (Major cases involving officials in Communist China). Hong Kong: Xiafeier guoji chuban gongsi, 1998.

———. *Zhonggong sifa heimu* 中共司法黑幕 (The inside dirt on the judiciary in Communist China). Hong Kong: Xiafeier guoji chuban gongsi, 1998.

Xiao Li 肖黎. *Soubu Wang Baosen de nüren* 搜捕王寶森的女人 (Tracking down and arresting Wang Baosen's woman). http://www.sinotimes.com/97/spw.htm (September 4, 2001).

Xiao Luntian 蕭倫添. "Fujian shengwei yuan fushuji Shi Zhaobin bei pan youqi tuxing 13 nian" 福建省委原副書記石兆彬被判有期徒刑13年 (Former deputy secretary of the Fujian provincial committee Shi Zhaobin is sentenced to 13 years' imprisonment). *Xinhuashe* 新華社, cable from Fuzhou, March 18,

2002. Site of the Anhui University of Technology CCP Disciplinary Committee. http://www.ahut.edu.cn/~jiwei/w/w-uvbbp.htm (August 13, 2004).

Xiao Xialin 蕭夏林. "95 nian fengqiyunyong xia de changpian xiaoshuo" 95年風起雲湧下的長篇小說 (The 1995 surge of full-length novels). *Wenlunbao* 文論報, March 1, 1996, p. 1. Reprinted in J3 4 (1996): 80–81.

———. "Zhuang zai taozi li de xianshizhuyi" 裝在套子裏的現實主義 (Realism caught in a trap) (in three parts). http://www.booker.com.cn/gb/paper21/6/class002100004/hwz40148.htm; hwz40150.htm; and hwz40153.htm (May 26, 2004).

Xiao Yang 肖揚 and Meng Jiangxiong 猛將兄. "Fanfuju nianmo turan fali; chengle shoushilü de dingpanxing 反腐劇年末突然發力；成了收視率的定盤星 (Anticorruption programs suddenly show strength at year's end; become ground zero for ratings). *Beijing qingnianbao* 北京青年報, November 27, 2003. http://www.people.com.cn/GB/yule/1081/2214561.html (June 2, 2004).

Xie Hong. "Xiamen Smuggling Case: The Lust Mansion." *The Straits Times* (Singapore), December 20, 2000. http://www.ccadp.org/laichangxing.htm (August 12, 2004).

Xin Dingding. "Crime Stories Disappear from Prime Time." *China Daily*, May 17, 2004.

Xinbao 信報. "Tanwu ji wanhuzhishouzui chengli; Chen Xitong bei pan tuxing shiliu nian" 貪污及玩忽職守罪成立；陳希同被判徒刑十六年 (His crimes of graft and dereliction of duty established, Chen Xitong is sentenced to 16 years in prison). *Xinbao*, August 1, 1998. Reprinted in Chen Fang, *Tian nu ren yuan*, pp. i–ii.

Xinhua News Agency 新華社. "Fantan zongju: Zhongguo fubai manyan shitou dedao youxiao xiezhi" 反貪總局：中國腐敗蔓延勢頭得到有效遏制 (General Antigraft Bureau: The spread of Chinese corruption has effectively been checked). October 14, 2002, release. http://news6.hotoa.com.cn/newsv2/2002-10-14/2/353678.html (December 15, 2003).

———. "Smuggler Sentenced to Death in S. China." December 20, 2002, release. http://www1.china.org.cn/english/government/51698.htm (August 1, 2004).

Xiong Yuanyi 熊園義. "Dangqian xianshizhuyi wenxue de xin tezheng" 當前現實主義文學的新特征 (New characteristics of the present realistic literature). *Wenyibao* 文藝報, June 24, 1997, p. 2. Reprinted in J3 9 (1997): 28–29.

Xiong Yuanyi 熊園義 and Dong Jieying 董傑英. "Lun dangqian xianshizhuyi wenxue" 論當前現實主義文學 (On the present realistic literature). *Dangdai wentan* 當代文壇 6 (1997): 15–20. Reprinted in J3 12 (1997): 46–51.

Xu Bin 徐斌 and Cheng Tiejun 程鐵軍, eds. *Shi da zhapianfan luowang ji* 十大詐騙犯落網記 (How ten major swindlers got caught in the dragnet). Haerbin: Heilongjiang renmin chubanshe, 1998.

Xu Jingbo 徐靜波. "Chen Fang tan *Tian nu* chuban jingguo yu Chen Xitong an" 陳放談《天怒》出版經過與陳希同案 (Chen Fang discusses the publication history of *Heaven's Wrath* and the Chen Xitong case). *Shibao* 時報 (Chinese-language paper in Tokyo), July 22, 1998. Reprinted in Chen Fang, *Tiannu renyuan*, pp. iii–ix.

Yan Yujiao 閻玉嬌. "Zhang Ping tan fanfu wenxue" 張平談反腐文學 (Zhang Ping discusses anticorruption literature). *Fan fubai daokan* 反腐敗導刊 8 (August 2002): 24–25.

Yan Zhaozhu 嚴昭柱. "Fanfu changlian de jiqing lizan—Ping Liu Ping de 'dang'an' xilie changpian xiaoshuo" 反腐倡廉的激情禮贊—評劉平的"檔案"系列長篇小說 (An enthusiastic eulogy on opposing corruption and furthering honesty—Critiquing Liu Ping's "dossier" series of novels). *Renmin ribao* 人民日報, March 24, 2002, p. 8.

———. "Yi qu fan fubai douzheng de liaoliang zhan'ge" 一曲反腐敗鬥爭的嘹亮戰歌 (A battle song, loud and clear, in the anticorruption struggle). In Zhang Ping, *Jueze*, second preface, 8 pp.

Yan Zhen 閻真. *Canglang zhi shui* 滄浪之水 (Deep blue breakers). Beijing: Renmin wenxue chubanshe, 2001.

Yang Binbin 楊彬彬. "Gei *Yuanhua daan* ranglu; Zhao Baogang *Zousi dang'an* yanqi paishe" 給《遠華大案》讓路 趙寶剛《走私檔案》延期拍攝 (Yielding to *The Great Yuanhua Case*, filming is postponed on Zhao Baogang's *Dossier on Smuggling*). *Jinling wanbao* 金陵晚報, October 16, 2001 (posted). http://ent.sina.com.cn/v/2001-10-16/60131.html (August 16, 2004).

Yang, Mayfair Mei-hui. *Gifts, Favors, and Banquets: The Art of Social Relationships in China*. Ithaca, NY: Cornell University Press, 1994.

———. "The Resilience of *Guanxi* and Its New Deployments: A Critique of Some New *Guanxi* Scholarship." *China Quarterly* 170 (June 2002): 459–76.

Yang Xia 楊霞. "Jiushi niandai guanchang xiaoshuo sanlun" 90 年代官場小說散論 (Informal discussion of the 1990s literature of officialdom). *Yishu guangjiao* 藝術廣角, March 2002. Abridged in *Xiandangdai wenxue wenzhaika* 現當代文學文摘卡, March 2003, pp. 8–9.

Yangcheng wanbao 羊城晚報. "Fantan xiaoshuo huobao Zhongguo" 反貪小說火爆中國 (Antigraft fiction explodes across China). *Yangcheng wanbao*, December 14, 2000. http://www.people.com.cn/GB/channel16/32/20001214/349657.html (September 12, 2003).

Yao Huanji 姚煥吉, rapporteur. "Changpian xiaoshuo *Chejian zhuren* yantaohui fayan jiyao" 長篇小說《車間主任》研討會發言紀要 (Digest of speeches at the conference on the novel *Shopfloor Director*). *Zuojia bao* 作家報, May 8, 1997, p. 2. Reprinted in J3 6 (1997): 136–38.

Yao, Shuntian. "Privilege and Corruption: The Problems of China's Socialist Market Economy." *American Journal of Economics and Society* 61.1 (January 2002): 279–99.

Yi Menglin 易孟林. "Wo de zhuixun yu Zhang Ping" 我的追尋與張平 (My quest and Zhang Ping). In Zhang Ping, *Zhang Ping wen ji*. Preface, printed in all volumes (8 pp.).

Yi Ming 佚名[pseud.]. *Chen Xitong qiren qishi* 陳希同其人其事 (All about Chen Xitong). http://www.weilaiw.com/book/shehui/chenxit (June 7, 2001).

Ying, Shang. "Regime and Curbing Corruption." *China Review* 4.2 (Fall 2004): 93–128.

"Yingpian ge an fenxi: *Shengsi jueze*" 影片個案分析：生死抉擇 ("Panoramic analysis of film" [English rendition of the original]: *Fatal Decision*). *Dangdai dianying* 當代電影 98 (September 15, 2000): 4–26.

You Di 尤鏑. "'Shuangzixing' Li Taiyin de rensheng sanbuqu" "雙子星" 李太銀的人生三部曲 (Double star Li Taiyin's own life trilogy). *Jiancha fengyun* 檢察風雲 (Shanghai) 12 (2005): 10–13.

Yu Jintao 于津濤. "Wang Yuewen: Wo dui guanchang fubai yijing liuqing" 王躍文：我對官場腐敗已經留情 (Wang Yuewen: I've gone easy on official corruption as it is). *Xingchen zaixian* 星辰在綫, September 18, 2003. http://www.csonline.com.cn/hxml/mlwenh/mlwangyw/about/t20030826_7500.htm (August 6, 2004).

Yu Kai. "Against Corruption." *China Daily*, January 7, 2004.

Yu Xiaoshi 俞小石. "'Fanfu xiaoshuo' xianzhuang kanyou" "反腐小說" 現狀堪憂 ("Anticorruption fiction" subject to worry). March 22, 2002. http://www.oh100.com/art/wenxue/eye/talk/200203/2207040703304.html (December 15, 2002).

———. "Naqi wenxue de wuqi" 拿起文學的武器 (Take up the weapon of literature). *Shenzhen shangbao* 深圳商報, March 10, 2001. http://news.fm365.com/wenhuab/20010310/221182.shtml (December 19, 2002).

Yu Yingrui 余瑛瑞. "Chumai linghun fubai duoluo—Xiamen teda zousi an tanguan lu" 出賣靈魂腐敗墮落—廈門特大走私案貪官錄 (Selling their souls in corrupt degeneracy—A register of corrupt officials in the enormous smuggling case at Xiamen). *Xinhua wang* 新華網, cable from Xiamen, September 5, 2001. Site of the Anhui University of Technology CCP Disciplinary Committee. http://www.ahut.edu.cn/~jiwei/w/w-xmbgt.htm (August 14, 2004).

"*Yuanhua daan* jiang cheng yingshi redian" 《遠華大案》將成影視熱點 (*The Great Yuanhua Case* to become a hot topic of film and television). *Jiangnan shibao* 江南時報, September 24, 2001. http://www.gog.com.cn/jqzx/j0108/ca48728.htm (August 16, 2004).

Yun De 雲德. "Hanren feifu de zhengqi ge—Du Lu Tianming changpian xiaoshuo *Cangtian zaishang*" 撼人肺腑的正氣歌—讀陸天明長篇小說《蒼天在上》 (A paean to vitality that shakes one to the core—Reading Lu Tianming's novel *Heaven Above*). *Wenyibao* 文藝報, March 8, 1996, p. 2. Reprinted in J3 5 (1996): 190–91.

Zeitlin, Judith, Charlotte Furth, and Hsiung Ping-chen, organizers. "Thinking with Cases," an international conference. University of Chicago, October 12–14, 2001. http://humanities.uchicago.edu/ceas/thinkingwithcases/ (January 31, 2002).

Zha, Jianying [查建英]. *China Pop: How Soap Operas, Tabloids, and Bestsellers Are Transforming a Culture.* New York: The New Press, 1995.

Zhang Aijing 張愛敬. "Maochu *Shiwei shuji*; *Shengwei shuji* zao yeman daoban" 冒出《市委書記》[;]《省委書記》遭野蠻盜版 (*Municipal Secretary* is illegally published; *Provincial Secretary* encounters uncontrolled pirating). *Renminwang* 人民網, September 13, 2002. http://www.people.com.cn/GB/wenyu/66/133/20020913/821613.html (December 19, 2002).

———. "*Shengwei shuji* ji zuozhe Lu Tianming jianjie" 《省委書記》及作者陸天明簡介 (Brief introduction to *Provincial Secretary* and its author Lu Tianming). *Renminwang* 人民網, September 25, 2002. http://www.people.com.cn/GB.wenyu/223/9103/20020925/830834.html (June 2, 2004).

Zhang Chenggong 張成功 and Lu Chuan 陸川. *Hei dong* 黑洞 (Black hole). Beijing: Qunzhong chubanshe, 2001.

Zhang Hongsen 張洪森. *Da faguan* 大法官 (The great judge). Ji'nan: Shandong wenyi chubanshe, 2000.

Zhang Jiong 張炯. "*Jueze*: Zhi mian xianshi" 《抉擇》: 直面現實 (*Choice*: Directly facing reality). *Renmin ribao* 人民日報, November 11, 2000, p. 6. Longer version in *Wenxuebao* 文學報, November 2, 2000, p. 3. Reprinted in J3 12 (2000): 4.

Zhang Lei 張雷. "Xin guanchang xianxing ji" 新官場現行[sic] 記 (New versions of *Exposure of Officialdom*). *Xinwen zhoukan* 新聞週刊, November 15, 2002. http://www.chinanewsweek.com.cn/2002-09-15/1/404.html (September 13, 2002).

Zhang Liang [pseud.], compiler. *The Tiananmen Papers.* Andrew J. Nathan and Perry Link, eds. New York: Public Affairs, 2001.

Zhang, Mei. "Official Role Models and Unofficial Responses: Problems of Model Emulation in Post-Mao China." In *Chinese Perspectives in Rhetoric and Communication*, D. Ray Heisey, ed., pp. 67–85. Stamford, CT: Ablex, 2000.

Zhang Ping. *Fa han Fenxi* 法撼汾西 (The law rocks Fenxi). Beijing: Qunzhong chubanshe, 1991.

———. *Guer lei* 孤兒淚 (Orphans' tears). Taiyuan: Shanxi renmin chubanshe, 1995. Beijing: Qunzhong chubanshe, 2001.

———. *Guojia ganbu* 國家幹部 (State cadres). Beijing: Zuojia chubanshe, 2004.

———. *Jueze* 抉擇 (Choice). Beijing: Qunzhong chubanshe, 1997.

———. *Shimian maifu* 十面埋伏 (Ambushed from all sides). Beijing: Zuojia chubanshe, 1999.

———. *Tian wang* 天網 (Heaven's web). Beijing: Qunzhong chubanshe, 1993.

———. "Xiaoshuo *Jueze* de zuozhe Zhang Ping renwei dui fubai baochi chenmo shi hen kepa de" 小說《抉擇》的作者張平認爲對腐敗保持沉默是很可怕的 (Zhang Ping, author of the novel *Choice*, believes that keeping silent about corruption is a terrible thing). Excerpted from *Nanfang zhoumo* 南方周末. *Fan fubai daokan* 反腐敗導刊 3 (March 2001): 20.

———. "Yi ge xianwei shuji de zibai" 一個縣委書記的自白 (A county secretary's self-vindication). *Beijing wenxue* 北京文學 6 (June 2001): 20–41.

———. *Zhang Ping wen ji* 張平文集 (The works of Zhang Ping). 6 vols. Beijing: Qunzhong chubanshe, 2001.

"Zhang Ping bei *Lü maozi* kunrao yu shang fating tao ge shuofa" 張平被《綠帽子》困擾欲上法庭討個説法 (Puzzled by *The Cuckold*, Zhang Ping is about to seek an explanation in court). http://bookinfo.net/chinese/toshi/c.8.28.02.htm (April 14, 2001).

Zhang Shuguang 張曙光. "Fubai wenti zai sikao" 腐敗問題再思考 (A reconsideration of the problem of corruption). *Dushu* 讀書 2 (February 10, 1994): 30–34.

Zhang Tianwei 張天蔚. "Cong *Jueze* dao *Shengsi jueze*" 從《抉擇》到《生死抉擇》(From *Choice* to *Fatal Decision*). *Beijing qingnianbao* 北京青年報, n.d., ca. August 2000? http://www.bookinfo.net/chinese/toshi/c.8.28.05.htm (April 14, 2001).

Zhang Xianhua 張賢華. *Fengbao: Chachu Xiamen teda zousi an jishi* 風暴：查處廈門特大走私案紀實 (Storm: Record of the investigation and prosecution of the great Xiamen smuggling case). Beijing: Zuojia chubanshe, 2001.

Zhang, Xudong [張旭東]. *Chinese Modernism in the Era of Reforms: Cultural Fever, Avant-garde Fiction, and the New Chinese Cinema*. Durham, NC: Duke University Press, 1997.

———. "The Making of the Post-Tiananmen Intellectual Field: A Critical Overview." In Xudong Zhang, ed., *Whither China?*, pp. 1–75.

———. "Nationalism, Mass Culture, and Intellectual Strategies in Post-Tiananmen China. In Xudong Zhang, ed., *Whither China?*, pp. 315–48.

Zhang, Xudong [張旭東], ed. *Whither China? Intellectual Politics in Contemporary China*. Durham, NC: Duke University Press, 2001.

Zhang Yifan 張一帆. "Chen Xitong an yu Zhongguo guanchang de fubai" 陳希同案與中國官場的腐敗 (The Chen Xitong case and corruption among Chinese officials). *Xinbao* 信報, July 28, 1998. Reprinted in Chen Fang. *Tian nu ren yuan*, pp. x–xiii.

Zhang Yiwu [張頤武]. "Postmodernism and Chinese Novels of the Nineties." Michael Berry, trans. *boundary 2* 24.3 (1997): 247–59.

———. "Quanqiuhua de wenhua tiaozhan" 全球化的文化挑戰 (The cultural challenge of globalization). *Wenyi zhengming* 文藝爭鳴 4 (1999): 66–71. Reprinted in J3 10 (1999): 15–20.

———. "Zhongguo baixing lanpishu: Wenhua" 中國百姓藍皮書：文化 (Blue book for the Chinese common people: Culture). Chinese Central Television, n.d. (since 2002). http://www.cctv.com/tvguide/tvcomment/tyzj/zjwz/2242.shtml (May 27, 2004).

Zhang Zhizhong 張志忠. "Guanchang wenxue cheng qihou" 官場文學成氣候 (Literature about officialdom comes into its own). *Shenzhen tequbao* 深圳特區報, May 27, 2002, B6. Reprinted in J3 7 (2002): 116–17.

Zhao Bing 趙兵 (moderator and *Renmin ribao* reporter). "*Shengsi jueze* daoyan yu wangyou jiaoliu" 《生死抉擇》導演與網友交流 (The director of *Fatal Decision* [Yu Benzheng] chats with web fans). *Renmin wang* 人民網, August 31, 2000. http://www.jcrb.com/zyw/n1/ca4788.htm (October 25, 2003).

Zhao, Henry [Y. H.; 趙毅衡]. "To Go Pop, or Not—That Is Beyond Question." *New Left Review* 2 (March–April 2000). http://www.newleftreview.net/NLR23613.shtml (September 5, 2003).

———. "The River Fans Out: Chinese Fiction since the Late 1970s." *European Review* 11.2 (2003): 193–208.

Zhao, Henry Y. H. "Post-Isms and Chinese New Conservatism." *New Literary History* 28.1 (1997): 31–44.

Zhao Lanying 趙蘭英. "*Zousi dang'an*: Jizai 'shehui aizheng' de bingli" 《走私檔案》：記載"社會癌症"的病歷 (*Smuggling Dossier*: Recording the medical record of a "cancer in society"). Xinhuashe 新華社 cable, July 31, 2001. *Jiefangjunbao* 解放軍報 web, July 31, 2001. http://www.pladaily.com.cn/gb/pladaily/2001/07/31/20010731001133_society.html (July 26, 2003).

Zhao Yiheng 趙毅衡. "Ershi shiji Zhongguo de weilai xiaoshuo" 二十世紀中國的未來小說 (Futuristic novels of the twentieth century). *Ershiyi shiji* 二十一世紀 56 (December 1999): 103–12.

Zhao, Yuezhi. "The Rich, the Laid-off, and the Criminal in Tabloid Tales: Read All About It!" In Perry Link et al., eds., pp. 111–35.

Zheng Bonong 鄭伯農. "Lun Zhang Ping" 論張平 (On Zhang Ping). *Wenyi lilun yu piping* 文藝理論與批評 5 (September 1999): 42–49.

Zheng Yefu 鄭也夫. "Fubai de zhengfu gongneng" 腐敗的正負功能 (The positive and negative functions of corruption). *Dushu* 讀書 5 (May 10, 1993): 81–85.

Zhi Hui 支慧. "*Tian nu* youle jiemei pian; Chen Fang yong xinwen shoufa xie xiaoshuo *Hai nu*" 《天怒》有了姐妹篇；陳放用新聞手法寫小說《海怒》(*Heaven's Wrath* has a sister work; Chen Fang uses journalistic techniques to write *The Sea's Wrath*). *Zhonghua dushubao* 中華讀書報, January 15, 2003. http://www.booktide.com/news/20030115/200301150043.html (September 6, 2003).

Zhiming youxi 致命遊戲 (Deadly game; television series). Liu Xiaobo 劉曉波, dir. Nanning: Guangxi minzu yinxiang chubanshe, 2001. 21 VCDs.

"Zhong Ji Wei fuze tongzhi tan dianying *Shengsi jueze*" 中紀委負責同志談電影《生死抉擇》(A responsible comrade in the Central Disciplinary Inpsection Commission talks about the film *Fatal Decision*). http://www.lcqz.com/zuanti/xiaohuang/ssjz/2304.html (July 31, 2004).

Zhong Xiaoyong 鍾曉勇. "Zhang Ping zai shuo *Shengsi jueze*" 張平再說《生死抉擇》(Zhang Ping speaks again on *Fatal Decision*). *Nanfang zhoumo* 南方周末, December 14, 2000. http://www.nanfangdaily.com.cn/ZM/0012/14/zmxw1401.htm (September 2, 2001).

Zhong Xinshe 鍾欣舍. "*Tian nu ren yuan* ji Chen Fang de aomi" 《天怒人怨》

及陳放的奧秘 (*Heaven's Wrath and Humankind's Resentment* and the mystery of Chen Fang). In Chen Fang, *Tian nu ren yuan*, pp. xxii–xxxii.

Zhongyang Dianshi Tai, *Xinwen diaocha, Beijing qingnianbao* 中央電視臺,《新聞調查》,《北京青年報》. "Xiamen Yuanhua an heimu: Qi ceng hong lou nei de shenmi 'meili'" 廈門遠華案黑幕：七層紅樓內的神秘"魅力" (Inside story on the Xianmen Yuanhua case: Mysterious "enchantments" of the seven-story red mansion). August 19, 2001. Site of the Anhui University of Technology CCP Disciplinary Committee. http://www.ahut.edu.cn/~jiwei/w/w-xmhl.htm (August 14, 2004).

"Zhongyang Jiwei, Zhong Zu Bu, Zhong Xuan Bu, Guojia Guangdian Zongju tongzhi yaoqiu" 中央紀委, 中組部, 中宣部, 國家廣電總局通知要求 (Notice of a request by the Central Disciplinary Inspection Commission, the Central Organization Department of the CCP, the Central Propaganda Department of the CCP, and the State Broadcasting and Electronic Media Administration). "Renzhen zuzhi guankan yingpian *Shengsi jueze*" 認真組織觀看影片《生死抉擇》 (Conscientiously organize viewings of the film *Fatal Decision*). *Zhengfu fazhi* 政府法制 98 (November 1, 2000): 1. (Reprinted from an August 18, 2000, Xinhua communique in Beijing.)

Zhou Meisen 周梅森. *Juedui quanli* 絕對權力 (Absolute power). Beijing: Zuojia chubanshe, 2002.

———. *Renjian zhengdao* 人間正道 (The righteous path on earth). Beijing: Renmin wenxue chubanshe, 1996.

———. *Tianxia caifu* 天下財富 (Riches everywhere). Beijing: Renmin wenxue chubanshe, 1997.

———. *Zhigao liyi* 至高利益 (The highest interest). Wuhan: Changjiang wenyi chubanshe, 1999.

———. *Zhongguo zhizao* 中國製造 (Made in China). Beijing: Zuojia chubanshe, 1998.

Zhou Mingjie 周明傑. "Wangyou ganshou *Da xue wu hen*" 網友感受《大雪無痕》 (Web visitors react to *The Blizzard Leaves No Trace*). *Beijing wanbao* 北京晚報, February 2, 2001. http://www.people.com.cn/GB/wenyu/223/2021/2554/20010202/387773.html (June 2, 2004).

Zhu Xiuliang 朱秀亮. "Qunzhong chubanshe zai maodun zhong rang 'fanfu' ticai re qilai" 群眾出版社在矛盾中讓"反腐"題材熱起來 (Caught in a contradiction, the Masses' Press lets "anticorruption" subject matter catch fire). N.d. [2001]. http://www.chinapostnews.com.cn/264/jc.01.htm (August 19, 2004).

Zhu Zhaolong 朱兆龍. "Tanguan heyi rezhong yu fan fubai" 貪官何以熱衷於反腐敗 (How could a corrupt official be so crazy about anticorruption?). *Zawenbao* 雜文報, October 17, 2003, p. 1.

"Zhuomuniao wenxuejiang" 啄木鳥文學獎 (The Woodpecker Literary Prizes). *Woodpecker* magazine website. http://www.e-woodpecker.com/wxj.htm (October 13, 2003).

Zou Jianwen 鄒建文. "Zhi yao ni xuanze dang he renmin, dang he renmin ye yiding hui xuanze ni" 只要你選擇黨和人民，黨和人民也一定會選擇你 (If only you choose the party and the people, the party and the people will definitely choose you). *Zhongguo dianyingbao* 中國電影報, June 29, 2000. Reprinted in J8 5 (2000): 29–31.

"Zuigao Jianchayuan guanyu xinghuizui li'an biaozhun" 最高檢察院關於行賄罪立案標準 (Standards for establishing cases of the crime of bribery of the Supreme People's Procuratorate). *Fazhi ribao* 法制日報, December 16, 2000. http://www.legaldaily.com.cn/gb/content/2000-12/16/content_10448.htm (February 24, 2004).

Character List

an zhong an 案中案
anfen leye 安分樂業
bai 敗
bai dao 白道
Bai de yaoyan de shijian 白得耀眼的時間
Bai Weihua 柏衛華
baihuai 敗壞
bailei 敗類
bailuo 敗落
Beijing Fazhan (Xianggang) Youxian Gongsi 北京發展（香港）有限公司
Beihun 碑魂
bu zheng zhi feng 不正之風
Cai Youqiang 蔡尤強
caimaochu 財貿處
Cao Keming 曹克明
Cao Wanshan 曹萬山
Cao Xueqin 曹雪芹
Cao Yu 曹禺
Changlong 昌隆
changzhang 廠長
chao (to make money illicitly) 炒
Chao Wanshan 鈔萬山
Chen Hu 陳虎
Chen Jian 陳健
Chen Jiayang 陳家揚
Chen Qiwen 陳啓文
Chen Xiaotong 陳小同
Chen Xinhao 陳心豪
Chen Xitong 陳希同
Chen Yan 陳雁
Chen Yongming 陳永明
Chi Li 池莉
chu 處
Chu Feng 楚峰
chuzhang 處長
Cui Yan 崔燕
Da Guan Yuan 大觀園
da lao te lao 大撈特撈
da qi 大氣
dageda 大哥大
Dangdai 當代
dangfeng 黨風
dangxing 黨性
Daoxianghu 稻香湖
dashu 大書
dazhong (wenhua) 大衆（文化）
dazhonghua 大衆化
Deng Bin 鄧斌
Deng Caigang 鄧才剛

deng kao yao 等靠要	Ge Ping 葛平
Ding Wufa 丁吾法	*gouwuquan* 購物券
Ding Wutian 丁吾天	*guan* 官
Dipingxian 地平線	*guanbenwei* 官本位
Dongjiao 東郊	*Guanchang xianxing ji* 官場現形記
Du Yu 杜愚	*guanchang xiaoshuo* 官場小説
duoluo 墮落	*guandao* 官倒
Dushu 讀書	*guanxiwang* 關係網
Ershiyi shiji 二十一世紀	*guanxixue* 關係學
fa sou le 發餿了	Guo Tao 郭濤
fan ji 犯忌	Guo Xiaoling 郭曉玲
fanfu (xiaoshuo) 反腐（小説）	Guo Zhongyao 郭中姚
Fanfubai daokan 反腐敗導刊	*Hai nu* 海怒
fanfubai (ticai) xiaoshuo 反腐敗（題材）小説	Haimen 海門
	hao han 好漢
Fang Hao 方浩	Hao Xiangshou 郝相壽
Fang Mingyuan 方明遠	He Chunlin 何椿霖
fanmian ziliao 反面資料	He Dun 何頓
fansi 反思	He Kedai 何可待
fantan xiaoshuo 反貪小説	He Ping 何平
fante 反特	He Qizhang 何啓章
fazhi wenxue 法制文學	*He shang* 河殤
fei zhuliu 非主流	*heimu xiaoshuo* 黑幕小説
Feng Aiju 馮艾菊	*Hong lou meng* 紅樓夢
Feng Minjie 馮敏傑	*Hongse kangnaixin* 紅色康乃馨
Feng Xiaogang 馮小剛	Hu Feng 胡風
fu 腐	Hu Xinhong 胡欣紅
fu chuzhang 副處長	Hua Jian 花建
fu ting 副廳	Huairou 懷柔
fubai 腐敗	Huang Jiangbei 黃江北
fubai fenzi 腐敗分子	Huang Jicheng 黃紀誠
fuhua 腐化	Ji Shengde 姬勝德
fuhua duoluo 腐化墮落	Ji Tao 紀濤
fulan 腐爛	Jia Qinglin 賈慶林
fushi 腐蝕	*jiamao fanfu xiaoshuo* 假冒反腐小説
fuxiu 腐朽	Jiang Zemin 江澤民
ganbu 幹部	*jiangshan* 江山
gao fubai 搞腐敗	Jiao Dongfang 焦東方
Gao Qiming 高啓明	Jiao Pengyuan 焦鵬遠
gaozhuang 告狀	Jiao Xiaoyu 焦小玉
Ge Fei 格非	Jiao Yulu 焦裕祿
Ge Huiyuan 葛會元	Jie Peiyong 接培勇
Ge Mengmeng 葛萌萌	Jin Jing 金晶

Character List

Jin ping mei 金瓶梅
Jin Yong 金庸
Jingdu 荊都
Jingnan 荊南
jinjin 僅僅
Jiu gui 酒鬼
Kewang 渴望
Lai Changxing 賴昌星
Lan Fu 藍甫
lao 撈
Lao She 老舍
li (subofficials) 吏
Li Boyuan 李伯元
Li Gaocheng 李高成
Li Hao 李灝
Li Haoyi 李浩義
Li Jizhou 李紀周
Li Ka-shing 李嘉誠
Li Min 李敏
Li Ming 李明
Li Mingxi 李明溪
Li Peifu 李佩甫
Li Peng 李鵬
Li Qiyan 李其炎
Li Rui 李銳
Li Runwu 李潤五
Li Shangmin 黎尚民
Li Taiyin 李太銀
Li Tuo 李陀
Li Weihuai 李偉懷
Li Xifan 李希凡
Li Xuejian 李雪健
Lin Chengsen 林成森
Lin Xianhan 林先漢
Lin Youfang 林幼芳
Lin, Yü-sheng 林毓生
lingdao banzi 領導班子
Linzhong 林中
Liu Bei 劉備
Liu Binyan 劉賓雁
Liu Bocheng 劉伯承
Liu E 劉鶚
Liu Feng 劉豐

Liu Jimin 劉濟民
Liu Jinsheng 劉金生
Liu Liying 劉麗英
Liu Qingshan 劉青山
Liu Xinwu 劉心武
Liu Zaifu 劉再復
Liu Zhenyun 劉震雲
Liu Zhongxia 劉仲夏
Liu Zifeng 柳子風
liumang 流氓
Longxing 龍興
Lu Chuan 陸川
Lu Xinger 陸星兒
Lu Xun 魯迅
Luo Ji 羅輯
Ma Zhongliang 馬忠良
Mao Dun 茅盾
Mei Yuqin 梅玉琴
Meici 梅次
Mi Jiashan 米家山
Mie Baozhu 乜保柱
minbenwei 民本位
Mo Yan 莫言
nuoyong (gongkuan) 挪用（公款）
paichusuozhang 派出所長
pangda de guanxiwang 龐大的關係網
peiyang 培養
Pi Deqiu 皮德求
Pi Jie 皮傑
piaozheng 票證
pinglun 評論
pingminhua 平民化
Qian shao 前哨
Qian Zhong 千鍾
qianze xiaoshuo 譴責小說
Qie Zuo Ting 且坐亭
Qin Jianzhong 秦建忠
qing guan (xiaoshuo) 清官（小說）
qing tian 青天
Qiu Huadong 邱華棟
Qiu Siyu 丘思雨
quanli xunzu 權力尋租
Qunzhong chubanshe 群眾出版社

qunzhong wenyi 群眾文藝
Ren Da 人大
renqing 人情
Ruoyou 若有
Shangdi 上帝
Shen Congwen 沈從文
Shen Shi 沈石
Shen Taifu 沈太福
Shengsi jiexian 生死界綫
Shi Tiesheng 史鐵生
Shi Zhaobin 石兆彬
Shiwei shuji 市委書記
shouhui 受賄
Shouhuo 收穫
shunkouliu 順口溜
Shunyi 順義
Si Mao 四毛
sirenhua xiezuo 私人化寫作
sixiang 思想
Song Huihui 宋慧慧
Song Jiang 宋江
suan fu 酸腐
Sun Qi 孫奇
tan 貪
Tan Yuan 覃原
tanwu 貪污
tanwu huilu zui 貪污賄賂罪
Tao Suling 陶素玲
Tegaote 特高特
tequan 特權
Tian Congyin 田聰穎
Tian Dongzhao 田東照
Tian Fengshan 田鳳山
Tian Manfang 田曼芳
Tian Weidong 田衛東
Tian Weiming 田衛明
Tian Xing 田醒
Tie Ning 鐵凝
Tie Ying 鐵英
tifa 提法
ting 廳
tongsu (wenhua) 通俗（文化）
touji daoba 投機倒把

tupokou 突破口
waishi 外史
Wan Yongnian 萬永年
Wanfang 萬方
Wang Anyi 王安憶
Wang Baosen 王寶森
Wang Guowei 王國維
Wang Meng 王蒙
Wang Qingxiang 王慶祥
Wang Yaozu 王耀祖
Wang Zhong Wang 王中王
Wangfujing 王府井
wangguo 亡國
Wanli 萬利
Wei Zhenliang 魏振亮
Weihui 衛慧
Wenhuibao 文匯報
wenren 文人
Wu Aikun 吳愛坤
Wu Aizhen (in novel) 吳愛珍
Wu Aizhen (in movie) 吳藹珍
wu gao 五稿
Wu, Helen Xiaoyan 吳小燕
Wu Mingde 吳銘德
Wu Woyao (Jianren) 吳沃堯 (趼人)
Wu Xiaoming 吳曉鳴
Wucai 五彩
wufa wutian 無法無天
Xia Zhiyuan 夏志遠
xiang 鄉
Xianggang Maofangqiang Youxian Gongsi 香港毛紡廠有限公司
Xiangmei 香妹
xiao qi 小氣
Xiao Yilei 蕭一蕾
xiaoshuo 小說
Xiaoshuo jie 小說界
Xinglong 興隆
Xinxing Shiye Zong Gongsi 新興實業總公司
Xiyuan 西苑
"Xuehun" 血魂
Xun qiang 尋槍

Yan Hongxing 嚴宏星
Yan Zhen (writer) 閻真
Yan Zhen (character in *Jueze*) 嚴陣
Yang Cheng 楊誠
Yang Fengrui 楊風瑞
Yang Qianxian 楊前綫
Ye Bingbing 葉冰冰
Yingxiong 英雄
You Fengwei 尤鳳偉
Yu Benzheng 于本正
Yu Dafu 郁達夫
Yu Haocheng 于浩成
Yu Jie 餘傑
Yu Shanshan 喻珊珊
Yuan Ke 袁可
Yuan Mingliang 原明亮
Yuanhua 遠華
Yuanhua daan 遠華大案
Zeng Li 曾俚
Zeng Mingna 曾明娜
Zhang Henshui 張恨水
Zhang Hongsen 張洪森
Zhang Jie 張潔
Zhang Tianqi 張天奇
Zhang Yimou 張藝謀
Zhang Zishan 張子善
Zhangtai 章台

Zhao Baogang 趙寶剛
Zhao Keming 趙克明
Zhao Lijiang 趙麗江
Zhao Ziyang 趙紫陽
zheng qi fenkai 政企分開
Zheng Xie 政協
Zheng Yanzhang 鄭彥章
zhiqingquan 知情權
Zhongguo zuojia 中國作家
Zhongxing 中興
Zhongyang 中陽
Zhou Beifang 周北方
Zhou Bing 周兵
Zhou Guanwu 周冠武
Zhou Huan 周寰
Zhou Senlin 周森林
Zhu Huaijing 朱懷鏡
Zhu Lin 朱琳
Zhuang Rushun 莊如順
Zhuge Liang 諸葛亮
Zhuomuniao 啄木鳥
zhuxuanlü 主旋律
Zijin 紫禁
Zouguo Liuyuan 走过柳源
zuofeng 作風
zuzhi (guannian) 組織(觀念)
zuzhixing jilüxing 組織性紀律性

Index

In this index an "f" after a number indicates a separate reference on the next page, and an "ff" indicates separate references on the next two pages. A continuous discussion over two or more pages is indicated by a span of page numbers, e.g., "57–59."

Allegory, 149, 155, 203n19, 223n75. *See also* Symbolism
Amoy. *See* Xiamen
Anderson, Marston, 23, 102, 146–49, 152
Anticorruption, 38, 64, 67f, 76, 127f, 166; as power struggle, 66–67; anticorruption tourism, 127; as discipline, 180–81; as evasion of social inquiry, 188–90; special journals on, 199n90
Anticorruption campaigns, 15, 66–67, 72, 99, 172, 174–75, 181, 189; as politics, 66–67, 174, 179
Anticorruption fiction and media, 6, 8, 10, 17f, 35, 45, 48f, 61, 72f, 89, 95, 105, 122f, 127, 144–45, 174–76, 188–89, 197n59; status of, 6, 144f, 157, 162–69, 222n58; rise of, 8, 14–18, 78f, 80, 104, 124, 127, 197nn68, 70; decline in, 8, 19–21, 127f, 163, 198–99nn84, 86, 90; realism and, 11–14, 45, 61, 154, 159, 168, 180, 196nn44, 49, 218n2; formulas in *Heaven Above*, 16, 22, 26, 36, 38–44; formulas in various works, 16, 70, 80f, 85, 88, 95, 111, 119, 122ff, 136, 140, 148, 161–62, 165–69, 176, 182, 187–88; forerunners of, 16, 150–52, 154, 163, 190, 197nn62, 65; and bureaucracy, 153–55, 159–60; fantasy in, 161–62; mass culture and, 162, 168–69; and law, 176–80. *See also* Lawsuits against anticorruption writers; Mass (popular) culture; Officialdom, fiction about; Realism
Auerbach, Erich, 10, 149, 159
Avant-garde, 5, 14, 16, 22, 105, 144f, 153, 155–58, 163, 165, 188, 218n1, 221n41, 223n68

Banking system, 7, 54, 61, 82, 84f, 87f, 126, 131f, 167, 186
Bankruptcy, 82f, 86, 129, 156, 181; novels about, 14, 20
Baoding, 79, 89, 214n57
Barmé, Geremie, 74
Becker, George J., 10–11
Beijing, 9f, 89, 125f, 134f, 175, 212n45; Chen Xitong scandal in *Heaven's Wrath*, 16, 48–77, 179; in other novels, 25, 32, 87, 107f, 129f, 132, 137, 185; Beijing Gang, 48, 70, 72. See also Chen Xitong; *Heaven's Wrath*; Massacre, Beijing; Wangfujing
Beijing Literature, 16
Bi Sihai, 17, 198n77
Blizzard Leaves No Trace, The (Lu Tianming), 45f, 200nn5, 7, 201n31
Bribery, 3f, 7, 19, 69, 74, 161, 171–73, 176f, 179, 188, 200n9; in *Heaven Above*, 26–29, 31; in *Heaven's Wrath*, 52f, 55, 58, 65–66, 68, 74; as social grease, 65–66, 68, 184; in *Choice*, 85, 87f, 92f, 183; in *National Portrait*, 108–10, 112, 186; in *Dossier on Smuggling*, 128f, 131–34, 137f
Brooks, Peter, 158, 168
Bureaucracy, 11–13, 21, 27, 29, 111, 117f, 139f, 181, 185, 190; as liar, the target of realism, 11, 13, 21, 43, 50, 84, 153ff; secrecy of, 45, 90, 175; as corrupting, 119–20
Bureaucratic capitalism, 30, 183f, 224n85
Bureaucrats, cadres, 39, 66, 76, 115, 119, 140ff, 152, 168, 173, 175, 181; as heroes, 5, 12, 16, 39–40, 62, 79, 82–84, 102, 106–10, 115, 123, 129, 136, 141, 190; speech, culture, 15, 30ff, 36, 44, 50, 54, 62, 76, 80, 90, 94, 104, 111–13, 117–19, 121–24, 135, 139, 167f, 177, 182, 226n26; abuse of power and privilege by, 28, 84, 118–21, 185–86; morale, 30; work style, 85–86. See also Corruption; Income, cadre; Officialdom, fiction about; Officials; Power

Cadres. See Bureaucrats, cadres; Chinese Communist Party; Corruption; Income, cadre; Officials
Cangtian zai shang. See *Heaven Above*
Cao Xueqin, *Hong lou meng* (Dream of the red chamber), 114, 147, 155
Capital flight abroad, 15, 25, 28, 52, 54–56, 61, 88, 94, 109f, 131f, 134, 167
Capital in Ruins (Jia Ping'ao), 150–51, 158f
Capitalism, 2, 6f, 12, 14, 43, 67f, 86, 95, 138, 141, 157, 164f, 168, 171, 175, 183, 220n30. See also Bureaucratic capitalism
Catharsis, 102, 147–49, 161, 219n17
CCP. See Chinese Communist Party
CCTV. See China Central Television
Censorship, cultural control, self-censorship, 1, 7f, 13, 20, 22, 41–45, 70, 95, 99–100, 103, 120, 123, 140, 142f, 154, 164, 196n48, 207n68, 211n32, 214n7, 220n38; of *Heaven's Wrath*, 48, 72, 79, 202–3nn9, 13, 14; in *Municipal Crisis*, 75–77; of *National Portrait*, 104f, 124
Central Disciplinary Inspection Commission, 25, 42, 59, 76, 99, 125, 178–79, 201n22, 203n10, 205–6n45, 211n38, 214n60; local branches of, 51, 109, 174, 181, 235
Central Propaganda Department, 99, 165, 174, 202n9, 213n46
Character development, 32–34, 97f, 100f, 114–17, 119, 121
Chen Fang, vii, 17f, 90f, 94, 124, 127, 163, 184, 198n75, 201n21, 206n49, 207n76, 208n85; self-censorship of,

75–77. *See also Heaven's Wrath*; *Municipal Crisis*
Chen Pingyuan, 150, 197n58
Chen Sihe, 163, 222n58
Chen Xiaoming, 194n18, 221n41, 223n68
Chen Xiaotong, 48f, 62f, 71, 202nn5, 7, 203–4n23, 205nn37, 39
Chen Xinhao, 17
Chen Xitong, 16, 44–77, 179f, 187, 211n38, 225n19; conviction of, 59; prosecuted for being powerful, 66, 68, 70, 77, 174–75, 225n19. *See also* Chen Fang; *Heaven's Wrath*
Chen Yuanbin, 17
Chi Li, 169, 221n52
China Central Television (CCTV), 132, 163
Chinese Communist Party (CCP), 3f, 6–9, 12–13, 23, 34, 36–37, 39, 41, 43f, 64, 66ff, 71, 76, 83, 90f, 94, 101, 113, 123, 138, 140, 167, 174f, 180f, 184, 190; insecurity of, 3, 12f, 41, 81, 90, 92ff, 176, 178, 180; 16th Congress, 7, 18f; as elite, 12–13, 138, 167, 181, 183; in relation to state and law, 12–13, 36f, 39, 62, 70, 73, 82, 91, 98, 100, 102, 104, 123, 168, 178–79, 184, 186, 200n7, 214n16, 224n86; literary interventions, 18–21, 43, 48, 79, 99, 105, 160, 164, 176–79, 181, 212n44; obedience in, 37, 41, 44, 62–63, 80, 97, 99, 178, 180f, 204n25. *See also* Censorship; Deus ex machina; Elites; Organization, "the"; Politics; Power; Protests; Regime change
Chinese Writers' Association, 20, 80
Chivalry and chivalric novels, 32, 75, 119, 135, 141, 158, 161–62, 164, 216n16, 220n49. *See also* Criminal culture, romantic
Choice (Zhang Ping), 19, 22, 42, 44, 74, 78–193, 162, 180, 182, 184–87, 189, 210n13; TV adaptation, 79, 99, 213n50; novel's style, 80, 88–91; film version, *see Fatal Decision*
Class, social, 5, 9, 43, 52, 60, 67, 90f, 92, 96, 118, 136ff, 141, 154, 157, 168, 174f, 181, 183–87, 220n30, 227n48
Classical Chinese, 101, 153, 158, 172–73, 202n7
Comedy, humor, 15, 28, 63, 88, 92, 107, 111, 114, 149, 151f, 155, 160. *See also* Farce
Commercialization, money values: of culture, 6, 8, 13, 15, 19f, 78, 103, 105, 127, 136, 141, 150–52, 163–64, 166f, 169, 222n60; of society, 116f, 151, 167–68. *See also* Consumerism, consumption
Communism, end of. *See* Regime change
Conspiracies (fictional), 36, 43f, 63f, 70, 73, 75, 85, 97, 131, 136, 160f, 206n51
Construction fraud, 24, 28–30, 58, 73, 111
Consumerism, consumption, 15, 86, 95, 163, 166–68, 183
Contagion, contamination, 31, 59, 178, 182f, 187, 224n4. *See also* Hygiene; Morality and immorality, *under* spread of
Corruption, 1–10, 14–21, 113, 120f, 170–90; discourse, 2–8, 17, 21, 23, 28–31, 35–41, 43, 50, 59, 64–70, 91–95, 102, 118–21, 136–40, 151, 166f, 170–90; public opinion on, 2–4, 7–8, 138, 175–76, 195n28; collective, 2, 35, 94f, 98, 120, 195n28; definitions, 3–4, 19, 170–73, 184, 187, 193–94n9, 226n27; cases, 3, 7, 17ff, 21, 23, 26–31, 45, 48–50, 54–62, 64, 70f, 73–77, 79, 84–88, 110–13, 118, 127f, 131–36, 138, 142f, 157, 172, 174, 179–80,

182, 199n93, 200n5, 203n18, 208n79, 216n11, 217–18n32, 226n31; as a social good, 31, 38, 50, 64–68, 92, 139, 171, 184; as hierarchical web, 36, 40, 42–43; rural, 58, 78, 91, 107f, 120, 186, 189, 198n79, 200n5, 207n75; intergenerational, 59–60, 182–83; "legalized," 70, 75, 184; *guandao*, 86, 172, 174; judicial, 177, 179. *See also* Anticorruption; Bribery; Contagion; *Fubai*; Hygiene; Misappropriation; Morality; Nepotism; Power; Privilege; Social change and dread of it

Crime, 2, 7, 28, 32, 34f, 48, 50, 53f, 59ff, 68, 70f, 77, 85, 93, 106, 118, 131, 137f, 176, 179, 181, 188; underworld, 25, 30, 32ff, 49–52, 60, 70–75, 106, 112, 131, 185; economic, 50, 110, 172, 177, 179f, 216n17. *See also* Crime and mystery fiction; Murder; Rape

Crime and mystery fiction: thrillers, 20, 22, 26, 39, 43–45, 49, 78ff, 98, 127, 135, 148, 157, 162–63, 181f, 185, 199n86, 220n38; genre devices, 32, 38, 41, 43f, 49, 61, 70, 80, 114, 135f, 157, 161–62, 182; private detective, 52, 58, 61, 176; Judge Bao, 96

Criminal codes and laws, 3f, 19, 27f, 61, 170, 172–73, 175, 179, 181, 187, 200n9, 225nn10, 11

Criminal culture, romantic, 65, 117, 131–33, 141, 161–62, 171

Criticism: Chinese, 5f, 11–21, 42, 45, 49, 71, 80f, 95f, 98–101, 103, 105, 110f, 115, 119, 124, 127, 141, 144–69, 194n22, 196n49, 198–99n84; Chinese elite, 6, 43, 144–45, 163–65, 168; other, 6, 10f, 121, 146–53, 156–59, 163f, 167; of mass culture, 144f, 158, 160, 162–69

Cultural Revolution, 44, 86, 136, 146f, 185, 189, 209n1

Da xue wu hen. *See Blizzard Leaves No Trace, The*
Dai Jinhua, 165, 214n61, 218n1, 223nn74, 84
Daqing oil field, 125
Decadence, 3, 59–60, 86, 101, 121, 161, 188f
Democracy, 2f, 7, 36, 45, 86, 92, 138–39, 164, 175, 184, 193n2, 221n43
Deng Bin, 53, 56f, 63, 68–69
Deng Xiaoping, 2, 7, 14–15, 47, 52, 68, 70, 181, 213n57
Dereliction of duty, 27, 59
Detective fiction. *See* Crime and mystery fiction
Deus ex machina, 34, 41, 62, 136
Discourse, 2, 34, 38, 50, 149, 153f, 167, 176–82, 188–90, 219n6; official (state propaganda), 5, 8, 13, 15, 17, 19, 29, 35, 39, 41, 43, 50, 59, 83, 88, 92, 98, 102, 120, 145, 153, 166, 174, 176, 178–82, 190, 293n15; nonofficial or popular, 8, 17, 29, 39, 41, 59, 94, 174f, 178, 180, 182; traditional, 59, 93, 160, 176, 183; official discourse of realism, 145. *See also* Corruption, discourse; Elevation; Foucault, Michel; Proportionality discourse
Doleželová-Velingerová, Milena, 146
Dossier on Smuggling (Liu Ping), 17, 43f, 73, 125–43, 162, 178, 182, 185, 188; sequels, 142
Duke, Michael, 146, 153, 219n5, 220nn29, 30
Dushi weiqing. *See Municipal Crisis*
Dushu (Reading; journal), 164, 206n53, 222n56

Index

Economic growth, 2, 9–10, 16, 38, 94f, 139–41, 162, 164, 171, 180; vs. ethics, 37–38, 130, 139
Elevation, Chinese literary discourse of, 75–77, 159
Elites, 29, 51–52, 77, 118, 148, 222n66, 223n68; CCP as, 12–13, 43, 181; in Chinese realism, 144f, 146; and popular culture, 164–65; power or ruling, 184–85. *See also* Class, social
Embezzlement. *See* Misappropriation
Enterprises: private, 9, 75, 95, 110, 139, 172–73, 185f, 194n11; privatized subsidiaries, 87–88
Entrepreneurs, 16, 66f, 86, 92, 106, 108, 118, 137–38, 141, 165, 185f; enterprise literature, 16
Epic qualities, 14, 38, 78, 105, 141, 149–50, 152, 156, 199n90, 212nn43, 44
Ershiyi shiji (*Twenty-first century*; journal), 164
Exile: Liu Binyan's, 15; Lai Changxing's, 136; He Qinglian's, 164
Exposure novels (late Qing). *See* *Qianze xiaoshuo*

Factories, 12, 14–16, 19, 23, 74, 81, 129, 156, 167, 176, 184, 186f, 189, 211nn25, 30; in novels, 23–25, 28–29, 39, 55, 80–102, 108, 112, 184. *See also* State-owned enterprises; Workers
Fanfu xiaoshuo, 17f. *See also* Anticorruption fiction and media
Fang Lizhi, 7
Fantasy, 16, 72, 152, 157, 161–62, 171, 210n18
Farce, 113, 149, 151
Fatal Decision (movie), 16, 72, 79–80, 104, 183, 185, 188, 193n8, 197n69, 210n10, 212–13nn43, 46, 50, 214nn59, 60, 61; comparisons to *Choice*, 81f, 86, 88–93, 95–103, 211n23, 213–14nn52, 55, 57; style, 99, 102
Fei du. *See* *Capital in Ruins*
Feng Xiaogang, 15, 212n44
Film studios: Beijing, 99; Shanghai, 99; Yuanhua (Xiamen), 126, 128f
Films, 3, 5, 15, 19f, 49, 52, 102–3, 143f, 147f, 161f, 165, 199n93, 212n44; anticorruption, 16, 45, 72, 79–82, 98, 144–45, 168. *See also* *Fatal Decision*; Film studios; *Xun qiang*
Formulas in popular fiction, 8, 49, 53, 61, 64, 73, 91, 97, 110, 114, 128, 136, 146, 176, 195n30, 223n76; anticorruption, 16, 20, 22, 38–45, 64, 79, 81, 91, 95–96, 104f, 110, 122, 127–28, 140, 182, 199n90; antispy, 73, 97, 136. *See also* Crime and mystery fiction, *under* genre devices
Foucault, Michel, 188, 194n15
Fubai, 4, 17, 173, 175, 179, 197n70, 225n14. *See also* Corruption
Fujian, 79, 125–26, 134; Fuzhou, 128f, 134f. *See also* Xiamen

Gallagher, Mary E., 184
Gang of Four, 136, 221n47; Zhongyang's, 82, 101f, 183, 185
Gangs, criminal, 25, 30, 32ff, 49–51, 60, 73, 80f, 131, 185f
Gao Qiming, 53, 56, 64, 74, 206nn49, 50, 207n76
Gao Xingjian, 160, 169
General Anticorruption Bureau, 7, 19
Gifts, 24f, 28f, 31, 58f, 85, 100, 106–8, 111, 113, 116, 118, 129, 132, 134, 137, 175, 188, 200n13, 204n34, 207n75, 217n22. *See also* Bribery; Guanxi
Good official, savior (stock character; *qing guan*), 5, 39ff, 43, 61, 74, 92,

94, 98, 102, 271; criticism of the device, 12, 189–90
Graft. *See* Misappropriation
Great Wall Company, 74, 203n18, 209n92
Guanchang xiaoshuo. *See* Officialdom, fiction about
Guanxi, 29, 31, 34–36, 43, 54, 64f, 111, 171, 182, 200nn12, 23; webs of, 29, 35, 64, 95, 107, 116, 136, 140, 160–61, 182, 185; and power, 35f; building, 75, 85, 106–10, 115–17, 119, 136–40, 159f. *See also* Conspiracies; Gifts; Local phenomena; Nepotism; Power
Guo hua. *See* National Portrait

Hao, Yufan, 183
He Dun, 12
He Ping, 60, 74, 205n40, 206n50, 208n81
He Qinglian, 164, 224n1
He Zengke, 164, 224n1
Heaven Above (Lu Tianming), 16, 22–46, 162, 197n70, 200nn6, 7, 201n31, 220n50; style, 22, 32–33, 38–39, 44; character development in, 32–34; comparisons to other novels, 49, 51, 53, 59, 64, 79, 82, 91, 94, 96f, 139, 145, 182, 184
Heaven Above (television series), 16, 42, 45, 79, 197n65
Heaven's Wrath (Chen Fang), 17–18, 47–77, 79, 167, 171, 174, 178, 182–85, 188f, 225n23; banning of, 48, 79, 202–3nn9, 13, 14; style, 49–50, 76; revision of as *Municipal Crisis*, 71–77, 207n70, 208–9nn87, 89, 90; comparisons to other novels, 80, 88, 91, 97, 110, 127, 136, 140f; law in, 179–80
Hegel, Robert E., 150
Hei dong (Zhang Chenggong), 216n11

Hero officials. *See* Good official
Hierarchy and its emblems, 31, 39–44, 62–63, 66, 76, 91, 117–19, 151, 168, 183, 226n26; clientelism, 28, 36, 58, 66, 184f; patriarchal protection, 35ff, 93ff, 97, 101, 185f, 188
Historical themes, 3, 44, 50, 64, 89, 96, 124, 138, 141, 155f, 158f, 161, 166, 170, 173, 189, 212n44; amnesia, 7, 189; on TV, 22, 45, 99
Hong Kong, 10, 19, 48, 52f, 56ff, 61ff, 66f, 69f, 72f, 77, 86, 126, 128, 132, 134f, 139, 142, 153, 205n40, 206n50, 207nn70, 72, 208n79, 226n36; stock market, 56, 74
Housing fraud, 17, 27f, 30, 32, 58f, 65, 131f, 187; luxury housing, 28–29, 77, 168; inferiority of commoners' housing, 28, 32, 65, 82, 93
Hu Feng, 159
Hu Jintao, 9
Humor. *See* Comedy
Huters, Theodore, 148, 219nn7, 16, 220n33
Hygiene, health, decay, discourses of, 2, 5, 7, 35, 92, 166, 177–78, 182, 188f, 226n28

Immorality. *See* Morality and immorality
Income, cadre, 28, 68, 75, 87f, 101, 107f, 112, 139; low salaries, 66ff, 92, 118–19
Industry, 8, 14f, 69, 87, 96, 131, 156, 187, 195n39. *See also* Factories; State-owned enterprises; Unemployment
Inequality, social and economic, 2, 9, 186, 222n58
Intellectuals, 11, 14, 58, 144, 160, 164, 166, 218n3, 222nn60, 66, 223n68; views of, 6, 138, 145, 158, 160f, 163–66; as novel heroes, 23f, 31; techno-

crats, 31, 36, 40, 45, 82, 102; reading habits, 61, 65, 164
Intelligence operatives, 50, 69f, 77, 126f. *See also* State Security apparatus
Internet, 5, 7, 105, 127, 162f, 167, 174, 213n48
Investment, 56, 66f, 74, 87, 94, 110, 138f, 167, 204n32; foreign, 7, 23f, 29f, 55, 63, 68, 74, 126, 128, 164, 184; in Ponzi schemes, 53, 56–57; overseas, 55, 69, 74, 77; bribes as, 66. *See also* Real estate; Stock markets

James, Henry, 13, 106, 121–23, 158
Ji Shengde, 126
Jia Ping'ao, 169; *Capital in Ruins*, 150, 158
Jia Qinglin, 126, 212n45, 213n55
Jiang Zemin, 47, 70, 76, 126, 181, 196n54, 212n44; and *Fatal Decision*, 19, 79ff, 92, 94, 99, 101; and Chen Xitong, 47f, 70, 72, 77
Jiang Zilong, 16, 44, 197nn65, 66
Jie Peiyong, 133, 217n22
Jin Yong, 158, 164
Jin Yuanping, 17, 198n77
Johnston, Michael, 183, 224nn4, 5
Journalism, reportage, 7, 15f, 18f, 48, 50, 58, 63, 68, 71f, 78, 126f, 140, 150f, 158, 160, 172, 174, 189, 202n7, 216n9; censorship of 7, 9, 13, 48, 71, 112, 159, 202n6, 220n38; fiction as a substitute for, 13, 19, 48, 50, 56, 71, 73, 77, 134, 140, 207n68; press criticism of anticorruption works, 19f, 162–63, 199n84; corruption of the press, 31, 63, 99, 107, 112f, 205n40, 209n1; reporters as fiction characters, 45, 60, 97, 108f, 115; Hong Kong, 69f, 77
Jueze. *See Choice*

Justice and injustice, 24, 44, 160, 171, 184; social, 4, 7, 37–38, 65, 111; obstruction of justice, 7, 30, 34, 38, 131, 179; legal/moral, 17, 40, 51, 79, 94, 97, 102, 128, 130, 141, 148, 153, 161, 174; cosmic, 38, 44, 171, 190; revenge, 51, 128, 136, 141. *See also* Law

Ke Yunlu, 16f, 198n77

Lai Changxing, 126f, 132–37, 140, 174–75, 208n79; fictional portrayal of, 126–42, 217n27; wife, Zeng Mingna, 134, 217n27. *See also* Liu Ping; *Dossier on Smuggling*; Yuanhua Group
Law, 4, 12, 19, 27f, 30, 69, 87, 170, 172, 174, 178, 181, 183, 187–89; rule of, 2, 88, 92, 138f, 178ff, 226n41; legal consciousness, 27, 39f, 53f, 62, 80, 119, 176–83; "law is useless," 29, 88, 93, 95, 111, 120, 138f; U.S., 74f; legal discourse, 177–80; dual nature, 178–79. *See also* Criminal codes; Justice; Lawyers
Law enforcement, 27, 31, 40, 62, 75, 83, 127f, 135f, 142, 171, 176, 200nn6, 7; heroes in, 19, 40, 44f, 49, 52, 128, 130; bad cops, 19, 106, 110, 112, 130
Lawsuits against anticorruption writers, 78f, 162, 200n5, 201n21, 203n40, 209n4, 210n7, 221n51
Lawyers, 56, 80, 119, 128f, 136, 138, 179, 195n24
Lefebvre, Henri, 11
Legal system literature, 17
Levenson, Joseph, 146
Lévi-Strauss, Claude, 5
Li Boyuan, 104f, 150ff, 220n27; *Guanchang xianxing ji*, 105, 150
Li Jizhou, 73, 126, 140, 208n79
Li Ka-shing, 52, 55f, 58, 68

Li Min, 52, 56, 63f, 69, 206–7n62
Li Ming, 69
Li Peifu, 17
Li Peng, 69f; his wife, Zhu Lin, 69
Li Qiyan, 51, 63f
Li Rui, 153
Li Tuo, 16
Li Weihuai, 53, 56, 74
Li Yi and Bi Hua, 153
Liang Qichao, 163
Lin Youfang, 126
Link, Perry, 146, 156, 194n19, 196n48, 219n5
Liu Binyan, 11, 15, 17, 71, 153f, 159f
Liu Kang, 165, 222n66
Liu Liying, 205–6n45, 211n38
Liu Ping, 17f, 127; works, 125–43, 218n37. *See also Dossier on Smuggling*
Liu Xinwu, 160
Liu Zaifu, 146
Liu Zhenyun, 15, 17, 104, 220n34
Local phenomena, 8f, 24, 36, 69, 74, 106–11, 125, 128, 136, 139f, 194n11, 207n75; local favoritism, 9, 26, 28, 111, 139, 174; townships, 29, 34, 91
Louie, Kam, 146, 219n5
Love (romantic), 33, 40, 45f, 51, 53, 61, 76f, 107, 114, 116f, 120, 127, 129–30, 133, 135, 141, 156, 159, 182
Lu Tianming, vii, 17, 61f, 71, 79, 104f, 163, 198n77, 199nn90, 1, 200n5, 207n68, 216n11, 218n2, 220n34; *Heaven Above*, 16, 22–46, 49, 52f, 59, 79ff, 94, 162, 182, 197n70, 207n68; and television productions, 45–46; *Shengwei shuji* (Provincial secretary), 45–46, 198n77, 199n90; son, Lu Chuan, 199n1, 216n11. *See also Blizzard Leaves No Trace, The*; *Heaven Above*; Television

Lu Xun, 11, 54, 113, 120, 145f, 149f, 153ff, 160, 219n18
Lubbock, Percy, 121, 215n20
Lü, Xiaobo, 224nn1, 2

McDonald's, 52, 55, 68
McDougall, Bonnie, 146ff, 219nn5, 15
Main melody, 43, 99, 104, 212n44, 220n34
Mandate of Heaven theory, 4f, 81, 91f, 175, 180, 183, 189; dynastic restorations, 176
Mao Dun, 15, 149, 155f, 189
Mao Zedong, Maoism, 9, 15, 67, 145, 152, 154–57, 165, 172, 187, 190
Market economy, 5–9, 12–15, 30, 43, 66, 84f, 90f, 170, 172f, 187ff; cultural market, 14f, 20, 71, 80, 136, 151, 157, 164ff, 168, 218n33, 223n68. *See also* Commercialization
Martial arts novel. *See* Chivalry and chivalric novels
Marx, Marxism, 15, 138, 154, 156, 159, 163, 170, 187; Engels, 157, 220nn36, 37
Mass (popular) culture, 1, 3, 5f, 15, 78, 80, 99, 103, 152, 158, 161–67, 174, 179, 187, 193n3, 194nn14, 18, 221n14, 222n64, 223n67; anticorruption novels as, 3, 6, 19, 22f, 38, 41, 49f, 79, 105, 127f, 135f, 141, 162–63, 165–66, 168–69, 195, 218n2, 222n58; corruption as entertainment in, 3, 13, 126–27, 143, 151, 161; criticism of, 5f, 105, 163–64, 150, 168; advocates of, 6, 144f, 163–66; mass audiences, 8, 11, 21ff, 26, 32, 114, 158, 160, 167, 199n87; in light of high, serious culture, 19, 105, 144f, 150, 158, 160, 165, 211n17, 218n1; and realism, 144f, 153, 156, 158, 160, 166; history of, 144, 150, 163, 165; compared to Western, 165, 169. *See also* Chiv-

alry; Crime and mystery fiction; Discourse, *under* nonofficial or popular

Mass media adaptations, 1, 3, 8, 20f, 26, 42, 79, 90, 98–103, 106, 158, 161f, 167, 186, 197nn65, 69, 200n7, 216n8, 217n28

Massacre, Beijing (1989), 3, 5, 7ff, 15, 47f, 78, 160, 164, 212n44

Masses' Press, 16, 20, 78, 157, 163, 168, 197n70. See also *Woodpecker*

May Fourth, 11, 13, 15, 97f, 163; realism, 146–49, 152–57

Melodrama, 13, 32, 39, 49, 73, 79, 81, 96ff, 100, 102f, 105, 114, 135, 148f, 160f, 163, 169, 186, 219n17

Military, Chinese, 74f, 84, 90, 125f, 131, 183, 196n45, 208nn83, 90

Ming fiction, 76, 89, 146, 151, 158, 203n19

Minority—"the corrupt are just a" claim, 35, 88, 92; opposite views, 64, 92, 118, 174f

Misappropriation (*nuoyong*), graft (*tanwu*), embezzlement, 4, 7, 17, 25–29, 47, 58, 65, 168, 171ff, 179, 187, 200n9, 225n11; cases (fictional), 25, 28, 32f, 86, 109, 161; cases (fictionalized), 53–58, 65–67, 74, 107, 109–11, 204nn30, 32, 205n37; cases (actual), 57, 59, 202n5, 204n28, 206n45, 225n17

Mistresses, 20, 40, 53f, 58–61, 107f, 129, 133ff, 177, 217n27

Mo Yan, vii, 6, 151, 153; and anticorruption, 15–16, 197n73, 222n58, 227n52

Modernism (literary), 152f, 156ff, 160, 221n45

Money, writing for. *See* Commercialization

Money laundering, 55, 74, 131

Monopoly, 29, 132, 139, 184; power, 67f, 112, 128, 167, 184; as corruption, 184

Morality and immorality, 7, 9, 12, 65, 92f, 97, 138, 149, 154, 170–73, 187, 190; in literature, 1, 4, 39, 51–52, 59, 81, 88, 90, 92f, 98, 110, 114, 120, 149, 159, 161, 179, 211n26; moral collapse, degeneracy, 2, 4f, 59–61, 121, 131–34, 187, 216n9; sexual, 5, 19, 59–61, 75, 86, 113, 121, 126, 159, 161f, 180, 188, 217n18; new morality, 9, 95, 98, 151, 220n26; characters and, 12, 26, 31, 34, 36, 59f, 64, 97–98, 113–16, 120; of CCP, 12, 67, 138, 175, 180–81; extralegal discourse of, 39, 53, 80, 88, 121, 171, 177–78, 180–83, 187; spread of, 43, 59, 61, 64, 93, 102, 175, 182–83, 188; corruption of, 44, 60f, 64f, 85–88, 90, 96, 113, 120, 150–51, 159, 171; crime of degeneracy, 59–60, 179f; moral economy, 64f; politics and, 98, 156, 159, 180f, 188; moralism in literature, 103, 110, 114, 132, 149ff, 156, 159. *See also* Contagion; Hygiene; Mistresses; Murder; Prostitution; Rape; Social change and dread of it

Movies. *See* Films

Municipal Crisis (Chen Fang), 72–77, 161–62, 180, 207nn72, 75, 208–9nn81, 87, 89, 90; new cases in, 73–75, 77, 126, 139f, 186, 208n79; self-censorship in, 75–77. *See also* *Heaven's Wrath*

Murder, 26, 30, 32, 45, 49, 51f, 54, 61f, 65, 73, 80, 100, 127, 130, 137, 142, 148, 157, 183. *See also* Crime and mystery fiction

National Portrait (Wang Yuewen), 104–24, 137, 140, 150f, 180, 182, 185f, 214n7, 215nn14, 15; style, 105, 114, 120–23

Nationalism, patriotism, 74, 99, 101, 103, 136, 144, 155, 162, 164–66, 168, 212n44, 216–17n18, 223nn68, 74
Nepotism, 29, 35–36, 86, 88, 111, 180, 186. *See also* Power; Princelings
New Left, 9
New Star (Ke Yunlu), 16
Ni Zhen (film critic), 81
Noir atmosphere, 99
Nostalgia, 188, 227n51
Nuoyong. See Misappropriation

Officialdom, fiction about, 14–19, 150, 168, 174, 197nn58, 72, 198–99n84, 200n11; compared with anticorruption fiction, 16–17, 44, 104, 159, 197n59, 198n79; Wang Yuewen's novels as, 18, 104–24. *See also* Anticorruption fiction; Bureaucrats; Discourse, *under* official; Officials
Officials: propaganda criticizing, 5, 13, 19f, 132f, 180–81; corruption of, 6ff, 19, 24, 30, 59–60, 65f, 108–14, 130–34, 139, 172–75, 223n75; traditional officials in life and literature, 6, 15, 89, 105, 118, 124, 142, 150, 181, 188; officials' views and mentality, 8, 12, 43, 66f, 93–94, 111–12, 138f, 141, 179f; aura, status, vocation of, 31, 80, 107, 111, 115, 137, 141, 190; "official [cadre]-centered" culture, 66, 94, 111f, 118, 121, 138, 141, 180, 183–86; factory manager as, 86; literati as counterweights to, 118; the term "official," 173–75. *See also* Bureaucrats; Chinese Communist Party; Discourse, *under* official; Good official; Income, cadre; Officialdom, fiction about; Power; Privilege
Organization, "the," 13, 36, 44, 52, 63, 118, 123, 130, 190, 200n14, 204n25; "sense of," 90, 180

Party School, 44, 51, 100, 109
Periodicals, Chinese mainstream literary, 16, 18f, 65, 78, 160, 164, 198n77, 203n10
Philanthropy, dubious, 113, 117, 128, 131–32, 137ff, 150, 172
Piracy of books and mass media, 10, 48, 72, 79f, 105, 124
Police (Public Security), 54, 58, 69, 78, 133, 157, 177, 179, 181f, 195n24, 200n6, 205–6n45, 216n11, 225–26nn25, 31, 34; corrupt, 9, 28, 30, 51, 58, 73, 75, 112, 125f, 188; fictional, 23–26, 28, 30, 51f, 56, 68, 70, 76, 83, 106–7, 112, 130, 176, 209n1, 217n19; private security, 70, 82, 86, 90, 106, 111f; Scotland Yard, 72. *See also* Intelligence operatives; Masses' Press; *Woodpecker*
Politics, 1f, 7, 31, 39, 92, 111; political novels, 3, 6, 16, 41, 46, 79, 97–100, 103–4, 122, 150, 156, 163, 166f, 218n2; political reform or lack of it, 5, 7, 12, 36, 39; postpoliticalism, 6, 165f, 168, 190; the system, 7ff, 12f, 35, 48ff, 64, 70, 92, 170, 175; political amnesia, 7; politics in command, 9, 66, 87, 174, 185; political themes in novels, 19, 23, 80, 104, 122f, 152, 158–60, 208n84, 212n44; politics of characters, 24, 26, 31, 33f, 37ff, 51, 53, 96, 99, 102, 104, 109, 139; political manners, 44, 94, 118–21, 139; state subversion, 50, 68–70; potted political discourse, 64–68; political attacks, pressure, 64, 66–68, 78, 87, 153, 174, 201n22, 225n16; politics and prizes, 80; as literary mission, 95, 156, 158–60, 166; factions, 96–98, 102, 108, 111, 113, 117, 119, 174, 180; corruption as a political discourse, 177–83. *See also* Censorship; Chinese Communist

Party; Democracy; Elites; Power; Reform; Revolution
Popular culture. *See* Mass (popular) culture
Pornography, 13, 19, 76, 179; "sex and violence," 19, 162–64; little in anticorruption fiction, 20
Postcolonial condition and criticism, 164, 166
Postmodern syndrome and criticism, 6, 12, 155, 161, 164, 166ff, 196n49, 218n1, 223n73
Postsocialist condition, 8, 166ff, 184, 195n31; postcommunist, 57, 170, 180, 184
Poverty, 2, 23, 32, 43, 82, 92ff, 186. *See also* Inequality
Power: concentration of, 3f, 17, 20, 29f, 43, 59, 67–70, 77, 128, 139, 154f, 167, 171, 174f, 178, 183f, 187, 190; as currency of corruption, 3, 9, 64, 105, 184f; struggles, 3, 66–67, 72, 93, 96, 100, 107, 111, 123, 127; of CCP, 7, 12, 91; of iron circles, 8f, 35f, 77, 93, 111, 118f, 129, 156, 174, 184–85; national, 10; abuse of, 10, 15, 20, 28, 35f, 59, 65, 118–21, 171, 178, 184; and law, 27f, 178; as a corrupting force, 30–35, 64, 67–70, 75, 77, 117, 123, 139, 182, 184f; more potent than money, 35, 64f, 68–70, 75, 77, 91, 116, 168, 170, 177, 184f, 187; nature of, attraction of, 36f, 93, 113, 122f, 137, 139, 141, 184f; local, praetorian, small-fry, 36, 50, 64, 109, 124; charisma, 40, 42, 48, 62, 83, 101, 106, 128; perks of, 59f, 93, 118, 168, 183; political literary mission, 95, 154, 156, 158–60, 166; consumer choice as, 168; resistance to authority, 171, 189; over women, 177, 187f. *See also* Censorship; Chinese Communist Party; Elites;
Local phenomena; Politics; Rape; Reform; Revolution; Women
Press. *See* Journalism
Princelings (children of high cadres), 15, 24, 28ff, 44, 49, 51, 56, 58ff, 62, 68, 84f, 87, 110, 116, 131f, 182–83
Private sector, 3, 9, 33f, 43, 75, 95, 110, 128, 139, 164, 176, 185f, 189, 194n11; corruption in, 43, 137, 140, 172–73. *See also* Entrepreneurs
Privatization, 4, 8, 12, 15, 30, 81f, 87, 161, 170, 173, 184, 186ff
Privilege, 7, 15, 21, 60, 68f, 111, 168; as corruption, 64, 119, 173, 175, 183–84; of CCP, 12, 181, 183–84, 186. *See also* Bureaucrats; Chinese Communist Party; Elites; Power, abuse of
Prizes, literary, 162; Mao Dun, 19, 80, 162, 210n13
Property rights, 55, 75, 167, 186–87. *See also* Privatization
Proportionality discourse (of censors), 41, 75, 157, 208n84, 220n38
Prostitution, 20, 53, 61, 74, 83, 86–88, 96, 110, 112f, 126ff, 187–88, 215n5
Protests, demonstrations, riots, 2, 4, 7ff, 39, 41, 86, 120, 161, 178, 184, 190, 194n23, 195n29; by workers, 15, 45, 74, 82, 89–93, 97, 101, 161, 176; by teachers, 23, 32
Průšek, Jaroslav, 146
Public opinion, 2–3; polls, 7–8, 175, 195n28. *See also* Discourse, *under* nonofficial or popular
Pyramid (Ponzi) schemes, 53f, 56–57, 68–70, 77

Qianze xiaoshuo (castigatory, exposure, or muckraking fiction), 15, 149–50, 152, 154
Qing dynasty, 15, 82, 166, 176; realistic fiction of, 11f, 15, 26, 54, 76, 80, 89,

104–6, 111f, 116, 121, 146, 148–52, 154f, 190, 195n4, 197n58, 219n6, 220nn26, 27
Qing guan. *See* Good official
Qiu Xiaolong, vii, 207n68
Qunzhong chubanshe. *See* Masses' Press

Rape, 25, 30, 32
Real estate, 15, 52, 55, 73, 77, 108, 126, 131–32, 138, 167, 173, 186f; speculation, 15, 82, 88
Realism, 3, 10–16, 21, 145–69, 176, 196n44, 223n76; definition, 10–11, 120, 144; classic Western, 10f, 13, 23, 32, 96, 106, 121–22, 147f, 157–59, 166f, 171; socialist or Maoist, 10f, 16, 90, 97f, 148, 152, 154f, 196n46, 219n16; China's own "classic," 10f, 13, 76, 80f, 88, 98, 106, 114, 122, 152–61; late Qing, 11f, 15, 146, 150f, 154f, 219n6; May Fourth, 11, 13, 15, 97, 146–49, 152–53, 157; Chinese compared to Western, 11, 13, 23, 32, 34, 96, 105–6, 114, 121–22, 146f, 155, 157–60, 166ff, 170f; limits on and of, 13–14, 20–23, 41–44, 50, 71, 73, 76, 81, 95–98, 106, 121–24, 136, 140–42, 145, 147, 149, 153, 178; Jamesian, 13, 106, 121–23, 158; new or "neo," 14f, 153, 196nn46, 49, 220n30; history of Chinese, 15–16, 145–53; in *Heaven Above*, 22f, 27, 31–37, 39, 41–46; in *Heaven's Wrath*, 49f, 56, 61–63, 65, 71, 76; in *Choice*, 80f, 88–91, 95–98, 100, 102f; critical, 105, 144, 151, 153f, 160f, 214n10, 220n30; in *National Portrait*, 105f, 114–18, 120–24; in *Dossier on Smuggling*, 127f, 134–36, 140–42; expectations for, 147–48, 154–61
Reform (system or economic), 2–4, 6, 8–10, 14–15, 30, 36, 39f, 55, 64, 66–68, 81f, 87, 94, 101, 137, 141, 151, 158–59, 164, 170, 173, 181, 189, 197n66. *See also* Market economy
Regime change, fall of communism, 3f, 12, 36, 39, 81, 91f, 93f, 176, 189. *See also* Mandate of Heaven theory; Revolution
Religion, 4, 6, 14, 38, 44, 54, 94, 96f, 108f, 111, 119, 151, 167, 171, 185, 188, 190
Rent (social science term), 68, 206n56, 217n30
Revolution, rebellion, upheaval, 10, 15, 23, 30, 39, 59, 90f, 93, 97, 145, 152f, 156, 161, 165f, 180, 182ff, 195n39, 212n44. *See also* Protests; Regime change
Roman à clef, 3, 48ff, 63, 71, 73, 77, 127, 132–35, 150, 210n7
Romance of the Three Kingdoms, 44, 132, 162, 209n90; Zhuge Liang, 24, 31; Cao Cao, 141f
Romanticism, 6, 146f, 149, 152f

Scandal fiction (*heimu xiaoshuo*), 19, 49
Schwartz, Benjamin I., 146, 219n6
Secretaries, personal, and subofficials, 58, 64, 77, 106–9, 111, 115–17, 137, 180, 206n51, 209n90
Shanghai, 10, 26, 99, 101, 207n68, 213nn46, 57, 226n33; Shanghai Gang, 47
Shanxi, 78, 209n1; Taiyuan, 79, 89
Shen Congwen, 149, 155f
Sheng Xue, 127, 215n5, 217n23
Shengsi jueze. See Fatal Decision
Shenzhen, 10, 26, 69, 112
Shi Zhaobin, 134
Shieh, Shawn, 216nn9, 11, 224n1
Smuggling, 19, 73f, 166, 179, 208nn79,

Index   287

83, 211n38, 217n30, 218n37; in Xiamen, fictionalized, 125–43
Social change and dread of it, 3f, 9–10, 14, 39, 81, 85–86, 90, 95, 120, 158–59, 171–74, 176, 181, 189; corruption as the new norm, 3, 5, 65, 88, 95, 151, 175. *See also* Mandate of Heaven theory; Morality; Regime change
Social science, Western, 3, 35, 38, 50, 64–66, 68, 92, 164, 170. *See also* Rent
Socialist realism, Maoist realism. *See* Realism, *under* socialist or Maoist
Squeeze, 68, 88, 186
State-owned enterprises (SOEs), 8, 16, 19, 39, 45, 82, 87f, 126, 184; restructuring of, 15, 86–87, 186–87; in novels, 16, 20, 30, 39, 45, 55, 79, 81–102, 128, 131, 166, 186–87, 196n49; organ/enterprise dichotomy, 39, 94–95; corruption in, 84–95, 186; subsidiaries, 87–88, 186
State Security apparatus, 69f, 206–7n62
Stock markets, 7, 15, 19, 28, 187; in novels, 26, 28, 45, 83, 189; Hong Kong, 56, 74
Suicides, 16f, 25ff, 30, 34, 44, 47ff, 51, 54, 56, 60f, 91, 97, 101, 207n75, 226n34
Sun, Yan, 195n28, 224n1, 2, 5
Superstition, magic, ghosts, 107f, 112ff, 117, 152, 161
Symbolism, 82, 87, 94, 98, 113, 139, 171, 188. *See also* Allegory

Taiwan, 16, 19, 67, 86, 129ff, 155, 217nn18, 31, 225n15
Television, 5f, 15ff, 48, 63, 79, 96, 99, 103, 112, 128, 158, 163, 199n87, 205n40, 213n47, 223n75; adaptations of fiction, 5, 16, 45–46, 72, 79, 89, 106, 124, 142–43, 167, 200n7, 201n28, 213n50, 217n28, 218n37; corruption themes, 8, 16ff, 19ff, 80, 142, 167, 194n19, 198n81, 210n5, 216n11, 222n58, 223n77; *Heaven Above*, 16, 22, 26, 42, 44f, 79; *Kewang* (Yearning), 16, 197n64; TV portrayed in fiction, 84, 86, 97, 109f, 113, 115, 118
Three Antis Campaign, 67, 174
Tian Dongzhao, 17
Tian nu. See Heaven's Wrath
Tie Ying, 74, 77
Todorov, Tzvetan, 5
Township and village enterprises (TVEs), 8, 25, 29, 39, 84
Transparency International (TI), 1–2, 193n2
Trials, secret anticorruption, 48, 66, 72f, 125–27, 132, 179–80, 202n6, 204n34
Typicality in realism, 157. *See also* Realism

Unemployment, 7, 14, 16, 87f, 90, 92, 94f, 112, 156

Wang, David Der-wei, 146, 149–52, 219n6
Wang, Jing, 168, 193n3, 218n1, 222n64, 223–24nn67, 85, 225n20
Wang Anyi, 6, 80, 153, 169
Wang Baosen, 16, 47, 49, 51, 56–59, 61, 74, 203n16, 204n28, 205n40. *See also Heaven's Wrath*
Wang Guowei, 147
Wang Hui, 195n37
Wang Lixiong, 214n7, 221n43, 227n52
Wang Shuo, 169, 222n59
Wang Yuewen, 17f, 106, 124, 140, 151, 214–15nn1, 3, 13; *National Portrait*, 104–24; style, 105–6, 121–23; *Meici*

gushi (Stories of Meici), 124. *See also National Portrait*
Wangfujing (Beijing neighborhood), 55, 68
Water Margin, 65, 93, 133, 141, 162
Wellek, René, 10, 155, 219n16
White, Lynn T., III, 3, 224n1
Wining and dining, 24, 29, 59, 75, 84f, 107–11, 116, 118, 126, 132, 137, 175, 183, 224n7
Women: authors, 5; as corrupted characters, 19, 22, 53, 73–74, 83, 85, 96f, 99, 110, 115, 131, 188, 212n45; in roles of power, 19, 22, 24, 52f, 60, 73–74, 83, 97, 99, 107, 109, 128f, 217n18; as corrupters, 19, 40, 83, 131ff, 187–88, 226n27; victims, 19, 25, 33, 148, 189; gendered viewing habits, 19, 199n87; heroines, 23f, 51, 53, 83, 97, 107, 128; wives, 24, 31–35, 40, 60, 83ff, 93, 99, 106ff, 110, 114, 121, 129, 131, 162, 188; role in anticorruption works, 40, 136, 176; feminism, 40; objects of control, 53, 177, 187–88; fiction's distorted gender relations, 56, 90, 136, 176; mothers, 98, 108; baby-makers, 129, 216n16. *See also* Love; Mistresses; Prostitution; Rape
Woodpecker (*Zhuomuniao*; magazine), 78f; literary prize, 198n75, 209n4, 210n13
Workers, 3, 9, 19, 29, 53, 81–97, 101f, 112, 131, 157, 163, 165, 176, 184, 186f, 211n30. *See also* Factories; Protests
World Bank governance indicators, 2
World Trade Organization, 9, 45, 177
Wu, Helen Xiaoyan, 82, 194n19, 224nn1, 7
Wu Jianren (Woyao), 104, 112, 150ff
Wu Jingzi, 151, 155, 220n33; *The Scholars*, 109, 151
Wuxi, 51, 56–57, 68–70

Xiamen, 73, 125–28, 162, 174–75, 211n38, 217n31; fictionalized, 128–43. *See also Dossier on Smuggling*; Smuggling
Xun qiang (Searching for the gun; film), 199n1

Yan Zhen (writer), 17, 198n77
Yang Qianxian, 125, 132–33, 216n9, 217nn21, 23
Yao, Shuntian, 183–84
Yu Benzheng, 99–102, 212n43, 213nn50, 52
Yu Dafu, 165
Yuanhua Group, 212n45; smuggling case, 19, 73, 79, 125–27, 132–33; fictionalized, 128–43. *See also Dossier on Smuggling*; Lai Changxing; Liu Ping; Xiamen

Zhang Chenggong, 17, 216n11, 222n59
Zhang Hongsen, 17
Zhang Ping, vii, 16–20, 35, 61, 105f, 152, 163, 209nn1, 4, 211n27; *Choice* and *Fatal Decision*, 19, 22, 44, 74, 78–103, 162, 182, 187, 210nn13, 14, 18; *Fa han Fenxi* (The law rocks Fenxi), 78, 209n2; *Tian wang* (Heaven's web), 78, 80, 202n7, 209n2, 210n13; *Shimian maifu* (Ambushed from all sides), 98, 196n51, 218n2; *Guojia ganbu* (State cadres), 98, 199n90. *See also Choice*; Factories; *Fatal Decision*; State-owned enterprises; Workers
Zhang, Xudong, 145, 160, 219n4, 222n66, 223nn71, 76
Zhang Yiwu, 196nn46, 49, 218n1, 221n41, 222n58, 223n69
Zhao, Henry Y. H. [Yiheng], 194n18, 223n68
Zhao Baogang, 143
Zhao Ziyang, 12

Zhou Beifang, 52, 55f, 63; his father Zhou Guanwu, 52
Zhou Meisen, 16f, 20, 104, 194n22, 197n68, 198n77, 210n5, 221n51, 222n58

Zhuang Rushun, 125, 217n19
Zhuomuniao (magazine). *See Woodpecker*
Zousi dang'an. *See Dossier on Smuggling*